Making Art

FORM & MEANING

TERRY BARRETT

University of North Texas

Professor Emeritus
The Ohio State University

Connect
Learn
Succeed™

For Jesse and Amy Barrett,
Erin Hazelroth and John Purdy,
and Michael Hazelroth

Published by McGraw-Hill, an imprint of the McGraw-Hill Companies, Inc., 1221 Avenue of the Americas, New York, NY 10020. Copyright © 2011 by The McGraw-Hill Companies. All rights reserved. No part of this publication may be reproduced or distributed in any form or by any means, or stored in a database or retrieval system, without the prior written consent of The McGraw-Hill Companies, Inc., including, but not limited to, in any network or other electronic storage or transmission, or broadcast for distance learning.

This book is printed on acid-free paper.

3 4 5 6 7 8 9 0 DOW/DOW 10 9 8 7 6 5 4 3 2

ISBN: 978-0-07-252178-8
MHID: 0-07-252178-3

Vice President, Editorial: *Michael Ryan*
Editorial Director: *William R. Glass*
Publisher: *Chris Freitag*
Associate Sponsoring Editor: *Betty Chen*
Director of Development: *Rhona Robbin*
Editorial Coordinators: *Elena Mackawgy & Sarah Remington*
Marketing Manager: *Pamela S. Cooper*
Media Project Manager: *Thomas Brierly*
Production Editor: *Leslie Racanelli*
Manuscript Editor: *Judith Brown*
Designer: *Preston Thomas*
Photo Research Coordinator: *Alex Ambrose*
Photo Researcher: *Deborah Anderson*
Illustrator: *Ayelet Arbel*
Production Supervisor: *Tandra Jorgensen*
Composition: *10.5/12 Times Roman by Prographics*
Printing: *70# Sterling Ultra Web Dulle by RR Donnelley*

Cover image: Sara Sze, *Still Life with Flowers,* 1999.

The credits section for this book begins on page 262 and is considered an extension of the copyright page.

Library of Congress Cataloging-in-Publication Data

Barrett, Terry.
    Making Art : Form and Meaning / Terry Barrett
        p.   cm.
    Includes bibliographical references and index.
    ISBN-13: 978-0-07-252178-8
    ISBN-10: 0-07-252178-3
    1. Arts.   2. Art Appreciation.   I. Barrett, Terry.   II. Title.

2009939915

The Internet addresses listed in the text were accurate at the time of publication. The inclusion of a website does not indicate an endorsement by the authors or McGraw-Hill, and McGraw-Hill does not guarantee the accuracy of the information presented at these sites.

www.mhhe.com

Contents

chapter six

Time and Motion   118

chapter seven

Words and Sounds   137

chapter eight

Directional Force, Size, Scale, and Proportion   150

chapter nine

Balance and Contrast   165

chapter ten

Repetition, Unity and Variety, Emphasis and Subordination   182

About the Author

TERRY BARRETT teaches in the department of Art Education and Art History at the University of North Texas. He is also Professor Emeritus, The Ohio State University, Department of Art Education, with an honorary appointment in the Department of Art where he received a Distinguished Teaching Award for his courses in photographic media, art criticism, and aesthetics. Dr. Barrett is author of the books *Why Is That Art?, Criticizing Photographs, Criticizing Art, Interpreting Art,* and *Talking about Student Art.* He is editor of the anthology *Lessons for Teaching Art Criticism* and former senior editor of the research journal *Studies in Art Education.* His chapters and articles on teaching art, criticism, and aesthetics are published in numerous anthologies and journals. He is serving as a Visiting Critic at the Academie voor Beelende Vorming (Academy of Art Education) in Amsterdam, the Netherlands; and has served as Visiting Scholar to the Getty Educational Institute for the Arts in Los Angeles; Visiting Scholar of Education at the Center for Creative Photography in Tucson; a consultant to the Lincoln Center Institute in New York City; a visiting professor at the University of Oregon and the University of Arizona; and visiting scholar, critic, juror, and educator at many universities and art museums nationally and internationally.

Preface

Making Art: Form & Meaning welcomes students to art making at the college level and to art worlds beyond the college curriculum. This book offers students a comprehensive overview of what is entailed in making art thoughtfully.

A Fresh Approach

A major premise of *Making Art: Form & Meaning* is that processes of art making are processes of making meaning. The book offers a framework for understanding how all the aspects of an artwork—subject matter, medium, form, process, and contexts—interact. It gives students a thorough look at the expressive possibilities of design elements and principles, including use of them in computer-based, time-based, and lens-based media. The book also expands the study of making art to include conceptual approaches that are basic to late-modern and postmodern art. In these ways, the book reflects an evolution in the study of art fundamentals.

Making Art: Form & Meaning supports a course in which the goals are to provide a foundation for both making and discussing art. It engages students intellectually in the study of art. The book tackles complex and abstract concepts in clear language with concrete examples, recognizing that this might be students' first encounter with art theory. Terms are boldfaced and defined on first use, and a boxed glossary, organized in the logical order in which terms occur in the text, appears as a preview in the chapters. After reading the book, students should have an understanding of modern and postmodern design concepts and vocabulary that will serve them well in future studio courses.

The book's examples are drawn primarily from the world of contemporary American art in its multicultural complexity because this is the world in which students live. The examples reflect a broad range of subjects, media, styles, and artists so that students can glimpse the diversity of the contemporary scene. *Making Art: Form & Meaning* also includes examples from past masters so students can see that form and meaning have always been interconnected. Many of the art examples are accompanied by quotations from artists, curators, critics, and educators that illuminate aspects of the artist's work being discussed.

Special Features

Making Art: Form & Meaning offers thorough coverage of design elements and principles. The book also features coverage of other topics that support the foundations curriculum.

- **Interpretations and Artists' Statements.** At some point in their coursework and in their later professional lives as artists, students will be asked to provide an artist's statement about their work. **Chapter 2,** "Meanings and Interpretations," helps students think about how they might direct viewers in thinking about their work. On a broader level, the chapter illustrates how the decisions artists make about subject matter, materials, composition, process, and context will affect how viewers interpret their work. The chapter offers an accessible introduction to issues in meaning, such as the core concept that a work can have multiple meanings and that viewers might arrive at meanings not intended by the artist. The chapter also gives students a framework for interpreting art that will be valuable throughout their lives, even if they do not ultimately pursue a career in art.

- **Contemporary Elements. Chapter 6,** "Time and Motion," is devoted to artists' uses of time and motion, especially important to performance art, much computer art, film, and video. **Chapter 7,** "Words and Sounds," discusses elements that play a major role in such artforms as text-based art, computer-based art, performance art, video art, and installation art. It shows how these elements, traditionally considered the domain of literature and music, are used expressively in art and design.

- **Postmodern Ideas.** *Making Art: Form & Meaning* gladly acknowledges that today modernism and postmodernism intermingle, compete, cooperate, and challenge each other. The book takes this to be a good thing and embraces both perspectives. Examples of postmodern art are often used to illustrate design elements and principles inherited from modernism and early traditions. In addition, **Chapter 11,** "Postmodernist Approaches to Making Art," adds another dimension to students' thinking about making art. This unique chapter is written with studio practice in mind, showing how postmodern ideas can inform artists' choices of subject matter, form, and technique.

- **Creative Processes and Practices.** Practices of making art vary from artist to artist and cannot be easily distilled into formulas. Still, students often find it helpful to know how other artists find inspiration, develop their work, and approach the day-to-day practice of making art. **Chapter 12,** "Artists' Processes and Practices," quotes professional artists and designers who suggest a wide range of approaches and perspectives. When students want to gain insights into art making from other working artists, or when they are in need of inspiration and motivation, they can refer to this chapter. *This chapter can be assigned at any time.*
- **Studio Critiques.** Critiques can be difficult for students, whether they are receiving or giving feedback on work. **Chapter 13,** "Studio Critiques," helps students make the most of critiques, explaining different types of critiques, offering quotations from students on what is and is not helpful, and describing the process using several real examples. *This chapter can be assigned at any time.*

Making Art: Form & Meaning is meant to be inspirational for first-year students. By taking art courses, students become members of larger communities of artists. The book welcomes them to such communities and asks them to contribute by becoming fully engaged in the processes of making and thinking about art and design.

ADDITIONAL RESOURCES

- **Online Learning Center (OLC).** Additional resources to supplement *Making Art: Form & Meaning* can be found online at **www.mhhe.com/ barrettart1e.** Student resources include quizzes, studio project ideas, chapter overviews, and vocabulary flashcards. An instructor's manual with teaching strategies and lecture PowerPoints is available on the instructor edition of the Online Learning Center.
- **MyArtStudio.** Students can access **MyArtStudio** through the Online Learning Center. This interactive site offers dozens of interactions that allow students to study and experiment with various elements and principles of art and to view videos of art techniques and artists at work.

Acknowledgments

I owe expressions of gratitude to the many people over many years who have helped bring the book to print. Joe Hanson, a former editor at McGraw-Hill, signed the contract for the book, and development editors Cynthia Ward and Karen Dubno have made significant contributions to the book. The book probably would not have come about without the continued support and confidence of Lisa Pinto, Executive Director of Development, and the caring guidance of the book's development by Betty Chen. Thanks also to the production team: Leslie Racanelli, production editor; Preston Thomas, designer; Alex Ambrose, photo research coordinator; Deborah Anderson, photo researcher; Ayelet Arbel, illustrator; Judith Brown, copy editor; and Tandra Jorgensen, production supervisor.

I extend sincere gratitude to the designers and artists who allowed their work to be reproduced and to the gallery and museum personnel who helped this to happen. I thank the student artists for their work and for participating in critiques that are quoted within. My former chairperson, Patricia Stuhr, and dean, Karen Bell, provided a supportive physical and psychological atmosphere in which I could write. My new dean, Robert Milnes, and new chairperson, Kelly Donahue-Wallace, continue such support. Georg Heimdal and Vicki Daiello, dear friends, encouraged me throughout. No one has read this book in all its iterations more often or with more enthusiasm and inspiring joy than my wife, Susan.

Many reviewers provided valuable suggestions and corrections, and I thank them for their insights:

Diane Banks, James Madison University
Emily Bivens, University of Tennessee
Laurie J. Blakeslee, Boise State University
Eileen Feeney Bushnell, Rochester Institute of Technology
Valerie Constantino, Pima Community College
Margaret Craig, Dutchess Community College
Michael Croft, University of Arizona
Kathy Dambach, Florida International University
Anna Divinsky, Penn State
Tracy Featherstone, Miami University
Janis Feldhausen, Milwaukee Institute of Art & Design
Christopher M. Gauthier, Utah State University
Michael Grothusen, University of the Arts
Anne Hallam, Metropolitan State College of Denver
Dan Henderson, The Art Institute of Atlanta
Kevin W. Hughes, Missouri State University
Brooke Hunter-Lombardi, Columbus College of Art & Design
Leah Klapperich, Marian University
Randall Lavender, Otis College of Art and Design
Nancy Magner, Bakersfield College
Sara Rochford Muzzy, University of Kansas
Cedar Lorca Nordbye, University of Memphis

Sue O'Donnell, Southeastern Louisiana University
Rick Paul, Purdue University
Michael Fremont Redfield, Santa Ana College
Gail Simpson, University of Wisconsin–Madison

Sherry Stephens, Palm Beach Community College
Gina L. Wenger, Minnesota State University, Mankato
Steve Willis, Missouri State University
Harry J. Wirth, Northern Illinois University

1
Making Art
AN OVERVIEW

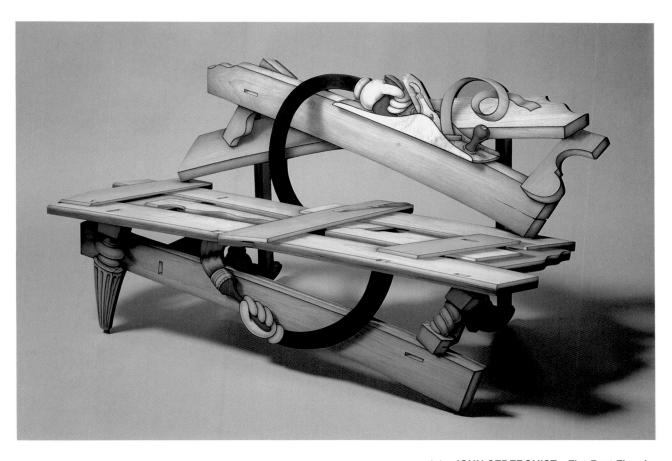

1.1 **JOHN CEDERQUIST** *Flat Foot Floogie Builds a Bench,* 2003. Litho inks, epoxy inlay, and aniline dye, 35 × 65 × 27 in.

Processes and Purposes
Subject Matter and Meanings
Choice and Uses of the Medium
Aspects of Form
Contexts
Conclusion: The Components and Meanings

All artifacts are expressive and carry meaning, whether they be comic strips or paintings, jewelry or sculpture, advertising campaigns or performance pieces, household objects or public spaces. The goal of this book is to aid you in making expressive and effective artifacts, whether your audience is yourself, your peers, the public, or a client. The concepts and principles the book describes apply to all the visual arts, "fine art" and "popular art" and "applied art," and objects and spaces designed for functional purposes. Rather than constantly distinguishing "work of art" from "designed object," I will, in general, consciously refer to human-made items as "artifacts," intentionally treating all human-made objects in a nonhierarchical manner so as not to privilege either design or art. Similarly, in general, the term "artists" includes those people commonly referred to as "designers."

Artists construct meanings in visual forms by the choices they make from the beginning through the completion and exhibition of their finished pieces. This book will make you more aware of those choices through an examination of knowledge common to artists and other artists' works. It will support your explorations into the expressive and functional possibilities of making artifacts. This chapter surveys the major components that you combine to create meaning and use in artifacts that you make, view, and use: artforms, processes, subject matters, media, design elements and principles, and contexts of showing and seeing artifacts.

Processes and Purposes

A finished artifact is the result of a series of activities and decisions that constitute a **process.** It refers to the ways that artists and designers think and work while making objects. There is no single, universal artistic or creative process; indeed, there are likely as many creative processes as there are artists and designers. However, some common activities are part of every project: conceiving of a work, deciding its purpose, beginning it, developing it, changing it, staying motivated in the face of problems, finishing the work, showing the work, and deciding its degree of success. At each stage, artists and designers make choices that help them discover new ideas and permeate their work with meaning for an audience.

The **purpose,** or intended **function,** for which some things are made plays a significant role in the creative processes of artists and designers. We look at four different creative endeavors in this section: a team of designers working on an assignment for a mass audience; an individual working on a journalistic self-assignment for a mass-market book; an individual artist expressing himself for a fine-art venue; and a craftsperson building a unique nonfunctional craft object for herself and others to enjoy.

Making Art Key Terms

PROCESS   The series of activities and decisions that lead to a finished artifact.

PURPOSE, FUNCTION   How an artifact is meant to be used.

SUBJECT MATTER   The representation of people, animals, plants, places, and things depicted in *representational art;* the shapes, colors, brushstrokes, and other elements in *nonrepresentational art.*

MEANINGS   Expressive content of an artifact and the artifact's inferred implications.

REPRESENTATIONAL ART   Artifacts that render figures, objects, or scenes as they appear in the real or visible world and as they might appear in the imagined world, with varying degrees of accuracy, distortion, and stylization.

NONREPRESENTATIONAL ART, NONOBJECTIVE ART   Artifacts that use colors, textures, shapes, and brushstrokes, for example, to express thoughts and feelings in themselves rather than to make *representational* artifacts.

MEDIUM, MEDIA   The material of which an artifact is made; also, an *artform,* such as painting, sculpture, or product design.

ARTFORM   A kind of artifact, such as a painting, drawing, sculpture, textile, photograph, product, or graphic design.

CRAFSTMANSHIP   The skill with which an artifact is made.

FORM   How an artwork is composed structurally according to its intended functional and expressive purposes, which affect its *meanings* and uses.

VIEWING CONTEXT   Where and how an artifact is placed for viewing.

INTERNAL CONTEXT   The juxtaposition of parts within a whole artifact and the *meanings* they evoke through proximity to one another.

ARTIST'S CONTEXT   The life history, experiences, and time influencing an artist's work.

SOCIAL CONTEXT   The time and place in which an artifact is made.

ART HISTORICAL CONTEXT   The artifact in relation to all other artifacts past and present.

INTERPRETATION   A process and result of deciphering what an artifact is about, means, or expresses.

All creators face constraints of time, materials, purpose, audience, and criteria for success. Yet individual designers and teams of designers typically work with different constraints than individual artists: designers accept assignments from clients, meet clients' needs with an outcome, within a specified budget and schedule, submit ideas for client approval, select materials, build and test a prototype, put the final work into production, and observe the market's response.

An illustration of how a creative process might work for designers is the challenge faced by the creative team at *Sesame Street,* the popular TV show for preschoolers. Over the years, the design team has consciously created a diverse, multicultural cast of puppets, but they were missing a girl Muppet with the draw of Big Bird, Cookie Monster, Bert, or Ernie. The team sought to create a female character who would make children laugh, but not at female stereotypes.

After nine months of research, the new character emerged as Abby Cadabby (**1.2**), a three-year-old fairy with a magic wand, tiny wings, and sparkles in her hair. The character's profile was turned over to the Jim Henson Workshop to be developed into a puppet. The Workshop brought sketches of the character and fabric swatches to the television team: among the

1.3   JOE SACCO   Panel from *Palestine,* 2001.

considerations was finding the right shades of pink and lavender to work with Elmo, who is red. The Jim Henson Workshop presented seventy-seven preschoolers with a sketch of Abby. The children made suggestions regarding hair, dress, and type of nose, and their recommendations were implemented. The television team created a ten-minute segment that they tested on fifty-three preschoolers, who were delighted with the character. Abby Cadabby made her premiere in the thirty-seventh season of *Sesame Street.*[1]

The very different creative process of Joe Sacco illustrates how someone working alone in a commercial medium might generate material and develop his work. His books blend journalism and entertainment to tell true stories. In one of his best-known books, *Palestine* (**1.3**), he offers a journalistic account of Israeli and Palestinian conflicts in the early 1990s. *Palestine* is a version of war reporting, but made in comic book form, Sacco's usual way of creating. He began in journalism as a high-school student in Oregon writing for his school newspaper. He made cartoons as a hobby. Eventually, as an adult, he combined professional written journalism within a comic-book format. Although some refer to *Palestine* as a "graphic novel," Sacco does not consider it one: "I don't feel what I do is fiction."[2]

In preparation for making *Palestine,* Sacco lived for two months with Palestinians in their territories occupied by the Israeli army and gathered specific anecdotes that would reveal a larger story. He interviewed many Palestinians and quotes their words in his narrative, humanizing their accounts in a way that a newspaper would not. His process of creating includes interviewing people, tape recording with their permission, and

1.2   SESAME STREET AND JIM HENSON COMPANY
Abby Cadabby, 2006.

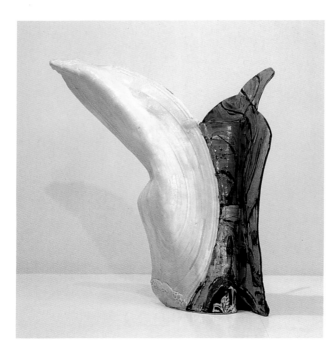

1.4 **BETTY WOODMAN** *Winged Figure Obi,* c. 1989. Ceramic, 27 × 14 in.

isn't well told and telling it honestly. In other words, if you're talking about the Palestinians, if you hear things that you don't feel like isn't good for their cause, you're still going to report that because that's just part of the story. You're being honest about the warts, but you are trying to present their story from their point of view."[5]

As an independent artist working on an expressive project of personal interest, John Cederquist need not face the challenges of appealing to a mass market or designing something that could be mass-produced. He makes one-of-a-kind sculptures that are shown in art galleries and sold to individual collectors or museums. *Flat Foot Floogie Builds a Bench* (see 1.1) is a three-dimensional bench made of wood that Cederquist imbues with life, humorously reminding us that materials have distinctive properties that contribute to the creation of the work, its function, and its visual appeal as an object that is delightful to look at.

Cederquist's title for his sculpture—*Flat Foot Floogie Builds a Bench*—informs us about his process and hints at his intended meaning. The sculpture is pertinent to the topic of artistic process because it seems to be about process and seems to express Cederquist's enjoyment in making artifacts. Although the sculpture is finished, the bench looks as if it is being built before our eyes. One cartoonish arm with gloved hand planes a board while another hand stains wood. Cederquist *did* shape the wood, stain it, and paint it to make the sculpture that seems to be making itself. We do not know to whom "Flat Foot Floogie" refers, but by use of this playful name, the artist indicates verbally that Floogie may not be the most adept of carpenters. Cederquist reinforces this understanding by showing a bench that looks as if it will not be very stable when finished. Nevertheless, Floogie enthusiastically goes about his work, the arms and hands expressing the joy of making.

Betty Woodman has been developing her artistic process and products for five decades. She began working in ceramics as a teenager. As a young craftsperson, she made functional objects such as dinnerware and vases or production pottery (systematically produced wheel-thrown pottery objects made by hand that are almost identical to one another) for daily use. She gradually shifted from functional to more symbolic and ritualistic objects. *Winged Figure Obi* (**1.4**), for example, is a vessel form, and although it could contain liquid, it would not function well. Its spout would not pour; the phallic protrusion is more like a handle than a spout.

Woodman experiments with different types of clay and methods of firing. She has significantly altered the surface treatments of her pottery. For many years, her husband, a painter, decorated the surfaces of her work. When he decided to stop doing this, she made pieces that she simply glazed in one color, undecided about how else she would finish them without copying what

photographing them or making quick sketches of them if he cannot take photographs. He tries to gather and remember visual aspects of what he is journaling for the drawings, which he will later make: what someone was wearing, details of where they live and walk. In the beginning of making *Palestine,* he thought his drawings were "a bit rubbery and cartoony," and it became clear to him that he had to push his style "toward a more representational way of drawing."[3] Part of his process is testing his drawings with people: for example, he would sit in someone's home in Gaza and show him the pictures he had made to see if they were understandable. A man in his seventies would look at the pictures and "he'd see pictures of the refugee camp, pictures of his life, or something he understood, and he'd get right away what I was trying to do." Sacco says, "Of course, I can never get it precisely as it was. . . . You reconstruct it to the best of your ability."[4]

Sacco's ability to produce the books he wants to make depends on successful negotiations with editors and publishers and his work's appeal to audiences. His books must make a profit in the marketplace. He published *Palestine* as a series of comics from 1993 to 2001, and based on their commercial success, he was able to have them published as a book. *Palestine* won the American Book Award. Nevertheless, the book has been criticized as being slanted to one side, and about those critics Sacco says, "They're right. . . . it isn't balanced. . . . I think of it as presenting one side that her husband had done. Eventually she has settled on very colorful and bold brushwork, much like an Expressionist painter of three-dimensional objects.[6]

In her work, Woodman engages in the endless debate about whether there is a meaningful difference between what is called "art" and what is called "craft." She continues making pottery but does not isolate herself from the arenas of painters and sculptors. She often throws cylinders on a potter's wheel, as would a traditional potter, but then cuts the cylinders in pieces and flattens them by dropping them on the floor. The flattened pieces retain the curvilinear spiral lines of her fingers on the clay as she shapes it on a turning potter's wheel. She shapes the slabs of thrown pieces into sculptural forms. She combines colors made from fired glazes with enamel paints added after firing the clay. Artistic processes and strategies for making art and other objects are further explored in Chapter 12.

Subject Matter and Meanings

In representational works of art, **subject matter** is the people, animals, plants, places, and things recognizably depicted. The subject matter of the photograph by Horacio Salinas (**1.5**) is a purse hung on a tree branch and bees on and about the bag.

Subject matter in nonrepresentational works of art may consist of a shape, a color, or a brushstroke. For example, the subject matter of Christopher Wool's painting *Untitled* (**1.6**) is smears of paint and lines that do not form recognizable objects that might be found in the world.

The **meanings** of an image or object are its expressive content or inferred implications. This distinction between what the work of art depicts (its subject matter) and what the work means or is about or expresses is very important. Subject matter is usually quite easy to determine: a purse, a branch, and bees in Salinas's photograph (see 1.5); smears and lines in Wool's painting (see 1.6). Meanings are harder to decipher than subject matter, and they require interpretive arguments based on evidence and reasons.

For instance, Salinas's photograph is made to evoke desire to purchase an object. Such a desire is prompted by the design of the purse, its brand name of Dior, which culturally implies sophisticated and expensive fashion. The photograph is made for an ad in a magazine published in spring. The

1.5 HORACIO SALINAS   Dior bag, 2008.

1.6 CHRISTOPHER WOOL   *Untitled,* 2007. Enamel on linen, 126 × 96 in.

1.7 **RICHARD SHAW** *China Cove,* 2001. Glazed porcelain with overglaze decal transfers, 15 × 9 × 7 in.

yellow of the purse and the bees evoke warm feelings of the summer to come. The photograph is accompanied by the tag line: "Killer bees: Catch more eyes with honey." The whole artwork, consisting of photograph, Dior bag, and text, is meant to appeal to women who may want to attract the admiring gazes of others.

Wool's painting seems to be about painterly qualities and an exploration of what he can do with a mostly black-and-white and gray color palette, using only abstract lines sprayed on linen, and wiping wet paint to make diverse marks and strokes. It seems to be about the joy of painting itself. It is open to other interpretations, as are all objects. The fascinating topic of meanings and interpretations is fully explored in Chapter 2.

When you work for a client, the subject matter may be broadly defined for you—for example, a commissioned portrait of a specific person, or, as in the *Sesame Street* example (see 1.2), a female Muppet. What the portrait and puppet look like and express will emerge in how you handle specific details as the project develops and while you meet the needs of your client.

Other times, you may choose your own subject matter, from observation or pure invention. In either case, your decisions about subject matter are central to meanings that viewers will construct about your work. You offer interpretations about your subject matter by how and what you choose to show and omit.

REPRESENTATIONAL WORKS OF ART

Based on observation of the world, **representational art** attempts to reproduce figures, objects, or scenes as they appear in the real or visible world and as they might appear in the imagined world (fire-breathing dragons or unicorns, for example), with varying degrees of accuracy, distortion, and stylization. Sometimes the term "figurative" is used synonymously with representational art. In more common usage, figurative refers to art that uses the human figure. We can refer to Norman Rockwell's painting (see 1.8) and Alberto Giacometti's sculpture (see 1.9) as both figurative and representational.

There are varying degrees of realism in art. Realistic or naturalistic art can even come close to deceiving the viewer, as in *trompe l'oeil* art, which stays so close to the ocular aspects of what it depicts that it "fools the eye," which is how the French term translates into English. Although *trompe l'oeil* was invented in the Baroque period (turn of the seventeenth century), artistic efforts to trick the eye reach far back in Western art history. An ancient Greek story tells of the artist Parrhasius, who is said to have painted a still life so realistic that birds flew to it to peck at its painted grapes.

Contemporary artist Richard Shaw continues working in the tradition of *trompe l'oeil,* but in ceramics (**1.7**). His gallery director attributes metaphorical meaning to the artist's work: "Houses of porcelain cards are built over porcelain containers that rest on porcelain books. Beyond his humor, Shaw intimates about the potential for imbalance in our loosely constructed real new world."[7]

Most representational art is somewhat less faithful to physical reality than *trompe l'oeil* paintings. Norman Rockwell is a master of realistically rendered subject matter, but we would not mistake it for the real. Look at *After the Prom* (**1.8**), for example, which he created in 1957 for a cover of the *Saturday Evening Post.* Dave Hickey, a contemporary art critic, describes Rockwell's choices of subject matter in careful detail, telling us that the artist chose the setting of a 1930s-era soda fountain, bathed it in golden light, and painted the models in 1950s-era clothing. Rockwell created a narrative with four characters: a young man and his date, the soda jerk, whom Hickey describes as the boy's older brother because of their facial similarities, and a male customer at the counter wearing a tattered bomber jacket and Air Force cap, whom Hickey describes as a veteran of

1.8 NORMAN ROCKWELL *After the Prom,* 1957. Oil on canvas, 31 × 29 in.

World War II, which ended twelve years before the date of the painting. Rockwell has the boy looking proudly at his older brother as the latter leans over to sniff the girl's gardenia. The veteran looks at the young couple and smiles.[8]

Because of the subject matter that Rockwell chose and how he portrayed it, the critic infers the meaning of the painting as a celebration of the freedom and safety of American youths after World War II. Hickey

explains that in the 1950s, parents tended to resent their children for having lives that were too easy and comfortable. The parents had endured the Great Depression and fought in World War II. Hickey believes that, in the painting, Rockwell uses the war veteran's response to the young couple to counter the attitude of their disapproving parents. In Hickey's view, Rockwell uses the veteran's smile to say, "This is what I was fighting for—this is the true consequence of that great historical

1.10   **SEAN SCULLY**   *Dark Light,* 1998. Oil on linen, 96 × 84 in.

1.9   **ALBERTO GIACOMETTI**   *Three Men Walking (II),* 1949. Bronze, 30⅛ × 13 × 12¾ in.

cataclysm—this moment with the kids and the gardenia corsage."[9]

Alberto Giacometti also depicts people in his bronze sculpture *Three Men Walking (II)* (**1.9**). The figures are representational men but look much less like men than if an artist like Rockwell had painted them. The degree of abstraction Giacometti achieves by elongation and gauntness affects our responses to the subject matter, although the figures are still representational. Giacometti's works are often interpreted as comments on life as empty and devoid of meaning.

NONREPRESENTATIONAL WORKS OF ART

Rather than depict objects in the real world, **nonrepresentational art** (also called **nonobjective art**) takes as its subject matter colors, textures, shapes, and brushwork, for example, that compose the formal pattern or structure of a work, and uses these to express

thoughts and feelings. Nonrepresentational paintings were the predominant style of modern art in European and American art by the mid-twentieth century. Sean Scully's painting *Dark Light* (**1.10**) has no people or places, and does not tell a story, but it does have subject matter of stripes and rectangles and colors and textures. Scully says he finds inspiration for his nonrepresentational paintings while walking the streets of New York when he sees painted stripes in a parking lot or new tar on top of old asphalt. A group of art students who discussed *Dark Light* saw references in it to a flag, a quilt, a patch, a rug, a mat, a piano, a beach blanket, a layer cake, a playing field, a game board, a textile, a window, doors, and a jail. They also listed several oppositional ideas that they thought the painting suggested: carnival/church, heaven/hell, tomorrow/today, day/night, war/peace, outside/inside, and good/evil.

Scully would likely be pleased with these observations and conjectures. He wants viewers to be involved in interpreting the subject matter in his paintings and what meanings it implies: "When you have something that, in a way, is incomplete, unfocused or unclear, the person looking at the painting is empowered to complete the painting."[10] *Dark Light* illustrates that non-representational art is not devoid of meaning or expression.

Jessica Stockholder is known for making temporary nonrepresentational sculptures for particular architectural environments. Her subject matter is things themselves, not representations of things, and materials she finds in discount stores. They were manufactured for a culture geared toward planned obsolescence, but before they outlive their life span she gathers them together and assembles them. In *Two Frames* (**1.11**), for example, her subject matter consists of plywood, plastic floor liner, glass, two pieces of a stucco-finished table base, a bookshelf, four metal table legs, a frame with Plexiglas, yarn, plasticine, zip ties, thread, shells, a rubber car mat, tape, and canvas from someone's oil painting. To these she has added oil paint and spray paint. Her subject matter is her materials and what she selects. They imply an acknowledgment and acceptance of our throwaway attitudes about items we purchase.

We can also infer meaning from the nonobjective logo designed for XM Radio (**1.12**). In this version, it is a simple design of lines in one color. From experience in our daily visual culture, we recognize lines in the middle as the letters *x* and *m,* and through our familiarity with advertisements, we likely know that the *x* and *m* stand in for the name of the company, XM Radio. We can also read the curved lines at either end of the logo as pulses, signifying that XM Radio broadcasts its sounds by satellite.

SIMPLE AND COMPLEX SUBJECT MATTER

Subject matter can be exceedingly simple. In some of her paintings, for example, painter Georgia O'Keeffe limited her subject matter to a single flower; sculptor Claes Oldenburg has used hamburgers and French fries as the subject matter for some of his soft sculptures; and William Wegman relies primarily on dogs for his photographs.

The subject matter of Laurie Simmons's photograph *Black Bathroom (April 16, 1997)* (**1.13**) is a common one in Western

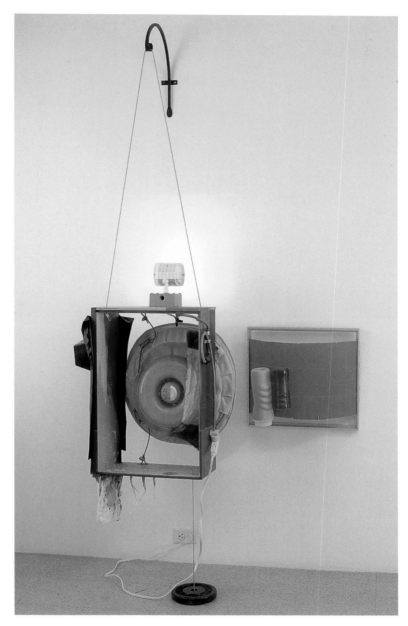

1.11 JESSICA STOCKHOLDER *Two Frames* **(detail),** 2007. Mixed media installation, 93 × 51 × 22 in.

1.12 XM Radio logo, 2008.

1.13   **LAURIE SIMMONS**   *Black Bathroom (April 16, 1997),* 1997. Cibachrome print, 28 × 40 in.

painting since the nineteenth century: a woman bathing. What is extraordinary in Simmons's work is that the "woman" bathing is a plastic mannequin with a wig. Simmons chooses the realistic medium and style of photography to make her fiction initially believable. The subject matter in *Black Bathroom* seems to be lifesize, but in this and in other similar images, Simmons uses little dolls in miniature environments she creates herself. Simmons's incongruous choice of subject matter (woman bathing) and materials (doll in a miniature environment) is central to her ideas about how women are imagined and represented in society. Her work illustrates the power and complexity of meaning that simple subject matter can evoke.

The triptych (three-paneled work) by Hieronymus Bosch known as *Garden of Delights* (**1.14**) illustrates that subject matter can be highly complex. Bosch was a Flemish artist who worked in the late fifteenth and early sixteenth centuries, in a time and place in which views of the world were very pessimistic, probably because Europe had been ravaged by plagues. Bosch shows us his vision of paradise and hell through a fascinating arrangement of people, plants, and animals, rendered in painstaking detail. In the left panel, God gives life to Eve as Adam looks on, but the setting is not an idyllic Garden of Eden. Bosch portrays it as a bizarre place: amid the seemingly normal creatures there is a unicorn, a three-headed lizard, a fish with wings, an amphibian reading a book, a monkey riding an elephant, and various creatures preying on others. Bosch has placed a strange pool and tree in the middle ground and strange architectural rocks in the background.

The left panel is a depiction of God presenting Eve to Adam.

The meaning of the middle and largest panel remains under dispute, with some recent historians understanding it as a moral warning and others understanding it as a vision of paradise lost. Bosch shows us a plain with rocky formations and monstrous mechanisms in or near the center of a lake. Naked men and women hide in eggs, seashells, spheres, domes, and transparent cylinders. Some of the figures caress and embrace gigantic strawberries, birds, and fish. Little people in the middle of the panel ride horses, pigs, goats, and a camel.

The right panel is a vision of hell. It is a dark place illuminated by fire and inhabited by a whitish monster with a broken egg for a body and tree trunks for legs: tiny people crawl in and out of him like vermin. The damned are impaled on musical instruments or are being eaten by monstrous animals. A city burns at the top of the panel.[11]

Although art historians have not arrived at a universally accepted explanation of Bosch's painting, its subject matter would have had symbolic meanings for his contemporaries. For example, we know that fruits symbolized carnal pleasure, eggs symbolized sex, rats symbolized falsehoods, and dead fish symbolized joyful memories of the past.[12] However, we are unsure of what these things mean in relation to the full ensemble. Bosch's painting is endlessly fascinating because of the questions it raises about views of the world when the painting was created and the fantastic ways Bosch visualized his subject matter.

When making art, you will have choices about subject matter: whether it will be representational or not or a mixture of both, what to include, in what amount of detail, and for what purpose. You will also need to consider whether your selection of subject matter, and your understanding of what it communicates, will resonate with viewers of your work.

More considerations of subject matter follow later in the book: uses of subject matter in postmodern art are discussed in Chapter 11, and in Chapter 12, artists offer their thoughts on their own individual choices of subject matter in their work.

1.14 **HIERONYMUS BOSCH** *Garden of Delights*; left wing: *Paradise (Garden of Eden);* central panel: *Garden of Earthly Delights*; right wing: *Hell (Inferno),* c. 1500. Triptych with shutters, wood, central panel: 220 × 195 cm.; wings: 220 × 97 cm.

Choice and Uses of the Medium

The material used to make an artifact is its **medium** (plural **media**). The media you choose and how you use them greatly affect how your artifacts will look, what they express, and how they may be used. Imagine the effect on meaning if Michelangelo's *Pietà* were made of Styrofoam instead of marble; if the Gateway Arch in Saint Louis, designed by Eero Saarinen, were made of translucent Plexiglas instead of opaque metal; if Maya Lin had designed the Vietnam War Memorial to be constructed of unfired red clay instead of polished black granite. As an artist, you will use materials to express yourself in form.

MEDIUM AS MATERIAL

As an artist, you need to be aware of the implications of the media you choose. No single medium is artistically superior to another; the point is how you use a medium to expressively meet the demands of an idea. The more media you explore and become comfortable with, the greater your options for media that best match your expressive ideas. You will also learn from experience that media are expressive in themselves and that artists both control the media they use and respect the peculiar characteristics of each medium they choose. As

the twentieth-century artist Pablo Picasso commented, "Painting is stronger than me—it makes me do what it wants."[13]

Designers are aware of the implications of the materials they choose for their products, seeking to manufacture environmentally friendly products, for example, through use of "greener" materials—those that have less negative impact on the health of the environment. Some clothing companies are reducing consumption of materials and waste by using recycled materials, printing clothing labels onto fabric rather than using sewn-on labels, and using fibers that can again be reclaimed.

MEDIUM AS ARTFORM

The term "medium" refers not only to a material but also to an **artform,** a kind of expression, such as sculpture, jewelry, ceramics, computer graphics, and so forth. Some artists choose to work within a single artform (medium) throughout their careers. Ansel Adams (**1.15**) worked exclusively within the medium of photography, mastering technical aspects of the still photograph as well as its potential for achieving beauty. Through his singular dedication to the medium, he produced a very large body of work that is collected and preserved by major museums throughout the world. In 1940 Adams helped establish the photography collection of the Museum of Modern Art in New York City, and in 1946 he established the first academic department of photography at California School of Fine Arts (later the San Francisco Art Institute). His disciplined study of the photography medium also resulted in his writing a series of authoritative technical books, *Basic Photo Series,* in the late 1940s and early 1950s, revised in the 1980s.[14]

Some artists work within a variety of artforms and with a wide range of materials. Louise Bourgeois, for example, has made very large metal sculptures for public sites, small hand-knit cloth sculptures, prints, drawings, and even jewelry. For the sculpture *Spider* (**1.16**), she used steel to construct the large spider that stands over a fenced cell containing mysterious objects made of silver, gold, bone, wood, glass, and tapestry. Her choice of media in the sculpture was not random. Bourgeois's work is partially autobiographical, and the individual materials have personal importance to her: tapestry, for example, is significant to her because as a young girl she helped her parents in their business of repairing and restoring old tapestries. She combines media in ways that are visually intriguing and emotionally evocative.

Today especially, categorizing artworks based on media (as artforms), such as drawing, sculpture, photograph, and so forth, can be arbitrary because artists sometimes purposely blur these divisions. Frank Stella's *La vecchia dell'orto (The Witch in the Garden)* (**1.17**) is labeled "mixed media." The term refers both to an artist's use of different materials in one piece of art—in this case, honeycombed aluminum, stretched canvas, and different kinds of paint material—and to the fact that it is sometimes hard to distinguish a work by labeling it one of the traditional artforms. Stella intentionally blurs distinctions between painting (a two-dimensional medium) and sculpture (a three-dimensional medium) by constructing aggressively dimensional painted works such as *The Witch in the Garden,* which is meant to hang on a wall.

MEDIUM AND CRAFTSMANSHIP

Consideration of media also entails how they are handled and made into expressive forms. When an artist has worked materials with considered skill and dexterity, the work is said to exhibit **craftsmanship.** There is not one particular way that any medium must be used; how a medium is used depends on the intent of the artist in making the piece and how the piece is meant to function. However, at a minimum, you would likely want to know or learn how to

1.15 ANSEL ADAMS *Aspens, Northern New Mexico,* 1958. Photograph.

1.16 LOUISE BOURGEOIS *Spider,* 1997. Steel, tapestry, wood, glass, fabric, rubber, silver, gold, and bone, 175 × 262 × 204 in.

make a work that will not fall apart, fade, or otherwise deteriorate, unless that is part of the intended meaning of the work. Careful consideration of how you craft any object will be expected of you by anyone who assigns, commissions, or collects your work.

The Kettering Skate Plaza (**1.18**) is a large-scale example of expert craftsmanship involving many kinds of skills with and knowledge of a variety of media. This skating plaza is designed for street skateboarding while also serving as a public square. It incorporates urban terrain elements such as benches, rails, and ledges and incorporates landscaping and art to create a multiuse park that is visually pleasing to the whole community.

Skate parks are best designed by landscape architects who are also experienced skaters. Poorly crafted parks can result in design and construction flaws due to lack of understanding of geological factors of climate and soil conditions, inappropriate concrete mixes, inadequate surface-finishing skills, and, especially, lack of knowledge of every aspect of the sport of skateboarding. Well-crafted parks result in durability over the years, functionality, and artistic and emotional appeal.

Some artists intentionally use craftsmanship in such a way that their objects will deteriorate, yet we do not consider it poor craftsmanship when it meets the expressive intentions of the artist making the work. For example, in 1960, Swiss painter and sculptor Jean Tinguely made the first of many self-destructive machine sculptures, *Homage to New York,* which battered

1.17 FRANK STELLA *La vecchia dell'orto (The Witch in the Garden),* 2000. Mixed media, 163 × 190 × 32 in.

1.18 Kettering Skate Plaza, Kettering, Ohio, 2005.

itself to pieces in the sculpture garden of the Museum of Modern Art in New York City.

Unintentional poor craftsmanship and the impermanence of materials present a major problem if makers or owners of such pieces want them to last. The twins Mike and Doug Starn, however, *intentionally* reject established conventions for making precious photographic prints that would extend the original look of their works and their stability over many years (**1.19**). Intentionally distressed in order to embrace time, change, and age, their work accepts photography's fragility. They use a variety of materials, including tape and pushpins, to hold their work together.

Museums employ scientifically trained conservators to clean work dirtied over many years. They also repair work damaged by the environment or purposely defaced with criminal intent. But some art can be lost forever due to craftsmanship that is not responsive to the effects of time and environmental factors.

Sarah Hood's piece *Malden Avenue East, Structural Series #1, Decomposition* (**1.20**) illustrates how the three concepts of medium as artform, medium as material, and craftsmanship can be successfully integrated. The piece plays with the concept of artform—it is jewelry, a necklace, but it is too delicate to actually be worn. Hood's choice of materials is a mix of fragile plant material and metal, juxtaposing suggestions of impermanence and permanence. She says that her use of the organic seedpods in her jewelry "comes from a desire to embrace the impermanence of the natural world around me. Rather than lamenting the transience of life, this jewelry celebrates it, transforming decay into beauty and lyricism, fragility into a strength of purpose."[15] The finely wrought silver sections evidence a high level of skill in the way the segments are fabricated, formed, and joined, yet much of the necklace has not been crafted by the artist, because she did not make the hanging pieces but instead found and used dried seedpods.

1.19 MIKE AND DOUG STARN *Blue Rose,* 1982–1988. Toned ortho print with Plexiglas, glue, frame, 11 × 14 in.

1.20 SARAH HOOD *Malden Avenue East, Structural Series #1, Decomposition,* 1999. Silver and Chinese lantern pods.

Aspects of Form

The physical structure of your work—its **form**—is the result of the processes you use to compose your materials according to your work's intended function and expressive purpose. Form can be used as both a verb (you form materials) and a noun (what you make results in a form; what you make has form).

Form is constituted by design elements, such as line, texture, shape, mass, volume, color, time, and so forth. These are the building blocks of any form. Design principles are ways that artists organize elements into form, by balancing them, emphasizing some elements more than others, establishing patterns, finding ways of unifying the elements, and so forth.

If you wish to make a calm and peaceful nonrepresentational sculpture, how will you express calmness and peace in the medium you choose? If you want to move a viewer to action through a political painting, how will you visually convey your idea so this happens? If you do not understand form, you may end up with a jarring piece that you meant to be calming, or a calming piece that you wanted to provoke action. Design elements and principles are the topics of subsequent chapters, but for the present, consider two well-formed works, Rockwell's *After the Prom* (see 1.8) and a motorbike (see 1.21).

Hickey, the critic, explains how Rockwell composed (formed) his painting according to an expressive intent. Hickey observes that the form of the picture welcomes us. He writes that Rockwell's view of the scene places us inside the store but not up at the counter: we are part of the society but not part of the community. "The clustered burst of white in the center of Rockwell's painting, created by the young woman's dress, the boy's jacket, and the soda jerk's hat and shirt, constitutes our gardenia; we stand in the same relationship to that white blossom of tactile paint as the soda jerk does to the young woman's corsage."[16] Hickey also tells us that the soda jerk that Rockwell posed leaning toward the girl is our surrogate: he inhales the fragrance of the flower that is the symbol of love. Rockwell shows him visibly responding. He shows the other figures responding to the soda jerk's response and to one another, and we respond to the totality of their responses. Rockwell has made a well-formed painting.

ENV (**1.21**), the world's first hydrogen fuel–cell motorcycle, relies in large part on its carefully designed form, and carefully chosen materials, for its high performance, which outstrips other electrically fueled bikes. The bike's structural form is lightweight, streamlined, and aerodynamic, designed to move quickly and efficiently as well as to look good. The bike produces minimal noise pollution, and its only emission is water vapor pure enough to drink. The bike can run for up to four hours before refueling. The surface finish of iridescent white and high-gloss black paint expresses the bike's dual nature: clean power and the excitement of a good ride. It is a well-formed machine.

Contexts

Meanings of artworks depend on context, the circumstances that form their setting. These circumstances in turn vary, from where and how an object is placed, to the way the parts of the object relate, to the history and experience of the artist and conditions in the outside world. We consider five types of context: viewing, internal, artist's, social, and art historical.

VIEWING CONTEXT

Where and how an object is placed—its **viewing context**—is crucial to how it is understood and received. Placing an American flag in the window of your dwelling signifies a positive view of America and its policies. Placing the same flag on the floor of an art gallery so that viewers must walk on it in order to see what else you have placed on the wall above it signifies criticism of the country and may be taken as an anti-American statement that will likely enrage some people, regardless of your artistic intent.

Similarly, if you take a piece of old discarded metal that you find visually interesting because of its shape, color, and texture and place it on a pristine gallery wall, it will be viewed as a work of "found art." That same piece of metal seen in an alley will be viewed as litter.

Viewing context includes an object's functionality, that is, how it performs in use. When the P'kolino Play Table (**1.22**) is featured in a design magazine, it appears as an interesting set of objects with an appealing palette of colors and shapes that are made inviting by their rounded edges. The two creators of the table (master's students at Rhode Island School of Design at the time)

1.21 Intelligent Energy ENV Bike, Great Britain, 2006.

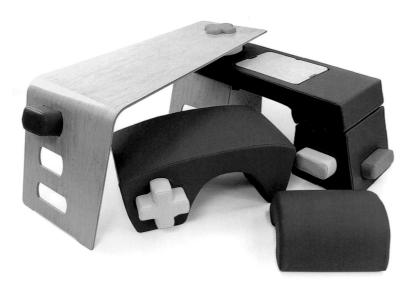

1.22   J. B. SCHNEIDER AND ANTONIO TURCO-RIVAS   P'kolino Play Table, 2004.

1.23   SARAH SZE   *Still Life with Flowers,* 1999. Mixed media, dimensions variable.

intend their product to be functional, as well as attractive, in homes where children learn and play: "We wanted to create play furniture that was designed for children (not miniature adults) and how they play and grow mentally, physically and socially . . . all while making the products beautiful (after all adults have to live at home too)."[17] The designers' play table avoids garish colors often used by designers who mistakenly believe that children need to be assaulted by bright colors to attract their attention. The colors of the P'kolino Play Table are pleasant and calming and avoid overstimulation of a household environment.

Other works your artifact is shown with will influence how viewers attribute meanings to your work. Curators thoughtfully place works beside one another, or distance works from one another, for interpretive reasons. For example, although most art museums show art in historical chronological order, some curators are hanging works from different times and cultures in the same gallery according to a theme, such as mother and child or social protest. They may also mix different media in the same gallery rather than in media-specific galleries: paintings, product designs, photographs, and other objects from the 1950s may be in one room, rather than spread throughout the museum into media-specific spaces such as a sculpture garden, a gallery for furniture, another for painting, and so forth. You too can influence how viewers will think about any one of your works depending on the context in which you show it, whether it is situated next to another of yours or next to someone else's.

INTERNAL CONTEXT

The juxtaposition of parts within the whole and the meanings they evoke through proximity to one another give an artifact its **internal context.** Sarah Sze makes sculptures, some ephemeral, some permanent, out of everyday small-scale household objects that she assembles for specific spaces. Museum educators for the Carnegie International Exhibition say that the items she chooses "respond to and infiltrate the surrounding architecture in which they are situated." She successively links small bits of discrete objects into a complex three-dimensional network (**1.23**). Each object affects the other objects near it, and "the interplay between individual components and overall structure allows Sze to explore the boundaries between art and everyday life."[18]

Everything in a work of art is altered by anything else in it. This will be apparent when we later consider how artists use design principles to change how design elements are understood according to how those elements are placed as part of an artifact. Some especially compelling examples in the chapter on color (Chapter 4) show how the same color against different backgrounds looks like different colors (see p. 84).

ARTIST'S CONTEXT

An **artist's context** is the life history, experiences, and time influencing the person whose work we are considering. We can enjoy *Untitled* by Wangechi Mutu (**1.24**) without knowing about her, but when we have access to facts about her life, there is more to think about when looking at her artwork. Like all artists, Mutu draws upon the personal facts of her life to express thoughts and feelings. She is Kenyan born, living in Brooklyn, and her work resonates with African imagery. She considers herself a multimedia figurative artist. When she was younger, a main source of her inspiration was discarded magazines she found on the street, her "poor man's paint." She chooses the female body as her subject matter and notions of beauty as a major idea for her work. Her works combine such diverse materials as cloth, ink, pearls, glitter, magazine fashion pictures, and medical imagery gathered from scientific texts. Mutu's life experiences are within multicultural settings, and she uses multiple representational conventions in her works. In *Untitled,* the head of the woman is in severe profile, as in ancient Egyptian representations of the human figure, although the torso of the figure is presented in the representational manner of Renaissance artists. Mutu's works reveal her ideas about contemporary society: "We live in a moment of collage, of splicing, entering another's space, of coexistence, or of forced coexistence."[19] In *Untitled,* Mutu has spliced ancient Egyptian and Renaissance perspectives with different media both old (ink) and new (Mylar), and she has given the woman a protective knife for a left hand, perhaps to indicate the need of women to defend themselves, and a prosthetic device for a right hand, perhaps to indicate the ravages of sexism.

Your own work will necessarily be grounded in the context of your life history. It can be a rich resource for your personal expression. Although we share commonalities of experience, no one has lived the same life. Your challenge as an artist is to transform your personal life experiences and insights into works that are understandable to others as well as meaningful to yourself.

1.24 WANGECHI MUTU *Untitled,* 2004. Ink, acrylic, photocollage, contact paper on Mylar, 36 × 24 in.

SOCIAL CONTEXT

The **social context** of a work of art is the time and place in which the work is made. To understand with some degree of confidence Leon Golub's painting *Try Burning This One . . .* (**1.25**), we need information about the social context of the United States in the first part of the twentieth century to accurately consider what the painting shows and implies. Golub (who died in 2004) based his paintings on political events. He pondered news media for themes and clipped out printed news photographs for his subject matter. His paintings are about his time in the world as he experienced it from his American perspective. He directly and consciously borrowed from the culture he lived in, and his art is often critical of it. To understand his paintings the way he meant them, we too must be aware of the paintings' social contexts.

In *Try Burning This One . . .* Golub portrays two standing male figures. One wears a T-shirt with an American flag and the words "Try burning this one . . . asshole." The other male next to him crudely and defiantly grasps his own crotch. The men, in their clothing, postures, and gestures, are threatening and

1.25   LEON GOLUB *Try Burning This One . . . ,* 1991. Acrylic on linen, 122 × 113 in.

confrontational. They look directly at you, the viewer. Their ideology seems to be one of an unenlightened patriotism that would protect the flag, with violence if needed, against any who would use it to protest policies of the U.S. government. Citizens of the United States have been divided about war and what it means to be patriotic in times of war, especially when wars are controversial. America's involvement in the Vietnam War from 1959 to 1975 was particularly divisive for Americans. Many demonstrations for and protests against the Vietnam War turned ugly. One way of protesting by those opposed to America's involvement in the war was to burn American flags, acts that oppositional elements considered highly offensive and unpatriotic. The Vietnam War and other American military engagements after it are frequent subjects of Golub's paintings. He was opposed to that war, and the wars in the Middle East that followed it, and took offense at those who considered calls for peace to be unpatriotic. *Try Burning This One . . .* is critical of those who think peaceful patriotism is cowardly and unmanly. Golub's political views, however, may not be easily inferred

by looking at this one painting.

Functional objects you design will likewise be seen within a social context of the time and place they are made, namely, within a segment of the consumer culture or the marketplace for your type of object. The designers of the ENV bike (see 1.21) are more aware of the precariousness of the natural environment than designers of earlier motorized vehicles when we were less conscious of the effects of products and their uses on the sustainability of the natural world.

Your work is in a competitive environment of products and services, whether or not you place it there, because consumers will. You will need to consider what social cues your own work is drawing upon, and whether you have presented them in ways that communicate your position on any given topic to an audience. If your references are too oblique or too ambiguous, misunderstandings of your work are likely.

ART HISTORICAL CONTEXT

When you make a work, it becomes part of an **art historical context** within the realm of all other artifacts throughout history. The history of art is often cast as a history of one artist referencing the work of another artist, sometimes to further a tradition, sometimes in a spirit of homage, and sometimes in a spirit of wanting to challenge a predominant style.

Robert Colescott based a painting he made in 1975 (**1.26**) on a painting Emanuel Leutze made in 1851 (**1.27**). Colescott's painting does not make much sense without knowledge of Leutze's painting. Leutze's is a historical painting of George Washington leading revolutionary troops in a surprise attack in 1776 against the British, who had invaded the American colonies. It was a bold attack that changed the momentum of the war in the colonists' favor and ultimately led to victory.

1.26 ROBERT COLESCOTT *George Washington Carver Crossing the Delaware: Page from an American History Textbook,* 1975. Oil on canvas, 84 × 108 in.

1.27 EMANUEL LEUTZE *George Washington Crossing the Delaware,* 1851. Oil on canvas, 149 × 255 in.

Colescott counts on viewers being familiar with Leutze's painting because it is frequently reproduced in textbooks about American history. Colescott implies this in the second part of the title of his painting: *Page from an American History Textbook*. Colescott's painting makes an ironic statement about history as presented in textbooks because, in Colescott's view, textbooks underrepresent and misrepresent the treatment of blacks in American history. Colescott has replaced George Washington with George Washington Carver and replaced the revolutionary soldiers with stereotypes of black people in minstrel-style blackface. His painting refers to tokenism—the inclusion of George Washington Carver as one of the few or the only important black person in many history textbooks for children—and to common stereotypes of black people in American culture.

Viewers will place your work into the context of past art and art currently being made and shown by other artists. They will want to know if your work is building on a past style, subverting one of them, or attempting to discard many. Your references to the art of others can be sophisticated or naive. If you are not well informed about the history of art, past and recent, you are at a disadvantage: those who know art will be consciously or subconsciously judging what you are doing by comparing it to what has already been done. Formal courses in art history are one way to acquire this knowledge, as is reading exhibition catalogs, period surveys, and monographs on particular artists. Instructors may ask you to make visual responses to the work of other artists in informed and creative ways.

Conclusion: The Components and Meanings

When you thoughtfully make a work of art or a designed object using subject matter, medium, form, and contexts, you will create meaningful objects. "Meaning" is an elusive term, but it generally refers to what the work is about or what it expresses. As we will examine in the next chapter, meanings of artifacts are multiple; thus we will use the word in its plural form, meanings. Works of art are not the kinds of objects that have single, correct, and immutable meanings.

Meanings are the results of interpretations. **Interpretation** is a process of deciphering what the work is about or expresses—not whether it is "good," but what it might mean to the maker, to the people for whom it was made if it is a historical artifact, and to its viewers in present time.

Work that you make will have personal meaning for you: it is based in your life experiences, and only you will know the significance of all the subjects or symbols you use. Thus not everyone may be able to fully access all the meaningful aspects of any work that you make. By being aware of an audience, however, you can choose creative processes and make choices about process, subject matter, media, form, and contexts to better communicate to others. By being consciously aware of your artistic choices, you will likely gain self-knowledge while expressing what you think about what you have experienced.

Let's look at one work of art, Frida Kahlo's painting *What the Water Has Given Me* (**1.28**) and see how the components of subject matter, medium, form, and contexts interact to allow us to formulate meanings about the work. The components and their interactions may be put into this simple but powerful formula for thoughtfully making your own art and considering the artworks of others:

SUBJECT MATTER + MEDIUM + FORM
+ CONTEXTS = MEANINGS

This formula need not be followed in any particular order: you can start with any of the components, but you should consider all of them and how they interrelate and inflect meanings. Although we can analytically separate subject matter, medium, form, and context in works of art and design, these components are interdependent, and all are simultaneously active depending on the artist's process of working.

With Kahlo's painting, let's start with *subject matter* because it is complex and dominates the painting. We see a bathtub. We see two sets of toes against the end of the tub and reflected in the water. The nails are painted red, thus are likely the toes of a woman. The big toe of the right foot is cut and bleeding. Below the right foot, a woodpecker lies on its back on top of a tree that is part of an island landscape. To the right of the bird, a skyscraper emerges from the center of an erupting volcano. At the bottom left of the volcano lies a man in a loincloth, perhaps a Jesus figure. At the bottom right of the volcano, a skeleton sits atop a hill. Under the left foot we can see a sailboat, a rock formation, a seashell with water pouring from it. There are sea animals in the water. Between the seashell and the island, a nude pregnant woman floats belly up in the water. Her eyes are closed, and she may be dead. A rope originates in the loincloth figure's hand, wraps around the woman's neck, then around the rock formation, and ends tied to another rock formation on the island. Insects, a dancing woman, and a snake are moving on the rope. A fancy dress floats in the water near the body. To the right of the nude body, a man and woman in formal wear stand behind large leaves. In front of the leaves, two nude women are on a bed: one woman is of darker skin than the other. Lush plant life with exposed roots and blossoms grows in the water at the bottom of the canvas.

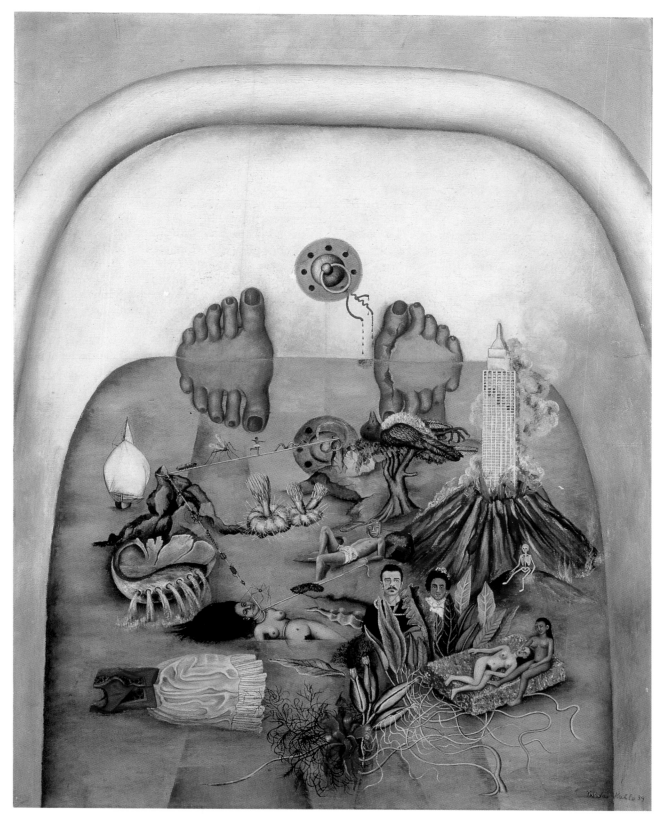

1.28 **FRIDA KAHLO** *What the Water Has Given Me (Lo que el agua me dio),* 1939. Oil on canvas, 69 × 88 cm.

Kahlo's choice of *medium* for this painting is oil paint on canvas. In *crafting* her painting, she does not draw attention to her technique of painting through noticeably thick paint and obvious brushstrokes as some painters do. Instead, she uses a simple representational style that does not distract the viewer from the painting's narrative content.

The *form* of the painting shows the feet and floating subject matter from the point of view of the woman taking the bath, although she is not shown. The figures and objects in the painting are not scaled realistically: the bathing feet are as large as the skyscraper, for example. Kahlo has rendered the scene and its objects with representational detail and realistic colors. The top of the canvas is calm in contrast to the bottom two-thirds, which contain most of the subject matter.

If we know of Kahlo's biography, which is well documented in recent history books, we know that all of her work is intensely personal because she investigates with honesty her life experiences. From *internal, artist's,* and *social contexts,* we can confidently infer that *What the Water Has Given Me* is a psychological self-portrait, a narrative of her life featuring selected memories and imaginings. Much of the subject matter is garnered from Kahlo's life: The floating nude woman, the darker woman on the bed, and the formally dressed woman look like photographs and other self-portraits of the artist. The floating woman's belly is swollen and may indicate pregnancy: Kahlo hoped for children but lost all her pregnancies due to a damaged pelvis—one of her injuries from a freak accident on a public bus. She suffered throughout her life after the accident and endured many surgeries. The man in formal wear looks like photographs and paintings of Diego Rivera, Kahlo's husband, a famous Mexican painter of large, politically motivated murals. The couple's relationship was emotionally tumultuous, with both having affairs, including Rivera seducing Kahlo's sister, and Kahlo engaging in lesbian relationships. The couple divorced and then remarried. Both artists were anticapitalist and pro-Marxist in their politics, which may account for Kahlo's rendering of the intrusive burning skyscraper in a natural agrarian environment. Kahlo is admired for being an early and influential feminist, an advocate of pride in one's ethnicity, and a promoter of social justice.

From artistic and social and *art historical contexts,* we know some of Kahlo's art-making processes. This painting is larger than most of her work. Her paintings are often small, partly because of the limitations of her body—she often painted while bedridden due to reparative operations following her bus accident. Kahlo was also attracted to small canvases by her knowledge of and preference for the fine detailing typical of the Mexican folk-art form known as the *retablos.* She strongly and proudly identified with Mexico's past and its indigenous people.

Although Kahlo distanced herself from the Surrealist painters of her time, her work is part of the Surrealist movement that explored the subconscious and revealed meanings beneath the surface appearance of things. We know that many of the things and situations represented in the painting are based on her actual life, but other things seem symbolic, floating above the water as if they were emanations of the bather's mind.

The intimacy of Kahlo's painting may inspire you to be more revealing when making your own works. Her bravery in self-disclosure may cause you to look more closely at your own life and at the stories you tell yourself to make sense of your life events: Are your narratives positive or negative, true or false, accurate or distorted? What would be the consequences of your changing your inner narratives into empowering stories? What if you shared these narratives publicly in paint or pixels?

As an artist or designer, you will express ideas, feelings, and attitudes in your work. Viewers of the objects you make will construct meanings and infer attitudes based on what they see when they consider your process and the choices you have made concerning subject matter, medium, form, and context. For perceptive viewers, everything counts in a work of art, even accidents and the unintended consequences of your choices. By deepening your understanding of the components of an artwork, you can knowingly exert greater or lesser control over your expressions and their effectiveness for viewers. The next chapter considers interpretation and meanings more fully and provides you with ideas about how viewers will construct meanings about the works you make. With this knowledge, you can better determine whether you are effectively showing your intent when making visual choices for your works.

2 Meanings and Interpretations

2.1 **MARTIN PURYEAR** *Ladder for Booker T. Washington,* 1996. Wood (maple and ash), 432 × 22¾ × (narrowing to 1¼ at top) × 3 in.

Making ideas and emotions visible in the artifacts you make requires that you think about what you make, how you make it, and most importantly, what consequences your work has for the world. You cannot always predict how viewers of your work will construct meanings, or interpretations, based on what they see, think, and feel, but you can provide direction by means of your choice of subject matter, media, and context.

Designers need to know and fulfill their purposes when designing for practical applications, and artists need to know what they intend to express when making works of art. We will see two examples of artists clearly communicating a verbal statement of their intents for making works. Then we examine four artists' expressed meanings in a sculpture, a photograph, a ceramic jar, and a painting. Artists as well as viewers can use a straightforward method for interpreting any artifact, keeping in mind that there is not one "right" interpretation—not even an artist's interpretation of her or his own work. You can use the open-ended set of principles at the end of the chapter for inferring meaning in works of art, both when you are making art and when you wish to reflect on what you have made.

Meanings and Interpretations Key Terms

ARTIST'S STATEMENT   A written commentary by artists about their own work to help them clarify their own *intent* and give viewers an entry point to understanding their artifacts.

SEMIOTICS   An area of study concerned with how a *sign* means.

SIGN   An entity that signifies another entity.

DENOTATIONS   What an image actually shows; its surface meanings.

CONNOTATIONS   What an image implies or suggests beyond what it shows.

INTENTIONAL FALLACY   The false belief that an artifact means only what its maker intended it to mean.

COHERENCE   The criterion that interpretations ought to make sense as thoughts in themselves independent of the artifact.

CORRESPONDENCE   The criterion that interpretations ought to match what we see in and know about an artifact.

COMPLETENESS   The criterion that interpretations ought to account for all that is in an artifact.

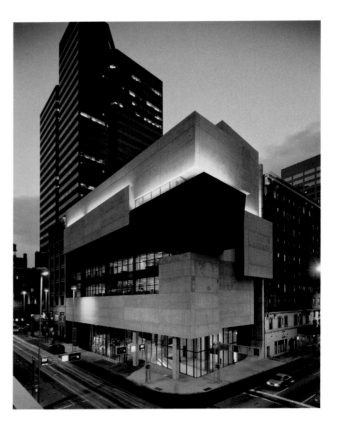

2.2   ZAHA HADID ARCHITECTS   Rosenthal Center for Contemporary Art, 1997–2003. Cincinnati, Ohio.

Designing with a Purpose

Architects, designers, and artists working under commission typically work within parameters established by the client who hires them. When accepting the commission of a design project for a functional space or object, you will need to be aware of such key factors as audience, purpose, and budget: an object or space must meet an audience's needs, fulfill a predetermined purpose, and be competitively priced. Craftsmanship is another essential component, whether the project needs to endure for generations or stand out for a moment in a crowd of competitors.

ARCHITECTURE: DESIGNING FOR A SMALL SPACE

Zaha Hadid, an Iraqi-born, London-based architect is the first woman to design a major arts building in the United States, the Contemporary Arts Center in Cincinnati (**2.2**). She designed the building as an "urban carpet" that would draw in pedestrian city traffic in a somewhat declining downtown.[1] The "carpet" is a poured seamless concrete sidewalk outside the building that continues into a mezzanine and curves upward into a wall in the building near a stairway that directs visitors up into galleries (**2.3**).

2.3 ZAHA HADID ARCHITECTS Interior, Rosenthal Center for Contemporary Art, 1997–2003. Cincinnati, Ohio.

2.5 FABIEN BARON Viktor & Rolf Flowerbomb, 2005.

2.4 Chanel No. 5, Photograph by Mitchell Feinberg.

The building has a small footprint because it needed to be built on a narrow plot of land. Hadid stacked six lively volumes that subtly shift atop each other, allowing 17,000 square feet of galleries, a lobby, a special space for children, a performance space, a coffee shop, a bookstore, and offices. The galleries seem to float over the main lobby and connect and interlock like a three-dimensional puzzle, allowing unobstructed views from all sides. The exterior of the building visually defines what Hadid designed as a flexible, functionally driven collection of interior spaces.

PRODUCT DESIGN: KNOWING HOW THE PRODUCT IS PERCEIVED

Within the highly competitive perfume industry, the look of the perfume bottle is integral to the image and appeal of *haute couture* fragrances. Many bottles are designed by artists and individually crafted by hand by artisans. Those within the industry refer to the bottle for Chanel No. 5 Eau de Parfum as "the Chanel square," and they acknowledge it to be the standard of excellence in the market (**2.4**). Executives at Chanel say that the bottle, designed in 1921, is influenced by the design of a gentleman's flask. They admire the bottle's simplicity, purity, and luxury as well as its functionality.

Fabien Baron designed a bottle for Viktor & Rolf's Flowerbomb fragrance (**2.5**), which debuted in 2005. Viktor & Rolf wanted the design of the bottle to begin with the name: "We wanted an explosion of a thousand different flowers, a flower bomb." Baron designed a glass hand grenade with pull pin. Victor & Rolf was pleased with the design, seeing it as a diamond grenade that combined "power and romance, preciousness and rareness,"[2] but critics of the design saw mangled bodies and severed limbs of soldiers and civilians, including children, and a cynical disregard of suffering by the protected wealthy and their fineries. Designers must be aware of what their designs actually suggest, no matter their intentions.

GRAPHIC DESIGN: INTEGRATING PURPOSE, FORM, AND PROCESS

Peter Chan designed a catalog and invitation (**2.6**) for an art exhibition by glass artist William Morris. To successfully complete the project, Chan first had to know what his clients wanted the design to accomplish. The client who first contacted Chan was the gallery owner. He was already aware of Chan's design work and wanted to commission him. Another client was the artist, William Morris. Chan sent samples of his designs to Morris, and upon reviewing them, Morris gave Chan free rein as designer. The artist's manager also approved of Chan as the designer.

All parties needed to agree on the purposes of the design. The invitation to the exhibit and the catalog of works needed to appeal to the gallery's audience of potential buyers. The glass sculptures are relatively expensive (between $30,000 and $150,000 each), and the potential buyers included museums and individual collectors. The pieces are one of a kind, and fifteen were to be exhibited. Each needed to be included in the catalog.

The clients commissioned Tina Oldknow, an established glass curator, to write the text for the catalog, and Chan suggested that the text tell the story of the works, how they came to be, and why they look the way they do. He wanted the artist's own words to communicate to the potential collector, and he obtained quotes from Morris in his own handwriting for use as a graphic element.

Chan wanted an easy and elegant flow of information for the catalog and decided on an accordion fold rather than a traditional sequence of pages. The catalog would be printed on two sides of two pieces of paper and wrapped in a heavy, textured brown sheet of paper.

Having decided that the artworks would look good against a black background, Chan consulted with the photographer of the works, asking that they be lit against a black background, from a consistent angle, and be of warm tone. The text would be printed in earth tones on a creamy white paper.

The quality of the graphic materials had to match the quality of the works of art. Choice of paper was crucial: how heavy, coated or not, recycled or made from virgin timber, textured or smooth? The grain of paper had to accept folds well. The choice of paper was also determined by the size of the catalog. Chan considered number of folds and size of the panels and decided on a seven-panel format. Based on the width of the panels, he determined what would be an elegantly proportional page height.

The catalog was printed in seven colors of ink and two varnishes that required two print cycles: on the first run through the press, cyan, magenta, yellow, black, a second black, and a dull varnish were printed; on the second run, metallic copper and green and a gloss varnish were added. The overprinting process maximized richness of color, a contrast between dull and shiny, and a rich black background.

The finished folded piece was hand-sewn together with a strip of leather. The invitation used the same paper and inks and matched the elegance of the catalog.

Each decision Chan made was meant not only to reflect the essence of the glass artworks as expressed by the artist and gallery

2.6   PETER KWOK CHAN   William Morris exhibition invitation and catalog, 1997.

owner but also to contribute to an expressive connection between the graphic design, the artworks, and the audience. After publication of the materials, jurors selecting the best graphic designs for the year awarded Chan's design a top prize for being "elegant and refined," "a beautifully tactile piece" with "sensitive typography, superior production quality," and said it was "interesting to read and exciting to look at."[3]

COMMISSIONED ART

Painters, sculptors, and other artists may have greater freedom than designers and architects, but they too work within the parameters of a project. The choice of media, subject matter, and intended message and such practical considerations as space to work, equipment requirements, and budget impose limitations on what you can create.

Artists who accept commissions from individuals or community groups must address the needs of those clients and keep them in balance with their own creative criteria as artists. Artists who accept commissions for public art face challenges similar to those faced by architects and other designers.

The federal government commissioned Richard Serra to produce a sculpture for the Jacob Javits Federal Building in lower Manhattan in 1981. Serra created *Tilted Arc* (Serra no longer allows the sculpture to be reproduced), which produced a public outcry and resulted in a public hearing in 1985. In 1989 the sculpture was dismantled and removed from the plaza and now sits in storage in a federal building. Serra designed the sculpture, oversaw construction of the monumental work that required great skill and craft, stayed within budget, finished the work on time, and made a piece that is consistent with his life's work. The citizens who worked adjacent to the plaza, however, objected to having to circumnavigate the 120-foot-long sculpture in order to cross the plaza. Public art, especially when paid for with tax dollars, is the frequent cause of controversy. In this case, Serra met his intent and vigorously defended his work and its placement in the plaza, but his choices were overruled by public opinion.

Nonetheless, rather than viewing limitations as negative impositions on creativity and expression, successful designers and artists willingly accept them as positive challenges and as needed constraints. Doing "anything you want" is much harder than starting with some guidelines, whether self-chosen or required by a client. In early coursework in art classes, many assignments start with certain constraints provided by the instructor. As artists progress, they usually impose their own guidelines on their work in order to structure their creative processes.

2.7 **TOM FRIEDMAN** *Loop,* 1993–1995. Spaghetti.

The Value of Knowing Your Own Intentions

Art instructors generally expect their students to think about what they are expressing and why and to be able to articulate their intentions. Knowing your intent is an essential part of the learning process. Oftentimes the instructor will supply the intent for your work in the form of a class assignment and evaluate the work on how well it meets the assignment. Beyond the classroom, however, you will find it essential to be able to discuss your work with others when you attempt to obtain gallery shows, apply for grants and other sources of funding for your work, or present your designs to a client.

Thinking about what you want to express will guide your creative process. Your idea will help you select appropriate media to express that idea, and will help you form your idea in media with appropriate attention to craft, while you consider your audience and where your work will be shown. In the following paragraphs, conceptual artist Tom Friedman, designer Maya Lin, and photographer Carrie Mae Weems express their thoughts on the value of knowing their intentions when they are making their artworks. Painters Eric Fischl, Jackson Pollock, and Miriam Schapiro say that they sometimes discover their intentions for works while they are making them.

Tom Friedman is an American conceptual artist who makes minimalist objects that are often wryly humorous, such as *Loop* (**2.7**), in which all the pieces from a 435-gram box of spaghetti were cooked, dried, and then connected end to end. The first piece connects to the last to form a continuous loop. Friedman has said, "You know, no one wants to look at art and have it not do anything."[4] He is aware of what he wants his pieces to do, and he clearly explains his intentions.

2.8 **MAYA LIN** **Vietnam Veterans Memorial, Washington, D.C.,** inaugurated in 1982.

Friedman's *Untitled* is a sculptural work from 1992 that does not reproduce well but is easy to describe. It consisted of one thin wire that protruded, perfectly erect, from the middle of a gallery floor. He made *Untitled* by placing the tip of the wire into a small drilled hole. He observed the long wire: When the wire bent over, he would cut it down slightly and straighten it. He kept cutting down the wire and straightening it until he found the exact height at which the wire would support itself without bending.

About this wire piece, Friedman said, "It was so sensitive that it would quiver with just the vibrations in the air, and it seemed to be defying gravity. It was almost invisible—you had to be shown where it was. I remember people would come into my studio, I'd point the piece out to them, and wherever they were, walking around my studio, they'd constantly have to orient themselves in relation to the piece. That's the kind of presence I was thinking about. Because of its fragility, people would have to consider it, hold it in their minds, and be sensitive to it so as not to damage it."[5]

From what Friedman says, we know that he was sure of his intent in making the piece. He wanted a presence for the wire and its fragility that would sensitize people to it. Viewers who experience the piece may well go away thinking about the implications of the piece, what it might mean for their lives. That is, they might interpret their experience of the work and build personal meaning about it: perhaps about the fragility of a moment, the preciousness of a blade of grass, the care they might want to provide for another.

Had Friedman not made the piece just right, figuring out just what he wanted the piece to do, choosing an apt medium for his idea, crafting it carefully so that the wire did just what he wanted it to do, placing the piece in the gallery where it would be seen, the piece would not have worked as he intended it to work. Also, if people walked into the gallery space, saw the wire, but pondered it no further, they would not experience a meaningful piece of art—they would just see a wire protruding from the floor. Both artist and viewer are engaged in an exchange of meaning making when works of art are successfully made and received.

Maya Lin designed the Vietnam Veterans Memorial (**2.8**) at the age of twenty-one while an architecture student and has designed other monuments and private homes as well as individual works of art. She starts her work by trying to anticipate the viewer's experience. The Vietnam Veterans Memorial is a V-shaped wall of black stone, etched with the names of 58,000 dead soldiers. It is now the most visited memorial in the nation's capital, but at the time of its planning and installation it was controversial because of its unconventional design. Many wanted a traditional sculpture of soldiers and viewed Lin's minimalist design as a protest against a controversial war. More political energy was devoted to stopping the project than implementing it. After the memorial was completed, a journalist reported, "Its political foes fell silent."[6]

Lin "creates, essentially, backward. There is no image in her head, only an imagined feeling."[7] According to Lin, she stripped the question of how she wanted the memorial to work to this: "How are all these people going to overcome the pain of losing something? How do you really overcome death?" During the development of the design, she remembers a skeptical veteran asking her, "What are the people going to do when they first see this piece?" She remembers telling him something like, "Well, I think they are really going to be moved by it." She adds, "What I didn't tell him is that they are probably going to cry and cry and cry."[8]

Carrie Mae Weems (**2.9**) worries about making her intentions for her photographs clear for viewers. She specifically addresses the problem of making a machine—a camera—express her beliefs:

> You know, we have to make art work for us within the context of our own individual belief systems. I've often thought about this. How do you do this with photography? How do you describe complex experiences in a photograph? What are the sights of it? What should it have to look like? What does it have to challenge? To whom is it challenging? You know, who's it for? All those kinds of questions are constantly shifting for me.[9]

Weems's answers to these questions guide her decisions when she makes her work.

In many of his paintings, Eric Fischl uses beds (**2.10**) as important subject matter. He acknowledges that the significance

2.9 **CARRIE MAE WEEMS** *Jim, if you choose to accept, the mission is to land on your own two feet,* 1988–1989. Gelatin silver print, 20 × 16 in.

2.10 **ERIC FISCHL** *Study for the Bed, the Chair, Head to Foot,* 2000. Oil on linen, 24 × 36 in.

2.11   LAUREN GREENFIELD *Annie, Hannah, and Alli, all 13, getting ready for the first big party of seventh grade, Edina, Minnesota,* 2002. Photograph.

of the bed image became clear to him only after he had been using it for years:

> When I was a student at Arizona State I was learning to paint abstract paintings *à la* Kandinsky. You know, arabesque forms and one edge of color bumping up against another and starting a different shape. I was having a horrible time with one painting. I didn't know what to do and I worked on it for weeks and weeks, painting and overpainting and getting really frustrated. I remember this one day, at the absolute limit of my tolerance, getting up and just drawing this form across the middle of the painting, then filling it in with white. When I stepped back, I saw that I'd painted a shape that looked like a white bed. And I had finished the painting as well. It was this weird painting in which there are flat abstract shapes and then this isometric "bed" sitting in the middle. I never understood it, but I knew it was done. It's always been a vivid memory for me. Then years later that bed started to appear and reappear until its presence became clarified to me.[10]

Jackson Pollock said, "When I am in my painting, I'm not aware of what I'm doing. It is only after a sort of 'get acquainted' period that I see what I have been about. I have no fears about making changes, destroying the image, etc., because the painting has a life of its own. I try to let it come through."[11]

Miriam Schapiro (see 10.1) said, "I see myself free in the studio inventing ways to bring out of the hidden crevices of my heart that which is stubborn and which asks for more and more strength and discipline for the extraction."[12] Making art for her is a way to discover something: she does not know ahead of time what she is going to do, but does it, and, in the process, finds her meaning.

We can draw important conclusions from these artists' thoughts about their intents in making works. Artists do think about and articulate the intended meanings of their work. Some artists form clear intentions from the start. Others do not always know with specificity what they mean to express when they begin a piece, and they are content to start with an ambiguous notion or a general direction and refine their idea in media as they proceed. Artists learn about the meanings of their works *after* they have finished them. Some of their intended meanings are very general and they do not offer explanations for particular works, but artists do concern themselves with what their work means to them and what they want it to mean to those who see it. Artists can discover their intents while making their works.

Writing an Artist's Statement

Eventually you will be asked to articulate what you make and why, by instructors, fellow artists, potential employers, granting agencies, jurors of competitive shows, and gallery directors. They will often request an **artist's statement**—a written introduction from your point of view to help the viewer understand and appreciate your work. Artists' statements often accompany exhibitions as signs on a wall near the entrance to the show or next to the artist's work. You need not use pretentious language or jargon when writing about your

2.14 JACQUIE STEVENS *Double-Spouted Jar,* 2001. Ceramic, 26 × 15 in.

2.15 ANNE SEIDMAN *Untitled,* 2002. Aquamedia on wood, 24 × 24 in.

glaze that contrasts with the outside color glaze. We recognize that the object is hollow and that it could be filled with a substance and that it could serve a practical function. Its form, however, suggests that the piece is meant to be more sculptural than practical.

Contexts. That *Double-Spouted Jar* does not have representational subject matter does not mean that it does not make *references* to things in the world. It certainly refers to other ceramic objects, indeed, to the history of ceramics, and to sculpture in general. More specifically, it refers to vessels, sacred and secular.

Stevens was born in 1949, in Omaha, Nebraska, of Winnebago heritage, and has lived in Santa Fe, New Mexico, since 1975. She has become a major figure in Southwestern ceramics. She discovered her talent for making ceramics while studying at the Institute of American Indian Art. Her innovations have been in form—unusual free-form shapes—as well as in her unique surface textures and bold use of color. In her objects, she often incorporates materials ranging from fiber and wicker to shell and leather. While maintaining her contemporary approach to pottery, Stevens also references her ancestry in designs that evoke the spirit of Winnebago basketry.[16]

Meanings. This pot attracts with its shape and its colors. It is welcoming, generous, and friendly. A Native American woman made it, and it seems to welcome non-Native viewers and all people who see it. It is a vessel that can hold something, but it looks to be more of a metaphorical than a practical vessel. By its form, it seems to ask that something spiritual be put within it, something for safekeeping that will be held with joy.

ANNE SEIDMAN'S *UNTITLED*

Anne Seidman's painting (**2.15**) presents interpretive challenges similar to those associated with Stevens's ceramic vessel. Can we construct meaning about such a nonrepresentational painting?

Subject Matter. The subject matter of Seidman's painting is the shapes and colors and textures of the paint she has used to make the work. It is an abstract painting that is nonobjective, that is, an artwork that does not depict objects in the world but, like Stevens's pot, refers to the world.

Medium. Seidman's medium is water-based paint that she has applied onto a surface of flat wood. She built up the paint so that the individual shapes are so heavily textured that they have a third dimension. By allowing the green drip to fall toward the red-orange shape, she shows the liquidity of her paint.

Form. The shapes of the painting descend and ascend from the top and bottom of the composition. Because they are cropped at both edges, Seidman implies that they continue, although we cannot see them.

An exhibition catalog for a gallery showing likened Seidman's paintings to strata of stacked earth, "tectonic plates," full of energy, tense with friction, piled along fault lines that could quake. Interlocking bits of shaped color are condensed into a limited space, and each one of these shapes holds its own against the other and against the edges of the composition. He sees that the artist has stacked "strata," or chunks, of organic material and has suspended them within a thick, white, textured field. Although the chunks share similarities, each one is distinct and unique in color, size, shape, and texture. Each holds its own identity in a pressurized field, yet they coexist, but with tension.

The drip of green from the bottom chunk of the top stack *almost* meets the orange chunk rising from the bottom stack. The ever-slight space that the artist left between the green and the orange is one "contested boundary." The artist has presented us with other tensions: at the top of the painting, ochre mesh contains green; a gray dot is contained by or atop its own green field; toward the lower middle of the painting, a bright green slides from its darker field, approaching, with peaceful or threatening intentions, the vertically aspiring pink beneath it. Most amazing is that the composition holds together even though it is clearly in danger of catastrophic collapse.

Contexts. Seidman has shown her paintings in art galleries that feature contemporary art. She exhibits this one painting with other paintings she made around the same time. Any single work in Seidman's exhibition is in dialogue with other works around it. Seidman knows that her work is also in dialogue with all abstract and nonobjective works of art made in recent art history. Seidman and the gallery assume and expect that viewers understand and appreciate nonobjective abstraction in art. Were one to walk into the gallery showing Seidman's paintings never having seen anything but realistic renditions of people and places in paint, one would likely be baffled. Such a viewer would lack the necessary context that Seidman's paintings presume and require.

Meanings. Seidman's painting does not present itself as a story or a political statement about current events. Rather, it presents itself as thick paint on board with nonrepresentational subject matter. Even though Seidman's painting presents itself as nonobjective and austerely abstract, the artist provides associations that may be personally relevant to viewers based on the shapes and colors and textures of paint on the board. The painting, as abstract and nonobjective as it is, delights in ambiguity. It is open to meaning by its lack of representational subject matter or narrative. Nothing in it prevents a viewer from building personally meaningful interpretive thoughts about the piece. The artist would likely be pleased to hear a viewer responding to *Untitled* with statements such as these: "My life is like this painting!" or "Our world is just like this, teetering on devastating collapse!" or "Sometimes I feel that the relationship between the two of us is just like the red and green shapes: I'm almost ready to touch you."

Semiotic Interpretations: Denotations and Connotations

A complementary alternative to the interpretive formula of Subject Matter + Medium + Form + Contexts = Meanings is a semiotic approach. **Semiotics,** an area of study concerned with *how* signs mean, in any medium, offers an effective means of interpretation. A **sign** is an entity that signifies another entity. In semiotics, signs are a combination of signifiers and signifieds. The words you are reading in this sentence are signifiers, that is, Roman letters that form English words that mean (signify) something to you because you read English. The signifieds in the sentence are what the words mean. Sign systems are apparent when we visit a culture with a language foreign to our own; otherwise, in our home cultures, we take signs and our decoding of them to be natural rather than learned. All sign systems, however, are learned, and all signs need to be decoded to be understood. Clouds in the sky, for example, signify predictable natural occurrences only to those who understand weather. In the United States, we have learned what is meant by a red light, a yellow light, and a green light when they are hung over an intersection of streets.

We are interested in semiotics here in order to refine our sophistication in decoding or interpreting visual signs made by people, especially in art. In every visual representation there is a *denotative level* and a *connotative level*. **Denotations** are what we literally see; **connotations** are the interpretive implications of what we see. To identify denotations is a descriptive process of listing all that we actually see in an artifact; to identify the connotations of what we see is to interpret what lies below the surface of an artifact. You can use denotations and connotations to interpret any written text and any object or image, including paintings, sculptures, buildings, and products, made by humans.

A class of college art students identified the following denotations, what they actually saw, in a magazine advertisement for Campari (**2.16**), an alcoholic beverage for adults:

Black background; vertical composition; red, white, and black color scheme; two voluptuous women, one dressed in white as an angel with wings and the other dressed in red as a devil with horns and tail; both women wear makeup; the angel holds a bottle of Campari in one hand and a glass of the drink in her other hand; the devil has one of her arms over the angel's chest and her hand approaches the angel's breast; the devil touches the angel's wrist; the devil's tail wraps around the thighs of the angel; the devil wears high heel shoes; the devil wears tight-fitting shiny vinyl from head to feet; the angel wears a tightly fitting gown, thrusts her hips forward, arches her back, and moves her shoulder into the devil; the angel's wings embrace the shoulders and back of the devil; the angel is blond; the devil's lips are parted, teeth revealed; the angel's face has an expression of expectancy; the word "Campari" is placed horizontally across the bottom of the photograph with white cap letters outlined by gold.

As a homework assignment, students wrote a paragraph that revealed what they interpreted to be the connotations, or interpretive implications, of the ad. Three samples follow.[17]

The Campari ad is clearly illustrating the theory that sex sells. The ad suggests that the angel is giving in to the devil's wishes and drinking Campari. The devil appears to be seducing the angel to such an extent that the angel is writhing in sexual bliss if not an out and out orgasm. The ad is implying that sex and alcohol go together hand in hand and is bringing out the beast in this otherwise angelic woman. The angel is in total submission to the temptation being elicited by the devil woman. The devil's firm hold over the angel is shown by the repetition of red elements found frequently throughout the ad such as the tail wrapped around the angel, the arm wrapped around her and the red liquid in the glass and in the bottle. In conclusion, this ad seems to be suggesting that women wanting to get loose, let their hair down and have a good time, may want to give Campari a try. And men wanting to have their way with their female dates may want to try offering up some Campari as a prelude to what most likely will turn out to be a night of unbridled bliss.

—SCOTT WITTENBURG

This image takes the traditional dramatic conflict between good and evil and restages it as a seduction. The devil, a sexy siren in red latex, entwines herself around our angel and insinuates herself in the erotic red of the Campari. Her shiny horns and mercurial hooves slyly punctuate her underlying danger. The Campari causes our angel to swoon ecstatically, caught both literally and figuratively in this devil's spell. But our angel isn't so innocent. Her lips reveal the slight glow of desire, her hair becomes a golden river of caresses, cascading down our devil's torso and pouring into her crotch. The angel's dress also plunges dangerously down her sides, revealing more of her inviting porcelain skin. At the bottom, her dress flows into a pool of excess and abandon. Her wings lightly clutch our devil. They are caught in a tension of fulfillment and desire, of feeling good by being naughty, of being seduced by seduction.

—MINDY RHOADES

Sex sells. The Campari ad, like many ads for many products, is counting on that. The product name is stamped boldly beneath the curvaceous, seductive embrace of good and evil. Two beyond-perfect women are selling the product. An angel,

2.16 Ad for Campari, 2006.

winged and beautifully gowned, holds the bright red nectar in her hands. She is in ecstasy. The devil, shiny and sleek, coils loosely around the angel. Sinful. Sin is bad but it feels good, and looks good. Campari is inviting the viewer to the other side. Not the dark, hideous side, but the shiny, well groomed, rich, sexy, exotic side, where mother told you never to go.

—DORI APPEL

"Right" Interpretations

We have examined interpretations of five images: a sculpture by Martin Puryear; a photograph by Hannah Wilke; a ceramic jar by Jacquie Stevens; an untitled painting by Anne Seidman; and a magazine advertisement for Campari. Each examination concluded with meanings. Which of these meanings are the *right* meanings? *The* single right meaning? None. Any single work of art can engender multiple meanings. No *single* meaning is *the right meaning*—even the artist's intended meaning.

When the artist who made a work provides the intended meaning for it—in an artist's statement, for instance, or an interview—this intent should not limit to a single meaning the many meanings that the work can have. The false assumption that a work of art means only what the artist intended it to mean is known as

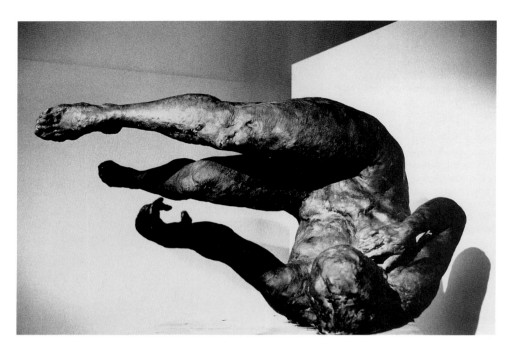

2.17   ERIC FISCHL *Tumbling Woman,* 2002. Bronze, life-size.

the **intentional fallacy.**[18] Works of art can mean more or less than or something entirely different from what their makers intended. The intentional fallacy reminds you that you need to purposefully decide what to include and exclude from your works so that they indicate to viewers a direction for interpretation. If you want to communicate a particular idea or evoke a particular response, you will need to consider all the expressive qualities of all the visual elements in your work and the context in which you place your work for viewing.

You might also show your work and get reactions to it while it is in process or after you have finished it. You can then match your intents for your work with viewers' interpretations of it and decide whether to alter your work or to let it be.

Eric Fischl was both surprised and hurt by how people interpreted and reacted to a sculpture (**2.17**) he made when it was displayed in Rockefeller Center in New York City to memorialize the victims of 9/11 one year after the attack on the World Trade Center. The bronze sculpture shows a life-size female nude falling, her legs in the air and arms outstretched when she hits the ground. Jerry Speyer, the Rockefeller Center landlord who had borrowed the sculpture from a gallery, quickly removed it and offered an apology when viewers complained and the *New York Post* condemned the sculpture. He added, "For centuries, the horrors of war have been sculpted by artists so that people would never forget. That was the intent of this sculpture, and that has been overlooked and misinterpreted." Fischl, the artist, also issued a statement, saying that the sculpture was "a sincere expression of deepest sympathy for the vulnera-

bility of the human condition, both specifically toward the victims of Sept. 11 and toward humanity in general."[19] Clearly the work meant much more than the artist intended.

As a graduate student in printmaking, Jonathan Fisher learned the consequences of intending one thing but unintentionally expressing something else through his choice of subject matter in *Merge— A Portrait of Jhierry* (**2.18**). The piece was one of a series of large signs, mounted on steel, that resemble signage on freeways for motorists. Fisher's intent was clear to him: he was using the highway-like signs as metaphors for people's life choices. About *Merge—A Portrait of Jhierry,* Fisher wrote

This particular piece was meant to feature Jhierry, a young man who has moved on an average of every three years during his adulthood. Jhierry uses his merging with traffic as a metaphor for his own experience with relocation. That is, he merges in with a new community for a temporary time. Then he exits as from a highway and eventually finds himself merging once again into a new community with new relationships and experiences. If traveling a stretch of highway can be a metaphor for life and passing years, then we could all be traveling our own highway. So, from there I placed Jhierry's photograph into a federal highway sign as Jhierry's road and life journey.[20]

When a class interpreted the work during a group discussion, however, they missed the metaphor that Fisher intended and instead saw the piece as a statement on racial profiling and harassment of blacks by police officers. The class had these reasons for their interpretation: a street map is in the background of the work, and a badge is prominently placed in the print, with the face of a black man in it. At the time the print was made, there was coverage in the media about how police officers stop black people, particularly black males, primarily because they are black and thus suspected of doing wrong, especially if they are driving through white neighborhoods. When Fisher heard the class's interpretation, he clearly saw how he had not communicated his intent for the piece. Because of this critique, Fisher resolved to show his future work to viewers while the work was still in progress to test their interpretations.

Interpretations are not "up for grabs"; a single artwork cannot mean *anything* anyone wants it to mean.

As an artist, you can set limits on what your works can mean by selecting certain subject matter, by using a medium in a certain way, by uniquely forming the subject matter and the medium, and by providing and referring to contextual clues. For example, Puryear's *Ladder for Booker T. Washington* cannot reasonably be interpreted as being about the September 11, 2001, attack on the World Trade Center. Puryear has limited what his sculpture can reasonably mean by contextual clues such as the title and the date: it was made years before September 11, 2001.

Are all interpretations equal? No. Because all interpretations require reasons, some interpretations will likely be more reasonable than others. Generally we do not say that an interpretation is "right," like the answer to an arithmetic problem may be right; rather we say that interpretations are insightful, enlightening, interesting, compelling, convincing, a good way to look at it, or, on the contrary, that some interpretations don't make sense, don't fit the work, are without evidence, or are nonsensical.

There are three criteria by which we can test interpretations:

- Coherence
- Correspondence
- Completeness

Coherence maintains that the interpretation ought to make sense *in and of itself.* You have likely heard interpretations that sound like mumbo-jumbo: on that basis alone, they are not good interpretations because they do not make sense in themselves.

But a thoughtful and coherent string of thoughts that makes sense in itself must also *fit the work* it is meant to interpret. This is the criterion of **correspondence.** We have all likely heard interpretations that sound sensible but do not seem to match what we are looking at. These are not convincing interpretations. A convincing interpretation has to make sense *and* clearly fit what we see in or know about the artwork.

An insightful interpretation has to account for everything in the work and how, when, and where it was made. An interpretation that leaves out something that is in the work is not likely to be compelling. This is the criterion of **completeness.** Completeness includes knowledge of the artist who made the piece and the cultural context in which it was made. When interpreting Hannah Wilke's photograph, it would be important to say, for instance, that Hannah Wilke had cancer and made art of her own body throughout her career.

2.18   JONATHAN FISHER   *Merge—A Portrait of Jhierry,* 2003. Digital paper print mounted on steel, 30 × 32 in.

As an artist, you can use coherence, correspondence, and completeness as criteria for making art that can be meaningful to others. Whether you begin with a preconceived idea or arrive at an idea while in the process of making a work, you can do a self-check to see if your idea itself is coherent. You can check to see that what you show actually corresponds to what you want to express. Everything in a work of art counts toward meaning: Are there distracting elements in a piece that you might eliminate for clearer communication? If you mean the piece to be ironic, will the viewer be able to decipher its irony? Is the work complete in the sense that it expresses what you want to express?

Deciding among Competing Interpretations

Who decides what is the best interpretation of a work of art when there are many competing interpretations of it? If it is your work that is being interpreted, you will likely decide which interpretation best fits your work while listening to what others have to say. In judging your own interpretations, you will apply the same criteria that you use to judge other interpretations: does your interpretation make sense in itself; do your thoughts and words match what you actually see in your work; does your interpretation cover everything you have included in your work? You must remember that just because you want a work to mean a certain thing, it does not necessarily mean that to other people. If communication through your art is important to you, you will be wise to get a variety of interpretive reactions to your work and consider them, especially if they are coming from people who are knowledgeable about art.

Should a work of art survive in the art world and become famous, the art community will decide what that work is about, and this interpretation will likely stand as the authoritative interpretation. Significant works of art receive considerations from many people over time: the artist who made the work, other artists who see the work, critics, historians, collectors, and so forth. Each one's interpretive opinion will slightly or largely influence other opinions, and we will have a "best interpretation" at any given moment, but that interpretation might be improved when others study the work and make further comments. Leonardo da Vinci's *Mona Lisa* continues to be interpreted in new and different ways centuries after it was made. We will never get a single right interpretation of it, nor would we want to: interpretations are a matter of ongoing discussions.

The Value of Having Your Work Interpreted

Many artists enjoy thoughtful attention when it is given to their art, as well they should. It is a significant compliment that someone would thoughtfully and carefully attend to a work of yours, seeking what it seems to mean to you and what it might mean to the viewer's life. As Carrie Mae Weems says, "I'm excited when my work is talked about in a serious manner—not because it's the work of Carrie Mae Weems, but because I think there's something that's important that's going on in the work that needs to be talked about, finally, legitimately, thoroughly."[21]

One of your goals as an artist should be to have your work interpreted by viewers. If paintings, for example, are made but not interpreted, they are then reduced to mere pigment on canvas. Without interpretive viewers, your art will not come alive or contribute to the world.

Artists sometimes think that their art is misunderstood. Although you may disagree with an interpretation, you can hear that interpretation, reflect on it, and decide whether to hold it and be influenced by it or let it float away as irrelevant. You can decide to change your work or to leave it as it is.

When you are aware that viewers will construct meanings about your work, you can guide and limit how your works will be interpreted by your choice of subject matter and how you present it, by the medium you use and how you use it, by the form of your work and your process of making it, by contextual clues you offer viewers, and by where and how you display it.

If a serious and knowledgeable viewer studies one of your artifacts and gives it serious interpretive attention but says that the work lacks coherence, you may learn from this and consider changing your work accordingly. You can learn from your viewers.

Art students who have experienced interpretive discussions about their own works in class discussions had this to say about those discussions:[22]

> The interpretive process in our class revealed how quickly and accurately a viewer can come to understand the work of the artist.
>
> —JONATHAN KETTLER

> I definitely thought that I learned a lot about myself. It was especially interesting hearing how others perceived my work in relationship to who I am and how I worked as an artist. It came to my surprise to hear how accurate they were.
>
> —JESSICA CHINN

> Interpretation of art is subjective and in some cases overlaps with the artist's original intent, and in some cases, fulfills the artist's intent of invoking emotion or meaning from the viewer in a specific way that could never have been anticipated in advance by the artist.
>
> —LESLIE O'SHAUGHNESSY

> Does it really matter if the responses are what the artist intended? I think it is more important that there was a response at all. Isn't that what art is all about? Opening a dialogue and allowing people to come to terms with their own feelings and connection to their world.
>
> —TISHA BURKE

Finally, the idea that all artworks have meaning does not necessarily mean that you must carry a burden to make profound works of art, tell complex stories, or communicate overt political messages. A work might simply be about the joy of making or the delight in materials. An exhibition review in the *New Yorker* stated this about Sarah Sze's work (**2.19**):

> For sheer joy in materials, no one can compete with Sarah Sze. Binder clips, bright blue Windex bottles, fake grass, PVC pipe, drinking straws, orange string—put it all together in the Whitney's moatlike sunken courtyard and you've got *The Triple Point of Water*. This refers to the solid, liquid, and gaseous states of H_2O and its ethereal title, but the elaborate installation is a marvel, a delicate, multilevel habitat, a miniature city or ecosystem animated by little fans and bubbling aquariums.[23]

Ideas like "sheer joy of materials" can be enough of an idea for a work of art.

Conclusion: Principles for Interpreting Art

The following list of principles drawn from the material we have just explored can serve as a summary of its

2.19 SARAH SZE *The Triple Point of Water,* 2003. Mixed media, dimensions variable.

main points. It is offered to help guide you when making meaningful artifacts and when interpreting work already made.[24]

- Artworks are always about something.
- Subject Matter + Medium + Form + Contexts = Meanings
- To interpret an artifact is to understand it in language.
- Everything in an artifact counts toward its meanings.
- Feelings are guides to interpretations.
- Artifacts attract multiple interpretations, and it is not the goal of interpretation to arrive at a single, grand, unified, composite meaning.

- There is a limited range of interpretations any artifact will allow.
- Meanings of artifacts are not limited to what their artists meant them to be about.
- Interpretations are not so much right as they are more or less reasonable, convincing, informative, and enlightening.
- Some interpretations are better than others.
- Convincing interpretations have coherence, correspondence, and completeness.

3 Point, Line, Shape, Mass and Volume, Texture, and Value

3.1 The Simpsons with Matt Groening, November, 1990.

Design elements are the basic visual components that you manipulate when creating images, objects, and performances. The most commonly identified design elements are point, line, shape, mass, volume, texture, and value; color (Chapter 4); space (Chapter 5); and time and motion (Chapter 6). To this traditional list we are adding words and sound (Chapter 7). Design elements may be thought of as the bricks of a building and design principles (Chapter 8) as the means by which you put elements together to construct a substantive building.

In any artifact you make, whether two, three, or four dimensional, you will use some elements of design. Occasionally you might use all of the elements in a single work. Design elements can be combined in an infinite variety of ways. This and the following chapters define the elements and show you many effective ways artists have used them in artifacts of all kinds. Here, we cover the basic elements of design and look at many examples of their use. Chapters that follow will cover additional, more complex design elements.

Knowledge of the elements of art and the ways artists use them can benefit you in two ways. First, you can make conscious decisions about which elements to use or omit, and to what effect. Second, you will communicate with others more effectively through the use of shared terms to describe, interpret, and judge the formal aspect of artifacts.

Point, Line, Shape, Mass and Volume, Texture, and Value Key Terms

DESIGN ELEMENTS   Visual components of artifacts, including *point, line, texture, shape, mass and volume,* space, color, *value,* time, motion, words, and sound.

POINT   A dot or small, circular shape.

LINE   A series of connected *points.* Lines can be actual or implied.

ACTUAL LINE   A series of *points* made by a tool moving across a surface.

IMPLIED LINE   A series of *points* that the eye recognizes as a line; a perceived line where areas of contrasting color or *texture* meet.

CONTOUR LINE   An *actual line* or *implied line* that defines the outer limits of a three-dimensional object or two-dimensional *shape;* sometimes synonymously used with "outline."

GESTURAL LINE   Line that conveys the energy of the artist's hand as it moves across the drawing surface.

HATCHING   A series of thin parallel lines.

CROSS-HATCHING   Crisscrossing straight lines, one atop the other.

CONTOUR   An actual or implied outline bounding a shape.

SHAPE   A two-dimensional area with defined or implied boundaries that can be measured by height and width.

GEOMETRIC SHAPE   A regular or standard shape such as a rectangle, triangle, circle, polygon, often human made.

ORGANIC SHAPE, BIOMORPHIC SHAPE   A shape that resembles irregular shapes often found in nature.

FIGURE   A *shape* on a background.

GROUND   A background on which marks, *shapes,* or *figures* are placed.

POSITIVE SHAPE   A dominant shape on a *ground.*

NEGATIVE SHAPE   A shape "left over" or around a dominant shape.

AMORPHOUS SHAPE   A shape that lacks clear edges and is ambiguous and indistinct.

MASS   Actual or illusionary three-dimensional bulk.

VOLUME   The measurable area that an object occupies— its height, width, and depth.

PLANE   A form that has height and width but very little depth; also a flat or level surface.

TEXTURE   The actual or implied tactile quality of a surface.

INVENTED TEXTURE   The illusion of tactility through the arrangement of lines, colors, and other design elements.

ACTUAL TEXTURE   The tactile quality of the material used to make an artifact.

IMPLIED TEXTURE   The tactile quality of elements in an artifact rendered in a way that gives the impession of texture.

VALUE   The relative degree of light or dark.

ACHROMATIC VALUE   Value without color, ranging from white to black, with variations of gray in between.

HIGHLIGHT   The area of an image that appears lightest to the viewer.

SHADOW   The darker *value* in an image in relation to the *highlight* of the image.

CONTRAST   The degree of *value* difference in an image; high contrast is a wide separation between dark and light; low contrast is a narrow range of values in an image.

3.2 Metrorail map detail, Washington, D.C., 2006.

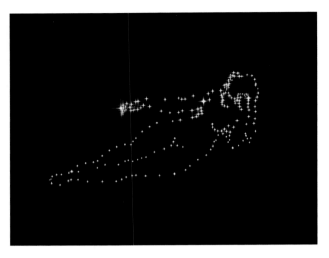

3.3 HANNAH WHITAKER *Constellation,* 2006. Photograph.

3.4 CHUCK CLOSE *Georgia Fingerprint (State II), Edition of 35,* 1985. Direct gravure etching, 32 × 22 in.

Point

A dot or small, circular shape is called a **point**. It is the simplest of elements, yet a single point can highlight important information, while a series of points can suggest linearity, and a cluster of points can suggest density. The Washington, D.C., Metrorail map (**3.2**) uses points to indicate the location of stations on the rail lines; larger points signify stations where commuters can transfer from one line to another.

While a graduate student, Hannah Whitaker made *Constellation* (**3.3**) out of points of light. At the time, she was immersed in studying the history of art, and she was particularly interested in classical portraiture, trying to reconcile her skepticism of it with her appreciation for it. She selected a historical painting of a classically posed reclining nude and drew it onto a piece of black construction paper, pierced holes in the paper, and photographed light shining through the paper with a star filter that diffuses light. She says, "In a loose sense, I often try to take advantage of the dramatic potential of loaded subject matter—in this case a naked woman, thinking about how it might fit my own contemporary voice."[1]

Chuck Close created a softly pointillist portrait of his daughter by using his fingerprints (**3.4**). *Georgia Fingerprint* is a comparatively small work, a print in black ink 22.8 inches high on a sheet of paper that is 30 inches high. Compare this to enormous canvases of faces Close has made with points, many more than

100 inches high. From a close view, his large paintings look like combinations of very abstract dabs of paint; from a distance, the images appear photographically realistic. Using his fingerprints to make a portrait of his daughter, Close adds emotional importance to the work for him, his daughter, and us: he is her biological

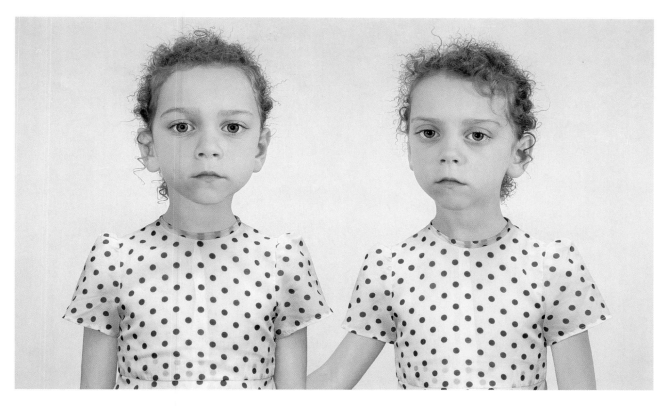

3.5 LORETTA LUX *Sasha and Ruby,* 2006. Ilfochrome print.

father and has re-formed her visually with his fingers.

In her photograph *Sasha and Ruby* (**3.5**), Loretta Lux uses the dots of the girls' dresses as compelling visual elements. The blue dots of the dresses are striking in themselves, but they also draw connections to the girls' blue eyes, dotlike amid the white of the artist's color palette. The dots also contribute to expressive meanings of the photograph. The girls are twins, and the dots that each wear are reminiscent of the genetic codes they share.

Line

Robert Smithson's massive earthwork sculpture *Spiral Jetty* (**3.6**) provides a dramatic example of a huge **line**—a series of connected points that make a length that seems to move in a direction. The spiral is composed of thousands of connected points, actually about 6,500 tons of black basalt rocks that he had placed in Great Salt Lake, Utah. From a distant aerial view of the sculpture, the individual points that Smithson gathered together merge into a continuous 1,500-foot-long and

3.6 ROBERT SMITHSON *Spiral Jetty,* 1970. 1,500 × 15 ft., Great Salt Lake, Utah.

15-foot-wide line that moves in a counterclockwise direction. Smithson's line, like all lines, has thickness—it is 15 feet wide. The 1,500-foot-long line also has a visible beginning and an end. Some lines, however, are continuous, such as a linear circle, with no apparent beginning or end.

3.7   **CY TWOMBLY**   *Untitled,* 1970. Oil-based house paint and crayon on canvas, 13 ft. 3⅜ in. × 21 ft. ⅛ in.

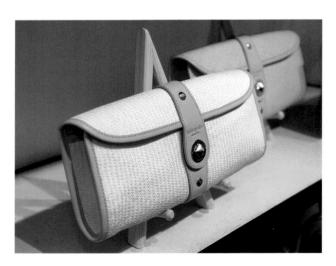

3.8   **Kate Spade, Handbag.**

Lines can be actual—made by a tool moving across a surface, as in Cy Twombly's *Untitled* (**3.7**). This is a clear example of the use of **actual lines,** made with white crayon by vigorous hand and arm movements on a piece of paper that he first colored with house paint.

Lines can also be implied—perceived, for example, where areas of contrasting color or texture meet, or when our eyes connect dots and perceive a line: hair-lines and tree lines are examples of **implied lines** in nature. A line is implied in the Kate Spade bag (**3.8**) where the woven white fabric meets the yellow leather. The yellow leather piping around the edges of the bag is another linear element that adds interest. The woven fabric of the bag is composed of lines of fabric moving over and under one another: These lines actually appear and disappear but our eyes tend to see them as continuous lines.

Thus lines can be "lost" and "found," or seem to appear and disappear: In this chapter's opening photograph of Matt Groening with his Simpsons (see 3.1), the contour lines of Groening's body disappear behind the cutout characters and objects that are in front of him. Each of the Simpsons is drawn with black contour lines. A **contour line** is an actual or implied line that defines the outer limits of a three-dimensional object or a two-dimensional shape.

LINE IN TWO-DIMENSIONAL ART

In two-dimensional art, a line is often a mark made by a pencil or other tool as it moves across a surface. Line is the predominant element in most drawings, although it is also essential to a wide range of art forms. The quality of line—controlled or loose, ragged or smooth, thick or thin—is expressive. That is, it has the power to suggest mood and feeling.

The quality of line in Jean Dubuffet's ink drawing *Parois d'Oreines* (**3.9**) is nervous and restless. Debuffet derived the line quality in part from his study of graffiti scrawls and scribbled children's drawings, examples of **gestural lines** that convey the energy of the artist's hand movements across the drawing surface. Twombly's *Untitled* (see 3.7) is an example of the use of gestural lines in a nonrepresentational work. Dubuffet has drawn *Parois d'Oreines* in a seemingly naive manner, but his uses of line are very expressive of the character's emotional state.

In strong contrast to Twombly's and Dubuffet's personal hand gestures in their works, Sol LeWitt's *Wall Drawing #260* (**3.10**) relies less on the artist's hand and more on the artist's mind. LeWitt intentionally reduces the meanings and emotional content of his work. Each of the lines is mechanical, and each is equally important, with no hierarchy in their use. LeWitt does not even touch his *Wall Drawing* works himself but sends directions to gallery staffs on how to install them. These are the artist's directions to the installer for *Wall Drawing #260:*

3.9 JEAN DUBUFFET *Parois d'Oreines,* 1964. Ink on paper, 12 × 9 in.

3.10 SOL LEWITT *Wall Drawing #260 on Black Walls, all Two-Part Combinations of White Arcs from Corners and Sides, and White Straight, Not-Straight, and Broken Lines,* 1975. Crayon on painted wall, dimensions variable.

3.11   MICHELANGELO BUONARROTI *The Holy Family with the Infant Saint John the Baptist (recto),* *c.* 1530. Black and red chalk with pen and brown ink over stylus, 11 × 15½ in.

3.12   VINCENT VAN GOGH *Portrait of Joseph Roulin,* 1888. Reed and quill pens and brown ink and black chalk, 12⅝ × 9⅝ in.

A 12-inch grid covering the black wall. Within each 12-inch square, a straight vertical, horizontal, diagonal right or diagonal left line or an arc from one of the four corners bisecting the square. All squares must be filled by one of the 8 choices. The direction or kind of arc or line in each square is determined by assigning each possibility a number (1-8) and by having the (wo)man pull those numbers 1-8 out of a hat. The drawing must begin with the upper left module, and end with the lower right.

The multiplicity and variety of configurations LeWitt achieves are particularly striking because the drawing relies on only two kinds of lines: straight and arched, without variation of thickness or other variables.

LeWitt's line drawing is purposely flat with no suggestions of representational subject matter or illusions of three-dimensional space on a two-dimensional surface. Line, however, is often used to create the illusion of three dimensionality and depth on a flat surface. Michelangelo's preliminary study for a sculpture, *The Holy Family with the Infant Saint John the Baptist* (**3.11**), illustrates several techniques dependent on line. First he made an underdrawing, lightly etching lines into the paper with a stylus (a sharply pointed tool) and no ink; then he went over those barely visible lines with red and black chalk lines, and then he added brown ink lines with pens. Through this layering of lines, he made the central figures seem three dimensional by suggesting volumes—spheres and cylinders—shaped by areas of light and shadow. Where light strikes the figures' shapes, Michelangelo's layers of line are thin; they are more thickly layered in shadowed areas.

Vincent van Gogh also layers lines in his ink drawing of his mailman, *Portrait of Joseph Roulin* (**3.12**). Van Gogh uses **hatching**, a series of thin parallel lines, and **cross-hatching**, or crisscrossed straight lines, layering one atop the other. Hatching can be seen in the man's hat and on his forehead; cross-hatching is prevalent throughout and is especially noticeable in the man's beard. Hatching and cross-hatching are also visible in Michelangelo's drawing, but they are subtler. Michelangelo's lines are delicate, whereas Van Gogh's are scruffy. Van Gogh's use of lines of different thickness is obvious: compare, for example, the thin lines in the background to the thick lines in the postman's coat. The denser areas of the drawing give the man bulk and a sense of physical substance. Thus you can use hatched and crosshatched lines for visual interest, to vary the tonality in your work, to build volume, to create the illusion of three-dimensional form on a two-dimensional surface, and to create highlights and shadows that occur when light illuminates a three-dimensional form. The different kinds of lines you can make approach an infinite number. Figure **3.13** gives you some initial variations, which you can continually modify for different expressionistic purposes in your work.

In his witty cover illustration for the *New Yorker* magazine (**3.14**), Saul Steinberg offers many examples of line in a single drawing. Steinberg's drawing is an especially effective example of how different types and uses of line can be expressive.

He has given the characters in the drawing different personalities, in part by the types of lines with which he renders them. He drew the seated woman with hatched lines only, and she appears flat, perhaps suggesting that she is a shallow person. The standing man is composed of simple and bold lines, while the seated man is composed of more subtle and nuanced lines, perhaps suggesting that he is the more sophisticated of the two men. Steinberg also made a woman with dots and no lines, suggesting that her personality is hardly formed. He used childlike lines to represent the child.

He also used lines in different media to achieve different expressive effects. The standing man in Steinberg's illustration is made with ink, which produces clear, assertive lines; the woman next to him appears to have been made with charcoal or some other soft medium that allows for smudging and blurring of lines. The child is made in the bold colorful lines of crayon.

Lines can be combined in a variety of ways to make different kinds of representations, from the more abstract to the more realistic, and in a variety of artistic styles. Steinberg's figures appear to exist in different worlds because each is rendered in a different style, yet they inhabit a single space and are likely family members.

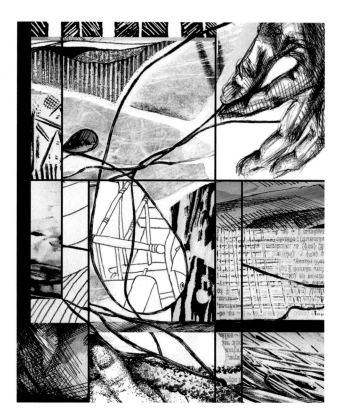

3.13   Types of lines.

3.14   SAUL STEINBERG   Cover illustration, *New Yorker* Magazine, November 23, 1968.

3.15 JIM SEAY Architectural model for Batman and Robin: The Chiller at Six Flags Great Adventure, New Jersey, 1996.

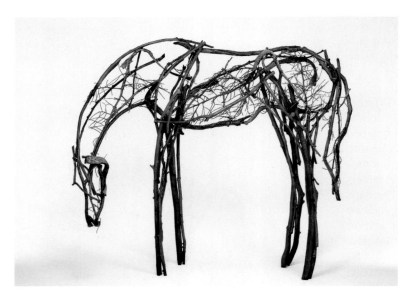

3.16 DEBORAH BUTTERFIELD *Ikebana,* 1995. Cast bronze, 79 × 86 × 40 in.

LINE IN THREE-DIMENSIONAL ART

In three-dimensional artifacts, linear elements are used as materials that structure objects, such as the linear form of the Batman and Robin roller coaster. Neither the model reproduced (**3.15**) nor the finished roller coaster is made of actual lines: the model is made of aluminum tubes and wires, and the finished ride is constructed of large tubular metal materials. The roller coaster, how-

ever, provides riders with an unbroken and fast linear journey of 2,700 feet that inverts them four times and drives them through thirty vertical curves and twenty-five horizontal twists in about sixty seconds.

Deborah Butterfield's sculpture *Ikebana* (**3.16**) is made of linear materials—in this case, sticks from trees. The horse is photographed in profile, and we can see its edge, or contour, quite clearly as a continuous, sometimes jagged, line. A **contour** is an actual or implied outline bounding a shape. Although she used linear materials that are not continuous and straight, she still creates a contour that resembles a horse. Butterfield initially constructed the piece from branches and sticks washed up along the Snake River in Idaho. Her use of irregular linear elements found in nature gives her sculpture a sense of spontaneity: *Ikebana* is like a drawing, although it is a large self-standing sculpture. Her use of driftwood gathered in the Wild West has metaphorical connotations of horses that run wild and free in unfenced nature.

Butterfield created *Ikebana*, after a real horse of that name, by selecting pieces of wood to convincingly model the structure and basic proportions of a horse in abstract form. Heavier and straighter long sticks serve as legs; lighter and curved sticks indicate the horse's neck and spine. She used smaller, crooked sticks in the interior of the horse, probably to suggest its circulatory system. When she had finished the wooden horse to her satisfaction, she disassembled it, stick by stick, so that each of the wooden pieces could be cast in bronze, and then she reassembled the stick pieces, now made of bronze, to make the final rendition of *Ikebana*. Butterfield began using bronze as a medium after discovering that humidity was altering her previously made wooden pieces in ways she had not intended.

Butterfield's use of line is not arbitrary but carefully considered. Several criteria influence her choices of linear material and how she selects and places it. She wants her sculpture to be convincing as a horse: although the sculpture is abstract and not anatomically correct, it has the size and mass and strength of a living horse. It is evident in looking at her sculpture that she understands the skeletal and muscular systems of horses. She also wants to preserve the integrity of the sticks and branches she uses as lines: she alters each piece of the material very little if at all. Finally, she uses her linear materials to suggest the grace, strength, and beauty of her subject matter.

Judy Pfaff's use of line in her sculptural installation *Gu-Choti Pa* (**3.17**) is different from Butterfield's in *Ikebana*. Butterfield uses lines to build an abstract sculpture that is recognizable as a horse. Pfaff's lines in *Gu-Choti Pa* do not represent; rather, they move our eyes in and through the intentionally chaotic space she has constructed. Pfaff says this about her use of line in her installations: "By attempting to achieve a certain type of speed that is traditionally reserved for painters, I'm reaching for a crossing over of ideas and a weaving of thinking and making . . . Most parts of my work are

3.17 JUDY PFAFF *Gu-Choti Pa,* 1985. Steel, wood, plastic, organic materials, bamboo, lattice, signs, veneer paneling, formica, steel grating, paint, 20 × 40 ft. diameter.

controlled and muscled into place, but there also exists a natural, beautiful line. It is important that the work has a balance of enough artifice and enough casualness, and enough surprise and enough reason."[2]

Line can be both functional and expressive in product design. The contour (line) of functional objects is a key feature. A member of Palm Computing's staff carried a block of wood the size and shape of the first Palm Pilot (**3.18**) that was released in 1996. The contour of the PDA (personal digital assistant) of Palm and other devices invented since is designed to comfortably fit the hand.

In her use of lines for a functional product, Marta Sansoni employs curved lines that invite a smile by their sense of whimsy. The design of her hand mixer (**3.19**) recalls the general form of a jellyfish, with the beaters suggesting tentacles in motion when the handle is turned. Sansoni says, "I like to design objects that are suitable not only for use but ask for playing with . . . I love objects that are capable of evoking emotions and feelings."[3]

3.18   Palm Pilot, 1996.

3.19   MARTA SANSONI   Hand mixer for Alessi, 1998.

Shape

Like lines, shapes can be actual or implied. A **shape** is a two-dimensional area with defined or implied boundaries that can be measured by height and width. The boundary of a shape can be defined by a line or implied by a difference of texture or color. Shapes have edges that can be sharp or soft. They are often referred to as either **geometric,** resembling simple rectangular, circular, or triangular shapes, often found in human-made things, or **organic** (also called **biomorphic**), resembling the irregular shapes often found in nature. However, natural objects often have geometric structures when perceived through the microscope, and many human-made objects and images can look organic.

Henri Matisse made many works of paper shapes. Late in his life, he created a series of "Blue Nudes." *Blue Nude II* (**3.20**) is made of paper painted with gouache, a water-based pigment, and then cut into shapes and adhered to canvas. The shapes are arranged to resemble a female figure in profile. The shapes are flat and organic. By overlapping some flat shapes over others, the figure appears to have dimensionality.

Lillie Mae Pettway is part of a community of African American women descended from freed slaves. Known as the quilters of Gee's Bend, they live and work collectively, making one-of-a-kind quilts, in the rural areas of Rehoboth and Boykin, Alabama. The quilts are made of simple geometric shapes, with a distinctive bold quilting style based on American and African American quilts. In their geometric simplicity they share an affinity with Amish quilts and modern art that is often based exclusively on shapes and colors without references to representational subject matter. The *New York Times* called the quilts "some of the most miraculous works of modern art America has produced."[4] The design of *Housetops Twelve-Block Half-Log Cabin Variation* (**3.21**) is the personal expression of Pettway. The sewing together of the pieced top with batting (stuffing) and its backing is performed communally.

FIGURE AND GROUND

When shapes are given equal emphasis, the result can be dynamic. Ellsworth Kelly's *Red White* (**3.22**)

3.20 HENRI MATISSE *Blue Nude II,* 1952. Gouache-painted paper cutouts adhered to paper mounted on canvas, 45.7 × 35 in.

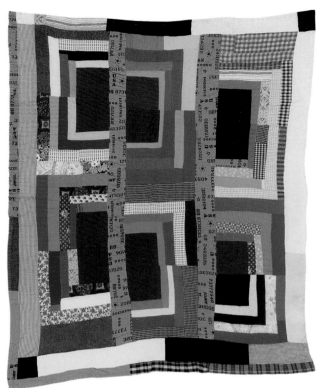

3.21 LILLIE MAE PETTWAY *Housetops Twelve-Block Half-Log Cabin Variation, c.* 1965. Cotton, wool, corduroy, 77 × 65 in.

is a painting of two interlocking shapes, one white and one red. The painting can be perceived as a shape, or **figure,** on a **ground,** or background. In the Kelly painting, which shape is the figure and which the ground? At first glance the red seems to be the figure and the white the ground, but we can easily reverse these mentally so that white is the figure and red the ground. This experience is known as figure/ground reversal.

POSITIVE AND NEGATIVE SHAPE

The CBS logo (**3.23**), popularly known as the "CBS eye," introduced in 1952, is one of the most readily recognized logos in the United States. The logo plays with a figure/ground reversal, as does Kelly's *Red White* (see 3.22). In the logo we can see an eye within a circle, or a circle containing an eye. It is composed of two positive black shapes, a small circle within a larger circle, and one negative white shape that resembles the shape of a human eye. When one shape is dominant, it may be called a **positive shape,** and the surrounding shape is called a **negative shape.** The CBS logo is an adaptation of René Magritte's painting *The False Mirror* (**3.24**), which combines geometric circular shapes with the organic shapes of a human eye.

3.22 ELLSWORTH KELLY *Red White,* 1961. Oil on canvas, 62½ × 85 in.

Brad Norr uses a positive (the lion) and a negative shape (the lamb) and a figure/ground reversal (we can concentrate on either the lamb or the lion) in his design of a promotional image and logo for the book *Transforming the Powers* (**3.25**). The "left over" space beneath the bulk of the lion and between his legs forms

3.23 CBS Broadcasting Inc. Logo, 2008.

the negative shape that represents a lamb. Norr's is a compelling use of positive/negative shapes that aptly evoke the content of the book, which is about changing oppressive regimes into peaceful global communities. Rather than devouring the small lamb, the powerfully large lion seems to protect it: the two coexist peacefully.

AMORPHOUS SHAPE

You can use **amorphous shapes**—those without clarity or precise distinction and of uncertain dimension with edges that are difficult to determine—when you wish to employ ambiguity and lack of specificity in your subject matter. In *Skulldiver 4* (**3.26**), Cecily Brown uses many amorphous shapes that lack clear edges and that blend into one another. Most of the shapes she uses seem nonrepresentational, but occasionally some of her shapes seem to represent a face with two eyes, an implied nose, and a mouth. Perhaps arms bent at the elbows are near the face, and perhaps she has suggested a distorted figure in the painting.

You can combine clear shapes with amorphous shapes in the same work. Philip Taaffe imposes clear shapes with distinct edges on top of amorphous shapes that form the background of the painting (**3.27**). The

3.24 RENÉ MAGRITTE *The False Mirror,* 1928. Oil on canvas, 21¼ × 31⅞ in.

amorphous circular shapes that form the ground of the painting blend into one another, forming one large ambiguous shape. The sources of Taaffe's shapes in *Painting with Diatoms* are accurate representations of spores taken from illustrations in botany books. His use of the actual shapes over the amorphous background implies triumph of order over chaos.

THREE-DIMENSIONAL SHAPE

Shapes in three-dimensional artifacts are implied through contour, imposed actual lines, and juxtapositions of colors and textures that define actual shapes or suggest implied shapes. Native American artist Nathan Begaye drew upon his Southwestern heritage in creating *Reconstructed Vessel* (**3.28**). He built it by combining different three-dimensional forms with distinct contour lines that reveal shapes. He has also applied distinct shapes onto the surface of the vessel. His technical decisions in making the pot are important to his intended expression:

> This vessel represents the many different facets of my world, the many different parts of me brought together. As a child I found pottery shards in the ruins and began to dream about ceramics popping out of the ground. It was magical. The reconstructed vessel recalls those fragments But there are also missing pieces, little empty spaces that are waiting to be filled, It is a metaphor for myself.[5]

When you consider using multiple shapes in a work, be aware that format itself is a shape. The designers of the packaging for Adobe Creative Suite 2 (**3.29**) contrast transparent organic shapes with the geometric forms of the boxes in which the software is packaged. The juxtaposition of the organic shapes on the geometric boxes is visually appealing, and the design implies a message: the product is organically intuitive and transparently understandable to users, and it suggests exacting standards in the making of its products.

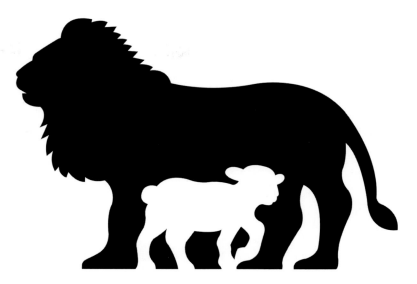

3.25   BRAD NORR   *Transforming the Powers* logo, 2006. Graphic design, size variable.

3.26   CECILY BROWN   *Skulldiver 4,* 2007. Oil on linen, 85 × 89 in.

Mass and Volume

A square is a shape; a cube is a mass; an open crate is a volume. **Mass** is the actual or illusionary physical bulk of a material that fills a volume. **Volume** is the measurable area that an object occupies—its height, width, and depth. Volume can also refer to an open area surrounded by material, as in a cup.

For product designers and architects, decisions about mass and volume are practical as well as aesthetic. The design of the Little Wing Kayak (**3.30**) required careful considerations of both use and visual appeal. Ted Warren and his design team made the kayak lightweight to provide easy transport to the water and buoyancy within it. Its dimensions balance minimal width and depth with maximum length so that the kayak is

3.27 **PHILIP TAAFFE** *Painting with Diatoms,* 1997. Mixed media on canvas, 54 × 66 in.

3.28 **NATHAN BEGAYE** *Reconstructed Vessel,* 1998. Polychromed earthenware, 11 × 10¼ in.

both fast and stable. The open "negative space" for the kayaker and the kayaker's gear was also a major consideration in the functionality of the design. At the fore and aft of the hull, the design integrates a **plane,** a form that has height and width but very little depth, in the form of flares, or "little wings," that stabilize the kayak in water.

Mass is the dominant element in Raoul Hague's wooden sculpture *Echo Lake* (**3.31**). Hague carves his sculptures from large pieces of solid walnut, and they are usually between 5 and 6 feet tall and very heavy. He moves the sculptures around on big wooden palettes with wheels, and galleries show them standing on similar wheeled dollies, emphasizing their mass. About *Echo Lake* one critic comments on the effects of the artist's use of mass: "The work is a massive bouquet of concave [curved like the interior of a sphere] and convex [curved like an exterior of a sphere] shapes that form radically dissimilar silhouettes as you walk around it. There are no punctures, and the piece meets the ground in a solid trunk-like way, but you can still feel the branching form of the original block like a phantom envelope around the sculpture."[6]

In two-dimensional artifacts, mass is a shape that appears to stand out from the space surrounding it or that appears to be a solid body of material. The illusion of mass and volume may be present in a two-dimensional image. Jenny Saville (**3.32**) depicts the illusion of mass in her paintings, which are often self-portraits that exaggerate her proportions. Saville says, "I'm not painting disgusting, big women. I'm painting women who've been made to think they're big and disgusting, who imagine their thighs go on forever."[7] By painting exaggerations of bodily mass, she explores the female body through a feminist lens, making social statements about how people can be conditioned by media messages in harmful ways. Mass is a primary visual element in her work: her paintings are very large, and she paints her subjects with illusions of mass that psychologically overpower the viewer.

Texture

The tactile quality of any surface is its **texture.** You can also create the appearance or illusion of tactile qualities, known as **invented texture.**

Sandy Skoglund's *The Cocktail Party* (**3.33**) illustrates both actual and implied texture. It exists in two formats: as a life-size three-dimensional installation in a museum and as a large two-dimensional color photograph. If we stood in front of the museum installation, however, we would see (and smell) mannequins, live models, furniture, and the corner of a room entirely covered with cheese doodles. The doodles make the actual texture of the installation crunchy. When looking at the large photograph of the installation, which Skoglund also displays as a work of art, we see the actual shiny texture of photographic paper and the implied texture of the cheese-doodled figures and room. Texture is essential to Skoglund's expression in *The Cocktail Party.* Her use of cheese doodles, for example, suggests that her intent is to imply "cheesiness," artificiality, and lack of intellectual nutrition that one may find at a cocktail party.

ACTUAL TEXTURE

In functional artifacts, the feel of a material may be critical to its success. Materials you use to make a work

3.29   Adobe Creative Suite 2, designed by MetaDesign, 2006.

3.30   TED WARREN   Little Wing Kayak, Warren Light Craft, LLC, 2006.

will have **actual texture.** Consider the importance of textural feel to a necklace, a blanket, or a steering wheel. Actual texture may also have a functional purpose. Skateboards (**3.34**), for example, have a rough texture on the deck for secure foot grip and a super smooth surface on the wheels for a smooth, fast ride.

Actual texture can repel or attract. Skoglund's use of texture in *The Cocktail Party* (see 3.33) does not invite viewers to touch it. However, Auguste Rodin's use of polished marble in his figurative sculpture draws people to its smoothness. Rodin carved *Danaïd* (**3.35**) from a block of marble. He brought the marble that represents

3.31 RAOUL HAGUE *Echo Lake,* 1978. Wood, 60 × 45 × 31 in.

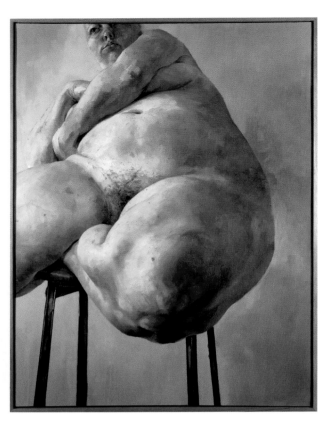

3.32 JENNY SAVILLE *Prop,* 1993. Oil on canvas, 84 × 72 in.

3.33 SANDY SKOGLUND *The Cocktail Party,* 1992. Installation and photograph, cheese snack food embedded in epoxy resin, furniture, sculpted figures from mannequins, and live models. (Sandy Skoglund, *The Cocktail Party* ©1992.)

the soft skin of the figure to a very smooth texture by giving it a high polish. It seems all the smoother in contrast to the rougher texture of marble on which the figure rests. The contrasts in surface also add visual interest. Rodin made the two textures with the right degree of difference: the figure is sensuously smooth, and the rock base is not so rough as to make us feel uncomfortable seeing the woman's body on it.

One of the most celebrated uses of texture in twentieth-century art that attracts and repels is Meret Oppenheim's surreal use of texture in *Object* (**3.36**), a cup and saucer with spoon, each covered in fur. The softness of the fur is inviting, but the thought of drinking from a fur-covered cup or eating from a fur-covered spoon is repulsive. Her work contributes to the Surrealist's artistic agenda of defamiliarizing the familiar with unexpected juxtapositions. In *Object,* she successfully accomplished this with the element of texture.

Texture will animate your work by engaging a viewer's sense of touch. In the fine arts, we usually do not want the viewer to literally touch our paintings or sculptures but rather to imaginatively experience their tactile qualities.

IMPLIED TEXTURE

In representational art, such as Rodin's *Danaïd*, texture contributes to the illusion of reality. The choice of textures can convey meanings as well as visual interest. The seventeenth-century Dutch painter Johannes Vermeer was a master at depicting with oil paint how light reveals textures. In *Girl Reading a Letter at an Open Window* (**3.37**), Vermeer presents a delicately rendered view of a quiet moment in a young woman's life as she reads a letter in the intimacy of her home. Vermeer shows the young woman in profile. Light from the window illuminates the smooth texture of her skin, and Vermeer subtly reveals the expression on her face in a dim reflection on the textured glass of the window. Note the virtuosity with which Vermeer renders the different surfaces in the scene: the plastered wall, the simultaneously translucent and reflective glass, the nap of the wool rug on the table with differently textured fruits on top of it, and the variety of fabrics, including the woman's starched white

3.34 **G2 Concave Pintail "The Lane" Longboard Skateboard,** 2006.

3.35 **AUGUSTE RODIN** *Danaïd,* 1884–1885. Marble, 15 × 28 × 21 in.

3.36 **MERET OPPENHEIM** *Object (Le Dejeuner en fourrure),* 1936. Fur-covered cup, saucer, and spoon, cup: 4⅜ in. diameter; saucer: 9⅜ in. diameter; spoon: 8 in.; overall height: 2⅞ in.

3.37 JOHANNES VERMEER VAN DELFT *Girl Reading a Letter at an Open Window,* 1657. Oil on canvas, 32¾ × 25⅜ in.

3.38 TOM LANG *Untitled,* 2002. Handmade paper. 22 × 16 in.

collar, her silky yellow dress, and the heavy curtains. The **implied textures** of the painting provide more than an engrossing atmosphere; they also indicate the varieties of goods available to the Dutch in the seventeenth century through their dominance in world trade as merchants in possession of a powerful fleet of ships. At the time the painting was made, it and its textures signified wealth and power to the Dutch; today it provides clues to a distant cultural context.

INVENTED TEXTURE

You do not have to depict real objects in order to create texture; you can invent texture, creating the illusion of tactility through the arrangement of lines, colors, and other design elements. Tom Lang's two-dimensional work (**3.38**) is made of cotton pulp. The actual texture of the piece is soft and pliable overall. Yet the viewer can also experience different implied textures in the work. The orange and black boxes on the left suggest a nubby texture through small dots of contrasting colors. The right side of the piece appears smooth, and the center suggests a texture somewhere between the two sides. *Untitled* is a nonrepresentational piece meant to delight the viewer primarily through the element of actual and invented texture.

Value

The relation of one part to another in terms of its lightness and darkness is its **value.** Thus, value is a relative term, and values without color, or **achromatic values,** which are discussed here, vary from white to black with limitless degrees of gray in between. Values are also referred to as "tones." Color also has value, and it is discussed in Chapter 4.

The eight vertical gray tones that stand between absolute black on the left and white on the right in Figure **3.39** could be expanded infinitesimally with very subtle gradations. You can see the relativity of the gray scale by noticing how the middle value running horizontally across the scale looks darker or lighter depending on its relationship to the other values near it.

Ansel Adams, the American photographer famous for his exquisite photographs of landscapes, was particularly concerned with the tonal range of a photograph, delighting in a full range from dark to light with subtle grays in between. A scientist of photography as well as an artist, he developed systems by which photographers could render black-and-white images in a variety of tonal ranges for expressive purposes. A **highlight** is the lightest portion of an image in relation to **shadow,** the darker portion. In Adams's *Moonrise*

(**3.40**), the foreground is in shadowed dark grays, and the highlights are the rising moon, the horizontal band of clouds, and the bright white walls of the adobe buildings that are lit by the sun setting behind Adams.

Artists who make achromatic images distribute light areas and dark areas to represent the illusion of spatial dimensions of what they depict. Käthe Kollwitz, working with charcoal (**3.41**), creates the illusion of three

3.39   A gray scale ranging from black to white with gray running horizontally through the middle of the scale to illustrate relativity.

dimensions through her use of a variety of values, with bright highlights on the woman's right forehead and cheek bones and the shadow to the side of her nose, cast by light striking the side of her face. The shadow above and behind her head separates the figure from the background, adding to the dimensionality of the drawing.

Contrast refers to the degree between lights and darks in an image. An image of high contrast uses a wide separation of values between lights and darks, and a low-contrast image has a narrow range of values. Sid Chafetz's print of Sigmund Freud (**3.42**) is rendered in high contrast, with the figure's hat and clothing in dark black against a light background. The artist's choice of high contrast enhances the authority of the subject's views and visually reinforces his stature as a significant contributor to the history of ideas.

Conclusion: The Power of Simple Elements

Point, line, shape, mass and volume, texture, and value are some design elements that artists use to express feelings and communicate ideas. The great abstract painter Wassily Kandinsky (**3.43**) meditates in writing about the power of simple elements and how artists use them. His compelling and passionate appreciation

3.40   ANSEL ADAMS   *Moonrise, Hernandez, New Mexico,* 1941. Photograph, silver gelatin print.

3.41 KÄTHE KOLLWITZ *Arbeiterfrau (Working Woman),*
1906. Facsimile of a charcoal drawing on laid paper. Impression
from the 1921 Richter portfolio, sheet size: 22¾ × 17¼ in.

for design elements is an inspiration for making and looking at all artifacts:

An empty canvas is a living wonder—far lovelier than certain pictures.

What are its basic elements? Straight lines, a straight, narrow surface, hard, inflexible, maintained without regard to anything but itself and apparently going on its own gait like a destiny that has already been fulfilled. Thus and not otherwise. Stretched, free, tense, evading and yielding, elastic, and indeterminate in semblance like the fate which awaits us. It could become something different, but abstains from doing so. Hardness and softness at once, and combinations of both that are infinite in their possibilities.

Every line says "Here I am!" Each holds its own, reveals its own eloquent features, and whispers "Listen, listen to my secret!"

A line is a living wonder.

A dot. Lots of little dots which are just a little smaller here and just a little larger there. All of them have their place within its compass, and yet retain their mobility—a host of little tensions ceaselessly repeating their chorus of "Listen! Listen!" They are little messages which by echoing each other in unison help to build up the one great central affirmation, "Yes."

A black circle—distant thunder, a world apart which seems to care for nothing and retires within itself, a conclusion on the spot. A "Here I am!" pronounced slowly, rather coldly.

A red circle—it stands fast, holds its ground, is immersed in itself. Yet it also moves because it covets each other place as well as its own. Its radiance overcomes every obstacle and penetrates into the remotest corners. Thunder and lightning together. A passionate "Here I am!"

A circle is a living wonder.

But the most wonderful thing of all is this: to combine all these voices with still others, lots and lots of them (for besides the simple basic forms and colors already mentioned, there are plenty more really), in one picture—a picture which thus becomes a simple and integral "HERE I AM!"[8]

Kandinsky wrote about his reverence for elements almost one hundred years ago, and he was making nonrepresentational paintings. Contemporary artists, including those making representational works, continue to acknowledge their awareness of design elements in their work today. Lorraine Shemesh's paintings (**3.44**) are frequently inspired by her fascination with water—"water was something that I was always drawn to"—and her fascination with the "formal aspects of the visual world, always trying to find a way to activate the figure/ground relationship in a more open-ended way."[9] In the following three chapters, we will continue to examine design elements, namely, space, color, time and motion, and words and sound.

3.42 SID CHAFETZ *Freud,* 1962. Woodcut, 17½ × 17½ in.

3.43 **WASSILY KANDINSKY** *Yellow-Red-Blue,* 1925. Oil on canvas, 128 × 201.5 cm.

3.44 **LORRAINE SHEMESH** *Link,* 1999. Oil on canvas, 67 × 66¾ in.

4 Color

4.1 **JULIAN SCHNABEL** *The Diving Bell and the Butterfly,* 2007. Film still.

Basic Color Physics
Color Schemes
Color Interactions
Color and Meaning
Conclusion: Beyond Color Theory

Julian Schnabel says, "Color colors meaning."[1] He speaks with authority earned through his accomplishments in different artforms. He is an American artist whose paintings are in major collections around the world, a director of four award-winning films, and the interior decorator of the Gramercy Park Hotel in New York City. Perhaps Schnabel's most pertinent film in regard to color is *The Diving Bell and the Butterfly*, based on the life of Jean-Dominique Bauby, an editor of the French fashion magazine *Elle*, who suffered a stroke and locked-in syndrome, a condition that left him awake and aware but paralyzed, only able to blink his left eye. With a therapist, he devised a system of blinking to indicate individual letters of the alphabet. Using this system, he wrote the book on which the movie is based.[2] Using vivid color, Schnabel cinematically reconstructs Bauby's memories and fantasies as written in the book of the same title (**4.1**).

Without light, we would see no color. Dan Flavin is an artist who spent a career investigating light and what experiences he could create with color by using simple neon tubes in different combinations to build light sculptures (**4.2**). Curators of his work explain that "by manipulating the formal, phenomenal, and referential characteristics

of light, the artist's installation asks viewers to consider a series of contrasts—between colors, intensities of light, structure and formlessness, the obvious and the mysterious, and the serious and the humorous."[3]

Color is one of the most important sensations that we experience: we see the impermanence of the physical world through the shimmer of color. Claude Monet, the famous Impressionist, painted the haystacks, poplars, fields, and gardens of Normandy, on the northwestern coast of France, in different seasons, weather, and times of day, capturing how their colors changed depending on the time of day and season. Wassily Kandinsky, who made color itself a subject matter in his own work (see 3.43), claimed that Monet's haystacks opened his eyes to the importance of color: "What suddenly became clear to me was the unsuspected power of the palette, which I had not understood before and which surpassed my wildest dreams."[4]

While artists and designers working in different media and time periods have recognized the expressive possibilities of color, as a contemporary creator you will practice in a world where the "power of the palette" is a given, and the array of color choices is vast. Colors

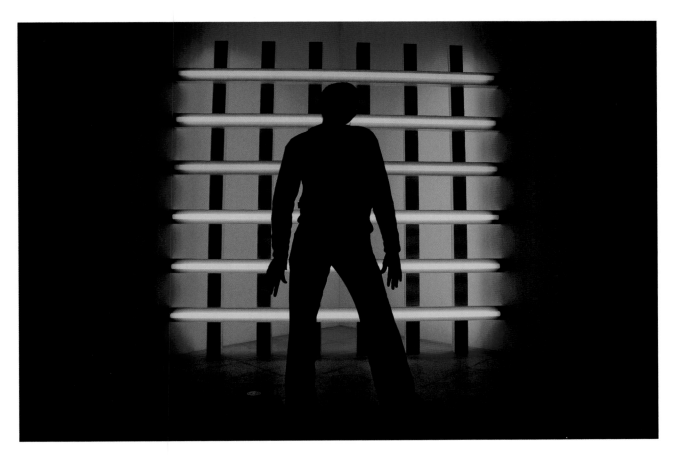

4.2 **DAN FLAVIN** *Untitled (in honor of Harold Joachim) 3,* 1977. Haywood Gallery, London, Wednesday, January 18, 2006.

Color Key Terms

COLOR The effect on our eyes of different wavelengths or frequencies of an electromagnetic spectrum that is infinite and continuous. Color consists of *hue, intensity,* and *value.*

COLOR SPECTRUM The portion of the electromagnetic spectrum that is visible to the human eye.

SPECTRAL COLORS Colors that become visible when white light passes through a prism: red, orange, yellow, green, blue, indigo, and violet.

SUBTRACTIVE COLOR PROCESS The mixing of *pigments* and *dyes* so that all colors of light except the desired color are absorbed (subtracted).

PRIMARY COLORS In a color system, the basic colors that cannot be broken down into other colors and that can be combined to create other colors.

SECONDARY COLORS The colors created from mixing two *primary colors.*

ADDITIVE COLOR PROCESS The mixing of colored lights so that when some colored lights shine on a surface, they combine (add) to make other colors.

OPTICAL COLOR MIXING Placement of different colors in such a way that the human eye mixes them to form new colors.

COLOR WHEEL A circular arrangement of the colors of the visible spectrum.

HUE A name of a color family or an area on the *color spectrum.*

VALUE (OF COLOR) The degree of lightness or darkness in a color.

VALUE SCALE A series of progressively changing values from light to dark or dark to light.

KEY Used synonymously with *value.* In a scale of values, high-key colors are lighter than colors in the middle of the scale; low-key colors are darker than colors in the middle of the scale.

INTENSITY, SATURATION, CHROMA The strength or weakness of a color.

TINT A color that has white added to it.

SHADE A color that has black added to it.

TONE A color that has gray added to it.

NEUTRALS Blacks, whites, and grays made from mixing black and white. In some media, earth tones are also considered to be neutrals.

PIGMENTS Ground-up color materials, such as powdered minerals, that are suspended in a medium such as oil or acrylic to make paint.

DYE An intensely colored compound that dissolves in a medium (usually water) and is absorbed by the material it touches.

OPAQUE Impenetrable to light; preventing underlying images and colors from showing through, or the illusion of this phenomenon.

TRANSPARENT Able to transmit light and underlying colors and images, or the illusion of this phenomenon.

TRANSLUCENT Penetrable to light but diffusing it so that underlying images are blurry, or the illusion of this phenomenon.

TERTIARY COLORS, INTERMEDIATES The products of mixing a *primary* and a *secondary color.*

MONOCHROMATIC COLOR SCHEME Variations in color based on one color.

ANALOGOUS COLOR SCHEME Variations in color based on colors adjacent to one another on the *color wheel.*

COMPLEMENTARY COLOR SCHEME Variations in color based on colors opposite each other on the *color wheel.*

TRIAD Three colors that are equidistant from one another (form an equilateral triangle) on the *color wheel.*

TETRAD Four colors that are equidistant from one another (form a square or rectangle) on the *color wheel.*

HEXAD Six colors obtained by choosing every other color on the *color wheel.*

CHROMATIC GRAY A neutral gray produced by mixing *complementary colors* in order to change *intensity* and *value.*

POLYCHROMATIC Many different colors in one composition.

SIMULTANEOUS CONTRAST An effect achieved by placing highly contrasting *colors, values,* and *intensities* next to each other; the contrast between colors increases when they are placed next to each other.

AFTERIMAGE An image that appears after looking away from a strong stimulus, such as seeing a halo after looking at a bright light.

LOCAL COLOR The color that an object reflects in the real world.

ARBITRARY COLOR A color chosen for expressive qualities other than representational qualities that correspond to the world.

SYMBOLIC COLOR Color that invokes cultural meanings, which can vary with time and place.

4.3 Apple iPod nanos, 2008.

are crucial to the design of popular consumer products (**4.3**). Companies employ color forecasters when designing products, recognizing that the right color can communicate "new," while the wrong color can say "dated," and that colors may suggest many other connotations such as seriousness or playfulness, luxury or practicality. Videographers, cinematographers, animators, and photographers

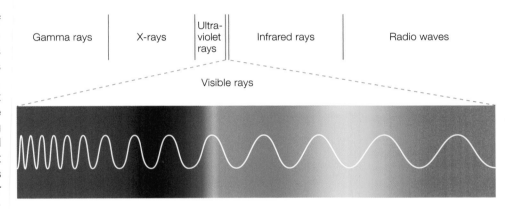

4.4 The electromagnetic spectrum with visible rays expanded.

carefully create or select lighting to create mood and atmosphere through color. Computer programs allow you to construct experiments to make color images, to visualize three-dimensional objects in color, and to design three-dimensional spaces in different colors that you can see under different lighting sources.

Color is a crucial and complex design element in all aspects of the visual arts. We respond to color both consciously and unconsciously. It affects our moods, thoughts, and actions. Color can raise or lower our heart rates, affecting our physical and psychological health. The more you learn about color, the more effectively you can create visual experiences, evoke emotions, provide insights into the world, and enhance people's experiences of life.

Basic Color Physics

A dictionary definition of color is "a sensation aroused in the observer's mind as a response to the stimulus of the radiant energy of certain wavelengths acting on

the eye's mechanism."[5] To paraphrase for our purposes, **color** is the effect on our eyes of different wavelengths or frequencies of an electromagnetic spectrum that is infinite and continuous. The **color spectrum** is that portion of the electromagnetic spectrum that is visible to the human eye, processed through the human brain (**4.4**). Every color has its own wavelength: red is the longest and violet the shortest. Wavelengths also travel at different speeds: red, for example, moves more rapidly than blue.

COLOR AND LIGHT

Without light, either natural or artificial, there is no color. In bright light, colors appear intense. In dull light, colors appear dull. In very dark light, we perceive shapes more than the colors of those shapes.

Light itself seems colorless to our eyes; however, when sunlight strikes moisture, such as rain or mist or a spray in Earth's atmosphere, we see the wonder of a rainbow, the optical and meteorological phenomenon that makes visible a continuous spectrum of colors. A rainbow spans a continuous spectrum of colors in the

4.5 White light distinguished as colors by means of a prism.

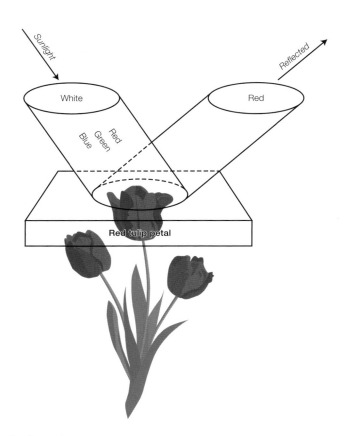

4.6 Seeing red.

sequence of red, orange, yellow, green, blue, indigo, and violet.

In 1666, Sir Isaac Newton, the British scientist, demonstrated that white light is composed of all the colors of the spectrum. He passed sunlight through a glass prism that separated the white light into the **spectral colors** in the sequence of those in a rainbow: red, orange, yellow, green, blue, indigo, and violet (**4.5**). This sequence of colors is sometimes taught with the mnemonic device of "Roy G. Biv": <u>r</u>ed, <u>o</u>range, <u>y</u>ellow, <u>g</u>reen, <u>b</u>lue, <u>i</u>ndigo (also known as blue-violet), and <u>v</u>iolet (rather than purple).

We see color on surfaces of objects in the world when those surfaces absorb and reflect waves of light: that is, color is produced by the surface of an object absorbing some wavelengths of white light while reflecting other wavelengths. When we see a red tulip in a garden, for example (**4.6**), all the colors of sunlight are shining on it, but the surface of the tulip's petals are absorbing all of the light rays except those rays that correspond to red, which are reflected through our eyes to our brain, and we recognize those rays as red. A surface that we see as black is absorbing all colors and reflecting none; a surface that we see as white is reflecting all colors and absorbing none.

As Monet showed in his paintings, as the quality of light changes throughout the day, so do colors. The red tulip may be a bright fiery red at noon and a dark maroon at sunset. The same absorption and reflection pro-

cess occurs when the surface of an artifact is painted, dyed, inked, or manipulated by other colorants.

We also see color as beams of colored light. Colored light forms the palette for much of contemporary art and design, including anything created for and displayed on a computer or television screen, in a movie theater, or on a lit stage for a performance.

ADDITIVE COLOR AND SUBTRACTIVE COLOR

The mixing of pigments and dyes is a **subtractive color process** (**4.7**). The **primary colors** (colors that cannot be broken down into other colors) of pigments and dyes are yellow, red, and blue; when combined, they form the **secondary colors** of green, orange, and purple. When primaries are mixed together and when secondaries are mixed together, the resulting color is gray. The colors of oil paintings are made with pigments suspended in an oil-based medium and applied to canvas. The color array of Apple's iPod nanos (see 4.3) is also based on the subtractive color process, with pigments mixed into the plastic shell. Most work in foundation art courses will likely be done with subtractive color materials such as paints, colored papers, and three-dimensional materials that are colored.

When artists use colored lights, they are using an **additive color process** (**4.8**); as mentioned, subtractive colors are made with paints and material colorants.

4.7 **The results of mixing the primary colors of pigments,** yellow, red, and blue, and obtaining the secondary colors of green, orange, and purple.

4.8 **The results of mixing primary beams** of red, green, and blue lights, resulting in the secondary colors of cyan, magenta, and yellow.

Both additive and subtractive color systems depend on primary and secondary colors. In an additive system of color, the primary colors are red, blue, and green, from which other colors can be made, such as the secondary colors of yellow, cyan, and magenta. When the three primary colors overlap, they make white light. Different combinations of colored lights create limitless variations of colors, as seen in Flavin's neon sculptural installation *Untitled 3* (see 4.2).

Kara Walker uses additive color in her projections of colored lights in some of her gallery installations (**4.9**). The black figures on the walls of the gallery are cutout silhouettes made of black paper adhered to the wall. The colors on the floor and walls of the gallery are overlapping projections of colored lights. Walker's projections of light function as a visually interesting element of the space, but perhaps most importantly, when viewers walk into the gallery, the lights cast the viewers' shadows onto the floors and walls, implicating them in the condition of racism that Walker portrays in her work.

In computer models of Prestige Forest Hotel (**4.10**), architects provide us with a graphically dramatic example of working with both subtractive and additive systems of color for a single structure. The architects

4.9 **KARA WALKER** *Darkytown Rebellion,* 2001. Cut paper and projection on wall, 14 × 37 ft.

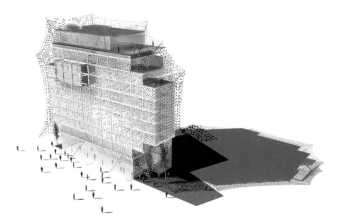

4.10   Prestige Forest Hotel, Barcelona, 2006. Computer-generated models of the hotel in daylight (above) and at night (right).

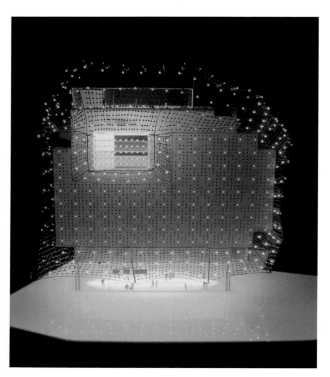

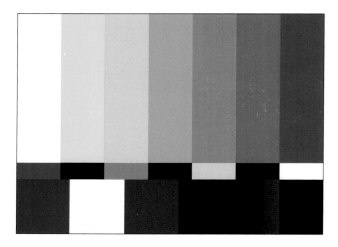

4.11   The colors that we optically mix when viewing a television program.

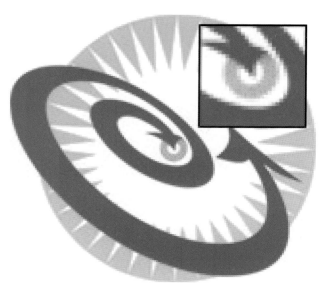

4.12   Pixels that we optically mix to view a recognizable image on a computer screen.

draped a stainless-steel mesh over the eleven-story structure. The mesh holds 5,000 LED-loaded polycarbonate discs. During daylight hours, the color of the hotel depends on the subtractive use of color: the mesh over the building subtracts (absorbs) all the colors of light except the colors the mesh reflects. At night, the additive color system is at work, creating interesting color effects by the LEDs emitting colored light. During the day, the building shimmers with subtractive daylight colors; at night, the building glows with additive electric colors.

OPTICAL MIXING PROCESSES

We constantly mix colors optically when we watch television (**4.11**), look at computer screens (**4.12**), and view printed images on billboards, magazines, and this book's color reproductions. **Optical color mixing** oc-

curs when bits of colors in an artifact are arranged in such a way that the human eye mixes them so they combine and produce another color that seems realistic.

The printing industry also uses a subtractive color process, whose primaries are cyan, magenta, yellow, and black (**4.13**). To print a color image, a piece of paper is run through a printing press, receiving four colors of ink successively. The inks do not literally mix together; instead the brain blends the tiny dots of primary colors into a very wide range of colors. A billboard 100 yards away appears to be a simple color picture, much like a large snapshot. If you stand close to the billboard, however, you can see that it is composed of clearly separated dots of cyan, magenta, yellow, and black.

COLOR WHEELS

After Newton discovered spectral colors of sunlight, he arranged the colors into a graphic diagram we commonly know as the **color wheel,** a circular arrangement of the seven colors of the visible spectrum (**4.14**). Today, there are wheels of eight, ten, and twelve colors, with the twelve-color wheel dominating current use, largely through the influence of Johannes Itten, the Swiss painter, designer, teacher, theorist, and author of *The Art of Color*.[6]

Itten's color wheel (**4.15**) provides us with a middle triangle composed of the subtractive primaries: yellow, red, and blue. Adjacent to the primaries are the secondary subtractive colors: orange, purple, and green. The outside circle contains the colors of the twelve-color wheel (primary, secondary, and tertiary colors): yellow, yellow-green, green, blue-green, blue, blue-violet, violet, red-violet, red, red-orange, orange, yellow-orange.

During the 1930s, artist Albert Henry Munsell developed a color wheel in the form of a three-dimensional color model or "color tree" (**4.16**). Munsell arranged ten colors on a three-dimensional model of the color wheel. There are five basic colors: red, yellow, green, blue, and purple. Unlike the Itten color system, Munsell's can better predict how the paint mixtures will actually look. Each of the ten colors of the Munsell color model has a "branch" of its own. The color chips on the outer edges of the branches are most saturated, or brightest, and gradually become less saturated, or dullest, as they approach the "trunk" of the tree. The colors at the top of the tree are arranged from lightest to darkest. Each chip is assigned a number, allowing designers and clients standardized precision in selecting colors.

The Munsell Color System is one of several systems used by industry to give designers and clients a common point of reference by alphanumerically standardizing different colors. Pantone is another system with alphanumeric precision for communication about and selection of colors. The Munsell and Pantone systems rely on essential characteristics of color called "hue," "value," and "intensity."

4.13 **The color separation process** of four-color printing.

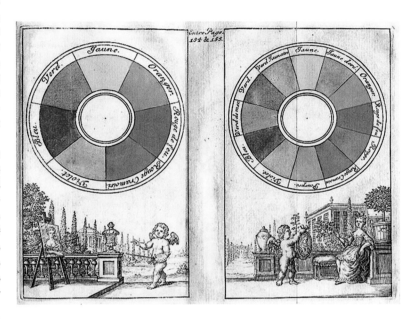

4.14 **A color wheel in use in Europe in the late seventeenth century** by an author known as C.B., based on Newton's color theory.

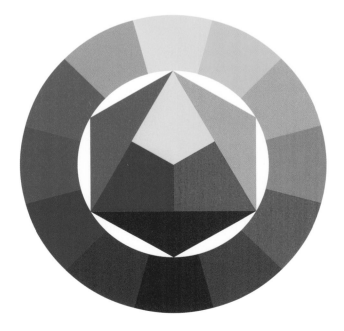

4.15 **Johannes Itten's color wheel.**

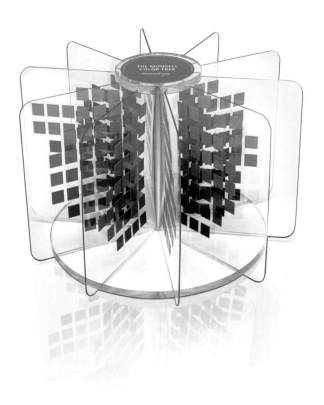

4.16 **The Munsell color system** in three dimensions.

PHYSICAL TRAITS OF COLOR: HUE, VALUE, AND INTENSITY

Each color has three separate, but essential, physical aspects, or properties, that can be measured by scientific instruments in terms of wavelengths but that are perceptible by the naked human eye: hue, value, and intensity, in light as well as pigment.

Hue corresponds to the common idea of color; it is the name we use to identify an area on the color spectrum. Some instructors also use *"hue"* to refer to a color family, using "blue hue" to refer to all blues, for example. Other instructors use *"hue"* to refer to a particular color among thousands of colors available to artists. American artist Ellsworth Kelly often limits himself to single colors on rectangular panels (**4.17**).

Value refers to the lightness or darkness of a color. Figure **4.18** shows an incremental **value scale** of blue, from dark to light. Some instructors use the words **"key"** and "value" synonymously. High-key colors are lighter than a middle value in a scale of colors; low-key colors are darker than the middle value.

As discussed in Chapter 3, achromatic value refers to lightness or darkness on a gray scale—a progressive series in which white is the lightest value, black the darkest, and variations of gray fall in between these extremes. When white or black is added to a color, it changes the color's value. From the standpoint of

4.17 **ELLSWORTH KELLY** *Blue Green Yellow Orange Red,* 1966, and *Orange Red Relief,* 1959. Installation view.

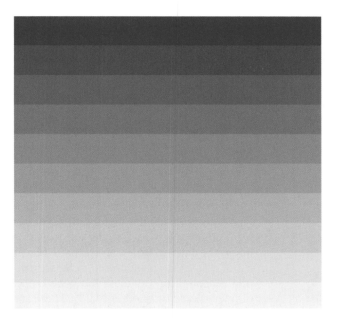

4.18   A value scale of blue.

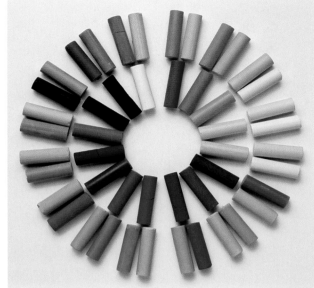

4.19   Prismacolor Art Stix in an array of intensities.

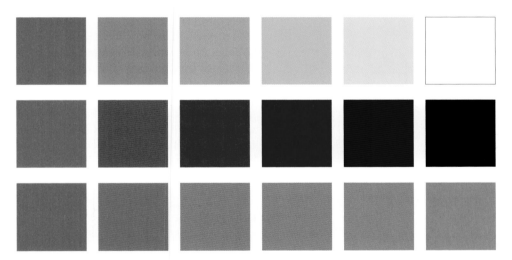

4.20   Tints, shades, and tones of red.

human perception, values may be as important as hues. In the darkness, we see values, not hues.

Intensity (also called **saturation** or **chroma**) refers to the strength or weakness of a color. The more closely a color resembles a spectral color, the purer or more intense the color appears to be. A strongly saturated color is vivid and bright. Colors range from saturated and intense to less saturated and less intense (**4.19**).

A **tint** is a color that has white added to it. A **shade** is a color that has black added to it. A **tone** is a color that has gray added to it (**4.20**). Adding white to a color lightens its value but diminishes its intensity. Adding black or gray to a color darkens its value but diminishes its intensity. A color may be darkened or lightened with the addition of another color to it, thus maintaining intensity in the new color.

NEUTRALS

Blacks, whites, and grays made from mixing black and white are achromatic (without color) and are referred to as **neutrals**. They differ from colors in the amount of light they reflect, and they do not resemble particular colors on the color spectrum. A white surface reflects all color wavelengths equally; a black surface absorbs all wavelengths. Many pigments obtained from the earth, such as raw umber, burnt umber, and raw sienna, are also sometimes called neutrals, especially in decorating schemes (**4.21**).

4.21   **Behr neutral color schemes,** red tone neutrals, 2008.

4.22   **Child's dress, tie-dyed silk,** India, twentieth century.

PIGMENTS AND DYES

Both pigments and dyes absorb some wavelengths of light and reflect others. **Pigments** are ground-up color materials, such as powdered minerals, that are suspended in a medium such as oil, egg, or acrylic to make paint. When applied, they tend to adhere to a surface but do not fully penetrate it. **Dyes,** in contrast, dissolve in a medium (usually water) and are absorbed by the materials they touch. Dyes can be natural or synthetic. Natural dyes can be obtained from animal and mineral materials, such as seashells and clay, and especially vegetable matter, such as berries, roots, bark, and leaves. When exposed to light, dyes can be less stable, or colorfast, than pigments. Knowledge of coloring materials helps in understanding the longevity of all artifacts (**4.22**).

OPAQUE AND TRANSPARENT COLORS

Some colors are **opaque,** preventing any underlying colors from showing through, and some are **transparent,** allowing underlying colors to show through and affect the top color. When a color is penetrable by light but diffuses it so that underlying images are blurry, we call it **translucent.**

Artists use these qualities of color to achieve expressive effects. Fashion designer Issey Miyake uses transparent dyes on fabric to reveal the texture of the fabric itself and to allow for the play of one color upon another (**4.23**). Glass artist Marvin Lipofsky uses transparent, opaque, and translucent colors to show the penetration of one volume by another (**4.24**). There are many methods of introducing color to a glass artwork. Some studios have furnaces containing molten glasses that are colored. The majority of glass studios use commercially produced colored glasses that come in rod, crushed, or pulverized forms.

Janet Fish is masterful at creating the illusions of transparency and opacity in her paintings, such as *Spring Flowers, Orange Tray* (**4.25**). Note that she is able to paint glass containers that seem to be transparent while they hold fruits and flowers that seem to be opaque. The pink geometric container is especially fascinating, because it is transparent and holds small solid glass objects that are both transparent and opaque.

Artists develop skill working with color by practice, through trial and error. When artists walk into an art store, they do not find tubes of paint labeled "primary yellow," "primary red," and "primary blue." Rather, they are faced with an array of reds, yellows, and blues with very many and sometimes exotic names. The names of the colors themselves are sometimes revealing and sometimes not at all helpful. Primary red, the red that matches the spectral red of sunlight, does not exist in a tube, can, bottle, or even in nature. Looking at and comparing basic sets of colors that have been gathered and packaged as "beginner's sets" reveal that no two manufacturers' basic colors are the same.

Given the number of choices on the market, consider starting by selecting a limited number of colors and working with them until you are comfortable with their properties and how they interact. Keep in mind that different color combinations of "primaries" will result in different secondary colors. For example, alizarin crimson, cadmium yellow, and ultramarine blue produce

4.23   ISSEY MIYAKE   *"PleatsPlease!"*, 2001.

4.24   MARVIN LIPOFSKY   *Untitled Glass Sculpture (Leerdam Series),* 1970. Blown glass, 8 × 16 × 11 in.

clear violets but less-than-clear greens and oranges that lack brightness. Cadmium red, lemon yellow, and cerulean blue produce bright greens, but the violets approach brown, and so forth. Some instructors offer this basic set of primary colors: cadmium red, alizarin crimson, French ultramarine, cerulean blue, lemon yellow, and cadmium yellow. Each has a warm or cool bias and in combinations provides truer and wider varieties of secondary colors that you will discover through experimentation.

Some color materials are very fugitive (likely to deteriorate or disappear) and should not be used if you want a work to remain unchanged. Low-grade construction papers, for example, fade quickly, as you have likely observed on bulletin board displays. Some color materials need not last long if they are used relatively soon and are to be reproduced in a more permanent color medium. Designers and illustrators use gouaches (opaque watercolors), for example, to make images that will be reproduced in books, posters, and magazines.

As you work in various media, you will gain a greater understanding of how to select and mix or layer colorants such as felt markers, ceramic glazes, silkscreen inks, and pastels. You will likely have the opportunity to learn how to digitally manipulate colors in images as well. Yet despite the differences in physical properties across media, some common principles apply, and they will become intuitive with practice.

SUBTRACTIVE COLOR MIXING

As discussed earlier, the primary colors for mixing pigments are red, yellow, and blue; when all three are intermixed equally, the result is close to black (**4.26**). The result is not a true black because there are no pure pigments that accurately represent the ideal primary colors.

When two primary colors are mixed together, the result is a secondary color. When red pigment and yellow pigment are mixed, the secondary color is orange; red and blue produce violet; yellow and blue produce green (**4.27** and **4.28**).

Tertiary colors (also known as **intermediates**) are the products of a primary and a secondary color. Basic tertiary colors are yellow-green, blue-green, blue-violet, red-violet, red-orange, and yellow-orange (**4.29**).

The primary, secondary, and tertiary colors are traditionally represented on a twelve-part color wheel (see 4.26). In this process of mixing pigments, known as a subtractive color process, the newly mixed color "subtracts" by absorbing the other colors that the new color does not reveal. Note that this is based on color theory. In practice, any given yellow mixed with any given blue might be a surprise that does not match the green of the color wheel.

Color Schemes

Artists and designers may choose to work with a scheme of one or more colors based on the effects that the combination creates. This is not to suggest that there is a formula for picking colors, because meaning depends on the interplay of all the compositional elements and subject matter. But knowledge of color relationships is helpful whether you wish to use them or subvert them. The most common color schemes are based on relationships across the color wheel and thus are focused on color. But keep in mind that value and saturation will also affect color relationships.

4.25   **JANET FISH**   *Spring Flowers, Orange Tray,* 2007. Oil on canvas, 48 × 60 in.

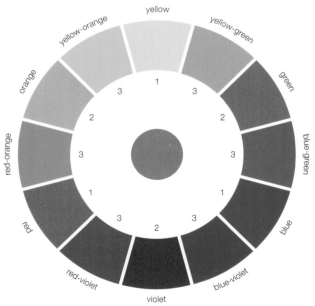

4.26   **The traditional twelve-part color wheel** for subtractive color mixing, with the primary colors numbered as 1, the secondary colors as 2, and the tertiary colors as 3.

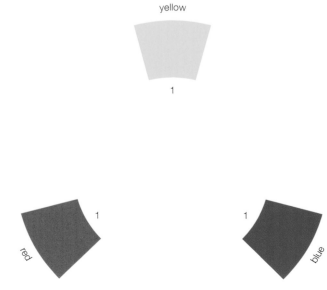

4.27   **Subtractive primary colors:** yellow, blue, and red.

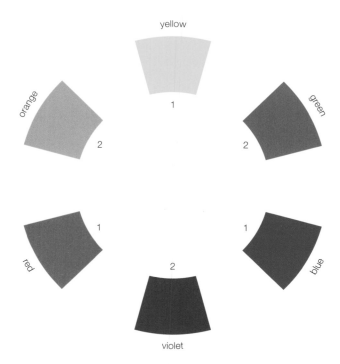

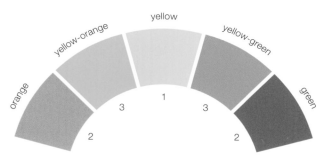

4.29 Primary yellow and secondary green mix to make tertiary yellow-green; primary yellow and secondary orange mix to make tertiary yellow-orange.

MONOCHROMATIC, ANALOGOUS, AND COMPLEMENTARY

Monochromatic color schemes use variations of one color. Monochromatic schemes often add intensity to a mood. Ross Bleckner's *Falling Birds* (**4.30**) is a monochromatic serigraph (a print produced with a silkscreen) in different values and intensities of blue. The blues give the image an ethereal quality. The falling hummingbird is an icy blue, suggestive of both the freezing weather that may have killed it and the mystery of death. The artist's choice of this monochromatic scheme adds emotional content to the painting.

Analogous color schemes employ several colors that are adjacent on the color wheel (**4.31**). They usually produce a harmonious effect. In his work from the 1950s, Mark Rothko often painted two to four rectangles of highly saturated analogous colors on a color ground with the intent of provoking an emotional response in the viewer, which they did, partially by the color schemes but also because of the hovering ethereal effect of the colors advancing and receding on the flat picture plane of the canvas (**4.32**). "The people who weep before my pictures," said Rothko, "are having the same religious experience I had when I painted

4.28 Subtractive secondary colors: primary yellow and blue combine to make secondary green; primary blue and red combine to make secondary violet; primary red and yellow combine to make secondary orange.

4.30 ROSS BLECKNER *Falling Birds,* 1994. Oil on canvas, 96 × 120 in.

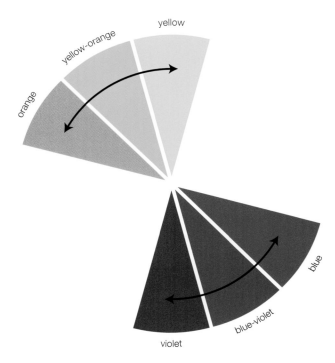

4.31 Samples of analogous colors.

4.32   MARK ROTHKO   *Orange and Yellow,* 1956. Oil on
canvas, framed: 93½ × 73½ × 2¾ in. (237.5 × 186.7 cm.);
support: 91 × 71 in. (321.12 × 180.34 cm.)

them. And if you, as you say, are moved only by their
color relationships, then you miss the point."[7]

Colors opposite each other on the traditional color
wheel are called "complements." Color schemes that
use such colors are called **complementary color
schemes** (**4.33**). Red and green, yellow and violet,
and blue and orange are examples of complementary
pairs. In a famous government poster from World War
II (**4.34**), a blue-orange scheme is both harmonious and
energizing, expressing its message in a simple, high-
impact composition.

TRIADS, TETRADS, AND HEXADS

To reinforce the desired expression you wish to make
in your work, you can construct harmonious or discordant colors using triads, tetrads, and hexads. Imagine
placing an equal-sided triangle within the color wheel;
the colors at each point of the triangle would form a
triad (**4.35**). A triad of primary colors—yellow, blue,
red—provides striking contrast. A triad of secondary
colors—orange, green, and violet—provides softer
contrast.

A **tetrad** provides a color scheme of four colors
based on the points of either a square or a rectangle inscribed in the color wheel, for example, yellow-orange,
green, blue-violet, and red (**4.36**). A **hexad** provides a
scheme of six colors, which means every other color
on the color wheel. As the number of colors and artist
uses increases, so does the potential for visual chaos.
Both tetradic and hexadic schemes are thought to bring
harmony and unity to a complex composition.

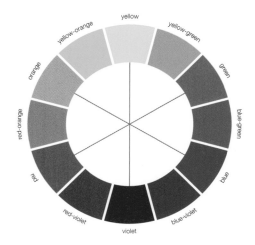

4.33   The traditional color wheel, with lines connecting
the complements.

WARM AND COOL COLORS

Color schemes can make use of the psychological association of colors with temperature. Colors on the red-yellow side of the wheel are warm, while the colors on the blue-green side are cool. Traditionally, many people have associated blue with sky and yellow with sun, green with water and orange with fire.

In two paintings shown here, Frederic Remington uses warm and cool schemes in narratives of the Old West. *His First Lesson* (**4.37**) is bathed in oranges and yellows, suggesting the heat of the southwestern sun. Even the shadows, made of **chromatic grays** produced by mixing complementary colors to change their intensity, have a warm tone. Compare the warmth of *His First Lesson* to the chill of *The Fall of the Cowboy* (**4.38**). The subject matter itself indicates cold through snow-covered ground, heavy clothing, and blankets. This sense of cold is further expressed through colors from the cool side of the color wheel—note particularly the blue-gray of the threatening winter sky. The colors express the emotional content of each painting—the first and earlier painting is optimistic in tone, while the latter suggests sadness about the fencing of the West.

Also, a cool blue may look cooler when placed next to a warm orange (**4.39a**). Warm and cool colors may also be used to indicate spatial depth and distance. This is because warm colors tend to advance toward the viewer, whereas cool ones recede (**4.39b**).

EARTH TONES

Beyond the conventional color wheel is a triad of yellow ochre, burnt sienna, and blue-gray, which produces the colors we associate with earth tones (**4.40**). Richard Misrach's *Dead Animals #1* works with this palette (**4.41**). The photograph contains a range of browns and grays, plus black and white for contrast, juxtaposing a harsh, ugly reality with a soft, pleasing color scheme. Misrach found the dead animals in an area of the U.S. where frequent nuclear testing has taken place.

4.35 **A triadic color scheme** using three tertiary colors that are equidistant on the color wheel.

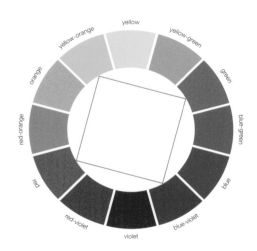

4.36 **A tetradic scheme** made up of two primary (red and green) and two tertiary (yellow-orange and blue-violet) colors. The square may be rotated around the circle to identify other tetradic schemes.

4.34 **J. HOWARD MILLER** *"We Can Do It!"* c. 1942.

4.37 FREDERIC REMINGTON *His First Lesson,* 1903. Oil on canvas, 27¼ × 40 in. Amon Carter Museum, Fort Worth, Texas, 1961.231.

4.38 FREDERIC REMINGTON *The Fall of the Cowboy,* 1895. Oil on canvas, 25 × 35⅛ in. Amon Carter Museum, Fort Worth, Texas, 1961.230.

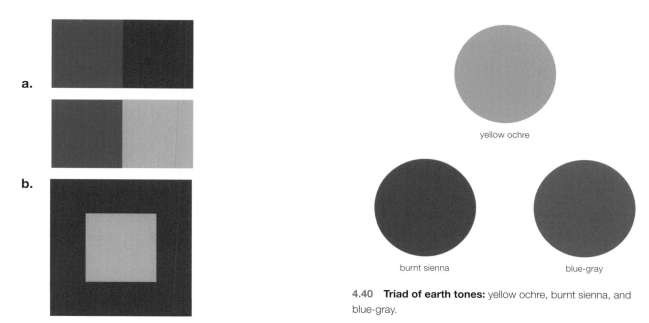

a.

b.

yellow ochre

burnt sienna

blue-gray

4.40 Triad of earth tones: yellow ochre, burnt sienna, and blue-gray.

4.39 Warm and cool color interactions. Notice how the blue seems to change when it is adjacent to different colors (**a**). The orange seems to advance, and the violet to recede (**b**).

4.41 RICHARD MISRACH *Dead Animals #1,* 1987. Color photograph.

POLYCHROMATIC SCHEMES

A color image that employs a wide range of colors in a variety of values is called **polychromatic.** The Adidas sneakers (**4.42**) are an example of an intense and vibrant polychromatic scheme of colors used to make a flamboyant fashion statement.

Trenton Doyle Hancock's large painting within an installation of smaller paintings hung in a wallpapered gallery, *For a Floor of Flora* (**4.43**), uses a polychromatic scheme of colors found throughout the color wheel. It mixes high- and low-contrast colors and colors with different degrees of saturation in a busily colored environment. Hancock calms the many diverse colors and complex patterning of the space with neutral colors.

Color Interactions

We rarely see one color in isolation from other colors. A warm "white" wall of a room is usually juxtaposed with a colder, brighter, white of the ceiling, painted that way to reflect more light in the room. We experience a minimalist sculpture of one color in relation to the colors of its surroundings and in relation to other works in its proximity. There are several kinds of color interactions.

SIMULTANEOUS CONTRAST

When complements are placed next to each other, they appear more intense. This optical effect is known as **simultaneous contrast.** In his installation *New Wall Drawings* (**4.44**), Sol LeWitt makes use of simultaneous contrast to blast the viewer with vibrating colors. On one wall, he places a saturated red against a saturated green, its complement; on the next wall, an analogous combination of orange, yellow, and red is activated by including the green complement in the composition. One art critic noted that as the eye adjusts to the intensity of the colors, the colors become almost restful, which suggests that artists can create dynamic color experiences for viewers.

Vincent van Gogh used simultaneous contrast with the juxtaposition of intense colors abutting one another in *Night Café* (**4.45**). He knew what he was doing when he made such a choice. Writing to his brother Theo, he referred to the painting as "one of the ugliest I have done . . . I have tried to express the terrible passions of humanity by means of red and green."[8] By his choice of simultaneous contrast in the painting, Van Gogh was evoking a heightened emotional response during a time in his life when he was seriously depressed with feelings of overwhelming isolation.

4.42 **Adidas ZX600 Multicolor,** 2008.

4.43 **TRENTON DOYLE HANCOCK** *For a Floor of Flora,* 2003. Installation, mixed media.

4.44 **SOL LEWITT** *New Wall Drawings,* September 3–October 12, 2002. Installation.

4.45 **VINCENT VAN GOGH** *Night Café (Le Café de nuit),* 1888. Oil on canvas, 28½ × 36¼ in.

You can create the phenomenon of simultaneous contrast with complementary colors and with any contrasts of hue, value, or intensity, making the colors in juxtaposition appear differently than they would apart. Josef Albers, perhaps the most influential color theorist of the twentieth century, observed: "A color is never seen as it really is—as it physically is. This fact makes color the most relative medium in art."[9] Albers conducted a number of color studies using squares of color superimposed on other squares of color to demonstrate some of the interactions. The three examples (**4.46, 4.47,** and **4.48**) are derived from his studies.

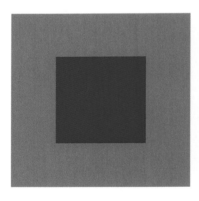 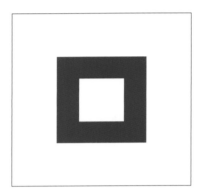

4.46   **The two green figures contained within the black and the white square** are the same color and value, but the appearance of their value is changed by their surrounding color.

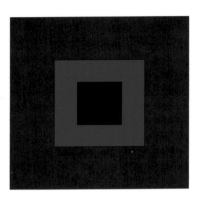 

4.47   **The two green squares** are the same, but the surrounding colors alter our perception of their size and color.

4.48   **The pink figures within the solid squares** are identical but appear different because of their surrounding colors.

AFTERIMAGE

You have likely had the experience of seeing a bright halo after looking away from a bright light. The halo is an example of an **afterimage,** an optical effect that also relates to color interaction.

Larry Poons uses the principle of afterimage in his painting *Sunnyside Switch* (**4.49**). If you stare intensely at the picture surface, focusing on one dot for fifteen to twenty seconds, you will "see" dots that are not really there. Moreover, if you look longer at the painting, with any movement of your eyes the afterimage dots will seem to jump accordingly. He places a motif of dots over a continuous color plane to provide us with an afterimage. Poons also made his dots elliptical, rather than round, and placed them on a diagonal axis. Thus the afterimage dots take on "direction" and seem to streak across the canvas. Because we have differing ocular sensitivities and view the painting with different eye movements, no two people experience or "see" exactly the same result.

ARTISTS AND OPTICAL MIXING

Impressionists as well as the pointillist artist Georges Seurat and more recently Chuck Close make paintings in which viewers mix colors with their eyes. For example, in *A Sunday on La Grande Jatte,* Seurat placed dots of colors next to one another that optically combine to make new colors in the viewer's eye. About a hundred years after Seurat, Close also employs optical mixing of colors in his paintings, prints, and images made of paper pulp.

Earlier we discussed optical color mixing in commercial printing and as used in electronic colors with computer screens and televisions. Painters and printmakers also use optical mixing on paper and canvas.

Emma (**4.50**), by Chuck Close, is a large woodcut of a baby's face. From a great distance, or if you squint at it, the print appears to be a likeness of a child's face. A close look at *Emma,* however, shows that the portrait is composed of thousands of small, abstract shapes of color ink. In the admiring words of one commentator, "Close's 'game' with color is exacting and demanding, requiring a knowledge of the optical effects of color mixing that is virtually unparalleled in the history of art."[10]

LOCAL COLOR AND ARBITRARY COLOR

The local color of a banana is yellow; the local color of grass is green. **Local color** is the color that an object reflects in the real world—although "real" color changes with the light and the reflections of other objects, as the Impressionists showed. When used in artifacts, local color helps create the illusion of reality. In his sculpture *Child with Puzzle* (**4.51**), Duane Hanson uses local color—blonde hair and light skin—to enhance the realism of a young girl made of polyvinyl.

Joel Meyerowitz is one of the earliest American photographers to use color in art photography when the majority of art photographers were making black-and-white images. Throughout his career in color photography, Meyerowitz was fascinated by local color and how light affected it. His first color book, *Cape Light: Color Photographs,* is a study of changes in color due to light in Cape Cod, Massachusetts.[11] In his photograph of a porch on an oceanfront home, he captures multiple light sources and effects in one frame: the hazy light over the ocean during a storm, the artificial light coming from the unseen interior of the house, and the lightning bolt striking parallel to the porch pillar (**4.52**).

Arbitrary color is the opposite of local color: it aims not to represent reality but to provide unexpected sensations, to enhance emotions, or to provide different visions of the world. The term "arbitrary" is misleading, because it wrongly suggests that the artist's choice of colors is without thought.

The Post-Impressionist painter Pierre Bonnard is recognized as a master of the use of arbitrary color to evoke feeling and mood. His *Nude in Bathtub* (**4.53**) uses rich, seductive colors in fanciful gradients that are not faithful to the actual color of his wife's skin or the surfaces of his bathroom. The photographer Brassaï saw Bonnard at work and described how Bonnard's use of arbitrary color was in fact quite deliberate as he focused on creating arbitrary color relationships on the canvas, especially with his facile use of yellow, which was not perceptible in the local scene he was painting:

4.49 LARRY POONS *Sunnyside Switch,* 1963. Acrylic on canvas, 80 × 80 in.

4.50 CHUCK CLOSE *Emma,* 2002. 113-color hand printed woodcut, 43 × 35 in.

4.51 DUANE HANSON *Child with Puzzle,* 1979. Life-size sculptural installation, polyvinyl with mixed media.

4.52 JOEL MEYEROWITZ *Porch, Provincetown, 1977,* 1977. Photograph.

4.53 PIERRE BONNARD *Nude in Bathtub,* *c.* 1941–1946. Oil on canvas, 48 × 59½ in.

I looked around for his easel, his palette. There were none. Nailed side by side on to the wall were several unstretched canvases on all of which, to my astonishment, Bonnard was working at the same time. Once he had collected a touch of *lacque de garance,* or cadmium yellow, with his nervous, deft fingers, he would then examine each canvas to find the one and only place to put it. In this way, he could nourish several canvases at once until they all came to life . . . By moving away from the canvases after each stroke, he was better able to judge the effect he was obtaining and to seize the color relationships, as well as to keep an eye out for any empty spaces.[12]

Contemporary African American artist Glen Ligon uses color for social purposes. The colors he uses in *Malcolm X, Sun, Frederick Douglass, Boy with Bubbles* (**4.54**) are politically charged. In the work, he uses both local color, such as yellow for the sun, and arbitrary colors to depict Malcolm X and Frederick Douglass, two of the most prominent African Americans in history, as white men with grotesquely colored hair and

facial marks of clowns. His painting can be read as an angry statement about race in America.

Color and Meaning

When used thoughtfully, color communicates messages, sets attitudes, and reinforces expressive content. Color draws attention to what is important in an image or object. It can affect mood and have cultural connotations.

MOOD AND EMOTION

Many performance artists particularly rely on colored light to enhance the mood of their works. Pioneer multimedia artist Laurie Anderson illuminated a concert stage with candles and theater lights to create a warm and inviting ambiance. In another piece, *Oh, Superman,*

4.54   **GLEN LIGON**   *Malcolm X, Sun, Frederick Douglass, Boy with Bubbles (version 2) # 8,* 2001. Paint and silkscreen on paper, 23 × 16½ in.

4.55   **LAURIE ANDERSON**   **Performance at Salisbury Festival,** 2005.

a video, CD, and live solo music performance, she illuminated her mouth with an electronic device she held within her mouth, creating an eerie effect when she spoke and sang (**4.55**). She has also produced her own light-projected colored figures to enhance her lyrics, both of which scarily referred to the overwhelming power of big industry in relation to the individual.

In *End Bad Breath* (**4.56**), graphic designer Seymour Chwast created a jarring and vitriolic antiwar poster with three colors on white. He altered the traditional red and blue of the American flag by using tints of the colors and made the face of Uncle Sam, whose mouth is full of airplanes bombing houses, a "sickening" green. The mood of the piece is repulsive for the viewer. The poster reveals the anger of the artist and is meant to arouse the viewer to antiwar action.

Jose Rementeria's poster (**4.57**) uses witty wordplay (human "beans" rather than "beings") and the local colors of various types of legumes against a stark red ground for a visual pun with serious humanistic intent. The red suggests urgency, and the harmonious colors of the dried beans imply peacefulness. The beans lie next

to each other in an earthy pod; although together in one pod, each retains its individual color and identity while coexisting peacefully.

COLORS AND CULTURES

Meanings of, associations with, and sensitivity to colors are culturally dependent and not universal. In fact, such **symbolic colors** vary with time, place, and culture. For example, the meaning of black and white in Western culture can be traced to the first lines of the creation story: "In the beginning God created the heaven and the earth . . . darkness was upon the face of the deep . . . God said, Let there be light: and there was light. And God saw the light, that it was good." The German poet and dramatist Johann Wolfgang von Goethe reinforced this view: pure light represented goodness and pure black, damnation.[13]

In some Eastern cultures such as those of Japan and China, white is associated with death, not goodness. At certain periods of history, white was not worn at funerals because it was associated with mourning. In the West, black represents seriousness, even death. When the governors of sixteenth-century Venice thought Venetian society was becoming too frivolous, they ordered that gondolas be painted black. The Puritans who emerged in Europe in the seventeenth century wore black, which they considered a subdued color. In many African communities, however, black has positive associations with life and protective ancestral spirits rather than negative associations with death or repression.

In some cultures, red is associated with both life and death. For example, in Comanche, a single word, *ekapi,* is used to designate "color," "circle," and "red," suggesting that in this Native American culture, red is something fundamental and all encompassing.[14]

Some cultures associate colors with status. The Incas represented themselves, their armies, and their powerful emperors with a deep purplish red. The ancient Romans also used red to indicate status and valued the color so much that taxes in some of their conquered lands were not to be paid not in gold or silver but in native materials that could be made into red dye.[15] The emperors of China were the only members of that society who were allowed to wear yellow, and their sunshine-colored robes were seen as a symbol of power.

Colors can also carry religious connotations. Catholics today generally associate blue with Mary, the mother of Jesus, and typically depict her in a blue veil.

4.56 **SEYMOUR CHWAST** *End Bad Breath,* 2004.

4.57 **JOSE REMENTERIA** **Poster** for the traveling exhibition "Coexistence."

4.58 UNIDENTIFIED ARTIST *The Nativity, c.* 1475. From the church of Saint Nicholas, Gostinople.

4.59 MICHELANGELO BUONAROTTI *The Entombment, c.* 1500. Oil on wood, 64 × 59 in.

This was not always the case. In Russian icons, Mary wears red, possibly symbolizing her giving birth (**4.58**). Byzantine artists of the seventh century dressed her in purple, perhaps to suggest mystery. She is sometimes adorned in sorrowful black because of her loss and in white because of her purity.

Sometimes color choice was not symbolic but based on the preciousness of the pigment itself. In fifteenth-century Holland, for example, scarlet was the most expensive dye, and artists therefore pictured Mary in scarlet clothing. In thirteenth-century Italy, ultra-marine blue arrived by donkey from its source in Afghanistan. Because it was very rare and precious, it was the chosen color for depictions of Mary's wardrobe. Michelangelo left a painting unfinished, waiting for the arrival of ultramarine that did not come soon enough for him. Most of *The Entombment* (**4.59**) is complete, but not the Virgin, outlined in the lower-right corner of the painting.[16]

In the Byzantine Empire during the eighth century, painters used natural materials, such as plants, rocks, insects, and eggs, to make colors, in order to glorify God and creation. Even today, Orthodox icon painters use natural rather than synthetic materials. The Or-

thodox tradition also emphasizes the light within every individual; thus artists carefully prepare the surfaces on which they paint, making them very white so that light will shine through the painted and gold-leaf figures represented in icons.[17]

Preferences for color are often culturally determined and can be turned into social values and notions of superiority of one group over others. For example, Europeans of the nineteenth century assumed they were superior to Africans, Asians, and Jews, who they thought demonstrated inferiority by their tastes for brilliant colors.[18]

Luis Jimenez often began public lectures about his work with the phrase, "I have an agenda . . ." Jimenez (who died in 2006) considered his primary audience to be the Chicano working class. He favored violent imagery and used garish colors that struck some viewers as inventively stereotypical and degrading. The artist, however, thought of his use of Chicano stereotypes as an effort to reclaim and redeem aspects of Southwest American history that have been ignored or erased by mainstream Anglo communities (**4.60**).

In *Color Blind Test* (**4.61**), Kerry James Marshall uses two different systems, one medical and the other aesthetic, to express social content with color. In the dotted background, the artist draws upon the Confusion Test, which is used to measure color blindness and other vision idiosyncrasies. The background also reproduces the red, black, and green colors of the Black Nationalist flag created by Marcus Garvey, leader of the Universal Negro Improvement Association. On the wall text next to the diptych, the Museum of Contemporary Art in Chicago offered this interpretation of Marshall's expressive use of color: "Marshall critiques the notion that our society sees colorblindness—ignoring the color of peoples' skin—as an ideal. Although some may purport to be 'colorblind', they still make distinctions based on race, and they fail to see the value in recognizing diversity."

Conclusion: Beyond Color Theory

Color is a complex art element. The theories discussed in this chapter are meant to help you understand some general ways in which color works in art. To truly develop an understanding of color, you will need to experiment with actual pigments, colored lights, and phosphor pixels. Even the renowned color theorist and artist Josef Albers recognized that factual knowledge of color theory alone is not enough: "Just as the knowledge of acoustics does not make one musical—neither on the productive nor on the appreciative side—so no color system by itself can develop one's sensitivity for color." He had little respect for factual identification of colors without sensitive seeing or an understanding of how the color acted within an artwork: "What counts here—first and last—is not so-called knowledge of so-called facts, but vision—seeing. Seeing . . . is coupled with fantasy, with imagination."[19]

4.60 LUIS JIMENEZ *Vaquero,* modeled 1980, cast 1990. Acrylic urethane, fiberglass and steel armature, 199 × 114 × 67 in. (505.5 × 289.6 × 170.2 cm.)

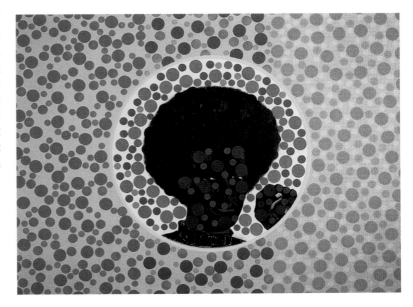

4.61 KERRY JAMES MARSHALL *Diptych (Color Blind Test),* left section, 2003. Acrylic on MDF panel.

5 Space

5.1 **TIM HAWKINSON** *Bear,* 2005. Granite, 23 ft. 6 in.

As a design element, **space** is an expanse of three-dimensionality that contains all things in which objects and events occur. It is a complex element, dependent on other elements that make it visible and perceptible. This chapter offers you ideas for and examples of constructing places, structures, and objects that are **three dimensional**—having height, width, and depth—and for creating the illusion of three dimensions on two-dimensional surfaces.

Actual Space

The three-dimensional space of the universe is infinite and ever expanding. We feel the infinite space of the universe on a dark, clear night indicated by a starry sky, the immense space of "big sky country" on an open Montana plain, the overwhelming canyons formed by towering skyscrapers in New York City, the expansive space of an auditorium, and the cramped space of a small closet. This is **actual space**—an expanse with depth, height, and width that surrounds an object or that an object occupies.

You are reading these words in an actual space, such as a room or some other interior space, or perhaps outdoors in a campus courtyard. In either case, you are reading in a three-dimensional space designed by people, unless you are in a virgin environment formed only by nature and relatively undisturbed by human intervention.

THE PSYCHOLOGY OF SPACE

The space in which you are reading has sensory qualities and psychological effects. The visual sensory qualities and their psychological effects are influenced by design elements such as texture, mass and volume, color, and light. We have different reactions to spatial elements that might increase anxiety or offer comfort. Each of us also carries a sense of personal space in proximity to others in which we feel comfortable, invaded when someone seems to come too close, or disconnected when a person stays too far away. Our responses to environmental and interpersonal space are both culturally and psychologically influenced. What is your experience of the space you are now in? How do you feel in it? What elements of the space affect your feelings?

Built spaces have psychological overtones, often designed for psychological and social effects: for example, some buildings of the state and the church are designed to maximize the impression of institutional power and to humble the visitor. Baroque architecture prevailed in Europe for 150 years during a time when new social and political systems concentrated power in the hands of individuals with absolute authority. Architecture affirmed individual and institutional power in

Space Key Terms

SPACE   An expanse of three-dimensionality in which objects and events occur.

THREE DIMENSIONAL   Having height, width, and depth.

ACTUAL SPACE   An expanse having depth, height, and width that surrounds an object or that an object occupies.

TWO-DIMENSIONAL SPACE   A planar surface area bound by height and width.

ILLUSIONAL SPACE   The appearance of depth, height, and width on a two-dimensional surface.

IN THE ROUND, FREE STANDING   Made to be seen from 360 degrees.

IN RELIEF   Meant to be seen from the front and sides, not *in the round*. Relief building or sculpting entails carving away or building up a flat surface.

POSITIVE SPACE   An area filled with elements of design.

NEGATIVE SPACE   An empty area surrounded and shaped so that it acquires form or volume.

VIRTUAL SPACE   Artificial, computer-based, three-dimensional environments and objects allowing viewer experiences that seem real.

FOREGROUND   On a two-dimensional surface, what appears closest to the viewer in a three-dimensional representation.

BACKGROUND   On a two-dimensional surface, what appears farthest from the viewer in a three-dimensional representation.

MIDDLE GROUND   On a two-dimensional surface, the area of a representation between *foreground* and *background* in a three-dimensional representation.

PERSPECTIVE   The illusion of *space* on planar surfaces, created by techniques for representing three dimensions on a two-dimensional surface.

ATMOSPHERIC PERSPECTIVE, AERIAL PERSPECTIVE   The technique of representing dimensional space by making objects close to the viewer appear crisp and vibrant and making them fuzzy and less intense in color and tone as they recede.

LINEAR PERSPECTIVE   A system of rendering the appearance of three dimensions on a two-dimensional plane by making objects appear smaller as they recede and by making parallel lines converge in the distance at a *vanishing point* on a *horizon line*.

VANISHING POINT   Where converging lines drawn in *linear perspective* seem to disappear into a distant dot on the *horizon line* of a three-dimensional scene on a two-dimensional surface.

HORIZON LINE   Where the sky meets the ground in the world or in a perspectival representation of it.

ORTHOGONAL LINES   Lines or edges in a picture that lead the viewer's eyes to the *vanishing points* in an illusional three-dimensional space.

PICTURE PLANE   The actual flat surface on which the artist makes marks or representations of three dimensions.

EYE LEVEL   The position from which an artist shows a scene.

CONE OF VISION   In linear perspectival rendering, a 45- to 60-degree angle that includes the artist's vision from the artist's point of view when depicting an illusion of a three-dimensional object or scene.

ONE-POINT PERSPECTIVE   The use of only one *vanishing point* on the *horizon line* of a representational picture made in *linear perspective*.

TWO-POINT PERSPECTIVE   The use of two *vanishing points* on the *horizon line* of a picture made in *linear perspective*.

THREE-POINT PERSPECTIVE   The use of three *vanishing points* on, above, or below the *horizon line* of a picture made in *linear perspective*.

BIRD'S-EYE VIEW   A point of view from a very high level looking down at a space or object.

WORM'S-EYE VIEW   A point of view from a very low level looking up at a space or object.

FORESHORTENING   In *linear perspective,* making things close to the viewer appear disproportionately large for expressive purposes.

ISOMETRIC PERSPECTIVE   A means of rendering three-dimensional objects without reliance on *vanishing points* or converging lines; scale of objects remains the same regardless of the distance from the *foreground* and *background*.

MULTIPLE PERSPECTIVE   More than one view of the subject simultaneously in the same picture.

the design of palaces, churches, government buildings, military installations, and residences of the wealthy and powerful. In their design of the residence Vaux-le-Vicomte (**5.2**), architect Louis Le Vau, designer Charles Le Brun, and gardener André Le Nôtre combined their efforts to extend the impression of wealth and power and authority from the building and its interior to the surrounding landscape into an expansive vista.

The words you are reading and the reproductions you are seeing are within an actual **two-dimensional space,** namely, a page, a planar surface bound by height and width that is structured by a graphic designer. The page has areas of positive and negative space. The verbal and visual information is printed in dark ink on light background so that there is sufficient contrast to allow you to distinguish between print and paper. The paper has texture that should allow ease of reading under different light sources. The weight and texture of the paper also influence the quality of the reproductions. The page is bound with other pages into a three-dimensional object, a book, that has mass.

The reproduction of Vaux-le-Vicomte is flat but provides **illusional space**—the appearance of depth, height, and width on a two-dimensional surface, in this case, of the three-dimensional palace and landscape. Thus space can be both actual and illusional.

How does the book look and feel? How does it open on a table or in your lap? With what impressions do the designer's choices for the book leave you? Does the physicality of the book facilitate or distract from your ability to understand its content? How and why?

ARCHITECTURAL SPACE

Designing architectural spaces can be a complicated and challenging experience for designers and artists, with real consequences for the people who use them. Any single architectural space is designed to be within a larger space—its context (see Chapter 1)—and both spaces ought to successfully interact aesthetically and functionally. Millennium Park (**5.3**) in Chicago is a complex example of successful contemporary design that incorporates buildings, works of art, landscape design, and city planning with the goal of being friendly to both viewers and the environment.

Chicagoans are striving to create a greener city. They annually plant about 30,000 trees; the city has seventy miles of highway medians planted with native flowers, grasses, and bushes; new homes, stores, and office buildings are required to have outdoor open spaces; and 200 of the city's buildings have energy-saving roofs planted with garden materials that cleanse the air and provide oxygen. All of these efforts are meant to conserve resources and energy, reduce storm water runoff, restore wetlands, and generate renewable energy. These overarching social, environmental, and aesthetic

5.2   LOUIS LE VAU AND ANDRÉ LE NÔTRE   Vaux-le-Vicomte, near Paris, 1661.

concerns had to be met by the designers and artists who completed the Millennium Park project.

With an expanse of 24.5 acres, Millennium Park is the largest green roof in America, covering an underground parking garage and railroad tracks. Among the park's prominent features are an outdoor concert venue, two interactive glass block towers that project video images of Chicagoans over a reflecting pool of water, gardens designed by landscape designers, and a large and shiny elliptical sculpture on the plaza. The park is an example of individual designers and artists working to achieve a harmonious result while maintaining the integrity of their individual projects. The design of this park is well beyond the scale of projects most young artists are likely to encounter, but even when working with smaller spaces, your design choices are parallel to those of the artists and designers who contributed to this park.

5.3   Millennium Park, Chicago, 2006.   A concert venue by Frank Gehry, a large elliptical reflecting sculpture by Anish Kapoor, two interactive glass towers that project images of Chicagoans over a reflecting pool of water by Jaume Plensa, and gardens designed by Kathryn Gustafson, Piet Oudolf, and Robert Israel.

5.4   Hopi National Elder Home, Hotevilla, Arizona, 2005.

Living spaces offer unique sets of problems and opportunities for creative solutions. Red Feather Development Group is trying to meet the overwhelming shelter needs of Native Americans, forty percent of whom live in overcrowded or substandard housing, as opposed to the national average of six percent. The obstacle to better living spaces for tribal members is

primarily economic. One solution is straw-bale homes (**5.4**), which are affordable and efficient and can be constructed by tribal members themselves. A straw-bale house is made by stacking bales of tightly packed straw on top of one another to make walls. The bales are then covered with stucco, which seals out moisture and prevents rotting. The walls, which can be up to 2 feet thick, provide high thermal resistance and a living environment that blocks out sound. The price of a bale house is less than half the cost of a traditionally built dwelling.

INTERIOR SPACES

When designing a building, architects make decisions about the exterior of the three-dimensional space it forms while also considering how it will define and contain the interior spaces. They design for a look, a quality of feeling to fulfill the functions for which the building will be used. They must be conscious of how people, air—both warm and cool—and light will circulate through the spaces they design.

About his design of the Guggenheim Museum in Bilbao, Spain (**5.5**), architect Frank Gehry said, "It's

5.5   FRANK GEHRY   Guggenheim Museum, Bilbao, Spain, 1997.

not just space—it's a kind of sculpture." He strove for an "ephemeral" form, so that "you won't be able to hold any form in your mind. It will constantly change, depending on your angle of view."[1] The curvy, undulating form of the art museum harmonizes with the hills behind it, and its organic form contrasts with the older rectilinear buildings on the street that approaches it. The interior space of the architecture is purposely designed to be open so as not to intrude on or limit the possibilities of displaying art within the museum.

Richard Serra's huge rolled and bent steel sculptures (**5.6**) are permanently installed in a gallery of the Guggenheim Museum, Bilbao. Note the size of the sculptures in relation to the people walking in and around them. The size of sculptures shows how one interior space of the museum can function. This particular gallery in the museum can hold huge and heavy sculptures that neither overwhelm nor are overwhelmed by the space.

ARTIFACTS WITHIN SPACES

If you are creating spatial works with separate parts, you must consider the interaction between the objects and the surrounding space. Serra's huge rolled steel sculptures such as those exhibited in Bilbao (see 5.6) are marvelous uses of space. Michael Kimmelman, art critic for the *New York Times*, considers the Serra installation "one of the great works of the past half-century." He praises Serra's sculptures especially for their use of space: "It is the spaces they define that really matter. You can perceive the works at each instant as you move through them—you can feel their walls closing in, forcing you along, or slowing your movement, or cutting off light, or thrusting outward." Kimmelman observed mothers cheerfully pushing strollers and children dashing through the sculptures. He also describes the expressive impact of Serra's uses of the element of space: "The narrowest spaces feel vertiginous, the openings like arenas, or bull rings, fields or pastures, places of shock or relief or repose, suddenly arrived at."[2]

Roxy Paine's *Conjoined* (**5.7**) stands in the backyard of the expansive grounds of the Modern Art Museum of Fort Worth, Texas. It is two life-size tree forms that

5.6 RICHARD SERRA Installation view of *The Matter of Time,* Guggenheim Museum, Bilbao, Spain, 2005.

5.7 ROXY PAINE *Conjoined,* 2007. Stainless steel and concrete, 46 × 42 × 28 ft.

5.8 RALPH BACERRA *Untitled,* 2002. Ceramic with glazes, 26 × 14 × 14 in.

5.9 Relief façade, Banteay Srei temple, Cambodia, tenth century.

are fabricated from stainless steel. As the title makes explicit, the two steel tree-forms are conjoined into one piece. *Conjoined*'s natural rhythm of lines are in marked contrast to the strictly geometrical lines of the museum's architecture of steel and glass. Viewers may see *Conjoined* from many angles within the building, and when they see it, they look through rectangles of glass over a geometric pond of water contained by steel, and over green grass on which *Conjoined* is situated. It is a spectacular sculpture made more magnificent by contrasts due to its placement.

THREE-DIMENSIONAL ARTIFACTS

When discussing the space of objects, depth is the crucial aspect of three-dimensional artifacts. The dimensionality of artifacts can vary from relatively round to relatively flat.

In the Round. Many artifacts are **in the round,** that is, they can be seen from all around, or 360 degrees. Such artifacts are also called **free standing.**

Tim Hawkinson's *Bear* (see 5.1) is an example of a huge sculpture in the round. It is a 180-ton teddy bear

over 23 feet high assembled from eight enormous un-carved boulders of granite. The piece is a delightful mix of what would seem impossible to unite. Teddy bears are soft and cuddly toys that children can hold in their arms. Hawkinson's teddy bear is hard and huge with the rough texture of unpolished granite. Yet the sculpture retains the joy of the toy. Although much too large to hold, viewers can literally run around it.

In marked contrast to the immensity of Wilkinson's *Bear, Untitled* by Ralph Bacerra (**5.8**) is a relatively small three-dimensional artifact. Its various sides and surfaces contain intricate details inspired by Chinese, Japanese, and Persian pottery and fabric designs. Many of these are lost to us seeing it only in reproduction because we can see only the one angle from which it was photographed. Although Bacerra's *Untitled* could be used as a pragmatically functional object, it can be appreciated as a sculpture. Bacerra plays with the three-dimensionality of the object by adding intricate two-dimensional patterns on its surfaces that seem to flatten the vessel's volume. The artist also draws attention to the three-dimensional mass and weight of the object by providing it with a delicate and complicated lid that results in tension: can the off-kilter base support the mass and weight of the object?

In Relief. Many three-dimensional sculptures are **in relief**—meant to be seen from front and side views and not in the round—and usually attached to a surface. A clock on a wall, for example, is an ordinary artifact that is hung on a wall and is meant to be seen from front and side angles. There are varying degrees of depth in relief artifacts, ranging from shallow to deep, sometimes referred to as "low relief" (also "bas-relief") and "high relief."

Relief sculpting is a method that entails carving away from or building up a flat surface. Sculptures in relief are common throughout the world and are often a significant aspect of a monumental building.

The bas-relief shown in figure **5.9** is part of Banteay Srei, a small Hindu temple in Cambodia that is considered a gem of Khmer art. The temple is dedicated to the god Shiva. The sculpture depicts Ravana, a powerful king, shaking Mount Kailasa, the residence of Shiva, the supreme god in the Shiva tradition of Hinduism. The relief is composed of many blocks pieced together to make the scene. Each is carved from red sandstone, a medium that allows delicate detail and withstands weathering.

Louise Nevelson is known for her innovative relief sculptures that she assembled out of found wood. *Dawn's Wedding Chapel IV* (**5.10**) is an example of high-relief sculpture. It is one of Nevelson's typically tall and wide sculptures, 13 inches deep, painted in white in this case, although many of her pieces are typically in black. Her choice of white makes the piece appear deeper than it is because of the shadows that it casts, which would be lost if the piece were all black. A lack of shadows would tend to visually flatten the piece.

Positive and Negative Space. In his design of a children's step-and-play storage unit (**5.11**), Michael Marriott uses **positive space** (an area filled with elements of design)—the structure itself on which children may climb and sit. It also has **negative space** (an empty area surrounded and shaped so that it acquires form or volume)—the empty spaces within the structure in which things can be stored. In his design of three-dimensional objects and spaces, Marriott follows the principle of "honest and appropriate use of material, process, and function." His mobile storage unit for children uses readily available and relatively inexpensive plywood.

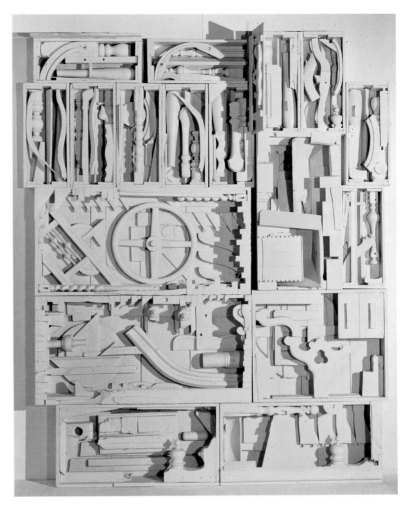

5.10 LOUISE NEVELSON Installation view of *Dawn's Wedding Chapel IV*, 1959. Painted wood, 109 × 87 × 13 in.

5.11 MICHAEL MARRIOTT Children's step-and-play storage unit, 2000.

He keeps the material "honest" by not painting or staining it so that it looks like what it is not. The material functions well for its intended use by children: it is sturdy and durable, and not a "precious" material that parents might worry about. He says, "The literal form of the end result is the outcome of a processing of ideas rather than an application of styles."[4] That is, its style comes from its intended function. The object has wheels for mobility and aesthetically corresponding curved corners for children's safety.

While Marriott uses negative space for functional efficiency, contemporary British artist Rachel Whiteread uses negative space for evocative expression. In her sculptures, she often casts the negative spaces of objects. In *Untitled (One Hundred Spaces)* (**5.12**), each component is composed of the space beneath an actual and ordinary chair. The negative space beneath a chair becomes a positive mass. She has made the invisible visible. She then aligned the components in a grid reminiscent of a classroom or gathering place. By representing the absent, she evokes what was once present and, by implication, the persons who occupied the chairs. By using subtly different colors and types of chairs, the installation also acknowledges differences of those who may have occupied the chairs.

The effect of Michael Heizer's use of negative space is said to be simultaneously sublime and terrifying.[5] The piece (**5.13**) is composed of four parts, and each is a rimless geometric pit of vacant space in the floor. Each part is 20 feet deep and lined with metal. Due to safety concerns, to walk right up to the edge of the pits and look into the forms, you must make an early-morning appointment; otherwise, during normal visiting hours, you will view the pits from behind a low Plexiglas barricade.

In *Afrum I (White)* (**5.14**), James Turrell uses actual negative space and light to create illusional mass. In the reproduction shown here and in the museum gallery, the white rectangular shape of *Afrum I* confounds us. The lustrous cube, which seems to be a suspended mass, is actually projected light interacting with a negative space cut into the corner walls. The piece is made of actual space (the cutout) and illusional three-dimensional mass (an apparent cube of light). The meanings of Turrell's work

5.12 RACHEL WHITEREAD *Untitled (One Hundred Spaces),* 1995. Resin, one hundred units of nine sizes.

5.13 MICHAEL HEIZER *North, East, South, West,* 1967–2002. Steel, each element 20 ft. deep, 142 ft. long.

with light and space are influenced by his Quaker faith, which he characterizes as having a "straightforward, strict presentation of the sublime." He intends his ethereal and illusionistic uses of space and light to express feelings of transcendence and a sense of the divine.[6]

Virtual Space

Virtual reality technology allows artists to design **virtual space,** a computer-constructed environment that appears three dimensional, allowing viewers expe-

5.14 JAMES TURRELL *Afrum I (White),* 1967. Projected light, dimensions variable.

riences that seem real. Virtual reality technology is primarily visual, but it can be enhanced with sound. Users can interact with the virtual reality by means of a keyboard, mouse, joystick, or multimodal devices such as a wired glove or a handheld wireless pointing device.

VIRTUAL ENTERTAINMENT SPACES

Virtual environments can be made to appear fantastical, such as *World of Warcraft,* or similar to a real-world environment, such as *Madden NFL 10* (**5.15**). Both are popular interactive entertainment games. *World of Warcraft* is a massive multiplayer online role-playing game in which players control characters within a fantastical game world, exploring landscapes, fighting monsters, and completing quests while interacting with other players online.

Madden NFL is simulated professional football informed and narrated by John Madden, a National Football League (NFL) Hall of Fame coach, winner of the 1976 Super Bowl, and recently retired television commentator. There are many options for game play, from playing a single game to playing a team for a whole season or over many seasons.

Madden NFL is interactive in many ways. As a player, you can choose to make instant decisions on behalf of the quarterback regarding the risk of a pass being completed or intercepted by the defense. You can also make choices for a runner, deciding his moves against a tackler. The football players in the computer

5.15 Madden NFL 10, Xbox 360.

5.16   Screen shot of Sims characters. Posted online by player BBKZ, September 15, 2008.

5.17   American period rooms, screen shots from the Metropolitan Museum of Art, New York City, virtual tour, 2008. Above: Renaissance Revival Parlor, Meriden, Connecticut, American, 1870. Below: Room from the Hart House, Ipswich, Massachusetts, before 1674.

game are simulated to mimic professionals who play the game in real life. The reality effect of the experience is enhanced through accurate modeling of how selected NFL players actually move on a real football field against real opponents.

The Sims (**5.16**) is a popular strategic life-simulation computer game without any defined goals like winning a football game. Instead, as a player, you make choices and engage in an interactive environment that you chose or created, and you help your virtual characters, Sims, make choices to reach their chosen goals and satisfy their needs and desires. You direct your Sims and have them interact with objects, such as furnishings in their residences, and with other Sims. Sims have a certain amount of free will and will engage in activities when left to their own devices. Sims with character flaws will be nasty to other Sims, insult them, or even slap them. There are consequences to their actions: for example, if they fail to pay their bills, their property will be repossessed.

SIMULATED SPACES FOR REAL-WORLD TRAINING

Relatively safe simulated environments are useful in the training of civilian and military personnel, especially when such training is prohibitively expensive or dangerous in actual environments. The Johnson Space Center has constructed simulated three-dimensional spaces in which real astronauts can prepare for shuttle missions.

Teams of experts painstakingly design virtual environments for serious gaming in which people can encounter real-life situations without putting themselves in physical peril. For example, the U.S. military collaborates with cultural anthropologists, specialists in gaming, computer animators, and actors to simulate real-world environments and situations for troops to experience before they are deployed to life-threatening situations around the world. Through recent warfare and peacekeeping engagements in the Middle East, the U.S. military has learned that violence can be greatly reduced when American troops acquire cultural knowledge of the people with whom they engage. Through sophisticated simulation games in virtual environments with virtual characters based on research of actual situations and real people, young American troops learn what to do and how to adapt to a foreign land and its people. The consequences of soldiers making choices in simulated environments are tabulated in points earned or lost, whereas in a hostile environment, consequences are lives lost or saved.

VIRTUAL EDUCATIONAL SPACES

There are many uses of virtual spaces for informational purposes. Some art museums, for example, provide simulated gallery spaces that the viewer can move through. An actual three-dimensional artifact in the museum may be made into a virtual object that allows a viewer to rotate it and see it in the round and from various distances, from close to far, without being in the museum. The Metropolitan Museum of Art in New York City, for example, provides an online virtual tour of its popular American period rooms (**5.17**), which offers an opportunity to see how Americans of earlier centuries furnished and decorated their domestic interiors. The virtual rooms are designed to succinctly show stylistic choices of different places and times with accurately reproduced furniture, accessories, paint, wallpaper, and fabric.

Illusional Space

Artists have been creating illusional space for thousands of years in many different cultures. The fifteenth-century book illustration *Yusuf Pursued by Potiphar's Wife Zulaykha,* by Persian artist Kamal Al-Din Bihzad (**5.18**), uses conventions of Persian manuscript painting to render a story told in the Qur'an. The narrative Bihzad depicts is also recounted in a mystical Persian poem, and the artist has written four lines of the poem into his representation of the palace. It is a story of failed seduction: resisting the amorous and adulterous advances of Zulaykha, Yusuf tears himself away from her grasp. The artist painted an elaborate architectural setting, with staircases leading to different levels. A Persian scholar writes about the effective use of space in the painting: "Bihzad's setting, with its receding, empty spaces, firmly shut doors, sharply angled walls, and zigzagging stairs, provides a brilliant visual embodiment of Yusuf's conflict."[7]

INDICATORS OF ILLUSIONAL SPACE

You can create the illusion of three-dimensional space on a two-dimensional plane with some basic indicators. They are foreground, middle ground, and background; and size, overlap, transparency, and placement, often used in combination.

5.18 **KAMAL AL-DIN BIHZAD** *Yusuf Pursued by Potiphar's Wife Zulaykha,* 1488. Watercolor, ink, and gold on paper, 12 × 8 in.

Foreground, Middle Ground, and Background. In two-dimensional representational artifacts, **foreground** is what appears closest to us. **Background** is what appears farthest from us, and **middle ground** is the space between foreground and background.

An unknown Indian artist working several hundred years ago painted an amorous encounter between Krishna, the Hindu god of love, and his beloved Radha (**5.19**). The narrative is based on Hindu tradition, and the scene is represented with Hindu conventions for depicting reality. To achieve the illusion of space, the artist depicted the trees larger in the foreground and smaller in the background, and placed the loving couple in the

5.19 **UNKNOWN ARTIST** *Krishna and Radha in a Bower,* c. 1775–1780. Watercolor and gold on paper, 6 × 10 in.

of foreground, middle ground, and background. In the foreground we see men carving stones for construction of a tower. The tower itself takes up the middle ground and most of the space of the painting. The artist has made it the central interest of the biblical narrative of the people of Babylon, in their pride, struggling to build a tower to heaven. The background consists of everything beyond the tower. Bruegel includes a cloud in the middle ground at the top of the tower to indicate how high the tower has risen.

Size. The use of size variations to indicate spatial relationships can be clearly seen in the special edition cover from *The Amazing Spider-Man #583* (**5.21**), produced in honor of the inauguration of President Barack Obama. The artists have placed the smiling face of the president in the middle ground, with his thumbs-up gesture in the foreground. Spider-Man hangs behind the president, taking his picture with a flash camera. The artists have made Spider-Man about the size of the president's head and shoulders. If the president and Spider-Man were both standing beside each other, they would be rendered as about the same size. By making Spider-Man small, the artists indicate that he is at a distance behind the president.

5.20 **PIETER BRUEGEL** *The Tower of Babel,* 1563. Oil on oakwood, 114 × 155 cm.

middle ground. The artist provides us with a special vantage point to view the narrative and brightens their intimate space. The artist also uses visual metaphors to express the lovers' desire in "the passionate undulation of entwining tree trunks, twisting leaves, and ecstatic flowers that in effect embrace the lovers in a cosmic nest."[8]

In another narrative based in religious beliefs, sixteenth-century Flemish artist Pieter Bruegel presents *The Tower of Babel* (**5.20**), also using the devices

Overlap. We have learned to see a thing that overlaps another thing as being in front of what it covers; therefore, you can also suggest depth through the placement of objects or shapes. *Trees* (**5.22**) is one of many preliminary studies Georges Seurat made for *A Sunday*

5.21   MARVEL COMICS   Cover of *The Amazing Spider-Man #583*, January 2009.

5.22   GEORGES SEURAT   *Trees* (study for *La Grande Jatte*), 1884. Black Conté crayon on white laid paper, laid down on cream board, 620 × 475 mm.

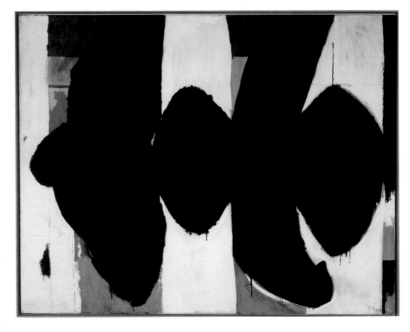

5.23   ROBERT MOTHERWELL   *Elegy to the Spanish Republic No. 34*, 1953–1954. Oil on canvas support, 80 × 100 in.

Afternoon on the Island of La Grande Jatte, 1884, his large painting famously made entirely of discrete painted dots. In *Trees,* Seurat uses overlap, as well as size, to indicate distance. The foreground tree appears closest to us because of its large size, and the other trees appear to be in the background because they are smaller, and this effect is heightened by the way the large tree overlaps the smaller trees.

Robert Motherwell also suggests spatial depth in his nonobjective painting *Elegy to the Spanish Republic No. 34* (**5.23**) by using overlap and size. The black shapes on the canvas appear closest to us because they overlap the white, yellow, red, green, and other shapes behind them. The black shape is also the largest shape in the painting. Motherwell's *Elegy* series commemorates the Spanish who were obliterated by fascist dictator Generalissimo Franco during the Spanish Civil War in the 1930s when they

5.24   **DINH Q LE   *Night Vision,*** 2008. C-print and linen tape, 49½ × 93⅜ in.

5.25   **GEORGIA O'KEEFFE   *Petunia No. 2,*** 1924. Oil on canvas, 36 × 30 in.

tried to form a democracy. Perhaps Motherwell metaphorically obliterates the smaller victims with the massive black shapes on top of them.

Transparency. Dinh Q Le, an immigrant to the United States from Vietnam, suggests special depth by use of transparency in his pixelated photograph *Night Vision* (**5.24**). On the right side of the composition, a distressed woman seems to be trapped behind a screen of enlarged pixels, seemingly attempting to push through the picture surface but unable to because of the obstacle that seems to be in front of her.

Placement. Another way to indicate illusional depth on a two-dimensional plane is to have elements near the top of a planar surface appear to recede, while those at the bottom seem to advance. Georgia O'Keeffe's painting (**5.25**) clearly illustrates this phenomenon. The petunia flower shapes at the bottom of the plane seems closest to us while the petunia behind the curved dark horizon line on top of them seems to recede in space.

Figure **5.26** visually summarizes ways of suggesting spatial depth on a two-dimensional plane. The techniques are effective in both representational and nonobjective artifacts.

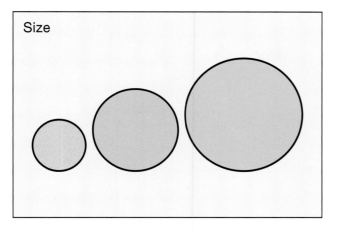

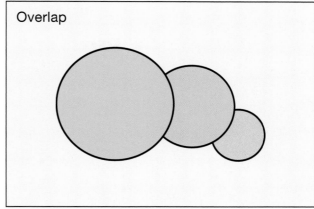

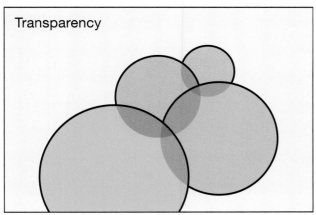

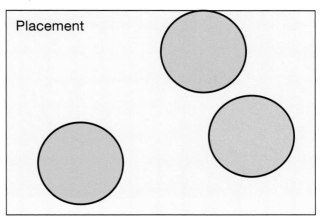

5.26 **The use of size, overlap, transparency, and placement** to indicate spacial illusions.

Types of Perspective

Artists through time and across cultures have invented and refined optical and mathematical conventions, or techniques, for indicating the illusion of space on planar surfaces. The general term for this is **perspective,** but it has many forms. Major perspectival devices include atmospheric perspective, linear perspective, isometric perspective, and multiple perspective.

ATMOSPHERIC PERSPECTIVE

Making objects that are close to the viewer appear crisp and vibrant, and making them fuzzy and less intense in color and tone as they recede from the viewer, is a technique called **atmospheric perspective,** or **aerial perspective.**

In actual space, things seem to diminish in clarity, intensity, and size the farther away they are from the viewer. Objects in the distance appear hazier and bluer, hues are duller, and tones are neither extremely dark nor extremely white. Textures appear coarse up close and fine from a distance. On a humid day, the moisture in the air diminishes clarity. Viewed from Chicago's

western suburbs, the John Hancock Building in the downtown area will appear light gray rather than its actual black. Even on a clear day, the whole Chicago skyline will appear softly textured, hazy, and bluish. On a misty day, it will seem to lack all color except light gray.

Annie Leibovitz's photographic landscape (**5.27**) captures the effects of atmospheric perspective. The birch trees that appear closest to us are the lightest in tone, and the ground appears darkest. As the trees behind those in front recede from our view, they appear gray. The textures of the branches of the trees closest to us are sharp, but as the trees recede from us, the textures in the background soften. She takes advantage of the natural effects of environmental conditions on the physical behavior of light, which cause the phenomenon of atmospheric perspective.

Just as humid days increase the hazy quality in the distance due to moisture in the air, high levels of pollution affect the color, contrast, and saturation of light traveling through it. You can deliberately reproduce these phenomena in order to suggest depth by lightening values and softening details and textures.

In his drawing of trees (see 5.22), Seurat employed atmospheric perspective when he made the foreground

5.27   ANNIE LEIBOVITZ   *Pitch Pines and Gray Birch in the Dwarf Pine Ridges, Ellenville, New York,* 2001. Black-and-white photograph.

tree crisp, the trees in the middle ground less crisp, and those in the background blurred. He made the textures of the leaves in the distance soft. The features of the trees in the background are less distinct than those in the foreground. Similarly, in the Spider-Man comic panel (see 5.21), the artists made Spider-Man in colors less saturated than those they used for President Obama.

LINEAR PERSPECTIVE

Use of linear perspective enables you to develop objects or figures of known size and to place them at various distances within the fictive space of a flat picture. Knowledge and use of linear perspective reach far back to ancient times. Research from the early Renaissance in the late 1400s by such artists as Filippo Brunelleschi and Leon Battista Alberti in Florence contributed to the science of depicting three-dimensional spaces on two-dimensional surfaces. Renaissance ideas were likely informed by prior research by Muslim scholars in Istanbul and Baghdad a century earlier, and these ideas were likely initiated in China as far back as the fifth century BCE. Modern-day cameras were invented to

render the illusion of three-dimensional space in linear perspective on a two-dimensional surface. Early experiments allowed images of the world to be projected on a wall in a dark room with such devices as a *camera obscura*. Later in history, through trial and error, artists learned to focus and fix otherwise fleeting images on chemically treated plates, such as a daguerreotype, and eventually on paper, which we now commonly call "photographs."

Thus, **linear perspective** is an invented system of rendering the appearance of three dimensions on a two-dimensional plane by making objects appear smaller as they recede from us and by making parallel lines converge in the distance at a vanishing point on a horizon line. A **vanishing point** is where converging lines seem to disappear into a distant dot on the horizon line of a three-dimensional scene on a two-dimensional surface. A **horizon line** is where the sky meets the ground in the world or in a perspectival representation of it.

The Road West by Dorothea Lange (**5.28**) is a photograph that clearly provides an example of a flat paper image of a three-dimensional space in the real world. The parallel lines of the sides of the actual road seem to converge in the photograph to one vanishing point where the land meets the sky in the distant horizon. Lange is effectively using the built-in perspectival rendering system of the camera for expressive purposes. Lange took a photo of this stretch of desolate land along U.S. 54 in southern New Mexico during the Depression. Many families took this route to look for work in California, which they found no more prosperous than the places they had left. Someone Lange met on the road said, "They keep the road hot a goin' and a comin' . . . They've got roamin' in their head."[9]

There are three major systems of linear perspective: one-point perspective, two-point perspective, and three-point perspective. All of them use **orthogonal lines,** that is, lines or edges in a picture that lead the viewer's eyes to the vanishing points in an illusional three-dimensional space (**5.29**).

In order to render space within the linear perspective system, you can imagine the flat, two-dimensional picture surface, or **picture plane,** as a window onto a scene. Looking straight ahead with your line of sight parallel to the ground, you focus one eye on a fixed spot in the distance, called a "fixation point." Your **eye level** (**5.30**), which represents the elevation of your eyes, establishes the horizon line, where you can place one or more vanishing points. When creating illusions of space that do not seem distorted, you are limited to drawing objects that appear within your 45-degree viewing angle, known as the **cone of vision,** which can be positioned from top, bottom, left, or right.

5.28   **DOROTHEA LANGE   *The Road West,*** 1938. Gelatin silver photograph, 11 × 14 in.

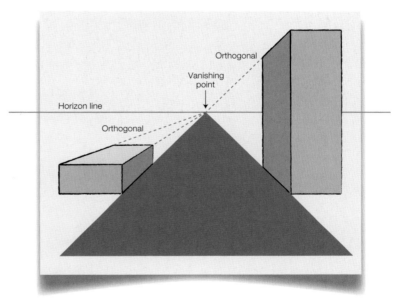

5.29   **Linear perspective** is achieved by using orthogonal lines that lead the viewers' eyes to vanishing points.

One-Point Perspective. In one-point perspective, there is only one vanishing point on the horizon line. The result can be dramatic, drawing the viewer into the scene. Pietro Perugino's fresco *The Delivery of the Keys* (**5.31**), in the Sistine Chapel, Rome, exemplifies such an effect. Figure **5.32** shows two cubes rendered in one-point perspective. The cube on top is placed above the horizon line; the cube on the bottom, below the horizon line. The orthogonal lines used to render both cubes have a single vanishing point.

The artists who created the Spider-Man panel (**5.33**) used one-point perspective. You can locate the vanishing point by following the cables on which the characters climb. They recede to a point where the cables meet the masonry of the bridge, towards the middle left of the picture.

Two-Point Perspective. Some renderings use two vanishing points in what is called **two-point perspective.** The use of two or more vanishing points allows you to depict an image from more than one diagonal direction (**5.34; 5.35**). This has the potential to make a scene livelier.

Ed Ruscha rendered *Standard Station* (**5.36**) in two-point perspective. Ruscha, the influential Los Angeles artist, is known for his visual explorations of words, images, and objects in landscapes. Through his dramatic use of two-point perspective, he turns an ordinary site into a mysterious symbol of the American vernacular landscape.

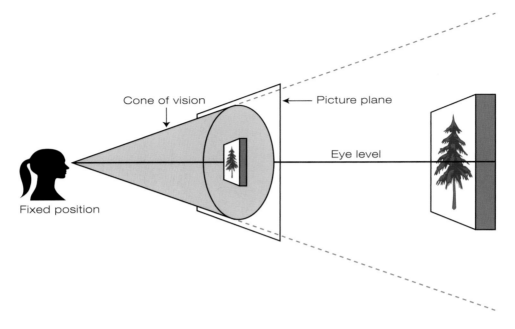

Cone of vision

Picture plane

Eye level

Fixed position

5.30   Rendering space within the linear perspective system.

CONTVRBATIO·IESV·CHRISTI·LEGISLATORIS

Vanishing point

Horizon line

Orthogonal

5.31   PIETRO PERUGINO   *The Delivery of the Keys*, 1481–1482. Fresco. Lines added to show one-point perspective.

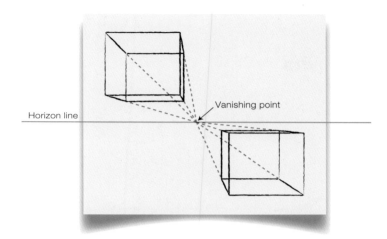

5.32   One-point perspective.

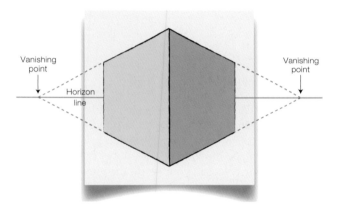

5.34   Two-point perspective. The orthogonal lines of this rendering of a cube merge at two vanishing points on the left and right of the horizon line.

5.33   MARVEL COMICS   COVER OF *Amazing Spider-Man #512.*

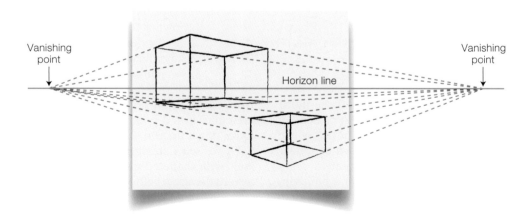

5.35   Two objects rendered in two-point perspective, one above and the other below the horizon line.

5.36   **ED RUSCHA**   *Standard Station,* 1966. Screenprint, printed in color composition, 19½ × 36¹⁵⁄₁₆ in.

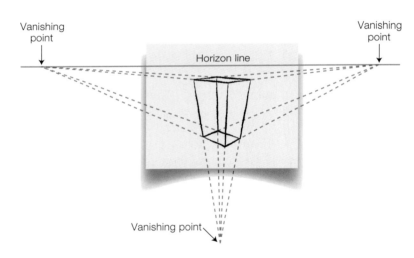

5.37   **An object rendered in three-point perspective** using three vanishing points at and below the horizon line.

POINTS OF VIEW

The eye level you establish in a picture will affect the viewer's understanding of the picture and emotional reaction to it. When you place the viewer's eye level below a figure or object in your work, the viewer will look up at the figure, and the figure will seem more powerful than if it were viewed from above. In narrative filmmaking, for example, the director commonly has the cinematographer place the camera in such a way that it looks up to a menacing character in order to make the character all the more intimidating. When the menacing character is defeated, the camera will conventionally point down at the figure, giving viewers a feeling of superiority. Thus relations of power and subordination are commonly built into chosen points of view in pictures of all kinds.

Three-Point Perspective. You can use **three-point perspective (5.37; 5.38)** when you wish to present an exaggerated point of view, usually above or below eye level. Three-point perspective is often used to render buildings from above or below. In addition to using two vanishing points, one for each wall of a building, you add a third vanishing point below the horizon line, and the walls then seem to recede into the ground. By placing the third vanishing point high in space, you can create a view looking up at a building.

Bird's-Eye View. As the name suggests, a **bird's-eye view** provides a point of view from a high level that looks down upon a space, person, or object. In figure **5.39,** we see Captain Marvel from above as he plummets with shattered glass from high up in a skyscraper toward the street below. The view from above heightens our sense of the danger of Captain Marvel's situation.

Worm's-Eye View. In a panel of a Spider-Man comic **(5.40)**, we see a superhero from a **worm's-eye view,**

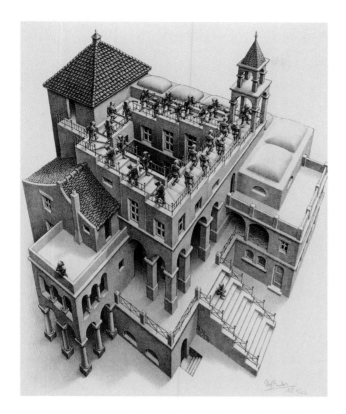

5.38 **M. C. ESCHER** *Ascending and Descending,* 1960.

5.39 **Bird's-eye view. Cover of *Captain Marvel #3,*** Marvel Comics.

a point of view from a very low level looking up at a space, person, or object. We see Spider-Man in action—his camera swings from his shoulder as he alights on a wall while removing his mask—from a low angle of view that makes him seem all the more powerful to us. By providing a worm's-eye view of Spider-Man, the artists imply his superheroic physical ability and psychological power.

Foreshortening. Through a technique known as **foreshortening,** you can create the illusion of an object extending back into space by making the part farthest from the picture plane smaller than it would be if the object were placed upright. You simultaneously render the part of the object closest to the picture plane larger. In an ad for Tony's Pizza (**5.41**), the artist uses foreshortening, or what some instructors refer to as "amplified perspective." By making the skates and hand very large in comparison to the head, the artist creates the illusion that the skater is airborne, skating above us, as he enjoys his pizza. The artist also rendered the slice of pizza disproportionately large, directing our gaze at the product being advertised. Exaggerated space is the dominant element in this image.

ISOMETRIC PERSPECTIVE

Another technical system developed to depict three-dimensional space on a two-dimensional plane is isometry, which means equality within measurement. Whereas in linear perspective, parallel lines are drawn to come together as they recede from the viewer, in **isometric perspective,** lines remain parallel, and no lines are parallel to the picture plane (**5.42**). Isometric perspective is useful for technical illustration and drafting. Architects, interior designers, engineers, and craftspeople commonly use it when they need to show all measurements in proper proportion at the same time. In figure **5.43,** the building is drawn in elevation, that is, flattened out with accurate dimensions of the building.

Although used primarily for technical purposes, isometric perspective can also be used for expressive purposes. The explosion of ideas in figure **5.44** is illustrated in the form of letters rendered in isometric perspective arising from a container, also drawn in isometric perspective. The illustration accompanies an article on new ideas of the year. The editors of the magazine ask us to "note the three-dimensional font created for the issue by the type designer Chester Jenkins, whose letters—inspired by the children's alphabet blocks that so often accompany the acquisition of language—seem to become legible and reveal themselves only when viewed from just the right perspective."[10]

5.40   Worm's-eye view. Spider-Man, Marvel Comics.

5.41   Foreshortening. Ad for Tony's Pizza, 2002.

MULTIPLE PERSPECTIVE

When you use one-point, two-point, or three-point perspective, you offer one consistent view of the subject matter; however, there are times when you might choose to use **multiple perspective,** more than one view of the subject simultaneously in the same picture. Picasso's *Guernica* (**5.45**), one of the most admired protest paintings, uses multiple perspective within one picture. Picasso was protesting the willful destruction of Guernica, a small town in the Basque section of Spain, by Nazi bombers in collusion with Spanish Fascists in 1937. Regarding Picasso's use of space and multiple perspectives, art historian Frederick Hartt notices "an explosion of shattered planes of black, white, and gray," and destruction depicted by "fragmentary glimpses of walls and tiled roofs, and flames shooting from a burning house at the right." The historian concludes that Picasso's spiritual message combines terror and resistance by effectively rendering the scene in multiple perspective.[11]

Al Held used multiple perspective to depict relationships of shapes in space. In *Phoenicia VI* (**5.46**),

he limited himself to lines of the same thickness while employing one-, two-, and three-point perspective, as well as isometric perspective, in one painting. The artist said his paintings are "metaphors for truths unavailable to direct perception. In the world we live in, nonobjective art is the unique vehicle to try and discuss things like: How do things come together? How do multiple and contradictory truths exist in the same place at the same time?"[12] The discordant perspectival schemes in his paintings are a spatial way for Held to explore coexisting and contradictory views of imagined objects and competing understandings of reality and how people perceive it.

Denying Illusion

Sometimes artists *deny,* or are simply uninterested in creating, the illusion of space in their artworks. This is the case especially since the 1950s in the United States when Jackson Pollock and Helen Frankenthaler, two Modernist painters, abandoned the long realist

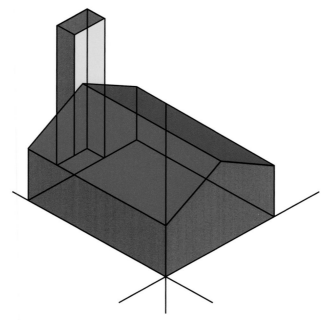

5.42 **Isometric perspective of a building.**

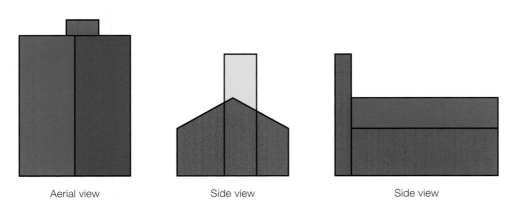

Aerial view   Side view   Side view

5.43 **Three views of a building** shown in elevation, one seen from the top, one from the side, and one from the back.

tradition of painting as a window and instead tried to make visually *flat* paintings. Influenced by each other and by the Formalist principles of the art critic Clement Greenberg, Pollock and Frankenthaler accepted and celebrated the fact that the canvas is flat and the paint physical, and asserted that they need not try to make a canvas look like an illusion of reality with spatial depth. Pollock famously applied his paint-dripping technique to make "all-over" compositions that were not meant to suggest a narrative or depict a scene in the physical world (**5.47**).

In *The Bay* (**5.48**), Frankenthaler poured water-based paint directly onto a raw and unprepared canvas, and as a result, the paint is not *on* the canvas but soaked *into* it, thus further resisting the illusion of three-dimensionality. Water-based acrylic paint helps intensify its color stains and reduces the glistening ef-

fect that oil paint often produces, thus further flattening the surface of the canvas.

Conclusion: Limitless Opportunities of Space

Working with space includes building environments in which to live, objects to use, and sculptures to contemplate. Constructing actual space, creating virtual space by means of computer technology, and representing three-dimensional space on two-dimensional surfaces offer you many opportunities for developing expressive content and communicating a message, whether you are creating functional space and objects, sculptures, or two-dimensional artifacts.

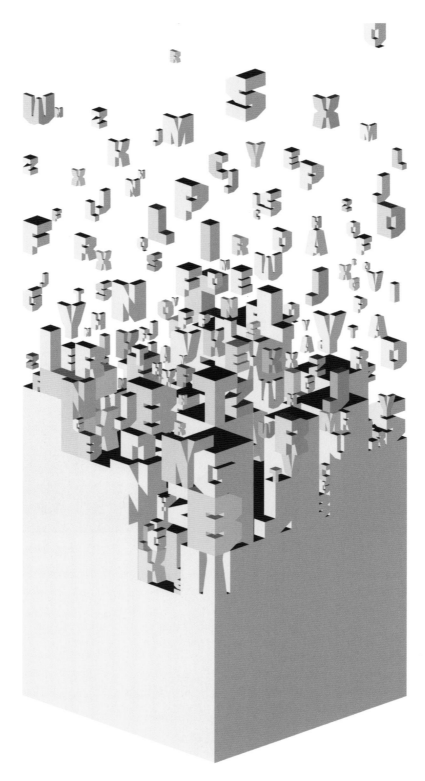

5.44 **CHESTER JENKINS** **Magazine illustration in isometric perspective,**
the Sixth Annual Year in Ideas. 12.10.06 in *New York Times Magazine,* page 14.

5.45 **PABLO PICASSO** *Guernica,* 1937. Oil on canvas, 11 ft. 5 in. × 25 ft. 5 in.

5.46 **AL HELD** *Phoenicia VI,* 1969. Acrylic on canvas, 114 × 114 in.

5.48 **HELEN FRANKENTHALER** *The Bay,* 1963. Acrylic on canvas, 60 × 122½ in.

5.47 **JACKSON POLLOCK** *Blue Poles (Number 1),* 1953. Oil, enamel, aluminum paint, and glass on canvas, 6 ft. 11 in. × 16 ft.

Time and Motion

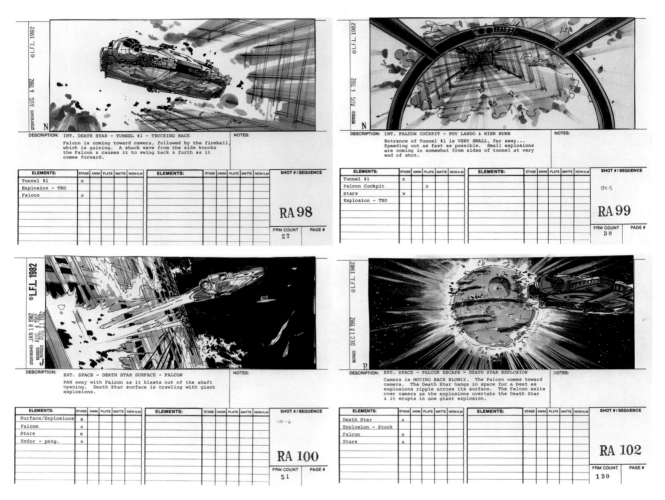

6.1 LUCASFILMS Storyboard for *Star Wars: Episode VI–Return of the Jedi*.

Indicating Time in Art
Indicating Motion in Art
Conclusion: Perspectives on Time and Motion

We are familiar with the elements of time and motion through our experiences with popular culture. We control speed and movement through a joystick, watch frame after frame flicker before our eyes on television and movie screens, and follow panels of drawings as a story unfolds in a comic book, graphic novel, or on a movie storyboard (**6.1**). The elements of time and motion are at work in the art gallery as well, when some interactive objects physically move and when the directional forces at play in a painting, photo, or drawing move our eyes over its surface. Whether you work in traditional or new media, in two dimensions, three dimensions, or four dimensions, the elements of time and motion offer many opportunities to make dynamic and meaningful artifacts.

American installation artist Robert Irwin's garden for the Getty Museum in Los Angeles (**6.2**) illustrates several aspects of time and motion. Irwin considered how visitors would move through the garden and designed walkways that would lead them from the top of the mountainside where the museum stands, down the hilly terrain, and

6.2 ROBERT IRWIN   Detail of the Getty Garden, 1997–present. .

Time and Motion Key Terms

TIME   The continuum of experience in which events actually or apparently take place. It is used to specify events.

CHRONOLOGY   The order of events as they unfold in time.

NARRATIVE   A representation of an event or story.

DURATION   How long an actual or recorded event lasts, or seems to last.

TEMPO   The speed at which an activity takes place, or seems to take place.

ACTUAL TIME   The *duration* of a real-time event as measured by a clock.

IMPLIED TIME   The illusion of time and its passing.

RECORDED TIME   *Duration, tempo, scope,* and *sequence* captured and preserved in media such as film, video, and computer-based technologies and in paint or ink.

SCOPE   A range of events shown or implied in a temporal artifact.

SEQUENCE   The order of a series of events or images.

STORYBOARD   A *sequence* of images representing the *shots* for a scene in a film or television show; a plan for a sequence of artifacts.

SHOT   In film or video, a continuous series of images of one action from one camera position.

CUT   In film or video, the immediate change from one *shot* to another; as a verb, to stop the camera from recording.

EDIT (IN FILM OR VIDEO)   To arrange a series of *shots* to convey and put in order a cohesive *sequence* or to convey a *narrative.*

RUNNING TIME   The *duration* of an event recorded on sequential media such as video or film; the duration of a performance.

MOTION   The actual or implied changing of position.

KINETIC ART   Artifacts that are designed to move.

IMPLIED MOTION   The illusion of movement and the passage of time or distance.

RECORDED MOTION   The capture of movement with lens-based media.

back up again, making the most of the view of city and ocean as well as of the garden itself. He also had to think of his design as one that changed over time, as his materials—the plants—grew and blossomed throughout the seasons. Irwin continues to add new colors to the garden's palette and new textures to its surfaces. He carved into the plaza floor the statement "Always changing, never twice the same," reminding viewers of both the dynamic nature of his work and the elements of time and motion in all our lives.

Indicating Time in Art

As an artist or designer, you will need to consider many different aspects of time when you create works. Product designers have to consider the desired life span of things they design. Graphic designers may want to be responsive only to the moment—news is quickly obsolete—or may want to make a piece that does not date itself. Painters and sculptors recognize that viewers will decide how long they wish to stand in front of an artwork, but artists need to think about how much time their work requires to be comprehended by viewers. Video and performance artists determine how long a viewer will need to watch an entire artwork. It takes viewers varying amounts of time, depending on size and space, just to walk through an architectural space or along an expansive sculptural work, such as the Vietnam Veterans Memorial (see 2.9) and Irwin's Getty Garden (see 6.2).

DIMENSIONS OF TIME

For our purposes, we will define **time** as the continuum of experience in which events actually or apparently take place. Time is used to specify events, which occur in a **chronology**—the order of events as they unfold in time. For example, one spring day many years ago, gardeners set young trees and shrubs into spaces in the ground designated for them in the Getty Garden (see 6.2). The gardeners watered them, the sun shone on them, and they continued to grow and change through summer, fall, winter; over the years they have become mature. A chronology is usually given in a sequence from beginning to end, or to the current time, and measures a length of time. In many art forms, this chronology is told in a **narrative**—a representation of an event or story—and narrators decide what and how to tell and show to viewers.

Time has dimensions of duration and tempo. **Duration** refers to how long an event actually lasts. We also experience duration in relative terms: some things that take an hour seem like they take "forever," while other things that also take an hour may seem to pass "in no time at all."

Tempo refers to the speed at which an activity takes place. Tempo, too, is a relative term: something can appear slower or faster in relation to something else. A rabbit moves more quickly than a turtle, but a turtle moves more quickly than a slug. Tempo can be measured, but tempo can seem faster or slower than it is, depending on the state of mind we are in when we experience something.

We can consider time as **actual time** measured by a clock or as **implied time**—the illusion of time and its passing. We also consider **recorded time,** that is, things in motion captured and preserved in media such as video, photography, and paint or in ink. Recorded time entails scope and sequence. **Scope** refers to the range of events shown or implied in a temporal artifact. **Sequence** is the arrangement of events, usually in a temporal order, especially in visual narratives. Sequence, however, need not follow time: Maya Lin arranged the names of military personnel on the Vietnam Veterans Memorial (see 2.9) chronologically by casualty dates from 1959 to 1982. She had other choices for sequencing the names: by military rank, by date of birth, or randomly. Each choice would carry interpretive connotations. Her choice of chronological arrangement by casualty dates not only allows visitors to find their loved ones but also visualizes the buildup and ebb of the war.

ACTUAL TIME

Artists who use actual time usually create works that have short durations, as the subjects and materials used are not eternal. These works, although ephemeral, demonstrate particular meanings about life that the artists wanted to carry out.

Many of Andy Goldsworthy's environmental sculptures are ephemeral. Their durations depend on nature. *Ice Pyramids in the Arctic Circle* (**6.3**) is or was an ephemeral sculpture that no longer exists or has been altered, if not destroyed, by time in the weather. It is also a photograph of an instant of time made into a permanent photograph by the artist, and it is accompanied by text that reads as follows:

Text, text, text here...................
Text, text, text here...................
Text, text, text here...................

Were we to go to the Arctic Circle where Goldsworthy built four pyramids of snow and ice, we would not be able to see the sculpture in its original form. It has likely been blown away or melted. Perhaps some remnant would remain. We do not know how long the sculpture lasted. *Ice Pyramids in the Arctic Circle,* the sculpture, had a duration of hours, days, weeks, or perhaps months. Its duration is an important part of its meaning, suggesting that sculpture can be fragile and fleeting and subservient to stronger forces, like life itself.

6.3   ANDY GOLDSWORTHY   Artist photographs his *Ice Pyramids in the Arctic Circle*. Color photograph with text panel.

For one of her first performance pieces, Laurie Anderson allowed her piece to be determined by factors of actual time. A classically trained violinist, Anderson played a violin on a New York City public sidewalk on a hot summer day while wearing ice skates that she had previously frozen into a block of ice. Her artwork endured until the ice melted, at which point she stopped playing, removed the skates, and walked away, ending the artwork. She used actual time to determine beginning, end, and length of her performance piece. The tempo of Anderson's violin piece depended on the pace of the music she chose to play in contrast to the melting of the ice block. The tempo of the whole performance was determined by the rate of ice melting that day. Her use of actual time suggests beautiful occurrences are often ephemeral in combination with human choices and the forces of nature, so notice them intently when they occur.

Vito Acconci used actual time and movements of unaware people as formal constraints that determined the duration, tempo, scope, and sequence of *Following Piece*. To make the piece, he selected an individual who happened to be walking by and followed that person until he or she went into a place that Acconci could not enter. Acconci's "following" could last minutes if the person got into a taxi, or hours, depending on where the person was going. The pace could be quick or slow, depending on how quickly or slowly the person moved. Acconci did this every day from October 3 to October 25, 1969. His intent was to examine the relationship of public and private spaces. *Following Piece* also showed the vulnerability of the followed and the potential of danger in public space. To preserve this ephemeral piece, composed of many parts, he wrote an account of each of his followings and sent them to different members of the art community.

Chris Burden, in his *Five-Day Locker Piece* (University of California, Irvine, April 2–30, 1971), lived in a locker for five consecutive days (the duration) and did not leave the locker during this time. He fasted for several days before he entered the locker. He estimated how much liquid he would need to consume while he was incarcerated, and he put five gallons of bottled water in the locker directly above him and placed an empty five-gallon bottle in the locker directly below him to receive his bodily wastes.[1] The sequence was straightforward, determined by actual chronology. The tempo was very slow, physically and psychologically. The scope was limited to one person in a very constricted space. Burden's locker piece tested the limits of the body and was part of the "body art movement" in the 1960s and 1970s.

6.4 **CHRIS WEDGE** *Bunny,* 1998. Stills from computer-animated film.

IMPLIED TIME

Artists immersed in filmic arts typically visualize their ideas, refine them, and promote them by means of a **storyboard,** a sequence of images for a scene in a film or television show. LucasFilms produced a storyboard for every scene of the *Star Wars* films (see 6.1) for producers to visualize what a scene might look like when staged and recorded with film or videotape in a setting with live actors. Each image represents a **shot,** that is, a continuous series of images of one action from one camera position that **cut** to another action or another shot from a different angle. The different shots would then be **edited** together to form a part of a narrative. Figure 6.1 is a portion of the storyboard for *Return of the Jedi,* 1983.

LucasFilms' storyboard for *Return of the Jedi* is a professional example of a skillfully rendered and colored storyboard for a project meant to be executed at great expense. However, you can make simple storyboards as a thinking process for filmic projects, even using stick figures.

Bunny (**6.4**), an Academy Award–winning computer-animated short film by Chris Wedge, took seven years of actual time to make. The film has a relatively short **running time**—the recorded duration—of seven minutes on the screen. Those seven minutes of screen time, however, imply eternity.

One night, Bunny, a tattered old rabbit, bakes a cake in her kitchen. As Bunny is making the cake, a pestering moth knocks her wedding photo off the wall. After Bunny thinks she has chased away the moth, she nods off in her rocking chair while the cake bakes. The tempo of *Bunny* varies but is generally slow and calming. Bunny is old and moves about her kitchen slowly; she beats the cake batter quickly; she rocks gently as she dozes off in her chair. She awakens suddenly to see a beautiful blue glow coming from the oven. She also sees the moth there, and joins it in the light, entering a mysterious otherworld, perhaps joining the young male rabbit with her in the photo that the moth had knocked off the wall. By its implication of eternal time, the film invites interpretations of a serious topic through cartoon characters.

Emmy and Golden Globe award–winning action drama *24* is a television series about the life of the character Jack Bauer, played by Kiefer Sutherland. He works with the U.S. government in a counterterrorist unit as it defends the country from terrorist threats, some of which are based on fact, and most of which are fictional (**6.5**). The series is an example of creative uses of duration, tempo, and scope in implied time that mimics real time. Each season is composed of one twenty-four-hour day; each episode, which is an hour long, covers an hour of that day. The duration of the narrative of the show over its lifetime of eight or more seasons expands significantly. The tempo of each episode and of the whole series is quick. The scope of action takes us to events in Los Angeles, Washington, D.C., and international locations, with a wide range of characters in tense situations.

The producers of a commercial for Diet Mountain Dew show a fictional narrative of a ferret with a chain saw attacking an unsuspecting couple as they are taking a walk in the woods. While the ferret chases the couple, and the woman jumps into the arms of her boyfriend (**6.6**), text appears on the screen that asserts: "Fact: Ferrets attack more people than grizzly bears." A commentator in a suit, witnessing the attack and holding a can of Mountain Dew, explains to viewers in a stage whisper that although the "fact" is surprising, "what is more surprising is that Diet Mountain Dew has all the intensity of regular Mountain Dew, but none of the calories." The commercial promotes the energy and irreverence that the brand is known for by its youthful target group. The actual duration of the spot is twenty-eight seconds. The implied duration is perhaps three scary minutes. The tempo of the frantic activity of the adults running from the demonic ferret with a chain saw is in marked contrast to the calm demeanor of the announcer touting the benefits of the soft drink. The scope of events is narrow but intense, with four characters. The commercial is sequenced according to the supposed chronology of the fictional event.

Duane Michals is known for his innovative uses of sequences of still images to indicate the passage of time in narratives set up for his camera. In *The Creation* (**6.7**), he alludes to the biblical account of how the world came to be. In the first three photographs of the sequence, he pictorally dramatizes creation through multiple exposures made in a darkroom. For the final three images, he made photographs of an apple and the apple with nude models, alluding to the episode of Adam and Eve in the Garden of Eden. Michals's handwritten numbers are part of his artwork, leading the viewer through the sequence. His sequencing of the images proceeds from a pre-time to recent time.

Gregory Crewdson is another photographer who creates implied time by fabricating his own moments in single, staged still images and then recording them. Influenced by narrative painters and filmmakers, Crewdson goes to great expense to build astonishingly elaborate sets for his still photographs (**6.8**). He directs a professional crew, including a director of photography, a camera operator, a production designer, a casting director, and actors. His photographs, large in size and lush in color, explore imaginary American suburban scenarios.

Crewdson's digital photographs look like instances in time caught on film in the real world, but they are constructed fictional tableaux, carefully enhanced in digital media during a postproduction stage. Crewdson makes what some theorists might call "simulacra"—a postmodernist term discussed further in Chapter 11— which means insubstantial forms or semblances of things that substitute for the real.[2] Like Duane Michals, he intentionally undermines our confidence in the credibility of the supposedly realistic medium of lens-based image making.

6.5 **24 promo, DVDs,** 2009.

6.6 **Mountain Dew television commercial,** stills, 2007.

RECORDED TIME

Bound between two covers, Sally Mann's book of photographs *Immediate Family* (**6.9**) presents a scope of events over eight years in the lives of herself and her children, Emmet, Jessie, and Virginia, as they grew up in a rural area of Virginia. Each photograph is a discrete instant in time: Emmet with a bloody nose, the three children playing a board game on the porch of their country home, Jessie acting as an adult posing with a candy cigarette. As we view the single instances in the book, the scope widens to a series of incidents that constitute one family's experience of childhood from toddler to teenager.

Photographs are instants of time and motion stopped. Photographic time can be considered a type of recorded time, but it has unique aspects. A photograph is the result of light reflecting off a surface through a lens, to a light-sensitive material within the camera, for a discrete bit of time. Whether the photographer records 1/1,000th of a second, one hour, or one day, the photograph is a record only of the instant the shutter is open.

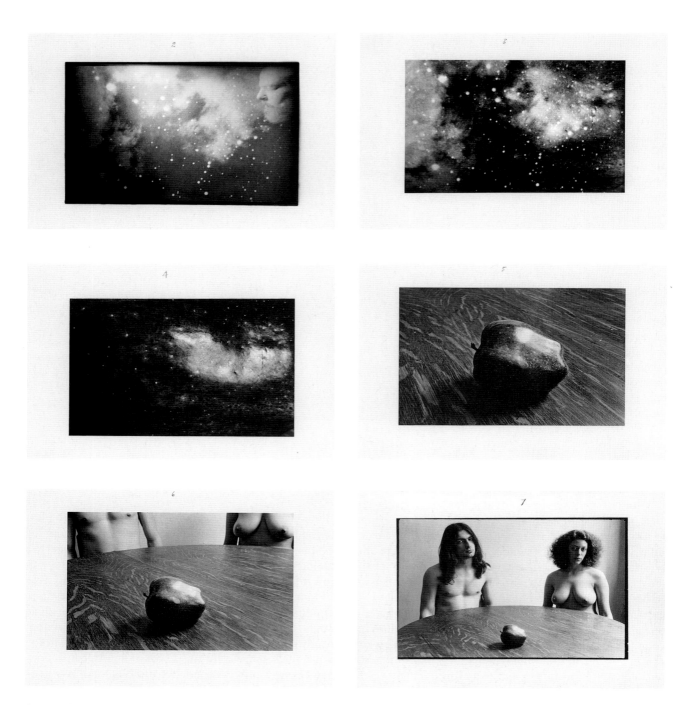

THE CREATION

6.7   **DUANE MICHALS**   *The Creation,* 1975. Photographs and handwriting.

6.8   GREGORY CREWDSON   *Untitled,* 1998. C-print, 50 × 60 in.

French photographer Henri Cartier-Bresson is known for making photographs of "decisive moments"—instances when many formal and narrative aspects come together to make an aesthetically pleasing picture. He said, "We photographers deal in things which are continually vanishing, and when they have vanished there is no contrivance on earth that can make them come back again. We cannot develop and print a memory."[3] Sometimes, however, the photographer stands and waits for such a decisive moment. In recalling his making of *Greece, Cyclades, Island of Siphnos* (**6.10**), Cartier-Bresson said that he recognized the geometric beauty of the architecture and the appeal of the sun and shadows, and waited for someone to pass into the scene. A priest wearing Greek Orthodox attire passed through, and Cartier-Bresson made a photograph of him but was not satisfied with it. He waited longer and captured a young girl in midstride. Her angular body posture visually corresponds with the architectural setting. This is the photograph Bresson selected for exhibition.[4]

Recorded time often contrasts sharply with actual time. A segment of a weekly TV sitcom that consumes days of work in actual time for actors and technicians will be seen by viewers in half-hour episodes.

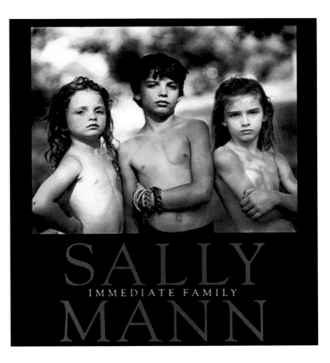

6.9   SALLY MANN   *Immediate Family,* 1993.

6.10 HENRI CARTIER-BRESSON *Greece, Cyclades, Island of Siphnos,* 1961. Photograph, 8 × 10 in.

6.11 WILLIAM WEGMAN Front and back slipcover for *William Wegman, Selected Video Works 1970–78.*

Recorded time can also have the same temporal duration as what it records; for example, William Wegman made videos of his dog Man Ray (**6.11**), one of which shows Man Ray lapping clean a small glass of milk. *Drinking Milk* begins when Man Ray starts to lap the milk from the glass and ends when the glass is empty and clean. The video is one continuous and unbroken exposure (one shot) with no edits. Wegman used one camera in a fixed position, starting the camera when the dog began lapping the milk from the glass and stopping the camera when the dog had lapped up all the milk. More often, however, videographers and filmmakers condense and expand time.

Sometimes film artists dramatically speed up motion or slow it down. To create film with "time lapse," the artist takes a series of pictures of something—say, a flower bud opening—at predetermined intervals and then shows the frames quickly, speeding up the process of nature. A flower bud may open over hours in real time, but we can see it open in seconds in filmic time.

Bill Viola has made many filmic works that dramatically slow down motion. *The Quintet of Remembrance* (**6.12**) is a cinematic work of a group of five people undergoing a range of emotions while a camera records every nuance of their physical reaction. *The Quintet of Remembrance* conveys the strong emotions of the people who vacillate between shock, grief, compassion,

6.12 **BILL VIOLA** *The Quintet of Remembrance,* 2000. Color video rear projection on screen mounted on wall in dark room, projected image size: 4 ft. 6 in. × 8 ft.

6.13 **LIÁN AMARIS SIFUENTES** *Fashionably Late for the Relationship,* 2007. Performance and film.

6.14 JACQUES-LOUIS DAVID *The Oath of the Horatii,* 1789. Oil on canvas, 10 ft. 10 in. × 14 ft.

6.15 ALEXANDER CALDER *Tower with Pinwheel,* 1951. Painted steel wire, painted wood, painted sheet metal, and string, 40 × 36 × 26 in.

rapture, anger, and fear. They share a close physical space, but each person is fully absorbed in his or her own emotions. Viola shot the actors' performance with 35mm film, which lasted approximately sixty seconds in actual time, and then extended the sixty seconds into about sixteen minutes for the finished piece. The movement is so slow and subtle that a viewer walking past the piece, which hangs on a flat screen on a wall, might not even know that the image is changing. When the viewer becomes aware of motion and observes the changes in the characters' expressions, the ultraslow motion accentuates the power and depth of each emotion.

Performance artist Lián Amaris Sifuentes and filmmaker R. Luke DuBois collaborated on the project *Fashionably Late for the Relationship* (**6.13**) that uses actual, illusional, and recorded time, and different rates of motion, for expressive and conceptual effects. In actual time, Sifuentes acted the role of a woman preparing for a date. She did this as a performance piece, in public view, on Union Square in New York City, for a seventy-two-hour period. Although Sifuentes performed in actual time, she moved very slowly to extend the time it would take her to prepare. For example, she had a glass of wine one afternoon and took seven hours to drink it. Passersby viewed her as she performed and became part of the piece as DuBois filmed Sifuentes continuously for seventy-two hours and then digitally compressed her performance into a film with seventy-two minutes of running time. In the film, the people who passed by or stopped to view the live performance appear as if they are moving very quickly as ghostly blurs, while Sifuentes no longer is moving slowly but at what seems to be a normal pace. Through different uses of motion, *Fashionably Late for the Relationship* plays with our conceptions and perceptions of temporal duration and tempo.[5]

The depiction of time in images is not limited to lens-based media. Historical paintings imply a chronology, although most do not show more than an instant of the historical narrative. "History painting" was especially important in Europe in the late 1700s, and such paintings drew upon mythology, religion, and human history as nobler than still lifes, landscapes, and portraits of powerful people.

Jacques-Louis David painted *The Oath of the Horatii* (**6.14**) five years before the French Revolution, seemingly prophesying it. We do not know the specifics of the story that it depicts, but it inspires ideals of duty to and sacrifice for a noble cause.[6] The painting foretells a bloody battle that will take place in the future and suggests past occurrences that have led to this dramatic moment.

Indicating Motion in Art

Like time, motion can be actual or implied, and it can be recorded. We will define **motion** simply as a changing of positions, but it has many complex uses in art.

ACTUAL MOTION

Many artists make objects and orchestrate events that physically move, using actual motion as a design element. In the performing arts, dance comes immediately to mind: dancers move. There are also plentiful examples in visual art of **kinetic art,** artifacts that actually move, such as Alexander Calder's mobiles (**6.15**). They move, usually gently, propelled by the movement of the air around them.

Ken Rinaldo designed and constructed *Autopoiesis* (**6.16**) to move through time and space in a gallery in reaction to viewers' movements. It is a group of fifteen musical and robotic sculptures that interact with the public and with one another. "Autopoiesis" is a term coined by Chilean biologists Humberto Maturana and Francisco Varella in their study of living systems: the term means "self-making," a characteristic of all living systems. When the sculptures sense the presence of a viewer in their exhibition space, they quickly move toward the viewer in a lifelike manner, stopping inches before they make contact with the person. The robots' arms capture video images of the viewer and project them onto the walls of the exhibition space, showing viewers what they look like to the robotic sculptures. The sculptures "talk" to one another and to the viewer in a musical language of audible telephone tones. They express fear with high rapid tones and calmness with low tonal sequences. Sometimes they simply whistle to themselves. They also compare their sensor data and react individually and as a group to the viewer, displaying behaviors of attraction and repulsion. *Autopoiesis* continually evolves its own behaviors in response to whatever unique environment it is in and to viewers' movements. Were the sculptures not able to move, their

6.16 KEN RINALDO *Autopoiesis,* 2000. Interactive artificial-life sculpture, Cabernet Sauvignon grapevines, infrared sensors, urethane plastics, custom software and hardware; each arm is 10 ft. long by 15 in. round, but dimensions vary with movement.

meanings would be radically changed. In Rinaldo's thinking, the robots' group consciousness creates a "cybernetic ballet" of people and machines sensing and responding to one another.[7]

IMPLIED MOTION

Most art causes our eyes actually to move; that is, when we look at a work of art, how the artist composed its elements causes us to look first at one part and then at another. But the artist does this through use of **implied motion**—the illusion of movement and passage of time or distance.

Alexander Calder made stabiles as well as mobiles (see 6.15). His stabiles look as if they should move like his mobiles, but they are designed to stay in one position, immobile. They do, however, "move" our eyes from element to element. *Vertical Constellation with Bomb* (**6.17**) is a stabile that implies motion: the small form on the top center of the sculpture points upward, suggesting upward movement.

In *Cloud 9* (**6.18**), Elizabeth Murray uses a series of blue shapes that snake around the border, and then she puts in blue squiggly shapes that take us into the interior of her composition. In the upper-left corner,

6.17   ALEXANDER CALDER   *Vertical Constellation with Bomb,* 1943.
Painted steel wire, painted wood, and wood, 30½ × 29¾ × 24 in.

6.18   ELIZABETH MURRAY   *Cloud 9,* 2002. Oil on canvas, 93 × 84 in.

she places red and purple shapes atop a red slide that moves our attention to other red shapes that then form an inner loop. With yellow, she marks the corners of an off-balance triangle, further animating the work and the movement of our eyes as we look at the painting.

The suggestion of motion is also possible in nonobjective works. Bridget Riley, an influential artist of the Op Art movement in the 1960s, made paintings with simple forms, some in black and white, others in color, that cause a planned retinal reaction in viewers' eyes. Her paintings convincingly suggest vibrant movement and depth. In *Cataract 3* (**6.19**), curving parallel lines seem to advance and then recede, creating a sense of fluctuating space. The series of diagonals produced by the thin lines appears to be moving to the gentle current of the sea. Riley's work illustrates how you might activate basic visual elements for complex effects.

Louise Bourgeois's sculpture *Arch of Hysteria* (**6.20**) moves our eyes in an endless orb that we can visually enter at any point, moving from fingers to heels, or torso to neck to arms, and so forth. Our eyes can also move through the negative spaces of the sculpture, and focusing on its shiny texture allows us to see our own reflection.

The choices Bourgeois made in order to get us to move our eyes were not arbitrary or based merely on personal taste. She uses many different styles in her work. In *Arch of Hysteria,* she particularly chose to represent a naked male figure in a pose representing extreme distress and vulnerability; it is usually the female body that is displayed with such sexual vulnerability. Bourgeois relies on psychoanalytic theory and her own insights to construct a sculpture that moves us to it, in it, and around it and invites us to gaze at the male body: "My intention is to put down, debunk the abstract male, whose image is constructed by society."[8] Her artistic choices affect social meanings.

Implied motion is important to the success of American painter Kehinde Wiley's works: the implied movement of his paintings is upward, joyous, and positive. In *Investiture of Bishop Harold as the Duke of Franconia, No. 2,* (**6.21**), the artist implies that the figure is gesturing toward us with his left shoulder. Yellow roses float freely in space in front of and behind the figure. Wiley uses settings familiar to conventional European portrait art, including religious imagery, and inserts young black males into his paintings. He subverts white European imagery with African American markers of identity, such as hairstyles, attire, and vividly colored backgrounds.

Implied Motion and Passage of Time. Marcel Duchamp's famous painting *Nude Descending a Staircase* (**6.22**) was directly influenced by photographers' early experiments in capturing and recording movement (see 6.26). To create the illusion of motion, Duchamp repeated and overlapped a female figure so many times that she appears to be stepping down a flight of stairs. Once we learn how to look at this painting, identifying the abstracted forms as a female figure and understanding the repetitions as implying a sequence, we can see the woman as if she were actually moving down the staircase, which would take time. Duchamp shows the illusion of movement and the passage of time in one still painting.

Marjane Satrapi's *Persepolis: The Story of a Childhood* is a graphic book (and subsequent animated movie) about growing up in Tehran during the Islamic

6.19 **BRIDGET RILEY** *Cataract 3,* 1967. PVA on canvas, 87 × 87 in.

6.20 **LOUISE BOURGEOIS** *Arch of Hysteria,* 1993. Bronze, polished patina, 33 × 40 × 22 in.

6.21 **KEHINDE WILEY** *Investiture of Bishop Harold as the Duke of Franconia, No. 2,* 2004. Oil on canvas, 82 × 72 in.

Revolution. It is an autobiographical account of the author's life between the ages of six and fourteen, when Islamic fundamentalists overthrew the shah's regime in Iran, and the country moved from secularism to religious rule. In a single narrative panel (**6.23**), the artist shows the implied motion of people hurrying. To achieve the illusion or suggestion of the passing of a period in the revolution when Iraq was bombing Iran in the 1980s, she uses several formal devices: repeated figures and forms, motion lines (above the backs of the three bottom figures), and a tall vertical format, to indicate the tiring motion of running upstairs and downstairs, into and out of bomb shelters.

Photographic Techniques in Implied Motion. The blurring of images can create the impression of motion. In his dramatic photograph of a soldier approaching the

6.22 **MARCEL DUCHAMP** *Nude Descending a Staircase No. 2,* 1912. Oil on canvas, 57⅞ × 35⅛ in.

6.23 **MARJANE SATRAPI** *Persepolis: The Story of a Childhood,* 2003.

6.24 **ROBERT CAPA** *Omaha Beach, Normandy Coast, France.* 1944. Photograph.

beach of Normandy, France, during the Allied invasion of Europe in World War II (**6.24**), Robert Capa probably achieved an unintentionally blurred effect due to circumstances beyond his control. He made the photograph in the midst of an intense battle and may well have moved the camera accidentally as he made the exposure. As a result, the soldier and the war materiel in the picture are blurred. That Capa's photograph is blurred adds to the emotional and cognitive effects of the image: both the soldier and the photographer were under fire from German gunners on the beach when the photograph was made. The same effect of blurring images can be achieved by using a slow shutter speed and not stabilizing the camera with a tripod.

Using a camera, you can create the illusion of motion with other effects. If you "pan" the camera (moving it left to right or right to left) at the same speed as a moving object, the object will be sharp, but the background will be blurred. If you use a slow shutter speed and a steady camera to photograph a fast-moving object, the object will be blurred and will visually indicate motion in a still image. Photographically blurred images have affected how artists show motion in two-dimensional

images, as we see in Duchamp's *Nude Descending the Staircase* (see 6.22).

If you "track" a movie camera or camcorder, moving it at the same speed as the moving object, the moving object will remain sharp, and the viewer will feel the effect of moving along with the object. If you "zoom" a camera lens while filming or recording, you will cause the viewer to have the illusion of moving in close to what you are showing.

Nathan Fox used lens-based imagery in hand-drawn images to imply motion in illustrations for a serious news story in the *New York Times Magazine*. In the hand-drawn panels (**6.25**), Fox illustrates an actual occurrence in the Iraq war. A group of American soldiers was leading a convoy of vehicles in the desert when an SUV suddenly appeared on the horizon. A soldier riding "shotgun" with a belt-fed light machine gun saw the distance between the SUV and the convoy closing rapidly. Thinking the SUV was probably an "idiot farmer," he fired warning shots. The SUV did not turn or stop. Acting on instinct, the soldier riddled the SUV with bullets and shot into the driver's windshield. The SUV jerked to the side and exploded in a blast that all but

6.25   **NATHAN FOX**   **"The Other Army,"** 2005. Illustration from *The New York Times Magazine.*

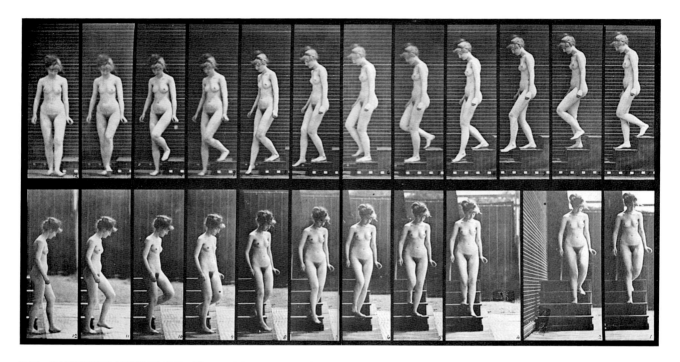

6.26   **EADWEARD MUYBRIDGE**   *Woman Walking Down Stairs,* 1872. Photographs.

vaporized it, but it had gotten close enough to demol-
ish a convoy vehicle. The SUV had been packed with
explosives and was driven by a suicide bomber.[9]

Fox visualizes all of that dramatic action in still pictures. He uses many different points of view to show
the story, much as a movie director would. The first
frame is from above and behind the soldiers' trucks.
Cut to a long shot (a shot including objects in the distance) of the approaching and unidentified SUV. *Cut*
to a medium close-up of the soldier as he faces us,
the viewers, and the SUV. *Cut* to an eye-level middle
shot from a side view of the soldier firing. *Cut* to a
close-up of bullets hitting in front of the SUV. *Cut* to
a close-up frontal view of the firing soldier, at our eye
level. *Cut* to an extreme close-up of the soldier's eye as
seen through his gun sight. *Cut* to the SUV being hit.
Cut to a long shot of the exploding SUV. In nine panels,
the artist has dramatically shown us the rapidity of decision making in an actual war.

RECORDED MOTION

Artifacts that use media such as film, video, and computer animation generally rely on **recorded motion**—
the capture of movement with lens-based media. Usually
the initial recording serves as raw material that the artist
then refines by editing and image-enhancing processes.

Early photographers studied actual motion by recording it with still photographs (**6.26**). Their efforts were meant to help us understand how people,
animals, and things move and then to show that
mobility in discrete increments. Eadweard Muybridge's *Animal Locomotion* consists of eleven volumes and contains more than 100,000 photographs
that he made between 1872 and 1885. Muybridge
also published *The Human Figure in Motion* (1901)
and invented the "zoopraxiscope," an early motion-
picture machine that re-created movement by displaying individual photographs in rapid sequence.

His studies clearly influenced Duchamp's *Nude Descending the Staircase* (see 6.22) and continue to inform other hand-rendered illusional motions, such as Satrapi's staircase drawing for *Persepolis* (see 6.23).

Harold Edgerton was an electrical engineer with a long and productive career at the Massachusetts Institute of Technology, where he investigated photographs in the service of new scientific knowledge. He invented the stroboscope, an instrument that produces short bursts of light during which he could capture on photographic film objects in flight that could not otherwise be seen by the human eye. He made thousands of such photographs, including still images of hummingbirds in flight and bullets shot from guns (**6.27**), using exposure times of less than 1/10,000 of a second.

Muybridge's (see 6.26) and Edgerton's uses of photography to study motion are reality based, made for scientific purposes with specialized equipment they each designed for scientific research, lending credibility to photography and other lens-based imagery. As we saw earlier, Michals's (see 6.7) and Crewdson's (see 6.8) use of realistic-looking photographs for fictional purposes, or as simulacra, undermines confidence in photographic media as truth-telling devices. Theoretical issues about the "truth value" of photographs are currently under discussion among scholars.

The Swiss artist team of Fischli/Weiss (Peter Fischli and David Weiss) created an elaborate sculptural artifact expressly to be recorded on film. They call the thirty-minute film *The Way Things Go* (**6.28**). To make the film, the two artists built an enormous and precarious structure about 100 feet long in an empty warehouse. They made the structure out of ordinary things one might find in and around a house, such as teakettles, tires, shoes, and scrap lumber. They set up combinations of these items and added fire, water, or chemicals to set off chain reactions. One thing bangs into another thing and knocks it onto another thing, which releases acidic foam that melts legs that unsteady a table and topple a can of something on the table onto a candle that ignites what was in the can, and so forth, for a full, mesmerizing, and tension-filled half-hour of carefully crafted and choreographed chaos.

The film reveals itself shot by shot as an unbroken sequence of moving events, but it took Fischli/Weiss

6.27 **HAROLD EDGERTON** *Queen of Hearts Playing Card Hit by a .30 Calibre Bullet,* 1970. Photograph.

6.28 **FISCHLI/WEISS** *The Way Things Go,* 1987. Still from thirty-minute film.

over a year to design and build and shoot the events on film and later to edit them together as a film. The tempo of *The Way Things Go* varies depending on the actual time it takes for the interactions and reactions of elements to happen: some happen quickly, others very slowly. A curator has interpreted the meaning of the film as the tension "between the chaos of a thing continually falling apart and the planning and control required to make it happen."[10] Each movement of the

6.29   FIREWORKS OVER CENTRAL BEIJING   Closing ceremony of the 2008 Olympic Games.

film is methodically set into action, and each seems as if it were accidental, but our knowledge that the actions are a planned expression by the artists opens up many metaphorical implications about life itself, our desire and inability to control life events, and the wonders and horrors of "destiny."

Conclusion: Perspectives on Time and Motion

Artists provide viewers with experiences that thoughtfully involve time and motion. In a basic use of time, they make decisions that affect how they want to move viewers' eyes about a space or object and for how long and at what pace. Will the artifact move the viewers' eyes or their whole bodies? Will the artwork itself move about or be in a restricted space? Will it be permanent or ephemeral?

Artists who involve themselves more directly in the four-dimensional arts that are essentially time based, such as live performances (**6.29**), videos, and computer games, make decisions about the duration of the entire piece and the time commitment asked of a viewer who wishes to experience it. They decide whether to make their work a narrative, and if so, how to sequence it, at what pace, and how large a scope of events it will include.

7 Words and Sounds

7.1 MICHAEL BIERUT/PENTAGRAM AND MARIAN BANTJES *Seduction: Form, Sensation, and the Production of Architectural Desire* **symposium poster** designed for the Yale School of Architecture, 2007.

Words and Sounds Key Terms

WORD   A *sound* or combination of sounds, or its representation in writing or printing, that communicates a meaning.

TEXT, COPY   In graphic design, a body of words, as distinguished from images, in a graphic artifact such as a book or poster.

TYPEFACE   A particular style of letters used in *typography* or *text*.

CALLIGRAPHY   The art of fine handwriting.

TYPOGRAPHY   The art of making and using movable type.

SOUND   A vibratory disturbance capable of being detected by the ear.

RECORDED SOUND   Sound that is saved to be replayed as part of an artifact.

IMPLIED SOUND   A depiction that suggests sound but is actually silent.

Words and sounds are not usually included in lists of elements of art, but they should be, because artists have used them as significant means of expression throughout the ages and across cultures, and they have become increasingly important in modern art movements such as Dada and postmodern art. Words and sounds are basic to many contemporary media: advertising, music video, animation, game design, Web design, graphic design, product design, illustration, cinema, and videography as well as sculpture, painting, printmaking, and other traditional media.

Words and Their Uses in Art

Use of words in art and design is commonplace throughout history and across cultures. Precursors to writing appear across cultures dating back about 12,000 years. Pictographs (symbols belonging to a pictorial graphic system of communication) and ideograms (pictures or symbols that illustrate a concept or idea rather than the object pictured) were carved or marked on stone walls and other surfaces. A **word** (or words) in art is a sound or combination of sounds or a representation in printed form that communicates a meaning.

Language of all kinds is an invented means of communication that is culturally specific. Contemporary artist Xu Bing reinforces the notion of communication as invented and culturally specific by a monumental work of invention. The work consists of one walnut-wood box containing four books of over 500 pages of hand-carved woodblocks of unrecognizable words that are hand printed on rice paper used for Buddhist books and hand bound with traditional Chinese binding techniques. Bing, however, uses a vocabulary of 4,000 false Chinese characters that he invented and hand cut onto wooden printing blocks. When presented as an installation piece entitled *A Book from the Sky* (**7.2**), the books are placed in rows on the floor and hung in scrolls from the ceiling. The artifact's body of words—the **text,** or **copy**—is illegible,

7.2   XU BING   *A Book from the Sky,* 1987–1991. Hand-printed books, ceiling, and wallscrolls printed from wood letterpress type using false Chinese characters, dimensions variable.

even to the artist, making every viewer illiterate. The artist heightens our awareness of language as invented and received within a cultural context.

Before Bing, Belgian Surrealist René Magritte made a painting that heightens our awareness that images of things are very different from the things they represent. With his painting *The Treachery of Images* (**7.3**), which shows a realistic rendering of a pipe with the words below it, *Ceci n'est pas une pipe* ("This is not a pipe"), he clearly marks the distinction between things and representationally realistic-looking images.

Artists working conceptually (in the sense that the idea they want to convey is more important than the work itself) often use words to draw viewers' attention to the meanings intended by their work. Their use of words forces interpretive thoughts in different ways than other elements, such as shapes and colors, would.

7.3   **RENÉ MAGRITTE**   *The Treachery of Images (La Trahison des images: Ceci n'est pas une pipe),* 1928–1929. Oil on canvas, 25 × 37 in.

Jenny Holzer was one of the first artists of recent times to use words exclusively as an art element in a series she called *Truisms* (**7.4**). Her *Truisms,* according to the artist, are informed by her study of Marxism, psychology, social and cultural theory, criticism, and feminism. To her, they are like "mock clichés," which she fashions herself. The sayings are meant to iterate a variety of existing viewpoints, both masculine and feminine and across the political spectrum. She designs them in uppercase (capital letters) in a particular **typeface,** or style of letters, with no punctuation, and in alphabetical order. Her earliest versions of the *Truisms* were printed in black text on white paper, about forty to sixty on a page. She first posted them anonymously in SoHo, New York City. Later she made them into LED (light-emitting diode) tube signs that she rented on Times Square in New York City, on London's Trafalgar Square, and in Las Vegas at Caesar's Palace. She has also put them on hats and T-shirts.

Holzer made a public art installation in Pittsburgh in 2005 that sends the texts of five books, written by authors with Pittsburgh roots, scrolling up hundreds of feet of the roofline of the Convention Center. The work uses more than 1,500 LEDs to scroll the texts twenty-four hours a day, seven days a week. The artist's intention is to give public attention to books that are usually read in private.

WORDS AS IMAGES

Many contemporary artists and designers use words as artifacts. Camille Utterback and Romy Achituv created *Text Rain* (**7.5**) as an interactive installation piece. To interact with the gallery piece, visitors stand or move in front of a screen on which they see a video projection of themselves combined with letters falling like rain or snow. The letters appear to land on the viewers and respond to the viewers' motions. Viewers can catch and lift the letters or let them fall. They can catch letters to make words. The designers have not selected random letters: the letters are from a poem about bodies and language.[1]

Bruce Nauman uses words as neon wall paintings, such as *One Hundred Live and Die* (**7.6**), which has four columns of twenty-five phrases in different colors that reflect onto the floor. Each phrase contains the words "live" and "die," but no two phrases are repeated. Examples of the phrases include "speak and die," "tell and live," "smile and die," "pay and die," and so forth. The phrases are both beautiful as sculpture and meaningful as texts, perhaps celebrating the diverse experiences of life.

Glenn Ligon's *Warm Broad Glow* (**7.7**) is a neon wall piece of the phrase "negro sunshine." It is considerably less joyous and less use of neon than Nauman's work (see 7.6). Ligon's neon letters seem to be of very dark light that shines light on the wall where it hangs. The light glows, as its title tells us. It is visually compelling as well as thought provoking about life as a black person. Sunshine typically conjures happy feelings, but if there is happiness in Ligon's piece, it is dulled by darkness.

Recent artists' works with words hark back to the history of **calligraphy,** the art of fine handwriting. Calligraphy has a long history in both Western and Eastern cultures. Words in representational form are

A LITTLE KNOWLEDGE CAN GO A LONG WAY
A LOT OF PROFESSIONALS ARE CRACKPOTS
A MAN CAN'T KNOW WHAT IT'S LIKE TO BE A MOTHER
A NAME MEANS A LOT JUST BY ITSELF
A POSITIVE ATTITUDE MAKES ALL THE DIFFERENCE IN THE WORLD
A RELAXED MAN IS NOT NECESSARILY A BETTER MAN
A SENSE OF TIMING IS THE MARK OF GENIUS
A SINCERE EFFORT IS ALL YOU CAN ASK
A SINGLE EVENT CAN HAVE INFINITELY MANY INTERPRETATIONS
A SOLID HOME BASE BUILDS A SENSE OF SELF
A STRONG SENSE OF DUTY IMPRISONS YOU
ABSOLUTE SUBMISSION CAN BE A FORM OF FREEDOM
ABSTRACTION IS A TYPE OF DECADENCE
ABUSE OF POWER SHOULD COME AS NO SURPRISE
ACTION CAUSES MORE TROUBLE THAN THOUGHT
ALIENATION PRODUCES ECCENTRICS OR REVOLUTIONARIES
ALL THINGS ARE DELICATELY INTERCONNECTED
AMBITION IS JUST AS DANGEROUS AS COMPLACENCY
AMBIVALENCE CAN RUIN YOUR LIFE
AN ELITE IS INEVITABLE
ANGER OR HATE CAN BE A USEFUL MOTIVATING FORCE
ANIMALISM IS PERFECTLY HEALTHY
ANY SURPLUS IS IMMORAL
ANYTHING IS A LEGITIMATE AREA OF INVESTIGATION
ARTIFICIAL DESIRES ARE DESPOILING THE EARTH
AT TIMES INACTIVITY IS PREFERABLE TO MINDLESS FUNCTIONING
AT TIMES YOUR UNCONSCIOUS IS TRUER THAN YOUR CONSCIOUS MIND
AUTOMATION IS DEADLY
AWFUL PUNISHMENT AWAITS REALLY BAD PEOPLE
BAD INTENTIONS CAN YIELD GOOD RESULTS
BEING ALONE WITH YOURSELF IS INCREASINGLY UNPOPULAR
BEING HAPPY IS MORE IMPORTANT THAN ANYTHING ELSE
BEING HONEST IS NOT ALWAYS THE KINDEST WAY
BEING JUDGMENTAL IS A SIGN OF LIFE
BEING SURE OF YOURSELF MEANS YOU'RE A FOOL
BELIEVING IN REBIRTH IS THE SAME AS ADMITTING DEFEAT
BOREDOM MAKES YOU DO CRAZY THINGS
CALM IS MORE CONDUCIVE TO CREATIVITY THAN IS ANXIETY
CATEGORIZING FEAR IS CALMING
CHANGE IS VALUABLE BECAUSE IT LETS THE OPPRESSED BE TYRANTS
CHASING THE NEW IS DANGEROUS TO SOCIETY
CHILDREN ARE THE CRUELEST OF ALL
CHILDREN ARE THE HOPE OF THE FUTURE
CLASS ACTION IS A NICE IDEA WITH NO SUBSTANCE
CLASS STRUCTURE IS AS ARTIFICIAL AS PLASTIC
CONFUSING YOURSELF IS A WAY TO STAY HONEST
CRIME AGAINST PROPERTY IS RELATIVELY UNIMPORTANT
DECADENCE CAN BE AN END IN ITSELF
DECENCY IS A RELATIVE THING
DEPENDENCE CAN BE A MEAL TICKET
DESCRIPTION IS MORE VALUABLE THAN METAPHOR
DEVIANTS ARE SACRIFICED TO INCREASE GROUP SOLIDARITY
DISGUST IS THE APPROPRIATE RESPONSE TO MOST SITUATIONS
DISORGANIZATION IS A KIND OF ANESTHESIA
DON'T PLACE TOO MUCH TRUST IN EXPERTS
DON'T RUN PEOPLE'S LIVES FOR THEM
DRAMA OFTEN OBSCURES THE REAL ISSUES
DREAMING WHILE AWAKE IS A FRIGHTENING CONTRADICTION
DYING AND COMING BACK GIVES YOU CONSIDERABLE PERSPECTIVE
DYING SHOULD BE AS EASY AS FALLING OFF A LOG
EATING TOO MUCH IS CRIMINAL
ELABORATION IS A FORM OF POLLUTION
EMOTIONAL RESPONSES ARE AS VALUABLE AS INTELLECTUAL RESPONSES
ENJOY YOURSELF BECAUSE YOU CAN'T CHANGE ANYTHING ANYWAY
EVEN YOUR FAMILY CAN BETRAY YOU
EVERY ACHIEVEMENT REQUIRES A SACRIFICE
EVERYONE'S WORK IS EQUALLY IMPORTANT
EVERYTHING THAT'S INTERESTING IS NEW
EXCEPTIONAL PEOPLE DESERVE SPECIAL CONCESSIONS
EXPIRING FOR LOVE IS BEAUTIFUL BUT STUPID
EXPRESSING ANGER IS NECESSARY
EXTREME BEHAVIOR HAS ITS BASIS IN PATHOLOGICAL PSYCHOLOGY
EXTREME SELF-CONSCIOUSNESS LEADS TO PERVERSION
FAITHFULNESS IS A SOCIAL NOT A BIOLOGICAL LAW
FAKE OR REAL INDIFFERENCE IS A POWERFUL PERSONAL WEAPON
FATHERS OFTEN USE TOO MUCH FORCE
FEAR IS THE GREATEST INCAPACITATOR
FREEDOM IS A LUXURY NOT A NECESSITY
GIVING FREE REIN TO YOUR EMOTIONS IS AN HONEST WAY TO LIVE
GOING WITH THE FLOW IS SOOTHING BUT RISKY
GOOD DEEDS EVENTUALLY ARE REWARDED
GOVERNMENT IS A BURDEN ON THE PEOPLE
GRASS ROOTS AGITATION IS THE ONLY HOPE
GUILT AND SELF-LACERATION ARE INDULGENCES
HABITUAL CONTEMPT DOESN'T REFLECT A FINER SENSIBILITY
HIDING YOUR MOTIVES IS DESPICABLE

7.4 JENNY HOLZER *Truisms* (detail), 1977–1979.

particularly important in Islamic cultures. Islam, one of the world's great religions, was founded among people of the Arabian Peninsula in the sixth century, and by the seventh century, Muslims had largely encircled the Mediterranean. Muslim scribes required long and arduous training, both artistic and religious, as a requirement for copying the words of the Qur'an, the sacred book of Islam. In long, flowing, stylized writing, with carefully shaped and connected letters reading from right to left, the scribes created abstract designs that are independent from the meaning of the sacred words. Calligraphy was extended to secular works, as in the page of Iranian poetry reproduced in figure **7.8**. The script on this page is symmetrically bordered and framed on the outer margins by starlike motifs and then on the inner band by lobe and leaf shapes to set off and harmonize with the text. The script itself is made by découpage—letters are not drawn but pasted on the page, like ceramic tiles, with astonishing craftsmanship.[2]

Typography is the art of making and using movable type. With the invention of movable type (around 1045 in China) and the printing press (around 1440 in Europe), great advances were made in preserving and advancing knowledge by printing books affordable to many people. Typographers are interested in the readability of typefaces (printable alphabets) they design and also in the expressive nuances conveyed by style: boldface, italic, simple, complex, serif (a stroke added to either the beginning

7.5 CAMILLE UTTERBACK AND ROMY ACHITUV
Text Rain (detail), 1999. Interactive installation, 4 × 5 ft.

or end of one of the main strokes of a letter), or sans serif (without such a stroke). Look at the many ways a college or university prints its name for different applications: official seal, T-shirts, sweatshirts, letterheads, signage for buildings, course catalogs, and backpacks. Some typefaces are likely athletically aggressive, while others may suggest scholarship. A typeface itself conveys meaning, apart from what the words say.

The Pushpin Group is a well-established graphic design firm in New York City, which published a design magazine called *Pushpin Graphic* from 1957 to 1981. Its masthead (**7.9**) combines gothic letters that announce the name of the magazine with flourishes of ink made with a pen. The Gothic typeface, developed in the twelfth century, is a highly stylized alphabet of compact and quite vertical characters with thick downstrokes and thin upstrokes bent back at the ends. Pushpin has a reputation for accepting many styles of illustration and design, and its magazine masthead expressed a playful and imaginative approach to traditional typography.

Artists Ann Hamilton and Ann Chamberlain and 200 volunteer scribes collaborated to make a mural of words about words for the new San Francisco Public Library that opened in 1996. Even before the old library was moved to a new building, the librarians had started switching its outdated card catalog system to computer cataloging. Hamilton and Chamberlain, with scribes under their direction, annotated 50,000 old paper cards with relevant information about the book to which the card directly refers, or made references that came to the scribe's mind by association: for example, on a card for a cookbook, a scribe wrote a recipe from another cookbook. The card reproduced here (**7.10**) references "*Lettering*, by Frank Thomas Daniel (1865–)," with hand-lettered script on the card. Some cards are political, others are funny, and some are straightforward. The two artists sequenced the inscribed cards and adhered them to walls in a patchwork collage they made permanent with a thin wash of transparent plaster. More than a dozen languages are represented in the mural. About the meaning of their public work, the artists say they are "interested in the labyrinth of associations that every book forms to other books in the subjective

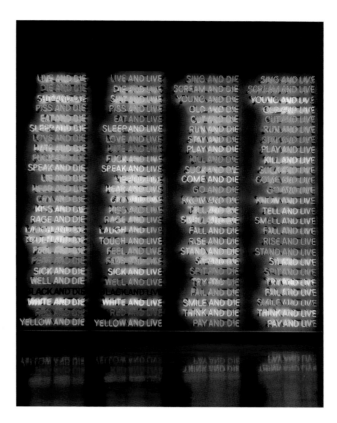

7.6   BRUCE NAUMAN   *One Hundred Live and Die,* 1984.
Neon tubing mounted on four metal monoliths,
118 × 132 × 21 in.

7.7   GLENN LIGON   *Warm Broad Glow,* 2005. Neon and paint, 4 × 48 in.

7.8 ARTIST UNKNOWN Calligraphic illustration of a page of poetry, Iranian or Turkish, Islamic, Ottoman period, c. 1280–1924, sixteenth century. Page of poetry from Amir Shahi of Sabzavar (d. 1453), *Anthology of Poetry,* artist Maulana Nur al-Din 'Abd al-Rahman Jami (1414–1492); author Nasir Khusrau (1003–c. 1066). Ink, colors, and gold on paper, lacquer binding. 8¾ high × 5¾ in. wide.

7.9 PUSHPIN GROUP Magazine logo, 1957–1981. Design by Seymour Chwast

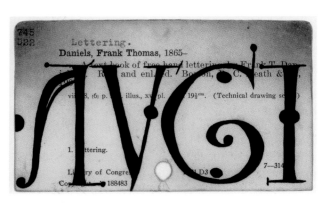

7.10 ANN HAMILTON AND ANN CHAMBERLAIN *San Francisco Public Library Public Art Project 1996* **(detail).** Annotated paper library catalog cards, size variable.

experience of the reader." They wished "to make a document of the collection and the readership during a time when the form of access was still largely spatial and tactile with the cards and the stacks."[3] Hamilton's and Chamberlain's project depends both on the beauty of letters as lines and shapes and on their evocative power as words.

Sculptor Malcolm Cochran uses letters as sculptures that combine to make words in a reflecting pool at the Ohio Supreme Court in Columbus (**7.11**). The exterior installation is called *Integrity,* and the word is spelled out in three-dimensional sculptural forms. Words integral to justice—reason, peace, honor, wisdom, compassion, justice, truth, equity, integrity, honesty—are literally "written in stone." Cochran had the letters that form the words installed just at or slightly below the full water line of the reflecting pool so that the text seems not only as solid as the granite from which it is cut but also as elusive as justice sometimes is.

WORDS AND IMAGES

Artists and designers working in many different media combine words and images in their creations. Lalla Essaydi, born in Morocco but educated in American art schools, returned to Morocco and the Islamic tradition of merging writing and design for an elaborate series of photographsshe calls *Converging Territories* (**7.12**). For the entire series, she posed her female models indoors, the realm that women occupy perforce in Islamic society. She spent weeks writing a continuous stream of diary-like texts in Arabic with henna (a dye women use to color the hair and body) on the white cloths with which she covered floors, walls, and ceilings. She also inscribed her models before making her photographs, giving them a voice that is often repressed in their own culture. By using excessive writing to cover what we see in her photographs, Essaydi implies that mere looking is insufficient for knowing: writing implies a need for interpretation, and interpretation is central to understanding. Yet Essaydi's photographs have a rebellious nature, too, since in the Muslim culture women are forbidden to practice calligraphy.

Sometimes you will be given words to work with, and at other times you might introduce words into your work on your own either for their abstract aesthetic value or to convey information. Words are particularly important in some narrative works of art. The story of Maus is a memoir by cartoonist Art Spiegelman, who recounts his father's struggle to survive the Holocaust as a Polish Jew. The Pulitzer Prize–winning graphic novel draws on his father's recollections of events he personally experienced and details ways the war reverberates through generations of a family. The tragic story is conveyed by words as well as by pictures. Neither words alone nor pictures alone would have the same impact as Spiegelman's combination of both approaches (**7.13**).

When words are expected, their absence can be powerfully expressive. Vicki Daiello made a sequence of four images composed of words, no words, small red squares, drawings, and black fields (**7.14**). The sequence plays with absence and presence, and meanings. Visually, the sequence moves from words ("Deconstruction" and "Silence") and a small red square on a black field, to three small red squares on a black field, to a totally black field, to an image that juxtaposes the words, the red square, and drawings. Conceptually, the sequence moves from the presence of words and a symbol (the small red square), to symbols and the absence of words, to black and the suggested "silence" of absence, and back to visible presence with the words, the symbols, and the drawings. To create the sequence, Daiello made graphite and ink drawings, scanned them, and used the software program Photoshop to select and manipulate

7.11 **MALCOLM COCHRAN** *Integrity,* 2002. Laser-cut white granite letters, 2 ft. square × 9 in. thick, in reflecting pool, Ohio Supreme Court Plaza, Columbus.

7.12 **LALLA ESSAYDI** *Converging Territories #12,* 2003. Color photograph, from a series.

7.13 **ART SPIEGELMAN** *Maus, A Survivor's Tale: My Father Bleeds History,* 1992. Page 31.

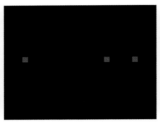

7.14 **VICKI DAIELLO** *Silences between words and world: Deconstruction and the evolution of an inquiry,* 2007. Sequence, digital media, PowerPoint.

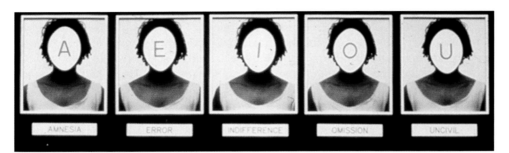

7.15 **LORNA SIMPSON** *Easy for Whom to Say,* 1989. Five color Polaroid prints, ten engraved plastic plaques, 31 × 115 in.

areas of the drawings. She used Power-Point to design the text, small squares, and black rectangles and to arrange the images into a sequence.

African American artist and photographer Lorna Simpson frequently uses words with photographic images, aware that images alone can be easily misread or under-interpreted. *Easy for Whom to Say* (**7.15**) addresses issues of language, race, gender, and personal and group identities. The face of the repeated female figure is hidden by one of five vowels, letters basic to the formation of English words. Words define others, and we define ourselves with words, frequently in the form of narratives. The words Simpson has chosen to associate with corresponding vowels [—amnesia, error, indifference, omission, uncivil—] have reference to the figure, which lacks visible identity. The words can apply to cultural narratives constructed about black women, to the figure's descriptions of herself, or to a combination. The artist's use of vowels and the words is an essential element in interpreting the work.

American conceptual artist Barbara Kruger almost always includes words in her works of art, juxtaposing text and imagery (**7.16**). She has standardized her choice of typeface and how it is presented, so that it is constant across her body of work. (She

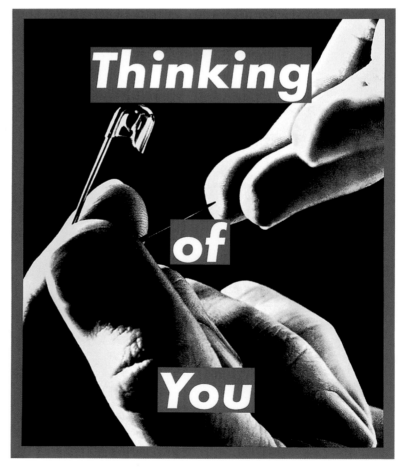

7.16 **BARBARA KRUGER** *Untitled (Thinking of You),* 1999–2000. Photographic screen print on vinyl, 123 × 101 in.

uses uppercase and lower-case white-on-red Futura Bold Oblique.) She takes images already in circulation in mass culture, crops them, alters their contrast, and changes their size, sometimes enlarging them to billboard size and sometimes reducing them to the size of matchbooks. She also takes words and expressions used in ordinary discourse, such as "thinking of you," a phrase that one might see on a greeting card. She subverts the phrases she uses, sometimes by altering how they are usually phrased so that they have a new bite and always by what images she puts them on top of, such as this menacing photograph of a fingertip about to be pricked. Her use of pronouns is intentionally slippery: who is the "you" to whom the print refers?

Typefaces and logos (corporate symbols) are closely associated. Sometimes logos are made of type only, and usually type accompanies logos in a variety of uses from business cards to signs on delivery trucks and even airplanes. José Luis Giménez del Pueblo offers a variety of sample logos

7.17 **JOSÉ LUIS GIMÉNEZ DEL PUEBLO** **Corporate Visual Identity Design,** 1980–2000: 1. The Ohio Arts Council, 2. Great Lakes Arts Alliance, 3. Fundesco Foundation, Spain, 4. Department of Interior of Spain, 5. The Basque Country, Europe, 6. Aldeasa, Duty-Free and Museum Shops, Spain and The Americas, 7. Vital Savings Bank, Euskadi, 8. Spanish Pavillion at the World's Fair, Seville, 1992, 9. TVE, Olympic TV Channel, Barcelona, 1992, 10. Channel 1 of the Spanish National Television Network, 11. National Soccer League of Spain, 12. Television and Communications Network Europe & the Americas, 13. Satellite TV Channels Network, National Broadcasting of Spain, 14. Symphony Orchestra and Choir, RTVE, Spain, 15. European Television Network, Televisa of Mexico, 16. Health Mutual Fund, Spain & the Americas.

(7.17) he designed for international companies over a twenty-year period, many of which incorporate design and type.

expressive content beyond the "quiet" elements of line, shape, texture, and so forth. Learning to be aware of the potential of sound in your work may give your pieces new dimensions for meaning and expression.

Sounds: Adding a Sensory Dimension

Some sounds are accidental, and others are designed or constructed intentionally. In either case, **sound** is a vibratory disturbance capable of being detected by the ear. When you incorporate sounds in your work, you add a sensory dimension and expand the possibility of

AUDIBLE WORDS

We often think of television, cinema, animation, and other lens-based and computer-based media as visual, but sound is an important element of these media. For example, the voices of many famous actors are a key element in the success of recent feature-length animated movies such as *Coraline, Bolt,* and *Kung Fu*

Panda. As Japanese *anime* (**7.18**) becomes increasingly popular on American television, quality English-language dubs are vital to the enjoyment of the animated experience: "A good one will enrich the story and bring the characters to life, but a badly dubbed show can be as grating as a concert performed off-key."[4]

Janet Cardiff's gallery installations are evocative especially because of her use of the spoken word, often delivered in softly spoken tones, seemingly to each individual viewer who enters one of her filmic spaces. *The Paradise Institute* (**7.19**) is an installation in an enclosed constructed space within a larger gallery. It shows video and uses audio to tell broken narratives about a cabaret singer, a nurse and a patient, and other characters through carefully placed speakers within the viewing space. In some versions, viewers put on headphones to listen to the **recorded sound** that the artist saves to be replayed during the projection. Filmmaker Atom Egoyan described how Cardiff's installation affected him: "I entered a room where a series of audio speakers mounted on thin metal stands emitted a soft murmur of conversation. As I got closer to each speaker, I could make out individual [aural] texts. At certain moments, my movement would trigger a projected image . . . It's difficult to express my excitement in this room. I had the sensation of being in the middle of a film that was still being formulated; that was still in someone else's mind."[5]

7.18 **Japanese anime,** 2006.

7.19 **JANET CARDIFF AND GEORGE BURES MILLER** *The Paradise Institute,* 2001. Wood, theater seats, video projection, headphones, and mixed media. 118 × 698 × 210 in.

NONVERBAL SOUNDS

Many of the artworks we have already examined incorporate sound without words as an important design element, for example, the sound of wind in Goldsworthy's snow pyramids (see 6.3), Wegman's use of a live microphone while making videotapes of Man Ray (see 6.11), sounds that Calder's mobiles (see 6.15) make as they move in the air, and the beeps and buzzes of Rinaldo's mechanical creatures in *Autopoiesis* (see 6.16).

Nick Cave is an American visual and performance artist and designer who works in many visual art disciplines, including clothing-based forms. The latter include the making of unique "sound suits" (**7.20**) that are both sculptures and costumes for live and recorded ceremonial performances. His sound suits are full-body costumes he creates out of apparently worthless objects that make noise when they move: sticks, bells, and garbage bag ties. He and all sorts of "non-artists" dance in the suits, sometimes in spontaneous street dances, at neighborhood bars, and other times in more conventional performance spaces. The costumes make sounds according to how those in the costumes move, greatly enhancing the rhythm and tempo of their movements. Cave plans to complete a series of fifty suits, display them as sculptures, and also record professional dancers moving in them and the sounds they make. Cave, an African American, intends his work to explore themes of skin and race. He considers the sound suits a second layer of skin that disguises and protects the wearer against the prejudices people of color encounter daily.

Jean Tinguely was a Swiss painter and sculptor in the Dada tradition who designed sculptures to move, and they usually move noisily (**7.21**). This is how the artist described his works:

To attempt to hold fast an instant is doubtful.
To bind an emotion is unthinkable.
To petrify love is impossible.
It is beautiful to be transitory.
How lovely it is not to have to live forever.
Luckily, there is no good and no evil.[6]

7.20   **NICK CAVE**   *Soundsuit,* 1998.

These succinct statements summarize many of Tinguely's beliefs about art and life. They can also help us interpret one of his early, artistically innovative sound pieces, *Radio WNYR*. This piece is part of the artist's experimentation with transient media, such as sound; he also used fire and water in some pieces. *Radio WNYR* tunes in and out of stations from one end of the radio band to the other. It is an ever-changing sound collage. The dial is controlled by a mechanical device, and the radio plays different sounds at different volumes by chance, including snippets of dialogue, music, and

7.21   **JEAN TINGUELY**   **(with left hand before his mouth) in front of one of his installations.**
Color photograph, 1985. Machine, bones, cow skull with horns, lightbulb, floodlights.

7.22 **NAM JUNE PAIK** *Megatron/Matrix,* 1995. Eight-channel video and two-channel sound multimedia installation with 215 monitors, approx. 132 × 396 × 48 in.

7.23 **EDVARD MUNCH** *The Scream,* 1893. Tempera and pastels on cardboard, 91 × 73.5 cm.

static. As a reflection of his statements above, *Radio WNYR* cannot hold fast an instant, bind an emotion, nor petrify love; it is always transitory, will not live forever, and does not distinguish between good sounds and bad sounds.

Nam June Paik was a South Korean–born American pioneer of video art, especially known for his expressive manipulation of TV sets and commercially broadcast images and sounds. For Paik, technology is a means of creative play, and television is not something viewers need to sit in front of and passively consume its force-fed content. *Megatron/Matrix* (**7.22**) is built of 215 monitors and is about the size of a billboard. The video is accompanied by a continuous loop of unrelated bits of sound captured from the Seoul Olympics mixed with footage of Korean folk rituals and modern dance. He arranged the monitors of this piece into two distinct but adjoining parts. *Megatron* suggests the global reach of media, while *Matrix,* the smaller section on the right of the piece, suggests media's impact on each of us. Museum educators write, "Smaller clips play simultaneously on multiple monitors, while larger, animated images flow across the boundaries between screens, suggesting a world without borders in the electronic age."[7] The display includes two partially nude women with whom he may be suggesting that our bodies are our primal connection to the world but mediated by media.

7.24 **MONTIEN BOONMA** *Lotus Sound,* 1992. Terra-cotta bells and lotus petals covered with gold, 300 × 300 × 300 cm.

Some artifacts depict people and events that suggest sound but are actually silent. Paintings, photographs, and sculptures, for instance, often imply sounds through visual representations. A famous example of **implied sound** in a painting is Edvard Munch's *The Scream* (**7.23**). It is a silent painting, but it implies sounds of horror emanating from the figure's mouth by the way Munch conceived and painted the image. The artist replicated in exaggerated form the physical characteristics the body would assume if a person were expressing extreme anguish through a scream.

Montien Boonma's *Lotus Sound* (**7.24**) is a silent sculpture that implies sound. He made the piece by stacking terra-cotta bells to make a curved wall. He covered terra-cotta lotus petals in gold and hung them behind the wall of bells. The wall of bells keeps the viewer separate from the lotus petals, but the spaces between the bells allow visual access to the petals. Both the bells and the lotus have significance in Buddhist meditation practices. The sculpture is meant to guide us to inner peace. Viewers would hear the bells in their minds while viewing the sculpture and thus be guided

to peace. The terra-cotta wall is transparent and opaque, solid and fragile. Although we can see the petals, the wall serves as a metaphorical barrier to them. We can achieve the peace that the lotus represents through the rhythm of meditative breathing.[8]

Conclusion: Combining the Elements

This chapter concludes our identifications, definitions, and exemplary uses of the basic elements of art: point, line, texture, value, shape, mass and volume, space, color, time, motion, word, and sound. Rarely will you make a work of art consisting of a single element. Most often, you will combine a few or many elements, and your challenge is how to do this in ways that satisfy you and that are communicative to others. The following chapter considers *how* you might manipulate and compose some or all of these elements in works of art to express your ideas and feelings in artistic form.

8 Directional Force, Size, Scale, and Proportion

8.1 **RICHARD MISRACH** *Unitled,* 2002. Color
photograph, 4 ft. 1 in. × 8 ft.

Design Principles
Directional Force
Size, Scale, and Proportion
Conclusion: Effective Uses of Size, Scale, and Directional Force

WWith this chapter, we begin an examination of design principles. Principles we will consider in this chapter are directional force and relations among size, scale, and proportion. Before considering these, we will first consider what design principles are, where they came from, and of what use they can be to you.

Design Principles

When artists and designers arrange the design elements (point, line, shape, mass, volume, texture, value, space, color, time, motion, words, and sounds), their arrangements are based on the expressive effects and ideas they want to make visible in visual form. Their artifacts, whether made consciously or unconsciously, methodically or intuitively, deliberately or by chance, are likely to reflect what have come to be known as **design principles**—strategies of organization for effective visual expression.

Design principles have been formulated through the ages. The ancient Greeks, for example, emphasized harmony, symmetry, and proportion as organizing principles of beauty in representational works of art. David Hume, the Scottish philosopher, wrote an important essay on art in 1757 that provided an open-ended list of qualities of beautiful things that included uniformity, variety, clarity of expression, and brilliance of color while adhering to representational realism. Art educator Arthur Wesley Dow taught art for thirty years in major art programs, including those at Columbia University and Pratt Institute, influencing many important designers and artists such as Max Weber, Edward Steichen, Alfred Stieglitz, and Georgia O'Keeffe. In 1899 Dow also articulated a set of principles of design to teach young artists how to compose "harmonious works of art." His principles were not dependent on accurate representations of reality, and they deemphasized hierarchical distinctions between "fine" and "applied" arts, or arts and crafts. His principles included subordination and rhythmic repetition, symmetry, opposition, transition, and notions of black and white values derived from his interest in Japanese prints.[1]

Thus design principles provide suggested ways to order, organize, and manipulate design elements by balancing them or destabilizing them, emphasizing some over others, establishing or disrupting patterns, unifying them, and so forth. People who study, make, and teach art continue to develop and teach design principles. Just as we have inherited some principles of proportion, for example, from the ancient Greeks and incorporated the syncopation of twentieth-century jazz music into variations of the principle of repetition, established principles are preserved, and new principles will be discovered now and invented in the future.

Directional Force, Size, Scale, and Proportion Key Terms

DESIGN PRINCIPLES   Compositional means by which artists arrange design elements of artifacts for effective visual expression.

DIRECTIONAL FORCE   Arrangements of elements that can move the viewer's eyes in, around, or through a work of art.

VERTICAL FORCE   An arrangement of elements along a vertical axis, often expressing height, power, and grandeur.

HORIZONTAL FORCE   An arrangement of elements along a horizontal axis, often expressing peace, restfulness, and stability.

DIAGONAL FORCE   An arrangement of elements along a diagonal axis, often expressing dynamism, agitation, and vigor.

CIRCULAR FORCE   An arrangement of elements along a circular path or radiating from a central point, often expressing fullness, harmony, joy, and inner stability.

TRIANGULAR FORCE   An arrangement of elements relying on a triangular structure that provides actual or illusional stability.

SIZE   The physical dimensions of an object or element of art.

SCALE   The comparative size of an element of art or object in relation to other elements or objects and expectations about what is normal.

PROPORTION   The relationship of the sizes of parts to each other and to the whole artifact.

GOLDEN RECTANGLE, ROOT 5 RECTANGLE   A rectangle derived by the ancient Greeks from the *Golden Section;* its length is the square root of 5.

GOLDEN SECTION, GOLDEN MEAN   A line sectioned so the ratio of the shorter section is to the larger section as the larger section is to the whole; the so-called perfect ratio in ancient Greek art and architecture.

Learning these principles of design can help you in two important ways. First, you will be able to use the strategies for making new and effective artifacts:

- What elements will you use in a work?

- How will you organize them?

- What effect are you achieving by using a certain element in a certain way?

- What are the implications for meaning when you do this rather than that?

- Are you strengthening your statement or weakening it by what you are repeating in the work?

- Is your work monotonous and lacking variety?

- Is your work too chaotic and lacking a dominant visual emphasis?

- Does your visual emphasis reinforce or dilute your expressive idea for the work?

- Are you diffusing the emotional impact of your work by overlooking one or more principles of design?

Second, you can use the principles of design to analyze and discuss aspects of artworks made by artists in the past, present, and future:

- What elements did the artist use most and least?

- How did the artist organize those elements?

- How does the artist get and hold your attention?

- Where does the artist direct your attention within the work?

- What does the artist emphasize most and least in the work?

On the basis of answers to questions like these, you can then answer important questions about artistic intent and effect: what do you want to show, make others think about, have others notice about the work, about the world, and about yourself in reaction to the work?

Principles of design are sometimes used in a prescriptive way, telling us that a work of art *should* be balanced, for example, or should use repetition to establish rhythm. Principles, however, can be read as *possibilities* rather than as *absolutes*. A useful and positive way to understand principles of design is to consider them as if-then propositions. For example, "*If* I want a sense of stability and calmness in my artwork, *then* perhaps I should consider using flat horizontal shapes." You can use a principle as a means of examining and reworking what you are making. For example, "I want a dynamic, energetic, and nervous expression, but I have many flat horizontal shapes that are working against my intended expression." Principles can also be used as a creative challenge: "Can I use flat horizontal shapes, which usu-

ally express peacefulness, to express instability and chaos?"

To use art elements and design principles successfully in your work, you must also consider the subject matter you are using, the medium you have chosen, your process, and the context in which you will show your work. When you view and interpret a work of art by merely identifying its elements without considering how and to what meaningful effect the artist has used them, you are engaged in a vocabulary exercise detached from aesthetic, personally expressive, and social meanings. Similarly, merely to identify design principles underlying an artifact without considering the meanings implied by the artist's use of those principles is to be engaged in a formal exercise detached from significant expressive purposes. As contemporary American artist Eric Fischl has observed, "It's important for a painter to have the formal means to deal with his vision of the world, but it also helps if that vision is an interesting one."[2]

There is no assurance to artists that applying one or more design principles when making a work of art will necessarily result in aesthetically successful or meaningfully expressive and functionally useful objects and images. As Roy Lichtenstein noted, "There is no neat way of telling whether a work of art is composed or not."[3] Nonetheless, design principles offer you a multitude of aesthetic and expressive possibilities. The principles we consider in this book include directional force, size, scale, and proportion (this chapter); balance and contrast (Chapter 9); repetition, unity and variety, emphasis, and subordination (Chapter 10); and postmodernist strategies (Chapter 11).

Directional Force

Once you make a mark or put three-dimensional material in place, directional forces come into play. A **directional force** is an arrangement of elements in such a way as to move the viewer's eyes in, around, and through a composition. A directional force can be vertical, horizontal, diagonal, triangular, circular, or a mix of many of these. Each directional force is commonly associated with its own expressive quality.

VERTICAL FORCE

Think of Greek columns, the Eiffel Tower, the Washington Monument, Northwest Indian totem poles: **vertical force** is an arrangement of elements along a vertical axis, often expressing height, power, stability, or grandeur. Verticality can also lift one's spirits upward, as in Gothic cathedrals and the Seattle Space Needle.

8.2   **GRANT WOOD**   *American Gothic,* 1930. Oil on beaver board, 30¹¹⁄₁₆ × 25¹¹⁄₁₆ in. unframed.

8.3   **GORDON PARKS**   *American Gothic,* 1942. Photograph.

Grant Wood's *American Gothic* (**8.2**) is one of the most famous paintings in the history of American art. It is a clear example of vertical force as a compositional device in painting. Its format is vertical, that is, its height is greater than its width. The figures in the painting are staunchly and stiffly vertical, and their verticality is reinforced by the three-pronged pitchfork, which is pointed directly upward. The architecture behind the couple also has an upward force, especially noticeable in the window, the pitch of the roof, and the lightning rod at the apex of the roof and painting. The painting is so straight, stiff, and rigid that educators at the Art Institute of Chicago, which owns the painting, wonder if the painting satirizes the narrow-mindedness and repression that has been said to characterize midwestern culture. Wood denied this interpretation. Many prefer to interpret the painting as "a glorification of the moral virtue of rural America."[4]

Regardless of Wood's intent, which we will never know with certainty, *American Gothic* is the subject of frequent parody. Gordon Parks, an innovative African American photographer, filmmaker, and social activist, made one of the first parodies in a photograph using Wood's title (**8.3**). Parks took a photograph of Ella Watson, who was part of a cleaning crew for a federal building in Washington, D.C. Parks was inspired to make the photograph after being subjected to repeated racism in restaurants and shops in the nation's capital, where he had come to accept a federally funded photography assignment. He posed Watson stiffly holding her broom upright with her mop beside her. The American flag looming behind and over her head dominates the photograph and significantly reinforces the verticality of the composition, which can be read metaphorically as oppressing the woman and by implication all black people in America. Unlike the white man and woman in Wood's *American Gothic,* who work for themselves on a farm that they presumably own, the black woman in Parks's *American Gothic* works for a government of a country that actively discriminated against people of color, particularly in 1941, decades before the civil rights movement to which Parks was an important contributor.

California artist Alison Saar's *Nocturne Navigator* (**8.4**) illustrates the directional force of verticality in a larger-than-life-size figure. Saar's woman is an escaped slave traveling at night along the Underground Railroad, guided by the stars. Her skirt has small holes of various sizes in it, arranged in the order of celestial constellations; neon behind the skirt shines through the holes, making them appear like the stars that aided the escapees on their dangerous journeys. Saar has emphasized the verticality of the female form by exaggerating the length of its legs beneath the skirt,

8.4   **ALISON SAAR**   *Nocturne Navigator,* 1998. Copper, wood, and neon, 144 in. high.

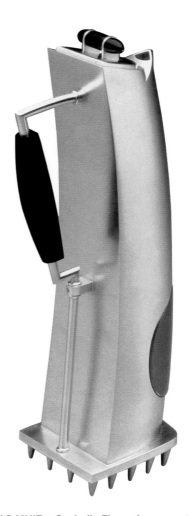

8.5   **THOMAS MUIR**   *Cycladic Figure Impregnated* (**coffee server**). Sterling silver, gold, anodized aluminum, and oxidized copper.

and the skirt itself is slightly raised off its pedestal, giving the figure a hovering effect. Palms raised, she gazes upward at the sky, a gesture both optimistic and prayerful. Wood (see 8.2), Parks (see 8.3), and Saar use verticality as a compositional device for social commentary.

Thomas Muir's sterling silver coffee server, *Cycladic Figure Impregnated* (**8.5**), is an excellent example of an artist using vertical directional force to express aesthetically elegant grace. The server sweeps upward from its rectilinear base with a gentle arch. The artist emphasizes the piece's verticality with a segmented tubular linear form that follows the curve of the vessel's body and serves as its handle. The oxidized copper circular form near the vessel's base draws attention by its red color, but the black anodized aluminum handle draws our attention upward, and the gold and black top of the server provides a culmination and visual resting point.

HORIZONTAL FORCE

An arrangement of elements along a horizontal axis produces **horizontal force,** which is associated with such attributes as peacefulness and tranquility. Think of reclining figures, split-rail fences, and a flat sandy beach. Grant Wood's *Spring Turning* (**8.6**) fills a horizontal format with its gentle rolling hills that expand to the left and right, off the canvas, implying great expanses of more verdant fields. Reinforcing the stability of the directional force is the orderliness of the rectangular and horizontal format of the Masonite on which the fields being plowed are depicted.

Eva Hesse's *Right After* (**8.7**) can be seen as an abstract landscape, with similarities to Wood's representational landscape (see 8.6). *Right After* undulates with a natural rhythm caused by gravity as it moves across space. The horizontal form of the piece enhances its calm mood.

8.6 GRANT WOOD *Spring Turning,* 1936. Oil on Masonite panel, 18¼ × 40¼ in.

8.7 EVA HESSE *Right After,* 1969. Fiberglass, approx. 5 × 18 × 4 ft.

8.8 **CHARLES CSURI** *Strawscape,* 2002. Computer-generated image, Unix environment, color ink on canvas, 38 × 52 in.

DIAGONAL FORCE

An arrangement of elements along a diagonal axis creates **diagonal force,** which brings a sense of nervous energy, vigor, and intense activity to a composition. Charles Csuri built his computer-generated image *Strawscape* (**8.8**) with diagonal directional force. Thousands of mathematically derived lines are crosshatched on diagonals. The largest mass of lines moves diagonally from upper left down to the middle bottom of the composition and then upward again in a diagonal to the right. The form at the top of the composition—more tilted lines that form a floating mass—may have blown from the forceful energy of the larger mass below it.

Cai Guo-Qiang's *Inopportune: Stage One* (**8.9**) simulates a car bombing in a dynamic sculpture consisting of nine real cars installed in the central rotunda of the Guggenheim Museum in New York City. Each car is diagonally positioned, and each car emits diagonally directed beams of light. Such angularity reinforces the suggested violence of the piece.

The programmers who constructed *Age of Conan: Hyborian Adventures* allow players of the game to control the characters in the game and the camera angles and distance from which they are viewed. The player who composed this screen shot (**8.10**) relied on many diagonals to enhance the excitement of a fight between a warrior and a spider creature. Both the player and the creature move along diagonal axes toward each other.

CIRCULAR FORCE

Notice the contrast between the violence of *Age of Conan* (see 8.10) and the peacefulness of *Figure of Budai Heshang* (**8.11**). Much of the contrast has to do with subject matter, but much of it also has to do with

8.9 **CAI GUO-QIANG** *Inopportune: Stage One,* 2004. Nine cars and sequenced multichannel light tubes, dimensions variable.

8.10 *Age of Conan: Hyborian Adventures,* screen shot, online game, 2008.

the diagonal forces in comparison to the circular force of the Buddha.

Circular force implies fullness, harmony, joy, and inner stability. You can achieve it by arranging elements along a circular path or radiating from a central point. The *Figure of Budai Heshang* presents the Buddha's stomach as large and round, and he has soft robes flowing over rounded knees. His smooth, round, full head and face evoke a welcoming response. In this incarnation, the Buddha is Qi Ci, a monk who lived in China's Zhejiang Province during the Five Dynasties (907–960 CE). Qi Ci frequented towns and begged for food wherever he saw it, talked with anyone who approached him, and slept wherever he found himself at night.[5] The roundness of the sculptured figure and its circular directional force give us a sense of peaceful centeredness. No angular forces jar us, as they do in the artifacts shown earlier (see 8.8, 8.9, and 8.10).

Judy Chicago's monumental installation *The Dinner Party* celebrates thirty-nine mythical and historically famous women, bringing them together at a table set with unique place settings made of ceramic plates and embroidered fabric, such as the one for poet Emily Dickinson (**8.12**). Chicago conceived the whole and individual parts of the piece and directed a group of women who meticulously crafted the pieces between 1974 and 1979. During these years, the feminist movement emphasized feminine traits of collaboration rather

8.11 *Figure of Budai Heshang,* China, early Qing dynasty (1644–1911), seventeenth century, Fujian Province. Dehua porcelain with clear glaze, 6⅞ in. high.

than masculine-centered worldviews emphasizing competition and domination. The collaborative effort also celebrates traditionally female artistic accomplishments, such as work with fabrics and china painting, that had been positioned as "domestic crafts" inferior to male-dominated "fine arts" such as painting and sculpture.

8.12   JUDY CHICAGO   *Emily Dickinson Place Setting, The Dinner Party,* 1974–1979. Ceramic and fabric.

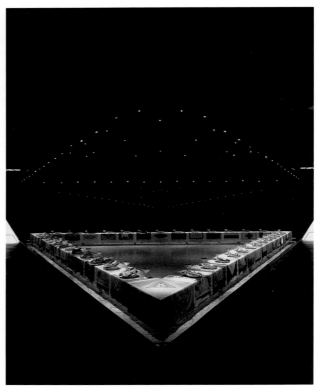

8.13   JUDY CHICAGO   *The Dinner Party,* 1974–1979. Installation view.

Circular motifs of the plates and the images on them are crucial to meanings of the piece, at a time when feminist theory celebrated biological differences of women, notably their ability to give birth. Thus the plates formally acknowledge the roundedness of the female body, especially its womb, and its receptive vulva in opposition to the aggression of the male body.

The circular plates and motifs in ceramic and fabric are positioned on a three-winged table that forms an equilateral triangle, which lends a structure of physical and psychological strength to support the circular elements. Although angular, the equilateral triangle connotes harmony rather than the conflict implied by unidirectional forces, as in the image from *Age of Conan* (see 8.10).

TRIANGULAR FORCE

The view of Judy Chicago's *The Dinner Party* in figure **8.13** shows how she used **triangular force,** an arrangement of elements relying on a triangular structure that provides actual or illusional stability. Think of the actual and psychological stability of a pyramid. Chicago's arrangement of the tables connotes the strength of the women represented in marked contrast to the circular

shapes of the ceramic plates, visually asserting that one can be both feminine and strong.

USING MULTIPLE DIRECTIONAL FORCES

In any work of art, more than one directional force is usually at play. For example, when you draw a simple horizontal line on a piece of paper, you have created a horizontal direction, but your horizontal line will also activate a sense of the verticality above and below it. The wooden African mask reproduced here (**8.14**) can be seen as primarily vertical, secondarily horizontal, and thirdly circular. The mask's verticality lends it strength and dignity; the horizontality of the eyes, brows, and lips provides a sense of serenity; and the ovoid circularity of the face gives us a sense of contemplative centrality. The mask was likely used to inspire awe in the young for their elders.[6]

Philip Pearlstein's painting *Two Models with Fan in Front* (**8.15**) mixes circular, diagonal, horizontal, and vertical forces to energize the languid pose of the two figures. The circular movement of the fan in the foreground is immediately apparent, and through it we see a stable triangle formed by the women. The women sit on an implied horizontal chair and floor that ought to provide a sense of rest, but the painting's horizon line is at an unsettling tilt for the mass of the embracing figures. The composition thus is directionally complex and dynamic, yet unified. Pearlstein consciously organizes the directional forces in his paintings:

> I look for a clash of the main axes of the primary forms. Diagonal, opposing movements result from the way the models are posed and how their forms move against the pieces of furniture. I rely on the angle where the wall meets the floor as a constant reference point, and against that I oppose the movements of the model's limbs . . . I would prefer to have my paintings "read" as moments in dance, in which the aesthetic of forms moving through space is seen as the motif, rather than as storytelling.[7]

Joan Snyder's mixed-media work *And Always Searching for Beauty* (**8.16**) has many directional forces, none of them particularly dominant. It approaches an "all-over" effect of works such as Jackson Pollock's drip paintings (see 5.47). The bright and light colors of her piece draw our attention toward the center of the painting, with the lightest section the focal point, but she diffuses the dominance of the highlight with diagonals moving upward as if toward a vanishing point. At the same time, the painting is fundamentally flat. She also uses horizontal and vertical forces with her placement of what seem like flowers distributed over much of the rectangle, which is full of vibrant energy.

8.14 Kakongo or Vili People's Mask, Zaire or Angola, late nineteenth–early twentieth century. Wood, pigment, fiber, 13 × 6 × 4 in.

8.15 PHILIP PEARLSTEIN *Two Models with Fan in Front,* 2000. Oil on canvas, 48 × 60 in.

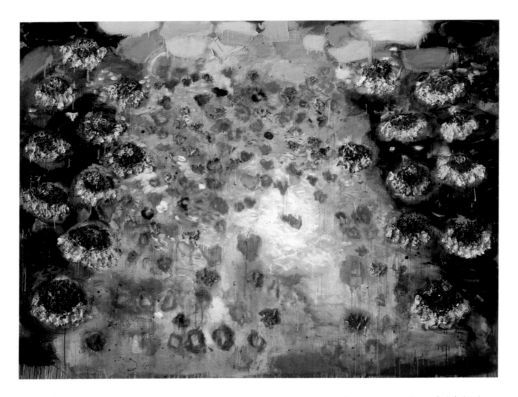

8.16   JOAN SNYDER   *And Always Searching for Beauty,* 2001. Oil, acrylic, papier-mâché, herbs on linen, 78 × 102 in.

8.17   GRETCHEN COCHRAN   *Pleasant Lake Bodice,* 1995. Crocheted wire, 3 × 2¾ × 1½ in.

8.18   JEFF KOONS   *Train,* 2003–work in progress. Operational replica of 1943 Baldwin 2900 class steam locomotive in stainless steel and aluminum, and Liebherr LR 1750 lattice boom crane, 160 ft. × 140 ft. 6 in. × 29 ft. 2 in.

Size, Scale, and Proportion

Three interrelated design principles having to do with the physical dimensions of an artifact and individual elements within the work are size, scale, and proportion. All three are properties of any artifact, and they can be manipulated for expressive purposes.

MAKING A STATEMENT WITH SIZE

The fixed physical dimensions of an object or element of art are a measure of its **size,** but we often think more generally of its smallness or largeness. Gretchen Cochran's crocheted wire sculpture *Pleasant Lake Bodice* (**8.17**) is shown here about actual size. The sculpture is only 3 inches high. Its small size directs us toward meaning and commentary. A bodice is a lace-up garment that sculpts a woman's torso, minimizing the waist in order to exaggerate the hips and chest. By making the bodice very small, the artist alludes to the discomfort of its restrictive function while also directing our attention to the network of wires that she has constructed. The size of the work forces us to move close to it, and this intimacy is also part of its meaning, asking us to consider the cultural pressures on femininity and the artist's implied social stance toward them.

Jeff Koons makes monumental sculptures in a renewal of the tradition of Pop Art. He is designing a 161-foot-tall outdoor sculpture (**8.18**) for the Los Angeles County Museum of Art. It will be an exact replica of a 1940s locomotive that will hang from an actual crane. Koons said the giant locomotive replica "will be absolutely so authentic a performance of a train, that it could fool an engineer who's worked on a train his whole life."[8] Museum administrators plan for the sculpture to dominate the museum entrance and to become a landmark for Los Angeles like the Eiffel Tower is for Paris.

PLAYING WITH SCALE

The comparative size of an element of art or object in relation to other elements or objects and to expectations of what is normal is its **scale.** Typically the standard of normal scale is the human body.

In Richard Misrach's photograph *Untitled* (see 8.1), the large horizontal format and the high angle of the shot reduce the human figure near the center of the im-

8.19 **CLAES OLDENBURG AND COOSJE VAN BRUGGEN** *Spoonbridge and Cherry,* 1985–1988. Aluminum, stainless steel, paint, 354 × 618 × 162 in.

age to the smallest possible scale. Misrach says that he uses scale to put people into proper perspective: "The huge scale enhances the beauty and the sense of the sublime but it also begins to expose our vulnerability and fragility as human beings."[9]

The sizes of the works by Cochran and Koons, and the size of *Spoonbridge and Cherry* (**8.19**), by Claes Oldenburg and Coosje van Bruggen, are absolute and stable. Each, however, also relies on scale. Comparing Cochran's *Pleasant Lake Bodice* to a woman's body makes the size of the sculpture meaningful. *Train* depends on the effect of its massive scale in proportion to the human body, which it dwarfs and overwhelms. The scale of *Spoonbridge and Cherry* depends on our knowledge of an edible cherry carried to one's mouth by a spoon.

Claes Oldenburg, a celebrated originator of the Pop Art movement, is best known for his ingenious, oversized, stuffed soft fabric sculptures of ordinary objects, such as hamburgers and ice cream cones, and for his monumental outdoor works in metals such as *Spoonbridge and Cherry*. Oldenburg has used the spoon as a motif in many of his drawings for sculptures. He and Coosje van Bruggen, his wife and collaborator, chose a spoon when they were asked to design a sculpture for the Minneapolis Sculpture Garden in Minnesota. The 5,800-pound spoon and 1,200-pound cherry were built at two shipbuilding yards in New England. The educators working on the sculpture garden refer to the work's "humorously gigantic scale." They attribute the cherry as Van Bruggen's contribution, referring to it as a "playful reference to the Garden's formal geometry, which reminded her of Versailles and the exaggerated dining etiquette Louis XIV imposed there."[10]

SEARCHING FOR PERFECTION IN PROPORTION

We refer to the relationship of the sizes of parts to one another and to the whole artifact as **proportion.** In his *Portrait of Claes Oldenburg* (**8.20**), photographer

8.20   DUANE MICHALS   *Portrait of Claes Oldenburg,* 1970. Photograph, 8 × 10 in.

Duane Michals (see 6.7) intentionally and meaningfully distorts the size of a portion of Oldenburg's face, disproportionately enlarging it by photographing him holding a magnifying glass in front of his face. Michals playfully mimics Oldenburg's key strategy in making his disproportionately large Pop sculptures.

When Jacob Lawrence painted *Typists* (**8.21**), he made the women's hands disproportionately large relative to the rest of their bodies, emphasizing the physicality of their labor. The women's shoulders and backs are bent forward toward their work, supporting this interpretation. The painting emphasizes the women's use of their hands and minimizes the use of their minds. Lawrence made the open file cabinets in the rear of the room all the same size, perhaps to suggest the routine drudgery of office work.

Classical Proportions. For many centuries, artists have tried to achieve harmonious compositions by developing formulas involving proportion. Through mathematical means, the ancient Greeks derived the **Golden Rectangle (8.22)**, which they believed to be the "perfect" rectangle—the rectangle that is most pleasing aesthetically. The Golden Rectangle is also called the **root 5 rectangle** because its length is the square root of 5.

The Golden Rectangle is derived from the **Golden Section** (or **Golden Mean**), a line that is sectioned so the ratio of the shorter segment is to the larger segment as the larger segment is to the whole (**8.23**). The ancient Greeks used this "perfect" ratio of length and width in architecture, book design, painting, sculpture, and many other artistic applications. The Parthenon (**8.24**), for example, is designed according to the requirements of the Golden Section.

Variations of the Golden Mean appear in art throughout the Renaissance, in later centuries, and in recent art. The Spanish Surrealist painter Salvador Dalí made *The Sacrament of the Last Supper* (**8.25**) inside a Golden Rectangle. He used the Golden Mean for positioning the figures. Part of an enormous dodecahedron floats above the table. The polyhedron above the table consists of twelve regular pentagons and has classical proportions.[11]

8.21   JACOB LAWRENCE   *Typists,* 1966. Tempera and gouache on paper, 22 × 29¼ in.

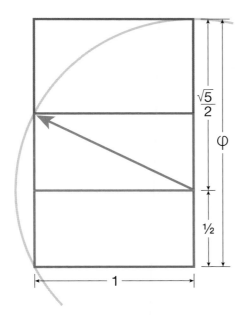

8.22 **Mathematical formula for the golden rectangle.**

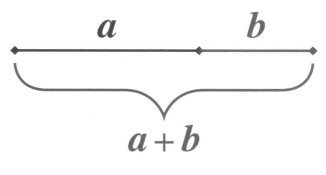

$a+b$ is to a as a is to b

8.23 **Formula for the Golden Section,** also called the Golden Mean.

8.24 **The Parthenon with a superimposed graphic** of the Greeks' use of the Golden Section to obtain the Golden Rectangle.

8.25 **SALVADOR DALÍ**
The Sacrament of the Last Supper, 1955. Oil on canvas, 65⅝ × 105⅛ in.

The Spiral. The Golden Rectangle also relates to the spiral (**8.26**), found in nature (**8.27**) in microscopic, human, and cosmic scales. The whorls on a pinecone and pineapple, the petals on a sunflower, and branches from some stems follow a geometrical harmony related to the Golden Rectangle.

A most striking feature of the Great Mosque of Samara (**8.28**) from ninth-century Iraq, is its winding minaret, which can be climbed by an exterior stairway, also based on the geometry of the spiral. Recall, also, Robert Smithson's *Spiral Jetty* on the Great Salt Lake (see 3.6).

Conclusion: Effective Uses of Size, Scale, and Directional Force

Size is an intrinsic property of any work of art. Every artifact also has scale in relation to its surroundings and to us. An artist's challenge is to be aware of the size and scale of his or her artifact and ensure that they are effective in relation to the intended meaning and expression. Similarly, when you arrange or use any design elements, you will likely be giving them one or more directional forces. By being conscious of the visual and psychological effects of directional forces, you can make your work more compelling. You can actually subvert your intended expression by not being aware, for example, of the peaceful connotations usually associated with horizontal forces and the more energetic connotations of diagonal forces in images and objects.

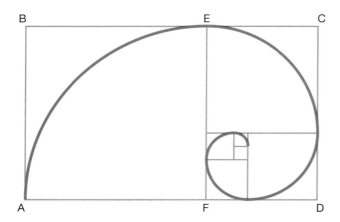

8.26 **The geometry of the spiral.**

8.27 **The spiral as found in nature.**

8.28 **The Great Mosque of Samara,** Iraq, ninth century.

9 Balance and Contrast

9.1 **PHILIP TAAFFE** *Desert Nocturne,* 2000. Mixed media on canvas, 8 × 102 in.

Balance occurs everywhere in nature in obedience to the laws of gravity. **Balance** is the equilibrium of weight and force, that is, a distribution of weight enabling someone or something to remain upright and steady. A standing upright tree growing in soil has balance established by its root system and by the directional forces of its trunk and branches; otherwise it would be uprooted by the unevenly distributed weight of its crown.

Construction cranes (**9.2**) have a long history, dating back to the ancient Greeks, and are a marvel of engineered balance. Designers of cranes are challenged by two major considerations: the crane must be able to lift a load, and it must remain stable when the load is lifted and moved to another location. Unfortunately, too often the news reports the loss of lives when construction cranes topple to the ground. Lack of balance has serious consequences.

Contrast is the use of opposing aspects of the elements of art, such as smooth against rough texture or a convex against a concave curve, to produce an intensified effect. The greater the degree of visual differences between the elements, the higher the contrast. Whether subtle or extreme, contrast is an aspect of any work. You can also use contrast as a way to balance an artifact visually and actually.

Balance and Contrast Key Terms

BALANCE   An equilibrium of weight and force; distribution of weight enabling someone or something to remain upright and steady.

CONTRAST   The use of opposing aspects of the elements of art to produce an intensified effect.

ACTUAL BALANCE   An arrangement of weight and force that allows a three-dimensional object to stand on its own.

ACTUAL WEIGHT   A measure of the heaviness of an object.

VISUAL BALANCE   The appearance of equilibrium in a work of art.

VISUAL WEIGHT   The appearance of heaviness of elements in a work of art.

SYMMETRICAL BALANCE   Visual or actual equilibrium of two halves of a composition mirroring each other in size, shape, and placement of elements of art.

APPROXIMATE SYMMETRICAL BALANCE   Equilibrium that is almost but not exactly symmetrical.

ASYMMETRICAL BALANCE   Visual or actual equilibrium of a composition not dependent on one side mirroring the other.

RADIAL BALANCE   Equilibrium achieved by elements emanating from a point, usually the center, in a composition.

SYMMETRY   Mirroring of elements on both sides of a horizontal, vertical, or diagonal dividing line.

VISUAL CONTRAST   Degree of visual difference among elements of art in a composition as a means of visual emphasis.

CONCEPTUAL CONTRAST   An implied opposition of ideas to emphasize unexpected differences.

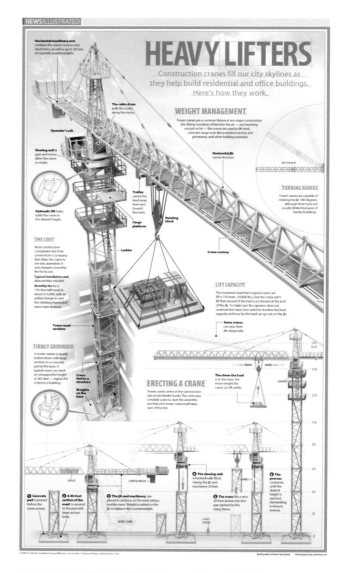

9.2   HIRAM HENRIQUEZ *Heavy Lifters,* 2008. Graphic illustration.

Balance and Weight: Actual and Implied

Balance as a principle of design regulates how artists and designers distribute weight and force within a work so that the work does not topple over, or appear to do so, because it is, or seems to be, heavier in one part or another. A work of art that has most of the prominent masses and shapes on one side and has no visual interest on the other side, for example, would seem unpleasantly lopsided and unbalanced.

In art, balance can be actual or implied. **Actual balance** is an arrangement of weight and force that allows a three-dimensional object to stand on its own. Artists using physical objects and materials must factor in the **actual weight** of materials: a measure of the heaviness or mass of an object, affected by gravitational force. **Visual balance** is the *appearance* of equilibrium in a work. Artists working in both three-dimensional and pictorial media must factor in the **visual weight** of the elements they use, that is, the appearance of heaviness or mass of those elements.

Andy Goldsworthy's *Penpont Cairn* (**9.3**) depends on equilibrium of actual weight and force to stand; were it not balanced, the cairn (a constructed mound of memorial stones) would topple to the ground in a heap. Goldsworthy selected stones from a quarry. The base stone for *Penpont Cairn* weighs six tons. After the stones were deliv its grain into slices, which he further broke up into more manageable pieces. He carefully shaped and then balanced each piece on pieces beneath it and across from it, as he raised the narrow oval from the ground, to its swelled middle, to its closed top.

Goldsworthy had built many cairns prior to building a permanent monument in his hometown of Penpont in Scotland. Some of his cairns were intentionally temporary, built on the seashore while the tide was out, and destroyed by the surf when the tide came in. He learned to build stable structures by trial and error, and many failed. He said, "The problem is that every stone has to be well supported or it will break, and it is not possible to use many very thin stones for leveling lest they crumble under the weight of the stone above."[1] You may also find that an intuitive sense of how to balance physical objects takes time to develop but is essential to working in many three-dimensional media.

Italian architect and designer Matteo Thun's sofa (**9.4**) has physical balance of weight and force; if it were not balanced—if, for instance, the backrest were heavier than the seat—it would topple over. It also has visual balance: the backrest is centered on the seat, and the two armrests protrude from opposite ends of the sofa. Although no components of the sofa are identical, they balance visually by the designer's use of similarity of shape and analogous colors.

In American artist Keith Haring's silkscreen *Untitled* (**9.5**), some elements look heavier or lighter than others, or equally weighted. The pyramid appears to be the heaviest object, because it is the largest and because we bring our prior knowledge of the heavy mass of pyramids to our viewing of the print. The spaceships seem lighter because of their smaller size and because they hover in the air. The woman is heavy in her pregnancy, but Haring portrays her as having a lightness of being by raising her arms and foot.

9.3 **ANDY GOLDSWORTHY** *Penpont Cairn,* 2000.

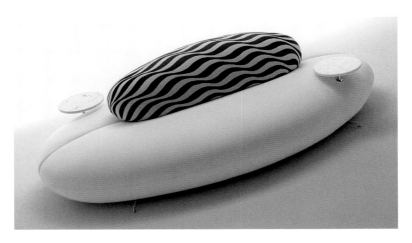

9.4 **MATTEO THUN** **Supersassi sofa, for Rossi di Albizzare,** 2000.

Haring visually balances his composition by the placement of objects and figure in his print and by his adept handling of proportional sizes. The visual center of the composition is the brightly colored pyramid, whose apex he placed at the vertical center of the image. He placed the base of the pyramid, however, to the right, and its two sides are not of equal size. He counterbalances the unequal distribution of size and mass to the right by placing the pregnant woman to the lower left.

9.5 KEITH HARING *Untitled* **(from the** *Fertility* **series),** 1983. Silkscreen, 106 × 127 cm.

Words are the names of people
you like:
Sally and Mary,
Thomas and Harry.
Words tell how you feel:
fine and dandy
and I like candy.

9.6 ANN RAND OZBEKHAN AND PAUL RAND *Sparkle and Spin,* 1957. Children's book, two-page spread.

The two-page spread from the children's book *Sparkle and Spin,* by the American husband-and-wife graphic design team of Ann and Paul Rand, provides an excellent example of balance in design (**9.6**). Each page is balanced, and the two facing pages present dynamic balance through contrast of large and small elements. The character's red face on the right side is massive on the single page. It is counterbalanced on the left page by the smaller red circle of the lollipop, the many small dots of candy in the upper left corner, and the narrative importance of the type placed above the lollipop.

A picture that seems unbalanced implies instability and creates tension. Documentary photographer Eugene Richards heavily weighted his photograph *Mariella, East New York* (**9.7**) to the left so that it looks unbalanced and effectively implies a lack of psychological stability in the subject's life. Richards's composition dramatically communicates the woman's desperation. The syringe, though relatively small in relation to the wide horizontality of the composition, emphatically angles downward, visually suggesting that it will pull the woman not only from the picture but also from life.

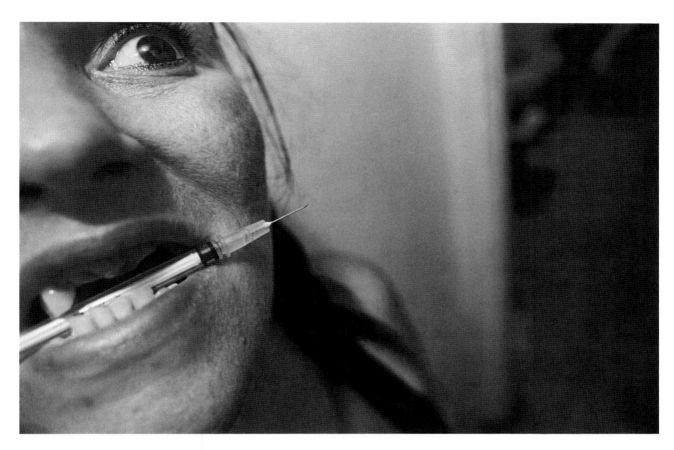

9.7 **EUGENE RICHARDS** *Mariella, East New York,* 1992. Photograph.

Kinds of Balance

There are four kinds of balance: symmetrical, approximately symmetrical, asymmetrical, and radial. **Symmetrical balance** refers to visual or actual equilibrium in which both halves of a composition mirror each other in size, shape, and placement of elements. When a work has an even distribution of weight, in a mirrorlike effect, but the symmetry is not perfect, it exhibits **approximate symmetrical balance.** If we surveyed all art, we would find that much of it is **asymmetrically balanced**—its visual or actual balance does not depend on one side mirroring the other. Last, a distribution of weight and force that emanates from a single point in a composition, usually in the center, exhibits **radial balance.**

SYMMETRICAL BALANCE

Symmetry is a mirroring of elements on both sides of a horizontal, vertical, or diagonal dividing line (**9.8**). Rorschach inkblots used in psychoanalysis are divided

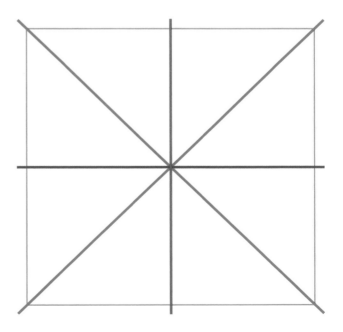

9.8 **An image can be symmetrically mirrored** along a vertical axis (red), a horizontal axis (blue), or diagonal axes (green), or along all axes simultaneously.

9.9 A solid tone rendering of the first of ten cards in the Rorschach inkblot test is a symmetrical design based on a vertical axis.

9.10 *Mandala of Guhyasamaja Akshobhyavajra,* Nepal, seventeenth century. Ground mineral pigment on cotton, 27 × 24 in.

along a vertical axis (**9.9**), thus they exhibit symmetrical balance.

Symmetrical designs can be very complex, as in Tibetan mandalas (**9.10**). In the Tibetan tradition, *mandala* literally means "center-circumference" and describes both the mandala's geometric structure and its religious significance. The center of the mandala is its essence, and the circumference is the grasping of the essence. Mandalas are representations of the spiritual embodiment of the Buddha; they are bodies of enlightenment. The basic structure of a mandala is symmetrical and carefully proportioned (**9.11**), but it also allows for many variations. The mandala's symmetry of shapes is simultaneously vertical, horizontal, and diagonal; however, the arrangement of colors is not precisely symmetrical. The symmetry functions to calm and center the minds and spirits of those meditating.

Symmetrical balance is also an organizational strategy in figurative work. Nivia González uses it to create a mood of calm contemplation. In *Angelita* (**9.12**), an imaginary line down the middle of the figure would divide both sides of the image in mirrorlike fashion. González's use of symmetry here is highly characteristic of her work. The artist usually makes images of women, often represented as ethereal beings and maternal figures. The figure's calmly downcast eyes and the muted palette of colors work with the symmetrical composition to reinforce this state of mind.

APPROXIMATE SYMMETRICAL BALANCE

Philip Taaffe's *Desert Nocturne* (see 9.1) looks at first glance to be symmetrical along its implied vertical axis up and down the middle of the painting, but it is not: the red linear shapes on the bottom left half of the canvas are different from those on the bottom right. If we imagine folding the painting in half along its vertical middle, the two sides do not match exactly. The burst shapes at the top of the canvas are symmetrically placed, but the changes in color make the symmetry of the placement of these shapes less obvious. Taaffe's painting thus plays with our initial assumption of exact symmetry, and the subtle variations add visual interest.

Apple Tree (**9.13**), by Russian artists Rimma Gerlovina and Valeriy Gerlovin, also has approximate symmetrical balance. The two artists work as a husband-and-wife team, modeling for their own photographs. Gerlovina is placed within the frame so that the part in her hair and the tip of her nose are mathematically centered along the vertical axis of the image. The two halves on either side of an imaginary fold down the center of the image do not, but almost, mirror each other. By placing the part in the figure's hair in the exact middle of the frame, the artists subtly move our visual attention from the hair, the face, hands, and apple to the trees and leaves in which the figure is embedded. The image is rich in connotations: Eve in the biblical Garden of Eden, seduction, "apple of my eye," and forming one's identity and future.

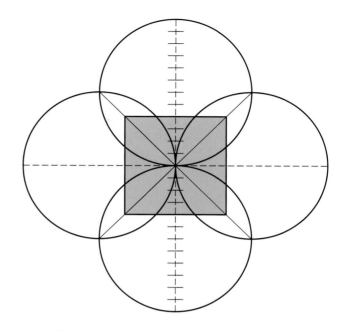

9.11 **The symmetrical geometry of a mandala.**

9.12 **NIVIA GONZÁLEZ** *Angelita (Little Angel),* 1995. Lithograph, 22 × 25 in.

9.13 RIMMA GERLOVINA AND VALERIY GERLOVIN
Apple Tree, 1995. Ektacolor photograph.

9.14 JOEL SHAPIRO *Untitled,* 1999. Bronze,
85½ × 67½ × 47¼ in.

ASYMMETRICAL BALANCE

Joel Shapiro's sculpture *Untitled* (**9.14**) is physically balanced—it is able to stand. It is made of bronze and is thus very heavy; it stands on one "leg," and it does not fall over. Its lack of symmetrical balance is one of the sculpture's most intriguing visual aspects because it gives the appearance of instability. The sculpture has no axis along which one side mirrors another. It has two "arms" and two "legs," but the arms are not the same in length, nor are the legs; yet it stands. The "figure" tilts forward but does not fall forward because its weight is distributed in asymmetrical balance. The expressive result of the sculpture's asymmetrical balance is dynamism and precariousness.

Sam Gilliam uses asymmetrical balance in his painting *Lullaby* (**9.15**). He employs six major sections in the painting, all of them of unequal size, and four of which expand the painting into more than a single rectangle. Nonetheless, he achieves a balanced composition by consistency of smoothly painted shapes over the whole painting. He also reinforces the balance of his composition by his placement and repetition of colors: blues and yellows visually hold the piece together.

RADIAL BALANCE

In nature, the shell of a sea urchin is radially balanced, as is the arrangement of seeds in a sunflower. Radially balanced objects are usually symmetrical or approximately symmetrical.

British artist Damien Hirst composed his montage *The Most Beautiful Thing in the World* (**9.16**) by adhering sets of actual symmetrical butterfly wings in a pattern that uses radial balance. The artwork has mirrorlike balance along any of its many axes, and its symmetry originates from its center and continues to its edges. The symmetry of the work is like the symmetry found in kaleidoscopic images created by the arrangement of mirrors. Hirst complements the natural symmetry of each pair of butterfly wings with his own symmetrical arrangement of all the butterfly wings.

In the *Changing Woman* tray by fiber artist Elsie Holiday, concentric circles that are woven together radiate around a center (**9.17**). The radial balance that Holiday employs is directly related to the intended meaning of the piece: *Changing Woman* symbolically depicts the positive energy emanating from the center of a young Navajo girl becoming a woman. Yet while the structure of the tray is symmetrical, its design is not. This, too, is symbolic—the girl's growth is irregular and asymmetrical, but she ultimately achieves a unified and centered wholeness.

Achieving Balance in Artifacts

Figure **9.18** illustrates six different ways of achieving balance. A larger shape is heavier than a smaller shape (**9.18a**), but darker colors can add weight to a shape (**9.18b**). Texture adds weight to a shape, and denser textures are heavier (**9.18c**). An irregular shape can balance a larger regular shape (**9.18d**). Two or more smaller shapes can balance a larger one (**9.18e**). A small dark shape can balance a large light shape (**9.18f**).

Susie Rosemarin achieves balance in *(#351) Blue Galaxy* (**9.19**) by color, texture, light, and symmetry organized with a subtle use of radial symmetry that is also symmetrical along both vertical and horizontal axes. She distributes various tones of blue evenly over the canvas. The lighter tones radiate from the lightest tone in the center of the painting. She achieves an allover pattern effect by use of a consistent visual texture over the whole canvas.

Julian Stanczak's *Mirrored* (**9.20**), as the title implies, is based on symmetrical balance along a vertical axis. With his use of transparent colors, he allows us to see through each layer of shape upon shape upon vertical lines that form the background of the painting. The transparency of the triangular shapes is reminiscent of folded paper that builds in density of tone, as one "fold" seems to overlap the one beneath it. The work is about mirroring and balancing made visible.

Ronald Bladen achieves actual balance in a large, 23-foot-tall aluminum outdoor sculpture, *The X* (**9.21**). The sculpture possesses a very stable symmetrical balance by the even distribution of actual weight and visual weight of the letter *x*. The thickness of the two-dimensional letterform also adds actual and apparent stability. The black paint on the aluminum reinforces the look of weight and mass and the work's strength and stability.

Sally Michel uses approximate symmetry to balance *Married Couple* (**9.22**). She has split the canvas in two by the separation of the two figures, visually

9.15   SAM GILLIAM   *Lullaby,* 2008. Acrylic on panel, 85½ × 47 × 4 in.

joined by their arms on the table they share. The male figure on the right is larger, bulkier, and takes up more space than the woman. His midsection is broader than the woman's, and a cat rests on his crossed legs, further adding to the mass of his shape. He thus carries more visual weight than the woman, but Michel balanced her composition with color, giving the seated woman more orange on her chair.

9.16   DAMIEN HIRST   *The Most Beautiful Thing in the World,* 2003. Household gloss paint with butterfly wings, 84 in. diameter.

9.17   ELSIE HOLIDAY   *Changing Woman,* 2000. Woven basket, 12 in. diameter.

a.

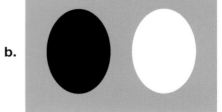

b.

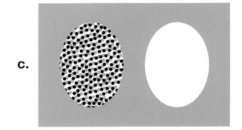

c.

d.

e.

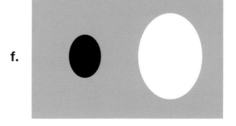

f.

9.18   Ways of achieving balance in artifacts.

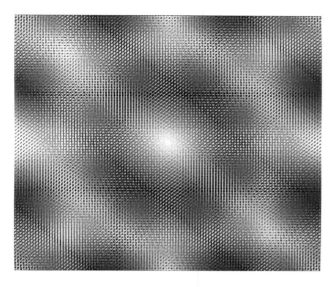

9.19 **SUSIE ROSEMARIN** *(#351) Blue Galaxy,* 2006. Acrylic on canvas, 72 × 84 in.

9.20 **JULIAN STANCZAK** *Mirrored,* 1971. Acrylic on canvas, 40 × 50 in.

April Gornik (**9.23**) employs asymmetrical balance in her landscape of dramatically stormy gray clouds that dominate the canvas. She balances the visual weight of the clouds with the light band of sunlight remaining on the plane of grass in the middle ground of the lower portion of the canvas. She also employs asymmetrical balance in her use of the trees on the right and left of the canvas. The three trees on the right of the canvas are visually heavier and more massive than the smaller tree to their left. With light and color, Gornik provides the smaller tree with emphasis: although it is small, the dark little tree stands out against its background, whereas the larger three trees stand against a dark background, reducing the attention the artist brings to them, achieving visual equilibrium.

Kay WalkingStick composed an asymmetrical canvas that she balances with patterning and space in *Orchide/Escaping the Garden* (**9.24**). She has positioned the dark legs of a couple to the right of the canvas. The legs are the darkest value in her painting, and because they are placed to the far right of the canvas, the composition would seem to be unevenly weighted to the right. However, she has balanced the legs with the patterning of plant life to the left of the composition. She balances the heavier one-third section with the two-thirds of the canvas to the left occupied by patterning.

9.21 **RONALD BLADEN** *The X,* 1968. Painted aluminum, 23 ft. tall.

9.22 **SALLY MICHEL** *Married Couple,* 1974. Oil on canvas, 40 × 50 in.

F. C. Ware's page from his graphic novel (**9.25**) symmetrically balances an arrangement of repeated colors while subtly communicating the routine monotony of time spent in hospital waiting rooms. Ware's choice of "institutional green," a muted color palette, and a symmetrical arrangement of panels reinforces his narrative. The balanced color composition (the green chair and bland yellow floor are symmetrically placed in each corner panel) contributes to the expressive meaning of his story.

Contrast

Contrast is juxtaposition. You can juxtapose different elements in a single artifact, such as types of texture, warm and cool colors, or light and dark tones, or you can juxtapose contrasting or conflicting ideas in a single artifact, such as war and peace. Contrast depends on comparisons that you cause the viewer to see and

think about. In a basic sense, every artifact must have contrast, some degree of visual differences between the elements, or else it would be invisible. Degrees of contrast vary, from high, stark contrast to low, subtle contrast.

VISUAL CONTRAST

The degree of visual difference among elements of art in a composition as a means of emphasis is termed **visual contrast.** Robert Irwin delights in contrast in many of his pieces. His Getty Garden (see 6.2) is a study in contrasts of plant materials' colors and textures: some of his juxtapositions in the garden are bold, and others are subtle. His piece *Untitled* from 1968 (**9.26**) is typical of many of his gallery installations that delight in subtlety. *Untitled* is done in very low contrast, consisting of dim light and shadows. Walking hurriedly through a gallery, you might not even notice it. *Untitled* is an actual convex, spray-painted disc held about a foot

9.23 **APRIL GORNIK** *Storm Field,* 2008. Oil on linen, 75 × 78½ in.

9.24 **KAY WALKINGSTICK** *Orchide/Escaping the Garden,* 2005. Oil on wood, 16 in.× 32 in.

9.25 **F. C. WARE** **Page from** *Jimmy Corrigan, The Smartest Kid on Earth,* 2000.

9.26 **ROBERT IRWIN** *Untitled,* 1968. Synthetic polymer paint on aluminum and electric light, disc: 60⅝ in. diameter.

from the wall by a central post. The disc is softly lit from four angles so that it creates a cloverleaf of shadows. The center of the disc seems to be right up against the wall, but it is not. Careful viewers need to spend time with the work to tell what is happening, to distinguish what is near from what is far, and what is solid substance and what is immaterial.

The installation view of three of Ellsworth Kelly's paintings on display at the Venice Biennale in 2007 (**9.27**) exemplifies stark visual contrast, in several different senses. The saturated colors are in stark contrast to the white walls of the gallery. Although Kelly's canvases are rectangular and horizontal in orientation, hung parallel to the walls, floor, and ceiling of the gallery, Kelly has shifted them to different degrees of angularity, severely disrupting the visual stability established by the 45-degree regularity of the room in which the paintings hang.

Mumbai-born English artist Anish Kapoor created a site-specific monumental installation for Nantes Museum of Art (**9.28**). He made the work of a huge red-wax mound that slowly moves through the museum, from the entry hall to a deep end of a patio, leaving dramatic smudges and scraps of red wax on the white pillars and floor. Its contrasts are many: white against red, circular against rectangular, and messiness in pristine museum spaces. The museum's educators interpret the piece by pointing out its various uses of contrast: "He works matter, light, space, using contrasts such as empty-full, male-female, concave-convex, inside-outside, material-immaterial, visible-invisible . . . This planned ambivalence gives his works, every time more monumental, a quality of mystery and infinity."[2]

John Tremblay uses radial symmetry in a fairly simple and straightforward composition, with uniform texture to create the striking sculptural painting *Major Stars* (**9.29**). Its effectiveness is due largely to contrast of shape and color. He uses strips of saturated colors against a white wall, enhancing the brilliance of the colors. The rectangular strips form a contrasting circle. The circle itself is in marked contrast to the rectilinear wall on which it hangs.

Ruari McLean's cover design for *The Thames and Hudson Manual of Typography* (**9.30**) relies on simple stark contrast: red, white, and black; a dominant directional force of verticality with thin and small horizontal bands of type; and lowercase type predominating over type with uppercase and lowercase. The starkness of the contrasty cover gets our attention and communicates clearly that the book is about type and how it can be used.

CONCEPTUAL CONTRAST

Contrast can also be used in the form of **conceptual contrast**—an implied opposition of ideas to emphasize unexpected differences. Meg Webster frequently makes rounded vessels, but *Melted Weapon Box* (**9.31**) deviates from her usually simple vessels into a strong social statement. She juxtaposes an assault rifle standing next to a vessel in the form of a cubic steel box that contains

9.27   **ELLSWORTH KELLY**   *Installation,* 52nd Venice Biennale, 2007.

9.28   **ANISH KAPOOR**   *Past, Present, Future,* 2006. Wax and oil-based paint, 345 × 890 × 445 cm.

an aluminum cube. She made the box and the cube by melting a rifle and reconstituting it into simple geometric volumes. She has contrasted the complex silhouette of the metal that kills into a simple container upon which one can calmly meditate. Out of the same materials she provides us with two very different objects with two very different sets of connotations. In the piece, she uses both visual and conceptual contrast.

Kara Walker is a contemporary American artist who makes use of both visual contrast and conceptual contrast to explore historical aspects of race, gender, sex, and violence. Walker cuts images from black paper and glues them directly on walls to create silhouette murals. The black paper on white walls provides stark visual contrast. Her choice of medium is also in stark contrast

9.29 **JOHN TREMBLAY** *Major Stars,* 2008. Acrylic on canvas, 143½ × 143½ in.

9.30 **RUARI MCLEAN** *The Thames and Hudson Manual of Typography,* 1992.

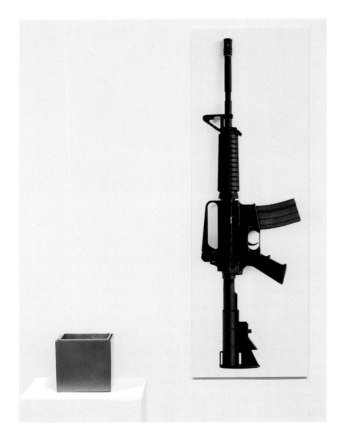

9.31 **MEG WEBSTER** *Melted Weapon Box,* 2008. Steel, aluminum, photograph, box: 4⅜ × 4⅜ × 4⅜ in.; photograph: 11¾ × 36¾ in.

conceptually to the subject matter of her images: nineteenth-century artists used black paper silhouettes to make flattering likenesses of their white subjects. Walker uses the medium to produce grotesque portraits of blacks and whites from that period. *Before the Battle (Chickin' Dumplin')* (**9.32**) shows a slave and a soldier engaged in a sexual act. The woman drops a "chickin'" drumstick, a stereotypic reference to blacks, as the soldier enjoys her "dumplin's."

Walker's use of absolute visual contrast of black against white is a perfect formal choice for her depiction of stereotypes: both silhouettes and racial stereotypes block out the particularities of details. Walker describes the method and intent of her work:

> Part of the reason my work is controversial is that it appropriates the male gaze: looking closely, not averting the eyes, facing things squarely. That means having to stare down all sorts of uncomfortable things, having to brave ugly situations with humor and distance. Distance is easy for me, being shy, but acquiring a sense of humor takes balls. My approach to making art is arguably female: I'm doing things—paper cutting, diary keeping, watercoloring, romance writing—that are steeped in second-class status. Silhouette cutting in its heyday was deemed a useful activity for women and invalids. But my method is sneaky, seductive, dark, and dangerous, because I'm using these seemingly harmless tools to face some really harsh truths about subjects like race and violence.[3]

Dutch designer Guido Ooms makes witty objects of contrasting materials and ideas. His computer memory sticks (**9.33**) are embedded in pieces of wood that he finds on the forest floor near his home. He thus contrasts nature (trees) and culture (computer technology) in the objects, playing on the name "memory sticks." His use of contrast is intellectually humorous, based on wordplay, and the contrast is of natural and human-made materials.

Conclusion: The Inherent Qualities of Balance and Contrast

Actual balance is crucial to healthy living. As infants, we learn to balance our bodies in stable sitting and standing positions and then learn to propel ourselves forward first with wobbly steps, frequently crumpling to the floor, until we can balance our weight and move forward with ease and nimbleness. As youngsters, we learn to balance objects, stacking blocks, for instance, or by playing games meant to develop our balancing abilities, such as carrying an egg on a spoon as we walk forward. As we age, yoga balancing postures can help us balance and strengthen our bodies to maintain physical as well as emotional equilibrium.

9.32 KARA WALKER *Before the Battle (Chickin' Dumplin'),* 1994. Cut paper and adhesive on wall.

Visual balance is also necessary to our sense of psychological equilibrium. As artists and designers, you have many ways to achieve actual and visual balance in objects and compositions when you design and arrange elements for functional, expressive, and communicative purposes. Actual balance can save or endanger lives (see 9.2). Actual and visual balance can bring calmness to your work, as in the symmetrically balanced image by González (see 9.12). Other ways of using balance add dynamic tension, as in Richards's photograph of the heroin addict (see 9.7). Awareness of the balance

9.33 GUIDO OOMS USB Memory Sticks, 2006. Natural wood and computer flash drives.

that you are using will aid you in achieving the physical and visual results you desire.

Although contrast is an inherent part of any work— any two elements contrast by nature of being different in some way—as an artist or designer, you can choose the degree of visual contrast you wish to use to create visual interest and to establish juxtapositions of ideas to make powerful conceptual artifacts.

10 Repetition, Unity and Variety, Emphasis and Subordination

**10.1 MIRIAM SCHAPIRO *Untitled,* *c.* 1975. Oil on canvas, 40 × 40 in.

Repetition
Unity and Variety
Emphasis and Subordination
Conclusion: Reflecting on Design Principles

One of the greatest challenges and joys for creators of artifacts is obtaining unity in a work—the feeling that a composition holds together well visually and is designed to be experienced as a whole—while also offering enough variety to add interest to the work. A thoroughly unified work may lack variety and may not hold our attention after its initial impact. A monochromatic painting, for example, will get our attention because of the oddity of having a painting of one color, or not even of a color, such as *Black Square on a White Field,* by Russian painter Kazimir Malevich (**10.2**). Malevich's painting is undoubtedly "visually unified," but any variations it may have, such as the mark of a brush, will not likely hold our visual attention for very long, although the painting may hold our mindful attention as we wonder about its significance in the history of art.

A time-honored and important means of achieving unity and variety is through the use of repetition in a variety of ways. Emphasis and subordination are two other design principles that will help you unify the works you make while also helping you achieve variety that will gain and hold viewers' attention.

Some instructors teach aspects of Gestalt psychology to account for and explain formal aspects of artifacts. **Gestalt psychology** is an aspect of cognitive psychology developed in the early twentieth century by German psychologists and philosophers investigating how the mind works to see unity and to seek closure in experiences. The German term *Gestalt* translates as "figure" or "form" in English and thus has implications for the mind's perception of imagery and spaces. The "gestalt" of an object or space refers to our recognition of wholes, rather than a collection of discrete parts, and to our response to whole images, objects, and spaces. In more familiar art language, sculptor Donald Judd made the summary observation that an artifact's "quality as a whole, is what is interesting."[1]

Rather than treat knowledge gained from Gestalt psychology as a separate and distinct means of organizing and recognizing artifacts, such knowledge is woven into the following discussions of repetition, unity and variety, and emphasis and subordination.

Repetition, Unity and Variety, Emphasis and Subordination Key Terms

GESTALT PSYCHOLOGY   An aspect of cognitive psychology developed in the early twentieth century by German psychologists and philosophers investigating how the mind seeks unity and closure. The "gestalt" of an artifact is the general feeling it evokes in viewers—their response to the whole object.

REPETITION   Use of any element or object more than once in an artifact in order to structure a viewer's experience of that work.

PROXIMITY   The relative distance between elements in an artifact.

PATTERN   A systematic *repetition* of an element in a work.

RHYTHM   The movement, fluctuation, or variation marked by a regular recurrence of related elements.

VISUAL RHYTHM   The ordered *repetition* of design elements within an artifact to move a viewer's attention.

IRREGULAR RHYTHM   A rhythm that omits expected stresses or adds unexpected stresses.

UNITY   The feeling that a composition holds together well visually and is designed to be experienced as a whole.

VARIETY   Visual diversity to avoid an unintended monotonous composition and to hold the viewer's interest.

GRID   A mathematically designed series of horizontal and vertical lines in which to organize elements.

EMPHASIS   Arrangement of elements of art to make some areas the primary focus of a viewer's attention.

SUBORDINATION   Arrangement of elements of art to support a larger visual theme, idea, or motif.

VISUAL HIERARCHY   Arrangement of design elements in terms of their importance to the expressive purpose of the work.

FOCAL POINT   An area of an artifact that grasps and holds a viewer's attention.

DIRECTIONAL LINES   Visible or implied lines that move the viewer's attention to an artifact's *focal point.*

10.2   KAZIMIR MALEVICH   *Black Square on a White Field,* *c.* 1923. Oil on canvas, 41¾ × 41⅞ in.

10.3   MUSEUM OF COMIC AND CARTOON ART logo, 2006. New York City. Design by Seymour Chwast.

Repetition

The design principle of **repetition** refers to the use of any element or object more than once in an artifact. Repetition can structure a viewer's experience of an artifact and can unify a design by repeating a shape. The logo for the Museum of Comic and Cartoon Art (**10.3**) is unified by the replication of round shapes for the character's head and torso, repeated again in the small *o* of MoCCA. The character's curvilinear tail reinforces the unity of the whole design. The designer's choice to leave space between the cartoon figure's legs and tail and black circle of a body also allows the viewer to mentally join the legs and tail to complete the figure. This use of an aspect of Gestalt psychology asserts the need for humans to bring closure and completeness to all experiences, including visual experiences.

American photographer Emmet Gowin uses repetitions of pairs in **proximity,** the relative distance between design elements, in *Barry, Dwayne and Turkeys* (**10.4**). In Gestalt theory, proximity is a means of establishing unity. The pairs in proximity that Gowin employs are in the title of the photograph, *Barry, Dwayne and Turkeys,* the two boys, and the two turkeys accentuated by two overturned circular objects behind them. Gowin also uses repetition of gesture: the smaller boy cranes his neck up to the other to tell him something, and one turkey turns its head to the other, like the boy. The differences in the gestures and positions of each member of the two pairs are the varieties that add interest. The two boys face in one direction and the turkeys in another. The photograph would not cause the delight

that it does were all the pairs posed or captured in symmetrical sameness.

Brazilian photographer and photojournalist Sebastiao Salgado's famous photograph of men working a gold mine in Brazil is about repetition, both in a formal sense and, more importantly, in a social sense. *The Gold Mine* (**10.5**) relies on repetition extensively, showing thousands of men as if they were a swarm of ants. Salgado explains that 50,000 mud-soaked men, called "mud hogs," like pigs that wade in dirt and slime, work the mines in the dry season from September through January. Nine men work each small plot, three digging and six carrying sacks of dirt weighing between 65 and 130 pounds up a myriad of ladders to the top of the mine where the gold is extracted from the mud.[2] Repetition is the primary design principle by which Salgado has communicated a miserable aspect of a human condition. So, while the repetition in *The Gold Mine* might be visually interesting, its use is a form of moral condemnation of an abusive labor practice.

Although repetition in artifacts is often pleasing, giving us a sense (a gestalt) of comfort in continuity, Salgado and Kiki Smith have used repetition for the opposite effect, one of discomfort. Smith's sculpture for a floor, *Jersey Crows* (**10.6**), relies on the repetition of twenty-seven fallen crows that forms a sense of chaos. The work is unified by the artist's use of repetition, but by placing the birds in the gallery in an unexpected and unpredictable way, with no apparent system, she adds mystery concerning the cause of the crows' deaths. The artist said, "I've had some of my sculptures in my house and they scare me."[3]

PATTERN

A systematic repetition of an element throughout a work forms a **pattern.** Carrie Ruby is an American designer who devotes herself to the creation of pattern designs. One of her patterns (**10.7**) repeats the subject matter of a crown in an abstract linear representation. The crowns form horizontal rows that slightly overlap into the rows above them. Vertical columns are aligned by the cross on top of the crowns with uniform white space in contrast to a consistently muted palette of colors.

Patterns are especially important in fabric design (**10.8**), upholstery material, carpeting, wrapping paper, wallpaper, and other applied uses. The interlocking poppies in Finnish designer Maja Isola's printed fabric for Marimekko form a striking pattern by her repetition of flowers and stems. There are variations in the individual flowers, but the repetition of the flower on a white ground of the fabric creates some variation in a bold visual motif based on repeated shapes, colors, and the subject matter of flowers.

The Ruby (see 10.7) and Marimekko (see 10.8) patterns are designed to be mass produced. There is a long tradition of handmade patterns through time and across cultures. A robe from nineteenth-century Liberia (**10.9**) is a beautiful handmade example of the use of pattern. The complex design is composed of many patterns in a single artifact. The vertical stripes of blues separated by thin stripes of white form the dominant pattern, which is accented with a checkered pattern of smaller rectangles of the same colors at the bottom of the robe. The dominant blue-striped pattern frames the more elaborate and intricate patterns joined together off center at the top of the robe as the central point of interest in the overall design.

REPETITION AND RHYTHM

Recurring elements that are related can move, fluctuate, or vary and create **rhythm.** Movement is an inherent aspect of rhythm, as in the fluctuation and speed of one's speech; the accent, meter, and tempo of music; the repetition in a narrative of a phrase, incident, character type, or symbol; or the effect created by the elements in a performance piece or a movie that relate to the temporal development of the action.

10.4 **EMMET GOWIN** *Barry, Dwayne and Turkeys, Danville,* 1970. Photograph.

10.5 **SEBASTIAO SALGADO** *The Gold Mine, Serra Pelada, State of Pará, Brazil,* 1986. Photograph, size variable.

10.6 KIKI SMITH *Jersey Crows,* 1995. Silicon bronze, twenty-seven units, each 16 × 19½ × 23½ in., installation dimensions variable.

10.7 CARRIE RUBY Pattern design, 2007.

Visual rhythm is the ordered repetition of design elements within an artifact with a systematic organization. It is a way of moving a viewer's attention.

Film directors, television producers, and their editors establish visual rhythms of shots in sequences that organize narrative material in ways that make sense, at a pace that fits the content of the production. Television producers of live events, such as football games (**10.10**), have the daunting challenge of instantly selecting which shot to show us on our television screens. A selection is provided to them instantaneously by many cameras situated at different distances and angles and focused on different aspects of a complex activity involving players on a field, referees, coaches and players standing on the sidelines, and thousands of spectators reacting to the events on the field. Producers of live events or directors and their editors establish rhythms of shots, from close to long to medium; from one player to another, to the interaction of a group of players, to crowd reaction; and so forth. Editors of actions that will be shown at a later date have the luxury of time to review and reedit the production for final viewing. Producers of live events have no such leeway and must make instant decisions that are transmitted in real time to viewers.

Lorna Simpson's *Easy to Remember* (**10.11**) is a work made to be experienced as a video installation on a gallery wall. It is a beautifully calming piece due to its use of rhythmic sound and moving pictures. Were we in its presence, we would simultaneously see fifteen close-up views in black and white of the mouths of African Americans and hear the men and women calmly humming nonverbal sounds for two minutes and thirty-five seconds. Its calm and consistent rhythm matches its gentle sounds and provides a mesmerizing meditative viewing experience.

Miriam Schapiro's *Untitled* (see 10.1) regularly and systematically repeats colors and shapes from one vertical edge to the other, forming a regular rhythm of predictably interweaving design elements. Schapiro's arrangement suggests a series of short, regular beats. This elegant piece with its visual delights of patterned shapes and colors has political content as well as formal beauty. It is usually women who sew, quilt, knit, embroider, and make decorative stitching. Artworks that rely on such media are often denigrated as merely "decorative," minor "crafts," lacking the seriousness and depth of "high art." Schapiro's fans celebrate these media while expanding

10.8　**Marimekko, fabric manufacturing plant.**

10.9　**Man's Robe, Liberia,** nineteenth century. Cotton and felt gown (kusaibi), 92 × 180 cm.

10.10　**Television production studio, interior view** during a live broadcast of an American football game.

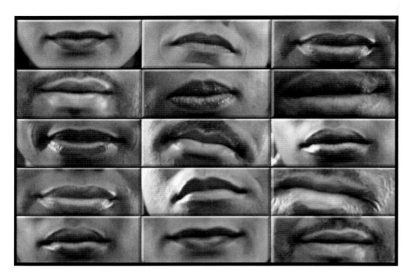

10.11   LORNA SIMPSON   *Easy to Remember,* 2001. Video installation with sound, 16mm black-and-white film, transferred to DVD, 2 minutes, 35 seconds.

notions of what can count as "high art." She is aware of such distinctions, but optimistically pursues her art, saying, "The art is successful for me when the passion is clear and the sensuous language is available to others."[4] In *Untitled,* Schapiro relies on a rhythmic pattern to achieve a sensuous language readily available to us.

In *Beaded Hair* (**10.12**), Amos Ferguson, an intuitive artist of the Bahamas, uses a regular rhythmic "beat" of triangles in the women's skirts and hair. The visual rhythms of the picture are established by shapes of triangles and dots and by regularly repeated color. The visual rhythm adds to the illusion of music that the women seem to be making: the one on the right plays a drum and each has a wind instrument in her mouth. The women's hips and dreadlocks seem to sway to the beat of their music. The horizon line dividing different tones of blue seems to indicate that they are on a beach.

Schapiro's (see 10.1) and Ferguson's (see 10.12) visual rhythms are regular, following a predictable pattern without deviation. **Irregular rhythms** are those that omit expected stresses or have less predictable repetitions. Such unpredictability can add variety and interest to a work. El Anatsui's *Fading Cloth* (**10.13**) is a weaving that uses an irregular rhythm. He made it out of flattened aluminum bottle caps that he has recycled into a large gorgeous wall hanging of discarded trash. His use of an irregular rhythm adds social meaning to the visual interest of his tapestry made of junk. Anatsui, a contemporary artist of Ghana, draws upon a broad spectrum of indigenous African cultures to make artifacts that express his concern for "the erosion of these inherited traditions by powerful external forces and the manner of their survival and transmission into the present. His deftly organized and sophisticated work represents an original synthesis of the many di-

verse histories of African art."[5] To achieve this synthesis of diverse cultures, he establishes a rhythm that he interrupts with another rhythm, and so forth, creating a kind of visual timeline of the development and decay of traditions.

Trenton Doyle Hancock, an African American artist, also establishes an irregular rhythm in his painting *Good Vegan Progression #2* (**10.14**), especially with the placement of trees and their varying sizes in proportion to the whole felt. We can begin to establish a count of four trees, from left to right, but that rhythm becomes less regular with unexpected stresses and spaces of both trees and colors. Nevertheless, the repetitive use of elements in a systematic way provides a sense of interesting wholeness in a complex composition. We could appreciate the whole composition as a score for a symphonic musical composition played out over time.

Unity and Variety

Through the use of **unity,** you can imply oneness, harmony, and the feeling that a composition holds together well visually. Pop artist Roy Lichtenstein expressed the importance of unity when he said, "Organized perception is what art is all about . . . I intend to unify."[6] You can use any or all of the design principles we have examined so far—from balance to repetition—to unify your artwork and clarify what you hope to communicate. Too much unity, however, may result in visual monotony. A solution is **variety,** the introduction of visual diversity in a composition. Too much variety may in turn result in undesirable chaos, suggesting that you balance unity and variety to suit the expressive purposes of your work. Design the work so that viewers experience it as a whole while its variations hold their interest.

Contemporary American artist Allan McCollum offers a monumental example of unity and variety in a work of large scope. *The Shapes Project* (**10.15**) consists of 7,056 framed prints, each different from the others, and each signed and numbered, which he displays in a gallery as an installation on the floor. *The Shapes Project* is McCollum's attempt to produce "a completely unique shape for every person on the planet, without repeating."[7] He began the project in 2005, and it continues. The project involves a basic vocabulary of 300 parts that can be combined with a computer program in over 30 billion different ways, one for every person on the planet when the world population is predicted to peak in the middle of the twenty-first century.

McCollum has used his system to make different-shaped artifacts in addition to monoprints, including sculptures in Plexiglas, plywood, rubber, and other materials, in different sizes. He maintains unity in the monoprints by consistent use of black on white, in a standard size, within standard black frames, set up in orderly rows. He achieves variety by changing each shape so that it is unique, as is each one of us.

Frank Stella's round canvas (**10.16**) is a delightful mix of unity and variety. The American artist has unified the circular painting with arcs and semicircles composed with both symmetry and proximate symmetry. The arcs and semicircles mirror each other along a horizontal axis cutting through the middle of the canvas. Stella then varies the symmetry of the composition with colors that do not mirror each other. He involves us in the pleasant activity of solving the visual puzzle of how he has unified and varied the piece.

Graphic designer Todd Roeth's *Seasonal Colors* (**10.17**) is unified by the verbal concepts of the four seasons that compose a year and by his use of a single size of one typeface, Rockwell Regular. He adds

10.12 **AMOS FERGUSON** *Beaded Hair,* 1984. Plio-lux enamel on cardboard, 35¾ × 29¾ in.

10.13 **EL ANATSUI** *Fading Cloth,* 2005. Aluminum and copper wire, 10 × 38 ft.

10.14   TRENTON DOYLE HANCOCK   *Good Vegan Progression #2,* 2005. Mixed media on felt.

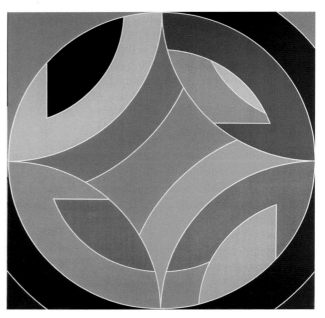

10.16   FRANK STELLA   *Flin-Flon IV,* 1970. Acrylic on canvas, 274.5 × 274.5 cm.

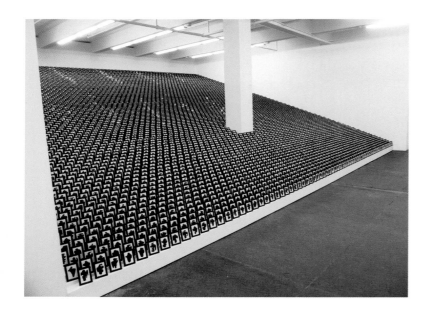

10.15   ALAN McCOLLUM   *The Shapes Project,* 2005–2006. Installation of 7,056 *Shapes* framed unique digital monoprints, each signed and numbered, 4.25 × 5.5 in.

Winter
Spring
Summer
Autumn

10.17   TODD ROETH   *Seasonal Colors,* 2008.

10.18   HANS HAACKE   *Wide White Flow,* 1967–2008. Installation, white silk fabric, electric fans, dimensions variable to space. Edition 1 of 3.

variety with a playful mix of colors of subtle grada-tions: "Winter" is a series of cool grays. With "Spring," he introduces pastels that are warmer than the winter colors, and he uses more variations of colors. The col-ors of "Summer" are saturated and the most varied of the four seasons. "Autumn" turns to earth colors that are more analogous than the colors for summer, getting us ready to repeat the cycle with analogous grays of winter. Roeth captures the variety of seasons with a pre-dictable and welcoming rhythm of change.

PRINCIPLES THAT UNIFY

Hans Haacke is a German American artist who has long been involved in investigating systems and processes, especially political and sociological processes. Early in his career, he created *Wide White Flow* (1967) at MIT and then reinstalled it in 2006 in a retrospective exhibi-tion in Germany (**10.18**). The installation stresses unity more than variety. A sea of white fabric gently moves

with the breeze from electric fans that are hidden so as not to disrupt the calm presence of the consistent gentle movement of the fabric. Haacke has said, "From the be-ginning the concept of change has been the ideological basis of my work. All the way down there's absolutely nothing static . . . nothing that does not change, or insti-gate real change."[8] *Wide White Flow,* however, empha-sizes change that is not disruptive but predictable and steady and soothing.

Tony Cragg is a British-born sculptor living and working in Germany. He uses a wide variety of materi-als in his work, including glass, porcelain, rubber, tree trunks, and metals, such as the bronze of *Red Square* (**10.19**). One commentator explains that Cragg's "sen-sitivity to different materials is and has been the start-ing point for his work. To a great extent, his choice of material has determined the form, which a sculpture has taken on. Different materials give different emotional experiences, both for the artist and for us as observ-ers."[9] *Red Square* is a unified organic, biomorphic, and

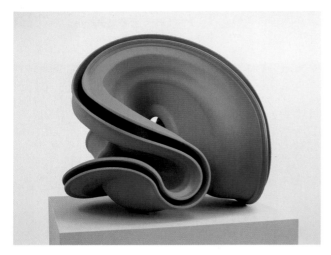

10.19 TONY CRAGG *Red Square,* 2005. Bronze,
167 × 73 × 70 in.

**10.20 STEVEN FINKE *Day 3: The Separation of the Waters Below
to Reveal Dry Land and the Creation of Plants; Day 5: The Creation of
Animals;*** and ***Day 6: The Creation of Humans,*** 1995. Mixed media, installation.

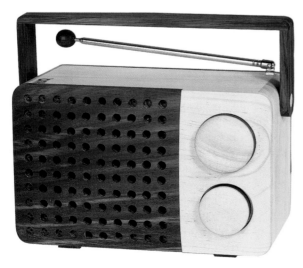

**10.21 SINGGIH SUSILO KARTONO Wooden radio wr01/
2bipod,** 2008. Pine and sonokeling.

abstract three-dimensional form in a single color, red,
made of a single material, bronze. The sculpture is one
continuous flowing and undulating form, smoothly
constructed, consistent with its curvilinear motif. Nothing distracts from its unified singularity.

Unlike Cragg's use of a single unified sculpture,
American artist Steven Finke's museum installation
about creation offers an example of unity and variety in
a grouping of many sculptures. Finke's challenge was
to create and arrange a variety of pieces into unified
works that interpret the seven days of creation as told
in Genesis (**10.20**). He achieves this with a sense of
whimsy. Each *Day* is unique while sharing a common
aesthetic sensibility through the handling of materials.

Day 3 refers to the day on which God com-
manded the waters to be gathered in one
place and land to appear and the earth
to bring forth grass, plants, and fruit-
bearing trees. Finke interprets this day
through a hand-hewn wooden table on
which rest obviously handcrafted symbolic
objects made of metal and glass. The symbolic objects refer to God's accomplishments on that day. The artist unified *Day
3* first by using the wooden table to create
a common visual background and a visual
container for the objects. All of the objects
are roughly the same size and share a diagonal directional force. All are made of
the same metal and glass and have a handmade look and feel, carefully crafted, but
not fussy.

Indonesian designer Singgih Susilo
Kartono created an aesthetically unified
functional object, a radio made of wood
(**10.21**), a material he chose for its environmental sustainability. He unifies the design
by use of a pattern in the form of a grid of negative dots
in the radio's speaker. He repeats and reinforces the
dot pattern by his use of circular knobs, a small sphere
on the end of the radio's antenna, light wood dowels
in the radio's dark handle, and rounded corners of the
rectangular object. The radio's wood grain flowing in
a horizontal direction is another unifying design element. The repetition of rounded forms gives the object
a pleasant visual and tactile appeal.

GRIDS: BASIC STRUCTURE
FOR UNITY OR VARIETY

You can subdivide a picture plane into smaller areas
using a **grid**—a mathematically designed series of horizontal and vertical lines. Grids allow you a basic structure to work with or work against: you can follow a grid
or use a grid for unity and deviate from it for variety.
Grids are especially useful in designing page layouts

for print and Web pages, providing a systematic structure in which you can place various elements such as headlines, body text, and pictorial elements. Grids are usually invisible in final production but are extremely useful in organizing space (**10.22**).

Grids are also a common means of making paintings, particularly in modern art. Chuck Close, for example, commonly uses a grid to structure his portraits in which each segment of his grid can be seen as an abstract composition in itself (see 3.4). American minimalist artist Agnes Martin made grids the subject matter of her work (**10.23**), seeing them as providing viewers with pure aesthetic pleasure.

Although Sitepoint and Martin follow the structures of their grids, American painter James Siena varies the grid, in a sense breaking it down or stretching its limits (**10.24**). Nevertheless, Siena's painting has a high degree of unity because of its grid structure. He also reinforces the unity of his painting by selecting a limited palette of muted color.

Iranian artist Shirazeh Houshiary and British architect Pip Horne also vary a basic grid structure in their design of a window as a major addition to a historically important church in Trafalgar Square in London. The original window was lost to bombs in the Second World War. At the center of the new window (**10.25**), the creative team has placed an ellipse, and from this ellipse they radiate a swirling, geometric grid of stainless steel frames. Their design is reminiscent of Christian symbols, such as Jacob's Ladder and the cross. A commentator sees political import to their use and variation of the grid structure of the window: "They

10.22   **Sitepoint: The Rule of Thirds,** variations of graphic material using one grid, 2008.

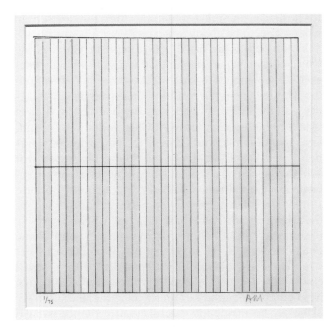

10.23   AGNES MARTIN   *Untitled,* 1998. Portfolio of 4 offset lithographs on GilClear paper, 12 × 12 in. Edition of 75, Details 1 and 4.

10.24 JAMES SIENA *Coffered Divided Sagging Grid (with glitch),* 2005. Enamel on aluminum, 29⅛ × 22¾ in.

10.25 SHIRAZEH HOUSHIARY AND PIP HORNE Window for St. Martin-in-the-Fields, Trafalgar Square, London, 2008. Etched mouth-blown clear glass and shot peened stainless steel frame.

have chosen a rather gynecological reworking of the ultimate symbols of Christianity and modernism—the cross and the grid." The "subtle curvilinear abstraction of the stained glass lattice feels very other and feminine, throwing the Church of England's slowly shifting conservatism towards matters of race, gender and sexuality into sharp relief."[10]

DESIGNING WORKS FOR VARIETY

Some artists, such as American sculptor and installation artist Sarah Sze, delight in pushing the boundaries of unity by going for variety. Sze makes site-specific temporary sculptural installations by gathering and assembling thousands of everyday objects that she arranges into fragile and expansive formations (**10.26**). Museum educators offer these insightful descriptions and interpretations of the artist's work:

> Sze's sculptures are flowing structures consisting of a conglomeration of small-scale household items that respond to and infiltrate the surrounding architecture. Like the information flow of the World Wide Web, her compositional language takes form by successively linking small bits of discrete information into a complex network. With an intensity born of a laborious patchwork technique that is at once painterly and sculptural, the interplay between individual components and overall structure allows Sze to explore the boundaries between art and everyday life.[11]

There is structure in her installation, but one must look for it, just as one must sometimes look for structure in what seems to be chaos in the world.

Fiona Rae is a British artist born in Hong Kong who makes abstract paintings that use seemingly random subject matter to create unexpected juxtapositions that challenge simple readings and understandings because of their lack of conceptual continuity. Her subject matter holds together visually while pushing the boundaries of unity far toward diversity. Of her ways of working, Rae says, "I like lively, heartfelt and witty art that can also be cool and ironic. Doesn't necessarily have to be painting, but that's my favorite thing, partly because I think it's the hardest way to be fresh and original in the 21st century." She admits to borrowing from "a dizzying range of sources, from abstract art to comic books." She believes that what is "common to all her work is the self-conscious juxtaposition of flat areas of color with dragged, daubed paint marks."[12] Although her compositions may appear accidental and arbitrary (**10.27**), she maintains careful control of her painted surfaces, and she has developed and maintained a distinct style. The title of her painting, *Cute Motion!! So*

10.26 **SARAH SZE** *Tilting Planet,* 2006. Mixed media, dimensions variable.

Lovely!!, is an acknowledgment that despite the seeming randomness of her imagery, she knows what she is trying to achieve—lovely and overdone motion.

Emphasis and Subordination

In order to achieve unity *and* variety, you must have one or more elements that dominate and another or others that are subordinates. You can create artifacts that are unified, but not so unified as to be too dull to hold your viewer's attention, by consciously emphasizing some aspects, which will then make other aspects subordinate to them.

Emphasis refers to the arrangement of elements of an artifact to make an area the primary focus of a viewer's attention. **Subordination** in artifacts refers to the arrangement of elements of art to support a larger visual theme, idea, or motif. There are ways that you can establish emphasis and subordination in your work, including use of a hierarchy of elements or aspects in a work, use of isolation, establishment of a focal point, consideration of placement of elements and aspects, and use of directional lines.

Elephant (**10.28**) provides an intriguing example of the use of emphasis and subordination in an artifact. Bansky, a pseudo-anonymous British artist, makes satirical political statements in drawings and graphic items that address issues of culture and ethics. He does not sell his work in commercial galleries, and he often uses public spaces to make his statements.

Elephant is a brightly colored but dark-humored piece that draws upon the notion that there is an elephant in the room that no one will acknowledge. The concept of "the elephant in the room" is often used in psychological counseling to point out to a patient that he or she may be ignoring a source of trouble that ought to be very apparent, such as an unacknowledged dependence on alcohol.

The major subordinate elements in *Elephant* are the woman and man relaxing on the couch, apparently unaware of the dominant, huge, red-upholstered elephant beside them. Subtler subordinate elements are the classical paintings hanging on the walls, which are altered, showing ominous events that are also apparently unacknowledged by the couple on the couch. Thus there is a **visual hierarchy** of elements in the work, an inclusion and use of elements in terms of their importance to the expressive purpose of the work. In *Elephant,* the red elephant is the emphasis and is more important than the people on the couch and the pictures on the wall, but each element is needed for the work to make sense. The interpretive implication of the elephant with its elaborate covering might be comfortable wealth in the world in contrast to poverty, hunger, or devastation of the natural environment, although the artist leaves the implications open to other interpretations.

10.27 FIONA RAE *Cute Motion!! So Lovely!!,* 2005. Oil, acrylic, and gouache on canvas, 91 × 75 in.

10.28 BANSKY *Elephant,* September 15, 2006.

Angela de la Cruz's sculpture of found and manipulated objects, *Upright (3 leg chair)* (**10.29**), provides us with an interesting example of equal distribution of emphasis and subordination. She has constructed a vertical sculpture. Its base is a four-legged stool with added stilts of wood to raise its height. De la Cruz has situated a chair with three legs on top of the stool, thus the descriptive title of *Upright (3 leg chair)*. The piece can be seen as one awkward-looking chair with its two parts tenuously cobbled together. It would be a precarious chair to sit on because the seat of the chair is tilted forward and the base does not look steady. She has made a nonfunctional chair out of two broken chairs, stressing the dependence of both on each other. The piece uses such an equal balance between emphasis and subordination that its composition could metaphorically represent a dysfunctional human relationship, a relationship of codependence in which each part is so enmeshed with the other that neither can function without the other, and both are not functioning well together.

EMPHASIS: FOCUSING VIEWERS' ATTENTION

The black shape in *Chartreuse* (**10.30**) dominates Mary Heilmann's painting. Its dominance is emphasized by its central placement, its size, and the heavy darkness of its color, which is accentuated by the lightness of the colors adjacent to it. It is the only shape in the painting that touches three edges of the composition.

American artist Georg Heimdal's *Sierra* (**10.31**) exemplifies emphasis and subordination, with a stress on emphasis. He uses many principles of emphasis, including establishing a **focal point** that shows where he wants his viewers to begin and return their attention, in this case, the tree stump. He uses a considered choice of placement of the stump, namely, where it best fits according to his expressive intents. He places it in the middle of the canvas. The stump is the largest single thing in the picture. It is also the most brightly colored object, thus reinforcing its hierarchy as the focal point. It is the emphatic object in the work supported by the subordinate craggy environment composed of rocks and sky.

If the stump were placed at an edge of the canvas, it would likely become subordinate to the rocks. If the stump were considerably smaller than the rocks, it would likely be subordinate to the rocks. By placing a small band of blue at the top of the canvas, the artist indicates sky, reinforcing the notion that this is a landscape. This adds an orienting bit of realism to a rather abstract representation. Were the sky to occupy the most space in the canvas, it would subordinate the rocks and the stump. The artist has also isolated the stump, drawing attention to it by providing no other trees or their remains to accompany it in the painting.

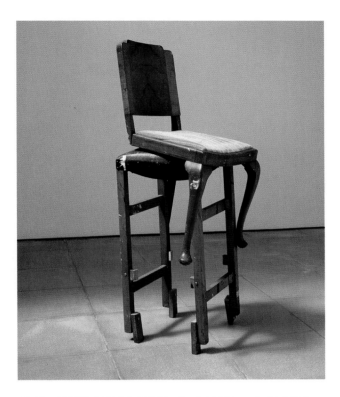

10.29 ANGELA DE LA CRUZ *Upright (3 leg chair),* 2004.
Mixed media, stool and chair, 130 × 50 × 45 cm.

The painting is simpler than it first seems because all its minor elements are successfully subordinated to its primary emphasis on the tree stump within its harsh environment. The color palette is strikingly limited. The painting is composed of thousands of discrete brushstrokes, so individual that they can be accurately counted, but the artist has not let his technique overwhelm the subject matter.

Heimdal, using restraint, subordinates composition, color, and brushwork to the subject matter and what it implies. We are challenged to wonder about the stump that was once a tree vital enough to survive in a very harsh growing environment and, further, to wonder why this simple thing is the subject of a meticulously constructed and executed painting.

Lulu (**10.32**), by American ceramic artist and printmaker Ken Price, provides an example of emphasis and subordination very different from *Elephant* (see 10.28) or *Sierra* (see 10.31) because Price's clay sculpture is one continuous form. Its emphasis can be identified as the waving shape, somewhat reminiscent of an arm with fingers, that rises out of what might be seen as a subordinate base. In a sense, it lacks a focal point—a center of interest—in favor of directing our eyes all around and over the piece. The artist directs our attention by using **directional lines,** another gestalt principle of unity, namely, that invisible and implied lines

10.30 MARY HEILMANN *Chartreuse,* 1987. Acrylic and watercolor on panel, 62½ × 66¼ in.

10.31 GEORG HEIMDAL *Sierra,* 1990. Acrylic on canvas, 36 × 36 in.

focus our attention. *Lulu* moves our eyes from the bottom portion of the sculpture toward the elbowlike curve in its middle and on through the handlike form at the sculpture's highest point. The small dark dots on the predominant red surface function as subordinate elements in the sculpture.

Bill Viola's *Acceptance* (**10.33**) has one dominant element that is supported only by a blank background, a type of subordinate element that stages the main and only event on the video screen. By having us concentrate solely on the figure, Viola enhances the emotional effect of the figure overwhelmed by relentlessly falling water. Anything else in the scene would be a distraction and detraction. The emphasis on the figure is made apparent by its off-center placement and isolation in the composition.

SUBORDINATION: SUPPORTING A LARGER THEME

Spencer Finch's airborne sculpture emphasizes subordination rather than domination, privileging nature over culture. *Sky* (**10.34**) is a collection of balloons filled with helium. In the reproduction shown here, the sculpture is floating in the sky amidst palm trees. The collection of balloons is monochromatic: purple. It is a bunch of balloons, reminiscent of a bunch of purple grapes. The piece is subordinate to the earth and the forces of nature, particularly gravity, and wind. The work is ephemeral: eventually natural winds will take it away from sight, or its helium will escape and the piece will wilt and fall to the ground. The sculpture is fragile; nature is strong and dominant. The subordination of the piece has metaphorical implications about fragility, impermanence, and dependence on forces greater than oneself in life on Earth.

The inside book jacket of Chris Ware's graphic novel *Jimmy Corrigan, The Smartest Kid on Earth* (**10.35**) is an example a very complex composition unified by subordination of many disparate elements to the dominant element of a representation of a map of the Earth. Ware's composition is a visual display that is amazing in its complexity and clarity. The graphic display is a kind of visual overview of the story he tells about himself and his estranged father. To see the display at all, you have to remove the paper jacket that covers the hardbound book, unfold it, and spread it out, much like a road map. To decipher all the images and texts in their proper orientation, you have to rotate the page 90 degrees four times.

The diversity of the design includes large and small shapes, single and multiple comic-book panels, pictures in black and white and in color, a flow chart, and text overlays. Ware has given us a tremendous amount of information on one piece of paper. If the page were not visually unified, we might well look away from it, overwhelmed by its density of information.

Ware, however, has masterfully unified the complexity through various compositional choices. He uses white negative space to allow the visual information to "breathe." He chooses a restricted palette of muted, harmonious colors, tending toward earth tones and grays, and complements them with blue. He uses overt directional lines, to direct our attention to and from the focal point of the composition, the map of the Earth. He uses the lines to point to events, places, and situations in the story that the book tells maximally in pictures and minimally in words. The lines themselves provide an element of graphic unity through use of repetition. He limits his choice of shapes to rectangles and circles of varying size, some of which incrementally change size, thus using a visual hierarchy.

Conclusion: Reflecting on Design Principles

Design principles have been developed through the ages, and when they were rearticulated as a set at the end of the nineteenth century, they reflected that century's concern for composing harmonious artworks. The approach to design principles presented in this and the preceding chapters includes the more diverse goals and sensibilities of contemporary artists, who are not always trying to achieve harmony and beauty. The principles offer a common vocabulary and general guides for making, viewing, analyzing, discussing, and writing about artifacts of all kinds. You will want to consider elements and principles in conjunction with your choice of subject matter and medium and the context in which your work is shown.

10.32   KEN PRICE *Lulu,* 2001. Ceramic, 11 × 13 in.

10.33   BILL VIOLA *Acceptance,* 2008. Black-and-white high-definition video on plasma display mounted on wall, 155.5 × 92.5 × 12.7 cm.

10.34   SPENCER FINCH *Sky (Over Coney Island, November 26th, 2004, 12:47 PM),* 2004. Fifteen to twenty-five balloons, string, brick, dimensions variable.

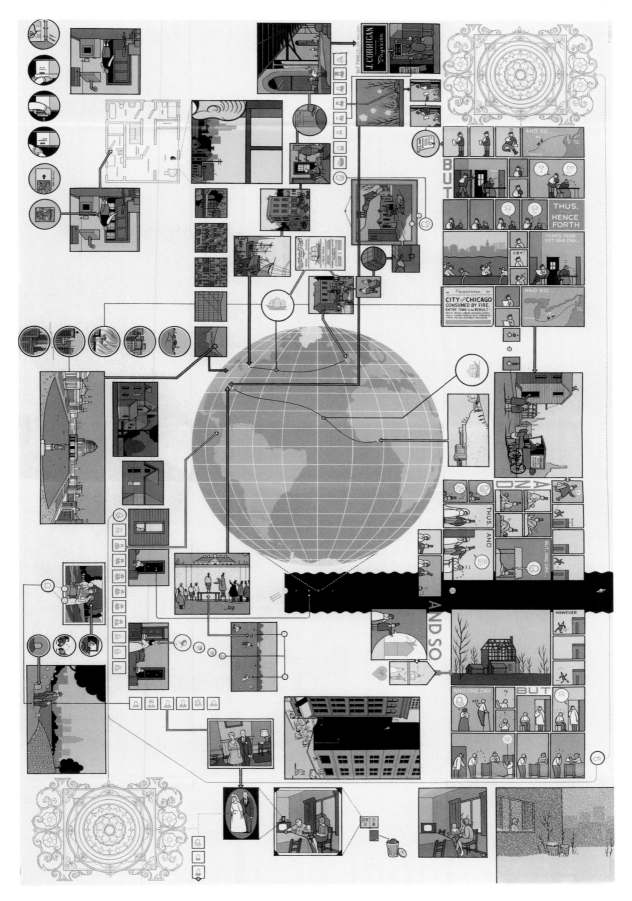

10.35 **F. C. WARE** *Jimmy Corrigan, The Smartest Kid on Earth,* 2000. Inside book jacket cover.

11 Postmodernist Approaches to Making Art

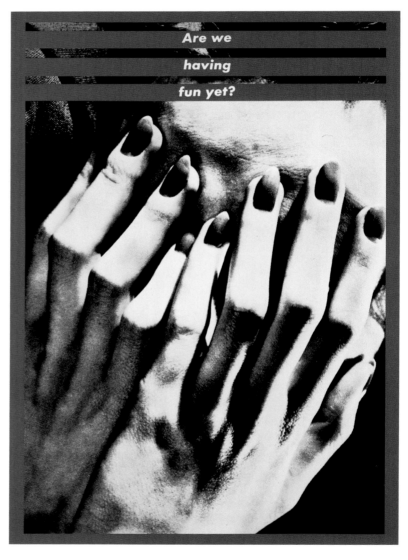

11.1 BARBARA KRUGER *Untitled (Are we having fun yet?),* 1987. Photographic silkscreen and vinyl, 147 × 103 in.

Art elements and design principles explored in previous chapters derive from sources throughout Western history. The ancient Greeks sought ideal beauty in the form of idealized realism, harmony, and exacting mathematical standards of proportion and scale. In 1757 philosopher David Hume listed the qualities of beautiful artifacts, which included uniformity, variety, clarity of expression, realistic exactness, and brilliance of color;[1] and in 1899 Arthur Wesley Dow proposed principles for "harmonious works of art" (subordination and rhythmic repetition, symmetry, opposition, transition, and Japanese notions of black and white mentioned in Chapter 8). Although these articulations of art elements and explanations of design principles were born and matured in times different from ours, we can still apply them to artifacts made in the past, in cultures across the world, and to objects, spaces, and events created very recently for daily living and for viewing in galleries.

Using elements and principles, we have examined artifacts, especially of our time. Current writers classify most of the works we have analyzed as examples of "modern art" or "postmodern art." We have mixed them without distinguishing between modern and postmodern, but this chapter concentrates on postmodern approaches to art making. We are already intuitively aware of postmodernist thinking because we have grown up with it, and it is part of our consciousness. Postmodernist thinking dominates the popular culture we experience in our daily lives and is also a dominant force behind much of the art we see in art-world venues.

Modernism and Postmodernism in Culture

Modern art and postmodern art grow out of and contribute to cultural modernity and postmodernity. Modernist and postmodernist thinking are broader and more expansive in time than their applications in modern art and postmodern art.

Postmodernism refers to both a period of time and a web of ideas, both of which resist specificity. Many scholars place the beginning of postmodernism in Paris 1968, when college students and some of their influential professors, joined by workers, revolted against what they saw as an oppressive French institutional system and, by extension, all established social and political structures. Art historians place the beginnings of postmodern art earlier than 1968, crediting especially the artist Marcel Duchamp (1887–1968) and the art movements of Dada (peaking around 1920) and Pop Art (beginning in the mid-1950s).

Postmodernist theory owes much to French theorists Michel Foucault, Jacques Lacan, Jacques Derrida, and Jean Baudrillard, who each in his own way radically reappraised modern assumptions about large ideas about history, culture, identity, representation, and language. Postmodernist thinking continues to influence all of the humanities, especially the study of literature in college departments of English literature. Postmodernist theory has both its proponents and its skeptics, but most instructors would agree that it cannot be ignored if we are to understand recent developments in the arts and humanities.

As a general set of beliefs, postmodernism is easiest to understand as ideas in relation to the ideas of modernism. Modernism began with the Enlightenment (the Age of Reason, *c.* 1687–1789), a European intellectual movement emphasizing reason and individualism rather than tradition. It was the basis of major social upheavals concluding with the French Revolution. Ideals of modernism continue into the present, where they exist alongside postmodernist ideas. Theoretical postmodernism is both a development of and a reaction against theoretical modernism. Some theorists and practitioners think of postmodernism as "antimodernism."

Modernism itself began as a radical reaction against an earlier set of values and beliefs. Modernists champion reason, science, and democracy to erase ignorance, superstition, and unquestioning support of church and state rulers. Modernists rally around the flags of freedom and individuality and the companion ideas of free enterprise, the Industrial Revolution, and capitalism.

Postmodernists argue that modernist beliefs have not led to a society free from poverty, political tyranny, and ignorance. They are less optimistic than modernists about the possibility of progress and the betterment of society. They are skeptical about the freedom of the individual, arguing that our actions are constrained by social context. They doubt that the power of reason alone can solve social problems. Postmodernist social critics assert that modernists did not deliver on their promises of a just society for all. They argue further that modernism oppressed workers under capitalist industrialization, excluded women and minorities from the public sphere, and colonized lands and peoples for economic and religious reasons.

Barbara Kruger's *Untitled (Are we having fun yet?)* (**11.1**) can be read as a rhetorical question that implies negative answers about how women and minorities have been and are being treated by dominant social groups. Kruger's use of a female subject can be generalized to anyone with less power in relation to those who dominate: a worker in relation to an employer, an indigenous people overtaken by a foreign power, and a society awash in sexist mass-media messages. In Kruger's sarcastic image, we are not yet having "fun," because we have not achieved social equity or embraced social justice.

Some postmodernists have lost hope, have despaired of the possibilities of achieving social justice, and have become nihilistic and paralyzed with pessimism. Many postmodernists, however, remain optimistic in the face

Postmodernist Approaches to Making Art Key Terms

ART WORLD   The people and institutions that circulate art and discourse about it.

HIGH AND LOW ART   A contested distinction between "fine art" and artifacts made for and used in daily living. Postmodernists collapse the distinction between "high" and "low."

WORK OF ART   A modernist term that implies a notion of an artifact as singular and unique and the product of isolated genius.

TEXT   A conception of artifacts as webs of references to other artifacts; postmodernists prefer it to *work of art* because the latter implies singular artifacts independent of other artifacts and ideas.

THE ABJECT   What is considered base about being human; things a culture thinks of as shameful and wishes to hide.

AESTHETIC EXPERIENCE   A unique reaction to an artifact or event that is disengaged, disinterested, and removed from practical concerns.

JOUISSANCE   A French term adopted by postmodernists to express the joy of losing oneself in an artwork; a term used in contrast to *aesthetic experience.*

COLLABORATION   Working as part of a team rather than as a sole creator.

APPROPRIATION   Possessing, borrowing, copying, quoting, or excerpting images that already exist, are made by other artists, or are available in the public domain.

SIMULATION   Imitating, copying, or reproducing an experience of the real.

SIMULACRUM, SIMULACRA   Representations of things that no longer have an original or never had one; insubstantial semblances of real things or events.

HYBRIDIZATION   Mixing diverse cultural influences in an artwork to make a new, distinct statement.

MIXED MEDIA   Different media used in a single work of art.

LAYERING   Placing images on top of images in artworks to make new associations and meanings.

MIXED CODES   Different conventional means of communication used in a single work of art, such as a combination of words and images.

RECONTEXTUALIZATION   Placing what is usually seen in one venue into a different venue to create new associations and meanings.

INTERTEXTUALITY   The shaping of one sign's meaning by other signs in a single work of art.

THE GAZE   Positioning the maker and the viewer of an image as the active subject, and what is represented as the passive object.

DISSONANCE   Lack of harmony or agreement between elements in a work.

IDENTITY POLITICS   Political action through artifacts to advance members of groups who are underrepresented, misrepresented, or oppressed because of race, religion, gender, and other social conditions.

METAPHOR   A direct comparison between two or more seemingly unrelated subjects; showing something with the attributes of another thing.

IRONY   The use of words and images to convey the opposite of what they say and show.

PARODY   A mockery of an artifact, an event, or type of representation.

---

of major social problems. They are willing to continue the struggle, with the help of art, to strive for what modernists set out to achieve. This chapter optimistically embraces postmodernists' hope for a better future, in part through art that challenges thinking made manifest in representations that question and critique social inequities.

Modern Art and Postmodern Art

Modern art, which was highly influenced by seventeenth-century Enlightenment views of the world, developed in the late nineteenth century into the twentieth century and continues to be influential today. Major movements of modern art include

Impressionism

Postimpressionism

Symbolism

Fauvism

Cubism

Expressionism

Dada

Bauhaus

Surrealism

Abstract Expressionism

Color field painting

Pop Art

Op Art

Hard-edge painting

Russian Formalism

Minimalism

Photorealism

Art photography

Socially motivated journalist photography

We have already seen some land art (see 3.6), performance art (see 6.13), and installations (see 7.22).

Modern artists are far too many to enumerate here. They fill our art history books and deserve careful study, and we have already seen many examples, such as Jacques-Louis David (see 6.14), Georges Seurat (see 5.22), Pierre Bonnard (see 4.53), Henri Matisse (see 3.20), Pablo Picasso (see 5.45), Kasimir Malevich (see 10.2), Wassily Kandinsky (see 3.43), Marcel Duchamp (see 6.22), Alexander Calder (see 6.15), Mark Rothko (see 4.32), Helen Frankenthaler (see 5.48), Georgia O'Keeffe (see5.25), Ellsworth Kelly (see 9.27), Al Held (see 5.46), Eva Hesse (see 8.7), Bruce Nauman (see 7.6), Sam Gilliam (see 9.15), Bridget Riley (see 6.19), and many others that you will pursue in your study of art history.

Critic and philosopher of art Arthur Danto summarizes the development of modern art as a series of "erasures." He described the development of modern art this way:

> . . . a dismantling of a concept of art which had been evolving for over half a millennium. Art did not have to be beautiful; it need make no effort to furnish the eye with an array of sensations equivalent to what the real world would furnish it with; need not have a pictorial subject; need not deploy its forms in pictorial space, and need not be the magical product of the artist's touch.[2]

In part due to the invention of photography, modern artists dropped realistic representations in paint; they distorted subject matter through Cubism; they eliminated subject matter as essential to art and turned to nonobjective works; they stopped hand rendering the illusion of three-dimensional forms on two-dimensional surfaces and accepted the purity of paint as a flat medium; they eliminated the need for the artist's touch by employing commercial fabricators; conceptual artists eliminated the need to have an art object at all, instead substituting ideas for objects; and Pop artists abandoned the need for art objects to be different from ordinary ones by introducing into their artworks everyday objects such as Brillo boxes and Campbell soup cans.

The term "postmodernism" first came into use to name a new stylistic direction in architecture that moved away from the principle "form follows func-

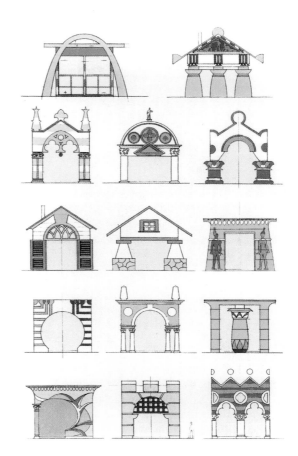

11.2 ROBERT VENTURI Eclectic House Series, 1977.
Colored plastic film on photomechanical print.

tion" articulated by American architect Louis Sullivan. That formulation had resulted in what many architects and critics considered the austere sparseness of rectangular steel grids and glass walls and a rejection of architectural ornament. In the 1960s, American postmodernist architect Robert Venturi opened architecture to the influences of multiple historical traditions, ordinary commercial buildings, and the influence of Pop Art. In his writings and in his buildings, he resisted what had become boring in modern architecture and introduced playfulness into modernist austerity. The sequence of elevations in his Eclectic House Series (**11.2**) "captures the firm's inclusive yet radical embrace of history."[3]

Postmodern artists also rejected notions of "progress" by moving from realistic representation to abstraction, turning to a pluralism of styles, and introducing great freedom and variety of expression. Like the Dadaists before them, they introduce humor and irreverence into art. Like the Pop artists who preceded them, they embrace rather than eschew the popular in culture. They reintroduced social, political, and ethical concerns into their artifacts.

11.3 **THE GUERRILLA GIRLS** "Do Women Have to Be Naked to Get into the Metropolitan Museum?" 1989. Poster.

Postmodern Attitudes toward Art

Postmodernism can be identified by a general set of attitudes toward art as well as characteristic approaches to making art. In this part of the chapter, we look at changes in attitudes about where art is placed, what constitutes "high" and "low" art, what is the purpose of art, and other aspects that distinguish postmodern art from traditional and modern art. After that, we will see examples of approaches that reflect these attitudes. If you have not already, you will begin to recognize postmodernist influences in visual books, advertising, product design, painting, sculpture, and all modes of art and design.

CHALLENGING THE ART WORLD

The people and institutions that circulate art and discourse about it constitute the **art world.** People in the art world include artists, museum directors, gallery owners and dealers, exhibition designers, publicists, connoisseurs, estimators, restorers, security guards, museum and independent curators, art critics, art collectors, art historians, art conservators and restorers, editors, writers, and advertisers. Art-world institutions include museums, commercial galleries, auction houses, private and public funding agencies, the art press, and centers for research and conservation. The art world is vast and global, with especially prominent centers in North America and Europe and also in Asia, South America, and Africa. Within North America, for example, there are important and influential centers, especially in New York City, but also in Los Angeles and Chicago and smaller cities throughout the continent. Most art that we see is brought to us by the art world.

Chuck Close (see 3.4, 4.50) views the art world as family: "Art is the other family. It's all family and friends. I consider the artworld family to be almost as important as my real family. It gives me a sense of belonging to something larger than myself."[4] Although he embraces the art world, and is highly successful economically and historically because of it, he is also critical of its ways:

> I hate the way, in terms of money and power and the government and stuff, I hate the way art is sold. I think it's really bad. They have to say that the reason art is important is that it attracts and brings more money into a community than sporting events; more people attend museums than go to sporting events, and it's good for the economy. Therefore, it's important to support art, and art should be in the community. The trouble with that . . . is that what's being missed in all this is not that art is just good for the economy and good for business, but that it's humanizing.[5]

Thus, although Close clearly benefits from the art market, he cautions us about its emphasis on money rather than on the betterment of humanity.

Another critique of the art world is that it discriminates against women and minorities. Emma Amos, an African American artist, says, "I am invisible as an African American woman artist. I show in February. Thank God for February. I show with other black artists in ghetto month shows that fulfill the funding needs of white institutions. Our few and far between shows seldom get shuffled into the other 11 months of the calendar."[6]

The Guerrilla Girls is a group of women, mostly artists, art historians, and arts administrators, who work collectively and anonymously for social justice in the art world. They appear at art events, unannounced and uninvited, wearing miniskirts, high heels, and great hairy gorilla heads. They frequently brandish phallic bananas. They produce politically charged messages on stickers, posters (**11.3**), magazine advertisements, holiday cards, and videotapes. The women continue to work collectively as a political force, and through the collectivity of their work, they attempt to foster solidarity among themselves and with other groups sympathetic to like causes.

ESCAPING THE CONFINES OF MUSEUMS AND OTHER TRADITIONAL VENUES

Some artists resist the confines of art museums and intentionally make art that cannot be housed within a museum's walls. Robert Smithson (see 3.6), an artist of earthworks too large to be housed in museums, was particularly critical of traditional art institutions:

> Museums, like asylums and jails, have wards and cells—in other words, neutral rooms called *galleries.* A work of art when placed in a gallery loses its charge, and becomes a portable object or surface disengaged from the outside world. A vacant white room with lights is still a submission to the neutral. Works of art seen in such spaces seem to be going through a kind of aesthetic convalescence. They are looked upon as so many inanimate invalids, waiting for critics to pronounce them curable or incurable. The function of the warden-curator is to separate art from the rest of society.[7]

Smithson made art directly in the landscape, in part to circumvent the commercial galleries. He also wrote passionately about the need to create works of art outside of the gallery and museum systems. He felt that the galleries and museums sanitized art to the point that it became nothing more than a portable object ready for consumption.

Barbara Kruger (see 11.1) and Jenny Holzer (see 7.1) often attempt to reach audiences beyond those that visit art galleries and museums by placing their works in public venues. Kruger has placed her pieces internationally, in different languages, on billboards, the outsides of buses, and T-shirts, matchbooks, and handbags. Holzer first displayed her now famous series of one-line sayings, *Truisms,* on sheets of copy paper that she pasted to walls in the SoHo district of New York City. She had also rented signage space in Times Square in New York; Candlestick Park in San Francisco during a baseball game; the marquee of Caesar's Palace in Las Vegas, where she displayed the Truism "Money creates taste"; and Piccadilly Circus in London, where she displayed "Protect me from what I want."

Bulgarian-born installation artist Christo and his Moroccan-born wife Jeanne-Claude are responsible for *The Gates* (**11.4**) in Central Park, New York City. They began working on the project in 1979 and finished in 2005. The installation consisted of 7,503 gates of saf-

11.4 CHRISTO AND JEANNE-CLAUDE *The Gates,* Central Park, New York City, 1979–2005.

fron-colored fabric, 16 feet tall, at intervals of 12 feet, over 23 miles of park walkways. After sixteen days of display, workers removed the gates and recycled the materials. Nine hundred workers participated in the preparation, display, and removal of the project. They received financial compensation and breakfast and a hot meal during the day. As Christo and Jeanne-Claude have done for their previous projects, they maintained their independence by financing the entire $21 million project themselves through the sale of preparatory studies, drawings, collages, and scale models. They donated merchandising rights for *The Gates* to a charitable foundation for the park. They accepted no sponsorship or money from the city. Their art necessarily depends on large sums of money because of the massive undertaking that most of their projects entail. Their seeking of alternative ways to fund their projects is an integral, acknowledged, and publicly visible part of their art making. Smithson (see 3.6), Holzer (see 7.4), and Christo and Jeanne-Claude invite you to consider showing your work in spaces other than museums and commercial galleries and seeking alternative means of funding your work. By placing their work beyond the confines of museums, they reach larger audiences.

COLLAPSING BOUNDARIES BETWEEN "HIGH" AND "LOW" ART

Postmodern artists seek to collapse boundaries that are important to modernists, who generally elevate art to a special, independent, autonomous sphere of its own. For modernists, true art transcends ordinary life. They believe true art is "high art," above "low culture" as

11.5   JEFF KOONS _Puppy,_ 1992. Stainless steel, soil, geotextile fabric, internal irrigation system, and live flowering plants, 486 × 486 × 256 in.

seen in popular objects and images. For example, modernist theorists such as Clement Greenberg disdain "kitsch," a term derived from the German word meaning "trash." Modernists label as kitsch what they consider to be cheap, tasteless, and tacky things often associated with middle- and lower-class visual preferences: Elvis paintings on velvet, lava lamps, and knickknacks of all kinds. Pop Art in the late 1950s is an important precursor to postmodernists' uses of popular culture to erase the boundary between **high and low art** by using popular images in their work—comic-book conventions, Campbell's soup cans, Spam cans, hamburgers and French fries, gas stations, celebrities, and so forth. Artists who began opening new possibilities for subject matter, medium, form, processes, and presentational contexts were part of postmodern thinking before it was identified as such.

Jeff Koons is known for making "kitschy art," a contradiction in terms, for modernists. Koons is especially known for his large sculpture _Puppy_ (**11.5**), made of live flowers, which he has installed at various worldwide locations, including its first incarnation in front of an eighteenth-century castle outside of Bad Arlosen (shown here), at Rockefeller Plaza in New York City, and near the Guggenheim Museum in Bilbao, Spain. Koons's _Banality_ series consists of greatly enlarged reproductions of small popular objects, such as statues of saints, cartoon animals, Hummel figurines, busty women, naked children, and a souvenir doll of pop singer Michael Jackson. These figures are meticulously crafted in porcelain and wood, painted and sometimes gilded in gold, by artisans whom Koons supervises in Italy and Germany.

Koons has also made explicitly sexual images of himself and his wife that according to some are pornographic and demean women by merely emphasizing their physicality. Also, the artifacts that Koons, Christo and Jeanne-Claude, and Judy Chicago (see 8.12 and 8.13) have fabricated for themselves in their names are criticized by some because the artisans who actually fabricate the works are not given sufficient credit for their highly skilled work.

Takashi Murakami, a contemporary Japanese artist, also embraces and celebrates popular imagery. He splits his time between Tokyo and Brooklyn, combines Japanese _anime_ and _manga_ images, high fashion, and _Nihon-ga_ (Japanese-style) paintings of the nineteenth century and has influenced Andy Warhol's Factory and Walt Disney animation. His work references religion, subcultures, and art history. In the fall of 2003, Murakami transformed New York City's Rockefeller Plaza into a fantastical pop cityscape with _Reversed Double Helix_ (**11.6**), a major display of sculpture that included a freestanding 30-foot-tall Buddha-like figure, "Mr. Pointy," with multiple arms and a pointed head, two giant floating "eyeball" balloons, and a forest of wide-eyed mushrooms for public seating. The "eyeball" balloons, each 30 feet in diameter, floating 60 feet in the air, surveyed the scene around Rockefeller Center. Murakami typically employs producers of hobbyist models rather than fine-arts craftspeople to execute his works. An important "low-art" aspect of Murakami's work is its commercial nature: many of his pieces sell as mass-produced consumer items. In 2000, Murakami curated _Superflat,_ an exhibition of Japanese

11.6 TAKASHI MURAKAMI *Reversed Double Helix,* 2003. Central figure 30 ft. tall, installation view, Rockefeller Plaza, New York City.

11.7 ELLIOTT EARLS *Abraham-n-Isaac,* 2004, Lamda photoprint, 80 × 42 in.

art, which acknowledged the influence of mass-produced entertainment on contemporary aesthetics.

Nan Goldin embraces an everyday style of photography. She merges a family snapshot aesthetic with "high-art" photography. Goldin photographically documents the lives of family members, friends, and acquaintances, initially in the Lower East Side of Manhattan and then in locations around the world (**11.8**). Goldin's work has been described this way: "Nan Goldin's color portraits of her bohemian community in the 1970s turned the intimate family snapshot into an artistic genre and valid photographic art."[8] Her work is similar in motivation and spirit to family snapshots and home videos, preserving memories of family, friends, and significant oc-

casions. Her subject matter, however, is intimate views of the private lives of her chosen "family," outsiders to the mainstream, such as lesbians, gays, and transgendered people. Her work is candid, direct, and close-up: she is part of rather than distanced from those she photographs. She likens her work to a diary. Goldin's use of the vernacular snapshot aesthetic is an intentional strategy: she is not simply elevating snapshot photos to the realm of high art. Hers is a socially aware and insightful use of the everyday camera to view subjects who have often been ignored in establishment art. Koons (see 11.5), Murakami (see 11.6), and Golden have opened possibilities for you to use the ordinary and everyday as sources of your own art making.

11.8 **NAN GOLDIN** Montage: *Cookie and Sharon dancing in the Back Room, Provincetown,* 1976; *Nan and Brian in bed, NYC,* 1983; *Nan one month after being battered,* 1984; *Self-portrait in bed, NYC,* 1981. Cibachrome color photographs, 30 × 40 in.

"TEXTS" AND "WORKS"

Modernists talk about a **work of art,** and postmodernists prefer the term **text,** borrowing a word from literary theory. In modernist thinking, artworks are often considered unique creations made by gifted individuals. In postmodernist thinking, however, artworks and all artifacts are more collaborative in nature and highly influenced by culture—that is, other works—which is why postmodernists chose a different word to refer to them.

Works are singular, speaking in one voice, that of the artist, which leads the viewer to look for the artist's singular meaning; texts imply that any artwork is a network of references and citations of other works from many disciplines. Postmodernists believe an artwork is a confluence of many voices that speak, blend, and clash, that images are influenced more by culture than we had previously thought.

Elliott Earls' image *Abraham-n-Isaac* (**11.7**) is an artwork, but it is more fully understood as a partial text rather than a singular and self-contained work. The image is part of a larger text called *Bull and Wounded Horse* that consists of an exhibition of photographs, objects, and large prints, and a performance piece that incorporates these objects. Making sense of the references in *Abraham-n-Isaac* requires knowledge of other texts upon which it draws: the Hebrew Bible, Hebrew text at the base of the image, and specifically the story of Abraham following God's command to sacrifice his son Isaac without question. The image is set in contemporary hip-hop style, with African Americans representing the two Biblical characters, one barefoot and in overalls, with a revolutionary hat and hairstyle, and the other in dress pants and two-toned leather shoes. Their tattoos are signifiers that carry cultural connotations as well as the specificity of what they show. Bling is abundant, around the neck of Isaac, and in the graphical symbols above the heads, which in turn reference the Star of David, a crucifix, the crescent of Islam, and a dollar sign. Blood spews forth. Through these multiple references to texts in sacred and popular cultures, Earls may be referencing black-on-black crime, as well as religiously based conflict in our post-9/11 world, and greed for money. It is not a simple or self-explanatory work but highly dependent on references external to itself.[9]

REJECTING ORIGINALITY

Postmodern artists attempt to free us from the pressure of being wholly original in our art making. In premodern times, such as the Middle Ages, artists were anonymous contributors to the community and self-expression was not an ideal, nor was the invention of new styles. However, in modern times, since the European Renaissance in fact, values shifted as the individual was honored and personal freedom was extolled. The "genius" artist was especially made to be a champion of the new, the first, the cutting edge. Postmodernists, on the other hand, are highly suspicious of the possibility of being original and do not hold originality as a value.

Many current artists encourage you to replace the pressure to be original with an awareness of the many visual texts that constitute your experience of the world, using this awareness to create your own art. As American artist Joyce Kozloff observes, "All artists lift from everything that interests them and always have—from earlier art, other work that's around, or sources outside art."[10] Such awareness allows you the freedom to quote from other sources as you add your own imprints and insights.

ACCEPTING THE ABJECT

A base aspect of being human, such as a corpse, excrement, vomit, and things associated with what a culture thinks of as shameful and wishes to hide, is known as **the abject.** Artists who accept the abject and use it in their work make art that might seem ugly or repulsive. They confront us with the totality of being human and ask us to accept the body and its functions knowingly and willingly.

From afar, Mona Hatoum's *Deep Throat* (**11.9**) looks like a pleasant table set for one. When you approach the table, however, you see a scientifically accurate videotape of the human digestive system at work on food that has been swallowed. The activity of digestion and elimination is a taboo topic while at the dinner table. Hatoum banishes the taboo and embraces by implication other functions of the body usually avoided in polite conversation. Her art asks us to see what we might prefer to ignore about life.

JOUISSANCE

The postmodernist version of the modernist aesthetic experience is *jouissance,* a French word meaning

11.9 MONA HATOUM *Deep Throat,* 2006. Installation with a video image on the plate giving a tour of the digestive system.

pleasure and enjoyment and carrying with it sexual overtones. The modernist **aesthetic experience** is a heightened awareness of an object while one is both *disinterested* and *distanced.* It is the enjoyment of something for its own sake without wanting to possess it. *Jouissance,* in postmodern usage, refers to viewers being so lost in a work of art that they lose all self-awareness and objective distance from the work being viewed. The concept of *jouissance* acknowledges a desire for possession inflamed by art. The two approaches to artworks are different, and the difference hinges mainly on personal engagement (*jouissance*) with a work of art versus a distanced and objective aesthetic appreciation of a work.

Vlado Mulunc's and Frank Gehry's *Dancing Building* (**11.10**), completed in 1996 in Prague, has a sense of *jouissance* about it. The architecture plays with and against modernist steel box and glass skyscrapers and their formal austerity and rectangular rigidity. *Dancing Building* collapses rigid modernist angles with sensuous curves. It destabilizes expectations of normality and makes us want to experience the inside of the building. In a metaphorical sense, modernist architecture is male and phallic, and postmodernist architecture embraces feminine aspects.

Postmodern Strategies for Making Art

All of the postmodern strategies for making art embrace to greater and lesser degrees the postmodern attitudes just discussed. These strategies include working collaboratively, appropriating, simulating, hybridizing,

11.10 VLADO MULUNC AND FRANK GEHRY *Dancing Building, Prague,* 1996.

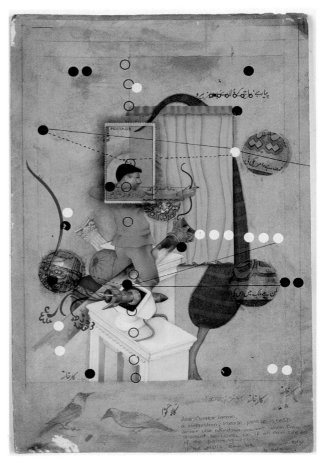

11.11 SAIRA WASIM, TALHA RATHORE, MUHAMMED IMRAN QURESHI, HASNAT MEHMOOD, AISHA KAHLID, NUSRA LATIF QURESHI *Untitled,* 2003. Gouache and mixed media on wasli (layered handmade paper), 10⅓ × 7½ in.

mixing media, layering, mixing codes, recontextualizing, intertextualizing, confronting the gaze, using dissonance, constructing identities, using narratives, creating metaphors, and using irony and parody.[11] Further, these approaches to making art overlap; although one may stand out in a particular work, none is used alone.

WORKING COLLABORATIVELY

In premodern times, artists often worked as part of a team; every artist had a specialty, and **collaboration** was an efficient way to produce works that needed many skills. In modern times, great value has been put on individual creations. Now, in the postmodern era, some artists are returning to collaborative working methods instead of being a sole creator. If you work in a design field, you are likely to be part of a team of artists and other creators. In the fine arts, you might find that some projects—large-scale sculptures, for example, or glassblowing—require collaboration, and others lend themselves to it.

In sixteenth-century India, a group of artists employed by the Mughal emperor Akbar produced exquisite miniature paintings using hand-ground pigments on handmade paper. *Khamsa,* the miniature book containing the paintings, illustrates age-old tales of love, war, religion, and political power. In 2003, six young Pakistani artists trained in the tradition of miniature techniques made *Untitled* (**11.11**), one of twelve exquisite miniature images that make up the Karkhana project (2003). The young artists are inspired by the Mughal court atelier, or *Karkhana,* where a group of artists would work together on a single painting. Following the Mughal tradition, the contemporary Pakistani artists also used handmade paints and papers, but included collaged photographic images, stencils, and rubber stamps. Rather than working in one studio, they worked across the globe, sending their jointly made paintings back and forth to one another between Melbourne, Chicago, Lahore, and New York City. One artist begins an image on a sheet of paper and mails it to someone else, who continues working on it before sending it to someone else. The contemporary group of six artists has a spiritual purpose in their collective art making. They are responding peacefully and creatively to cultural conflicts by working collaboratively and across cultures in contrast to the rise of political and religious violence worldwide following September 11, 2001.[12]

APPROPRIATING WHAT ALREADY EXISTS

The most direct and clearest challenge to modernist notions of originality and works made by individual artists is **appropriation.** To appropriate is to possess, borrow, steal, copy, quote, or excerpt images that already exist, made by other artists or available in the public domain and general culture. Appropriation art of the 1980s and after is especially informed by French artist Marcel Duchamp's "ready-mades," most famously *Fountain* (**11.12**), an ordinary urinal that he signed and exhibited as a work of art in 1917. Duchamp's gesture was conceptual: he was challenging the prevailing definition of art as pleasing aesthetic objects.

11.12 **MARCEL DUCHAMP** *Fountain,* 1950 (replica of 1917 original). Porcelain urinal, 12 × 15 × 18 in.

11.13 **RICHARD PRINCE** *Untitled (Cowboy),* 1989. Ektacolor photograph, 50 × 75 in.

Contemporary American artists Jeff Koons (see 11.5) and Barbara Kruger (see 11.1), discussed earlier in this chapter, are both involved in appropriation as art. Koons uses cultural icons such as Hummel figurines, pop star Michael Jackson, artifacts of the NBA, and mundane household items. He insists he is sincere in his work and that he is not critical toward what he displays. He rejects hidden meanings, believing that there is no gap between your perception of the work of art at first glance and any deeper meaning in the artifact itself. Kruger's work is informed by feminist theory and is overtly and obviously critical of social injustices. She appropriates photographs from popular culture, crops them, heightens their contrast, and adds text. The texts she uses are also appropriated from popular culture, but she subverts the texts with ironic twists of phrasing and word choice, juxtaposing words and pictures. Like Duchamp, both Koons and Kruger take material from popular culture and use it for conceptual ends: Koons wants to celebrate that culture, and Kruger wants to make fundamental changes in it.

The Metropolitan Museum of Art in New York owns a work of appropriated art by American postmodernist Richard Prince, *Untitled* (**11.13**). He made it from one of the images of a successful TV and print advertising campaign for Marlboro cigarettes. Prince selected a portion of the image and enlarged it, thus diminishing its original sleekness and exaggerating its mechanical means of production. The Metropolitan refers to Prince's piece as "a copy [the photograph] of a copy [the advertisement] of a myth [the cowboy]." The museum interprets *Untitled* as "a meditation on an entire culture's continuing attraction to spectacle over lived experience." Through his "rephotographing" of images, Prince intends to reveal that mass-media images are "hallucinatory fictions of society's desires," undermining their seeming naturalness.

Art critic Hal Foster tells us appropriation art reveals that "underneath each picture there is always another picture." Foster argues that the importance of appropriation is that it entails a shift in position: "The artist becomes a manipulator of signs more than a producer of art objects, and the viewer an active reader of messages rather than a passive contemplator of the aesthetic or consumer of the spectacle."[13] Foster's remark relates to seeing any artifact as a text rather than as a solitary and original work, as discussed earlier in this chapter.

SIMULATING THE "REAL"

The process of imitating or copying is **simulation.** The related concept of simulacra, developed especially by Jean Baudrillard, a French theorist of postmodernism, is a prominent theme explored by postmodernists. **Simulacra** (singular **simulacrum**) are representations of things that no longer have an original or never had one

to begin with, insubstantial semblances of real things or events. The idea of the simulacrum asserts that we are no longer able to distinguish between the real and the simulated "hyperreal" of television, advertising, video games, role-playing games, and all kinds of spectacles in contemporary society. In Baudrillard's thinking, the distinction between the real and the representation collapses, and all we know are the signs of popular culture and media. Any image moves from being a reflection of reality, to a perversion of reality, to a mask of the absence of reality, to pure simulacrum—having no relation to reality at all.[14]

Betty Boop (**11.14**), a popular sexual icon, can serve as an example of a simulacrum. The animated cartoon character appeared in a series of films produced by Paramount Pictures in the 1930s and has remained popular ever since. She is based on a real singer, Helen Kane, who herself rose to fame by imitating Annette Hanshaw, a jazz singer in the 1920s. Betty Boop, a copy, survives both Kane and Hanshaw, actual people—she is a copy that no longer refers to an original but that has taken on an independent life of her own.

Photography, a medium based on copying, with the property of realistic-looking duplication, lends itself especially well to playing with simulation by contemporary artists. Gregory Crewdson, for example, is a photographer who uses the conventions, techniques, and technicians of cinema to produce convincing-looking simulacra in the form of still photographs. *Untitled, Winter* (**11.15**) is a photograph that Crewdson made with the help of a set designer, cinematographer, and professional actors. The image is a composite of two different shots: he used one central scan for the bedroom and the man, and another scan for the woman. The postproduction work with Photoshop software to refine the image was elaborate but adds to the realistic look. A professional crew may be beyond your art budget, but Crewdson's idea of using realistic images to subvert viewer trust in the truth of images is open to you.

HYBRIDIZING CULTURAL INFLUENCES

The process of mixing diverse cultural influences in an artwork is **hybridization.** In postmodern terminology, it refers to "the processes and products of cultural mixing which articulates two or more disparate elements to engender a new and distinct entity."[15] Artists and theorists who want to disrupt simplistic divisions of complex cultural generalities—such as Western/non-Western, black/white, male/female, gay/straight—share this meaning.

Sangeeta Sandrasegar is an Australian-born artist of Indian-Malaysian descent who explores in her artwork the intersection of diverse cultures in her life, relationships, and body. She brings together vastly divergent sources: Indian cultural myths, legends, and iconography; Japanese *manga* pornographic images; the romance of Hollywood films (from the Indian film industry); and the sex and violence of Hollywood cinema. Her usual medium is paper cutouts of couples and singles that are influenced by the traditional henna designs applied to the hands and feet of Indian brides. In this way, she reflects on traditional customs and gender roles in Indian society. As in the example from the series *Goddess of Flowers* (**11.16**), Sandrasegar hangs ornate paper cutouts a little bit away from the wall in dimly lit spaces and projects overhead lights onto them, illuminating the cutouts and projecting shadows of them on the wall. The artist's overlay of paper images, space, and projected shadows reinforces the complexity of cultural conditions and how we perceive them: we have materiality (red paper), projections of it (light-red shadows), and conceptual space in between (white negative space).

Masami Teraoka is from Japan and lives in the United States. His art reflects his experiences of two distinctly different cultures. In the watercolor reproduced here, *AIDS Series / Vaccine Day Celebration* (**11.17**), Teraoka draws upon the tradition of Japanese *ukiyo-e* wood-block prints to show a couple picnicking on a beach in

11.14   BETTY BOOP

11.15   GREGORY CREWDSON   *Untitled, Winter,* 2004. Digital C-Print, 64¼ × 94¼ in., image size 57⅕ × 88 in., framed size 66⅜ × 97⅛ x 2½ in.

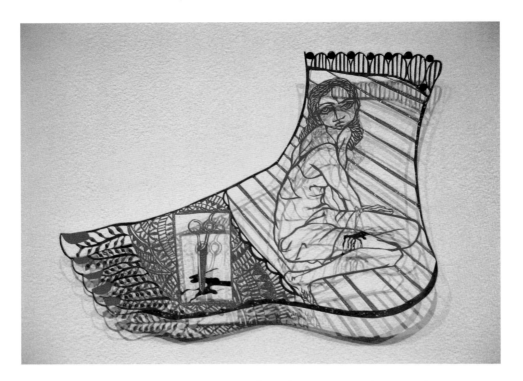

11.16 **SANGEETA SANDRASEGAR** *Untitled (no. 22),* from the series *Goddess of Flowers,* 2003–2004. Paper, glue, sequins.

11.17 **MASAMI TERAOKA** *AIDS Series / Vaccine Day Celebration,* 1990. Watercolor study on paper, 29 × 43 in.

11.18 ROBERT RAUSCHENBERG *First Landing Jump,*
1961. Combine painting: cloth, metal, leather, electric fixture,
cable, and oil paint on composition board, with automobile tire and
wooden plank on floor, 7 ft. 5⅛ in. × 6 ft. 8⅞ in.

Hawaii. They have just received a fax that announces
Vaccine Celebration Day. They dance, and he plays a
samisen (three-stringed instrument) and flies a kite that
reads "Celebration." Faxes and condoms blow away
in the sea breeze along with cherry blossoms, reflecting the artist's hope for good news about AIDS.[16] The
painting, a pastiche of cultures and times, raises consciousness of an epidemic with global effects.

All of us are members of many cultures, whether,
like Sandrasegar and Teraoka, we have a mixed national
or ethnic background, or whether we belong to different groups based on shared values, beliefs, norms, and
customs. You can make cultural influences visible in
your work and explore ways to bring different cultures
together to create a new, more complex entity.

MIXING MEDIA

Many modernists uphold the ideal that any specific art
medium ought to be used purely, that is, artists ought
to discover and exploit the nature of any given material. An artwork made of wood should look like wood;
plaster and concrete need not be disguised as something
else, because they are beautiful media in themselves.
Some kitschy materials, such as glitter and Day-Glo
paint, are not the stuff of art.

A corollary modernist principle is that each artform
does a certain thing best: for example, photographs
should not be made to look like paintings; paintings
ought to exploit their flatness; and architecture ought to
reveal its function and thus not hide heating ducts under
a false ceiling.

Modernists also tend to avoid mixing different media into conglomerates that ignore the individual and
"pure" identities of each. Each medium ought to be explored to determine what can be done with it and its
unique qualities.

Postmodernists reject these restrictive principles and
attitudes and freely employ **mixed media,** different
media in a single work of art. Robert Rauschenberg
began defying the restrictions with his "combines," art
objects for which he intentionally mixed painting and
sculpture. In *First Landing Jump* (**11.18**), Rauschenberg mixed various media (cloth, metal, leather, electric
fixture, cable, and oil paint on composition board) and
ordinary objects (an actual automobile tire and wooden
plank) with an art object (painting on canvas), and he
makes the "painting" project off the wall like a "sculpture." Today the mixing of media in one work of art is
common, but it was not always so.

LAYERING IMAGES

Because of photomechanical reproduction, images
are cheap and plentiful. In a process called **layering,** some artists pile images on top of each other,
changing the meanings of each of the images from
what they originally meant or were intended for. To
make *See* (**11.19**), for example, Rachel Hecker layered images of Tubby from the 1950s comic book
Lulu and a digital sign with the word "see" over an
airbrushed female nude. The woman's torso is from
a 1950s painting manual, and it is suggestive of soft-
core pornography. Tubby reacts to it, from a "two-
dimensional, dwarfed, and infantilized"[17] male point of
view on his phallic surfboard. The word "see" in digital
style is prominent. Each single image is clear enough: a
cartoon character, a nude, and the word "see." By layering these simple images, the artist has complicated each
and made a new painting whose meanings are ambiguous, posing questions such as these: See Tubby engage
with a woman? See the male gaze at the female body?
See the woman's breasts and lips fragmented from her
body as if only some of her parts are valuable?

China, China (**11.20**) employs layering to communicate an idea about personal identity. It is one of more
than thirty porcelain busts made by Ah Xian, a Chinese
artist who fled to Sydney, Australia, in 1990 for political reasons. The busts are of anonymous men and
women, young and old, heavy and slight. Bust 14, pictured here, is life-size, molded directly from the woman
who modeled for Xian. On the eyes of the figure the

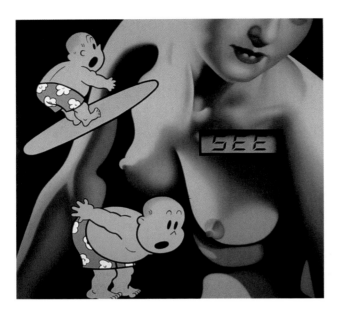

11.19 RACHEL HECKER *See,* 1984.

11.20 AH XIAN *China, China,* **Bust 14,** 1999. Porcelain in overglaze polychrome, enamels with flowers of the four seasons and butterfly design, 14½ × 13 × 9 in.

artist has layered a bright orange butterfly; he covers her lips with flowers. He has layered similar subject matter on her head and shoulders. The sources of the images are traditional Chinese patterns found on plates and bowls and vases in the Ming (1364–1643) and Qing (1644–1911) dynasties. Through these busts and the images he places on them, Xian visually expresses the thought that Chinese culture is part of a Chinese person, no matter where he or she dwells.[18]

MIXING CODES

A "code," in postmodern discourse, is a system of signs and a set of conventions for how the signs are to be used. Signs within a culture are arbitrary, not natural. We communally agree, for example, that at a traffic intersection, green means go and red means stop. A problem with codes is that we use them so effortlessly that they seem natural rather than invented. All images rely on codes, but usually we are so aware of the codes that we do not even think about them. A driver's license from a state in the United States is coded: it contains words; the state symbol; a series of short black lines that we know as a bar code, but the content of which we cannot readily decipher; other numbers; abbreviations; and a colored picture of a head without a body that we read as an identification photograph. Some artists make us consciously aware of codes in everyday life and how they shape our perceptions by mixing them together and juxtaposing them.

Michael Ray Charles, an African American artist, uses **mixed codes** to unmask racist biases. In *Cut and Paste* (**11.21**), he appropriates a coded system from pa-

per doll kits but uses a racist image of a black man as the doll, with various stereotypical props. The props visually signify racist attitudes with signs that are used to denigrate African Americans: a football, a hair pick, a gun, a banana, a tie, a handbag, a chicken, and a knife. Within our culture, most of us know how to read these signs, or "signifiers": the football can be associated with racist notions of blacks' supposed superior athleticism and inferior mental capability; the gun with the imagined threat of violence posed by black males; the handbag with purse snatching by black males; and so on. The figure itself is coded with oversized lips, braided hair, and white minstrel gloves and shorts similar to the ones Walt Disney's Mickey Mouse wears (Mickey Mouse himself is a derivation of a black minstrel figure). By mixing the code of paper doll workbooks made for children into the image, Charles suggests that racism is learned at home and at an early age.

RECONTEXTUALIZING
THE FAMILIAR

Related to the mixing of codes, another postmodernist strategy is **recontextualization,** "positioning a familiar image in relationship to pictures, symbols, or texts with which it is not usually associated in order to generate meaning in an artwork."[19] Fred Wilson is a contemporary master of recontextualization. He forages through museum collections and rearranges objects to give them power through unusual juxtapositions. In a detail from his exhibition *Mining the Museum* (**11.22**), he has placed a wooden post used for whipping slaves alongside wooden furniture of the same period from the collection of the Maryland Historical Society. Similarly, Wilson's juxtaposition of steel shackles and silver tea sets in other works displays the brutality that coexisted with gentility in slave owners' lives.

Yolanda Lopez appropriated the widely displayed sacred image of Our Lady of Guadalupe and recontextualized it into a political artwork, *Portrait of the Artist as the Virgin of Guadalupe* (**11.23**). The artist says that her series of Virgin images is her way of "questioning a very common and potent icon of the ideal woman in Chicano culture":

> At a time in our history when we were looking to our past historically and culturally I wanted the Guadalupes to prompt a reconsideration of what kinds of new role models Chicanas need, and also to caution against adopting carte blanche anything simply because it is Mexican. By doing portraits of ordinary women—my mother, grandmother, and myself—I wanted to draw attention and pay homage to working-class women, old women, middle-aged over-weight women, young, exuberant, self-assertive women. Church groups that were offended by the work were absolutely correct. The works are also an attack on the authoritarian, patriarchal Catholic church.[20]

By changing the context of a known image, you can radically alter the image's original meanings and uses.

INTERTEXTUALIZING SIGNS

The term **intertextuality** refers to the shaping of one sign's meaning by other signs. Each sign constitutes a text to be read. Many postmodernist strategies of art making rely on intertextuality, especially hybridizing, layering, mixing media, mixing codes, and recontextualizing. For example, Masami Teraoka's *AIDS Series / Vaccine Day Celebration* (see 11.17), which illustrates hybridizing, uses the sign of cherry blossoms drawn from traditional Japanese pictures, pictures of faxes that refer to AIDS, and representations of condoms. Each of these signs has many conventional associations, and when they are mixed into a single work, they then shape the meaning and significance of the other signs in the work. In Japanese visual culture, cherry blossoms signify positive aspects of spring and romance, but in Teraoka's watercolor, such a reading is confronted by the dangers of unsafe sex in an age of AIDS.

To construct meanings about works with multiple references, we need to know to what those references

11.21 MICHAEL RAY CHARLES *Cut and Paste,* 1994. Acrylic on paper, 60 × 35 in.

refer. We need to be aware of a variety of texts and how they interact in an artwork or design. The ad agency knows the references of its ad for condoms (**11.24**), and it also knows its target group, namely, young people who are or will be engaged in sexual activity. The ad plays with references to animals made of balloons, namely, rabbits, which are known for prolific procreation. The ad is inclusive of multiple gender roles, showing rabbits engaged in ways of procreating that are not biologically accurate for the animals. Its use of balloon-like condoms, with pastel colors, is a humorous appeal for safe sexual practices. Its audience will be able to read its multiple texts.

11.22 **FRED WILSON** *Cabinet Making* (detail: *Whipping Post*), 1820–1960, from *Mining the Museum: An Installation by Fred Wilson.*

11.23 **YOLANDA M. LOPEZ** *Portrait of the Artist as the Virgin of Guadalupe,* 1978. Oil pastel on paper, 32 × 28 in.

CONFRONTING THE GAZE

The concept of **the gaze** originated in film theory in the 1970s and was first identified as "the male gaze"—the tendency of Hollywood films to represent women in ways that heighten the sexual or erotic aspects of their bodies, because that was believed to be the way men looked at women. Such representations usually position the maker, and thus the viewer, as the active subject and the woman as the passive object. Film theorist Laura Mulvey argues that the female body in film too often has a "to-be-looked-at-ness." The male gaze is also pervasive in mass-media advertising, used to sell any and all kinds of products and services.

Art critic John Berger sees the gaze at work in many paintings and sculptures of the past as well. He argues that these images are the result of men's desire to legitimately eroticize and then stare at women. Worse yet, male painters and patrons sometimes cast the blame for the pleasure on the woman. Berger writes, "You painted a naked woman because you enjoyed looking at her, you put a mirror in her hand and you called the painting *Vanity* (**11.25**), thus morally condemning the woman whose nakedness you had depicted for your own pleasure."[21]

Postmodern artists do not adopt the tradition of the gaze so much as confront it. Cindy Sherman's large series of photographs *Untitled Film Stills* brings critical attention to the male gaze. In each of the works, Sherman appropriates the look and feel of unnamed Hollywood movies and dresses and poses herself as their vulnerable female characters (**11.26**).

Since the late 1970s, feminists have considered the possibility of "the female gaze," whereby the female is in the position of a subject who actively desires males or females. Some female artists, such as Britain's Tracey Emin, make work based on their own sexual lives. Emin made a blue tent she called *Everyone I Have Ever Slept With 1963–1995* (**11.27**). Appliquéd to the inside walls are names of her many sexual partners. Later, she made *My Bed,* an installation that includes a mattress with white rumpled sheets and pillows, pantyhose, and a towel. Heaped at the bottom of the bed are vodka bottles, slippers, underwear, cigarette packs, condoms, Polaroid self-portraits, and a fluffy white toy. Her works are both confessional and confrontational concerning her role as an active sexual subject rather than a passive sexual object. The work of Sherman, Emin, and others challenges you to a greater awareness of the implications of how you represent women in your own work.

USING DISSONANCE

Lack of harmony or agreement between elements in a work causes tension referred to as **dissonance.** As we saw in Chapter 5, clashing colors can create visual dissonance in a work. In what *Print* magazine calls a personal project, Cecilia Cortes-Earle created an award-winning poster (**11.28**) employing dissonance between a plaything for a young girl—a would-be page from a cutout book—and young girls as playthings in the international sex market. The text at the bottom of the page lists statistics of young children involved in the international sex market.

Contemporary Dutch painter Robert Smit (**11.29**) combines dissonant images to open the possibility of new meanings. His strategy of painting is directly influenced by his reading of the important German philosopher Georg Wilhelm Friedrich Hegel (1770–1831). Influenced by the philosopher, the artist says, "What I do is join contrary, opposing, diverse images together in order to construct new meanings that reach a new level."[22] Smit is engaged in an ongoing ambitious project that will eventually compose one massive work on a wall that will be a grid of sixty-four squares, 7 by 7 feet each, made up of thirty-two pairs of images. Each diptych is composed of two canvases of divergent imagery, allowing the artist and the viewer to construct a new conceptual and emotional synthesis of the two canvases. Smit paints one of the two adjoining canvases. He generates the other piece photomechanically and has it digitally printed onto a similarly stretched canvas. When he puts the two square canvases of the same size next to each other to form a diptych, Smit then decides whether and how to alter each part of the pair for an effective synthesis.

GET IT ON. durex®

11.24   Ad for bunny condoms, 2008. Designed by Fitzgerald & Co. Advertising, Atlanta. Art Director: Fernando Lecca; Copywriter: Jerry Williams; Photographer: Arian Camilleri.

11.25   HANS MEMLING *Vanity,* c. 1485. Central panel from a tryptic, oil on oak, 20.2 × 13.1 cm.

Smit both digitally appropriates imagery from sources within popular culture and makes his own digital photographs. The diptychs include Photoshop manipulations, oil, acrylic, and tempera, and elements of collage. His painted and digital subject matter makes reference to significant social issues as well as personally important biographical incidents with which the viewer might identify. With a postmodernist attitude that challenges authorial voice and the unique hand of the artist, he invites the college students he teaches to add to what he has done or contribute a square of their own, which he accepts or further modifies.

CONSTRUCTING NEW IDENTITIES

The characteristics that define you or another person constitute identity. White Anglo-Saxon female is one identity. Identity can be socially determined by membership in a group according to such markers as race, ethnicity, religion, gender, or sexual orientation. When you take political action to advance the interests of members of a group thought to be oppressed and marginalized by virtue of a shared identity, you are engaging in **identity politics.** Artists working with identity politics make art based on issues regarding race, gender, ethnicity, and social issues rather than on aesthetic appeal. Many of the artists already discussed in this chapter—Kruger, Goldin, the Guerrilla Girls, Sandrasegar, Hecker, Xian, Charles, Wilson, Lopez, Sherman, and Emin—are to a greater or lesser extent and in different ways involved in identity politics in their artworks.

ACT UP (Aids Coalition to Unleash Power) and Gran Fury, two activist collectives, assert their members' gay and lesbian identities in confrontational graphic images and slogans such as "We're here, we're queer, get used to it." The initial goals for ACT UP were "to publicize the [AIDS] crisis, to get drugs into bodies, and to end the AIDS crisis."[23] They organized (**11.30**) and mobilized government support of research and policies to end the AIDS epidemic nationally and worldwide, relying especially on use of confrontational graphic designs.

Melissa Shiff is a contemporary individual artist also working with important social issues in the context of her Jewish heritage. *Elijah Chair* (**11.31**) is an antique rocking chair with an embedded

11.26   **CINDY SHERMAN**   *Untitled #71,* 1980. Color photograph, 16 × 24 in.

11.27   **TRACEY EMIN**   *Everyone I Have Ever Slept With 1963–1995,* 1995. Appliquéd tent, mattress, and light, 48 × 96 × 84 in.

video monitor that shows doors opening into various homes—rich, poor, and in between. She intends the chair to serve as "a meditation on unconditional hospitality and the unequal distribution of wealth in urban America."[24] Shiff made *Elijah Chair* as part of her larger social project entitled *Times Square Seder, Featuring the Matzoh Ball Soup Kitchen*. The work took place in three storefront windows on Forty-second Street in New York City. The whole work, of which the chair is a central part, consisted of readings, performances, video projections, art installations, and a soup kitchen for the homeless. For the chair, Shiff drew upon Jewish customs related to the prophet Elijah: the opening of the door for Elijah and the setting aside of a chair for him. The artist created the chair to employ the prophet in the service of social action. For Shiff, the piece "documents the staggering divide of wealth in this city of extremes in an effort to show that Elijah signifies the hospitality and openness to the Other that must occur."[25] Shiff embraces her religion and her politics in her art that confronts Jews as Others, and she shows in her artifact that the Jewish tradition embraces otherness.

Guillermo Gómez-Peña is a performance artist, writer, activist, and educator intensely involved with issues of his identity. He was born in Mexico City and resides in the United States. He explains the conflicts he experiences negotiating the politics of mixed identities:

> Today, I wake up as a Mexican in U.S. territory. With my Mexican psyche, my Mexican heart, and my Mexican body, I have to make intelligible art for American audiences that know very little about my culture. This is my daily dilemma. I have to force myself to cross a border, and there is very little reciprocity from the people on the other side. I physically live between two cultures and two epochs. I have a little house in Mexico City, and one in New York, separated from each other by a thousand light-years in terms of culture. I also spend time in California. As a result, I am a Mexican part of the year, and a Chicano, the other part. I cross the border by foot, by car, and by airplane. My journey not only goes from South to North, but from the past to the future, from Spanish to English, and from one side of myself to another.[26]

The still photograph from a live performance by Gómez-Peña (**11.32**) shows the anguish of being Mexican and American, concerns with his interface between Mexico and the United States, North America and South America, and border conflicts between the two countries and immigration and the political ramifications of his brown body.

11.28   CECILIA CORTES-EARLE   Poster, 2007.

ADAPTING LITERARY DEVICES TO VISUAL ART

Literary theory heavily influences postmodernist art theory. Thus it is not surprising that contemporary artists are increasingly using literary strategies when making visual artifacts.

Using Narratives. Recall from Chapter 6 that a narrative is a representation of an event or story. Storytelling, or narration, is an ancient practice of oral tradition and an old practice in the history of art, dating to the ancient Egyptians or earlier. "History painting," the depiction of an event from biblical or classical history, achieved high status during the Renaissance. Nineteenth-century painting and sculpture reveled in dramatic history stories and sometimes in sentimental family dramas. However, modern painters of the late nineteenth and early twentieth centuries turned away from storytelling in art, believing narratives were more suitable for writers than for visual artists. By the 1960s, abstraction ruled in the mainstream art world, and narrative art making was taboo. During that decade, artists rebelled against such strictures on their

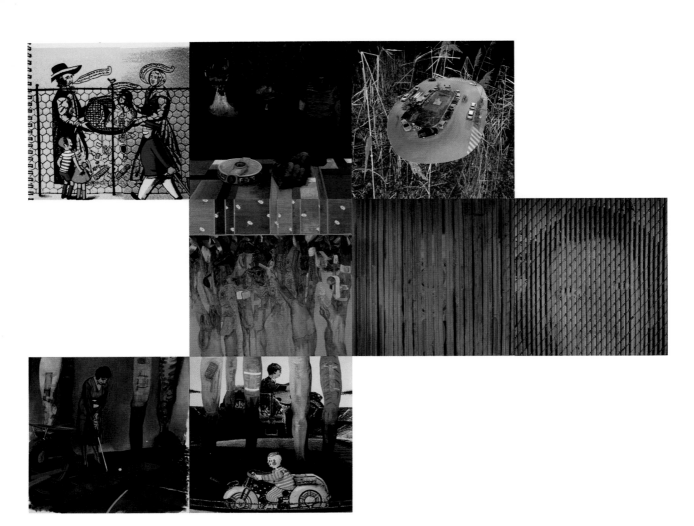

11.29 ROBERT SMIT *No Meaning* (detail), 1998–present. Grid of diptychs, each square painting, 6 ft. 7 in. × 6 ft. 7 in.; total grid upon completion, 53 ft. 6 in. × 53 ft. 6 in.

11.30 ACT UP, photograph of a protest.

creative practices and reintroduced narrative into their artworks.[27]

Charlotte Schulz makes highly detailed images based on narrative fragments:

> My avenue of pursuit is in stories. I want to be affected by the larger flow of history—the history of stories. I see my own experience as a narrative that speaks about the past and present as well as the quotidian themes throughout human history. I am incorporating stories told both through words and images as a way to bring these "memories of the world" into my present realm.[28]

Schulz says that the telling of her stories in the space of a canvas or sheet of paper is formally the most challenging aspect for her as an artist: "The almost magical transformation of bringing the three-dimensional world into the physical space of a flat surface completely engages me. Spatially, I am interested in how painting can link modern cinematic vision with the stilled and timeless vision of the Renaissance. The whole is experienced by moving from picture to picture within the painting as well as viewing it in one look."[29]

Panel #6, with its long literary title (**11.33**), is one of many detailed charcoal drawings that Schulz displays as part of a grid of framed drawings on a wall. Each detailed drawing shows a dreamlike narrative that is open to multiple interpretations. When she refers to a "cinematic vision," she is referring to how each drawing can be likened to a scene of a complex movie or a fragment of an entangled and complex dream.

Narration is a common strategy in advertising on television and in print media. Producers of television commercials are adept at telling stories, sometimes based on humor, other times on sex or fear, in thirty seconds. An Altoid Mints print ad (**11.34**) on the back cover of a magazine suggests a narrative with one posed photograph and a tag line. "Oh, the shame" accompanies the intrusion of a mother into her son's bedroom at an implied inopportune time. The ad suggests the intense pleasure of curiously strong mints.

Creating Metaphors. As in "All the world's a stage," when we attribute the qualities of one thing (the world) to another (a stage), we are creating **metaphor.** As explained in Chapter 1, in a general sense, all images are metaphors because the qualities of the image are attributed to the thing being depicted. A Frida Kahlo self-portrait (see 1.28), for example, is a metaphor for an aspect of Kahlo's persona. Her selection of details shapes our interpretation of her self-image.

11.31 MELISSA SHIFF *Elijah Chair: Art Ritual and Social Action,* 2002. Sculpture and video installation.

11.32 GUILLERMO GÓMEZ-PEÑA Photograph from the performance Binational Boxer.

11.33 CHARLOTTE SCHULZ *The maximum of all possible hate is realized in the eternal moment . . . Panel #6,* 2005. Charcoal on paper, 22 × 28 in., installation of drawings, 75 × 113 in.

Many modernist artworks minimize metaphoric meaning in favor of aesthetic meaning, referring to powerful arrangements of elements in the work whose meaning tends to be self-referential or to refer to other works of art. Postmodernists, on the other hand, often refer directly to events outside of art itself and explicitly use metaphors to do so.

Korean sculptor and installation artist Do-Ho Suh's sculpture *Public Figures* (**11.35**) is overtly metaphoric. It depicts hundreds of tiny human figures holding up a relatively huge pedestal of the type typically found in a public setting, such as a park. Importantly, Suh placed no figure atop the pedestal; the figures supporting the pedestal are the only figures in the sculpture. Suh's sculpture is a metaphor for many unrecognized individuals who support societies' heroes. He explains his work:

> I just want to recognize them. Let's say if there's one statue at the plaza of a hero who helped or protected our country, there are hundreds of thousands of individuals who helped him and worked with him, and there's no recognition for them. So in my sculpture, *Public Figures*, I had around six hundred small figures, twelve inches high, six different shapes, both male and female, of different ethnicities.[30]

11.34 ALTOIDS MINTS **Advertisement** in *Interview* magazine, October 2006, inside back cover.

11.35 DO-HO SUH *Public Figures,* October 1998–May 1999. Fiberglass and resin, steel pipes, pipe fittings, 120 × 84 × 108 in., installation view, Metrotech Center Commons, Brooklyn, New York.

11.36 STEPHEN ALTHOUSE *Clamps,* 2003. Photograph, 41 × 60 in.

11.37 JANINE ANTONI *Gnaw,* 1992. Six-hundred pounds of chocolate, gnawed by the artist, 24 × 24 × 24 in.

Some visual metaphors are open to a wide range of interpretations due to the lack of specificity in their references. Stephen Althouse's *Clamps* (**11.36**) shows two antique wooden C-clamps holding a ribbon of torn fabric. It suggests general themes such as control and restraint, hardness and delicacy. One possible interpretation is that the image is about relationships: two people hold something between them that is fragile, trying not to crush it, but not letting it slip away or unravel due to a lack of careful holding.

We have already examined how the use of formal elements, such as line, shape, and texture, contributes to the meanings of artworks. An additional way for you to communicate ideas about your subject is through the creation and use of metaphor.

Using Irony and Parody. You can use words and images to convey the opposite of what they say and show in a technique called **irony.** While this strategy is not new, many contemporary artists are reemploying it to engage viewers in questioning what they have received as knowledge. Knowing whether something is ironic is essential to understanding works of art, as we can clearly see in Michael Ray Charles's *Cut and Paste*

(see 11.21). Some fear Charles's images will be misunderstood and taken as straightforward *reinforcements* of racist views that actually encourage what they are meant to resist. If you use irony in your own work, you have the challenge of letting the viewer know what your work is for and against without it being overly didactic and preachy.

Native American performance artist James Luna attempts to communicate his views through parody. A

parody is a mockery of a literary work, an event, or type of representation. In a street performance piece, *Take a Picture with a Real Indian,* Luna, a Luiseño Indian, invites passersby on the street to have their picture taken with a life-size image of Luna wearing one of three native costumes: contemporary, basic breechcloth, and a fictitious "wardance" outfit. The work explores the fascination that the general public has for "their" Indians, a fascination that often ignores the reality of American Indians today. Luna explains his art-making strategy:

> One of the primary reasons I make art is to inform others about Native peoples from our point of view—a view that because of history is rich in native cultural tradition, and both influenced by and influential in contemporary American society. I truly believe that Native Tribal peoples are the least known and most incorrectly portrayed people in history, media, and the arts. I want to change those perceptions.[31]

For viewers to realize the meanings and impact of an ironic work of art, they need to know what the work is quoting or referring to. In the 1993 Whitney Biennial exhibition, for example, New York–based artist Janine Antoni exhibited a sculpture called *Gnaw* (**11.37**). It is a very large, solid block of chocolate that the artist has chewed, breaking down its edges and corners, and softening its rigid form and hard planes. Its massive and simple form refers to the tradition of minimalist sculpture of the 1960s that was nonrepresentational, with no explicit references to social reality. It is also, however, a piece that "thematized contemporary female obsessions with overeating and dieting, beauty and thinness, and the masochistic longing for love that propels such obsessions."[32] So it appropriates minimalist form but adds strong social content. When making ironic works of art, if you give indications of your work's references, you will give viewers more to understand and think about your work.

Conclusion: Are You a Postmodernist?

You were born into an era that is now called postmodernist. This overview of some of the attitudes and approaches of working artists who are fluent in and contributing to current art making can help you consider your own art making. You are likely already using many of the approaches that are discussed here: they are of our lifetime.

12 Artists' Processes and Practices

12.1 **ADIDAS GROUP** *Football Heaven,* 2006. The foyer of the main train station in Cologne, Germany.

Artists' Motivations and Ideas for Making Art
Artists' Practices of Making Art
Conclusion: Keep Yourself Motivated

This chapter is a collage of quotations from contemporary artists and designers who share their motivations, sources of ideas, and their practices for making art. The statements provide an authentic look at art making from many insiders' viewpoints, and they provide a range of possibilities, as there is not just a single way to be an artist. They are meant to be a source of inspiration for you to consult anytime you are faced with difficulties in starting a work or completing it. The source of each quote is provided so that you can delve further into the processes of those artists who most inspire you.

The diversity of the voice and style of writing should put you at ease and help you realize that you don't have to use pretentious language or jargon when talking or writing about your work. Clarity and simplicity will suffice.

Artists' Motivations and Ideas for Making Art

In this section, a wide range of artists and designers talk about where they get their ideas to explore and create and what motivates them to make things. Their insights are delightfully diverse. Their statements reinforce themes that we have been exploring from the beginning of the book.

Adidas Group (see 12.1). "We are consumer focused. That means we continuously improve the quality, look, feel and image of our products and our organizational structures to match and exceed consumer expectations and to provide them with the highest value. We are innovation and design leaders who seek to help athletes of all skill levels achieve peak performance with every product we bring to the market" (from its website, www.adidas.com).

Karim Rashid (1960–), Industrial Designer. "I believe every new object should replace three. Better products edit the marketplace. I believe objects should not be obstacles in life but raptures to experience. I try to develop de-stressors—objects that bring enjoyment and simplify tasks while increasing our level of engagement and of beauty. Our lives are elevated when we experience beauty, comfort, luxury, performance and utility acting seamlessly together."[1]

Peter Schreyer (1954–), Automobile Designer. "The technical prerequisites of all products are becoming increasingly similar. At present this is the case with cars, computers, watches and even vacuum cleaners. Design forms not only the product itself, it stands equal to the label. The diverse world of products is an indication of our liberty. Design has its place more on the psychological level. Good design sells emotions, creates identification with a label and ultimately influ-

ences someone's position in society. You can reach extraordinary design only with visions, which exceed the imagination of today's customer. It is visionaries that have always contributed to the cultural, scientific, and sociological successes of our society. We would still be living in the Stone Age if it were not for visionaries."[2]

Scott Henderson, Designer, Architect. "As a parent, you simply tolerate all of these primary colors and blocky shapes around the house. Why can't baby stuff be highly functional and elegantly or cleverly designed? What about space efficiency? There's a huge opportunity out there."[3]

Erik Adams, Graphic Designer, Product Designer. "I want to use storytelling to make design more meaningful. For me, writing is important—the way writing and imagery work together. I want design to become a more intelligent and emotional process, a vehicle to communicate other things. My three main goals are to make my work instructive, edifying, and uplifting."[4]

Cybu Richli (1982–), Graphic Designer. "Unfortunately, a lot of infographics aren't informative or appealing. Making a great graphic requires functional thinking but also aesthetics, independent-mindedness, even stubbornness to find that really innovative way of explaining things."[5]

Anne Seidman (1950–), Painter (see 2.15). "I paint because I strongly feel that individual expression confirms our existence."[6]

Julian Schnabel (1951–), Painter, Filmmaker (see 4.1).

Q: "What's the worst thing you can do as an artist?"

A: "Try to get people to like you."[7]

John McCracken (1934–), Artist. "The only art worth doing is the art that makes things better. More actually advanced. More enjoyable. A key: genuine happiness. All around. So, make art that comes out of your own sense of what's actually best, and advanced, and supercool."[8]

Mierle Laderman Ukeles (1939–), Artist. "I believe that art is the articulation of human freedom. Remember, above all, you are the boss, The Boss, of your freedom. No one else. Your art, if it is original and worth something, expands all human freedom.

"Art, after it comes through you, will be different. Art comes from you, you all by yourself, unique among anyone who has ever lived in the history of the world; AND, art comes from you in *your* world with the choices you make as a free being, and the glue, even, with the relationships that you create and stick to; AND art comes from you as a citizen *in* the world; AND you *within* history and in nature."[9]

Roger Brown (1942–1997), Painter. "In America—in Chicago—we are living in a constantly growing and changing environment, one that is to a large extent devoid of masterpieces of older art. In a strange way this is good, because not having the great works of European art as constant reference points gives us the opportunity to make fresh art—art that derives from our own experience."[10]

Stephen Shore (1947–), Photographer. "I believe that art is made to explore the world and the culture, to explore the chosen medium, to explore one's self. It is made to communicate, in the medium's language, a perception, an observation, an understanding, an emotional or mental state. It is made to answer, or try to answer, questions. It is made for fun. In short, it is made in response to personal needs and demands."[11]

Barbara Jo Revelle, Photographer. "I make art because it is a way of communicating with other human beings. For me, art making is the best way to express the ideas that form in my brain . . . Art is about creating meaning and I think meaning lies in the relationships between things. For me single images, like glimpses of life from an elevated train, are poignant, but have little to do with understanding. A long time ago I began to construct meanings by combining images. First I combined photographs. Then I began to put pictures with all sorts of other things: words, audiotaped stories, animal noises, gravestones, eggshells, wedding cakes. Film with food. One's experience always exceeds one's vocabulary, so art making is a way to name the unnamable or make visible something that wasn't visible before."[12]

Philip Taaffe (1955–), Painter (see 3.27, 9.1). "The painting should say there's another world. It's a utopian position that I have, but I am actually trying to lay the groundwork for some kind of paradisiacal situation on earth. I think about what's going on in the world, and whether my painting can conceivably have any impact on the situation."[13]

Howard Finster (1916–2001), Painter. "God called me into the minister's work to . . . get acquainted with the Earth people from this world. . . . Then I was in my last church, and I'd been there fifteen years and three months. And I asked them that night what I preached on that mornin', and there wasn't but one man in that church that could tell me my text from one service to another. And I thinks to myself, my God, they ain't listenin' to me. And that's why I retired from preachin'. I tried to think of Billy Graham's messages, and I been hearin' 'em for years, and I couldn't even think of one

of his messages. And I said to myself, I'm like that, they're like that, and everybody's like that. Now I've gotta reach the people, so God called me to sacred art. Now when I write a message, that message is not goin' away with the wind. And the people not gonna forget it from one service to another. And that's why I'm in folk art. I'm preachin' in thousands of homes alayin' here on my bed."[14]

Mark Ryden (1963–), Painter. "I like for viewers of my paintings to feel presence of meaning and story but I like for them to come up with their own interpretations. I think if I explain too much of a painting away the painting loses a sense of mystery and curiosity. Some of my imagery comes from something specific, some of it is more subconscious. Some meaning I consciously imbue into my art, some meaning comes from outside my self."[15]

Ida Applebroog (1929–), Painter. "While I am a woman, and an artist with feminist concerns, my subject matter is universal. Thus, my source materials come from everywhere. I am really an image-scavenger; I will use images and ideas from television, films, newspapers, magazines, the *National Enquirer*—whatever is at hand. I then recycle and repackage the images, and if things work well, the painting makes itself. I would also like to note that I am not exclusively a painter; I also do books, sculptures, videotapes, and films. Basically, I am an art maker."[16]

Jimmie Durham (1940–), Sculptor. "I have lived in Europe, New York City, and Mexico as well as on Indian reservations. It is kind of a duty to be free, intellectually and in any other way, to break totally out of the isolation in which we are kept.

"I cannot sit in my studio, in my private world, and think up good art ideas, make them, and shove them in the world's face; I must make my art socially, for common use and the common good. But if I do not speak well, if I am not serious about myself, I cannot make anything useful to society.

"It also seems necessary to me, for the same reasons, to try to combine the art world—the galleries, museums, and art magazines—with the rest of the world. Art has real functions in human life. We know things and we know in ways through art that we cannot know through what we call language. If we could say art or write art we would not make art."[17]

Sean Scully (1945–), Painter, Printmaker (see 1.10). "My paintings are about power relationships, or they are about things having to survive within the composition . . . the composition is a competition for survival. It's interesting that something tall can stand up and be in a composition, dynamically, and have to deal with something much bigger."[18]

David Levinthal (1949–), Photographer. "I grew up in the 1950s. I loved cowboys as a young child. My mother has told me that I had a favorite shirt and she would stay up late and wash it so that I could wear it the next day. And I wouldn't go out without my Red Ryder gloves. I remember going to the movies with my father on Saturday and seeing bad Westerns. (I knew they were bad; they must have been God-awful to him.) . . . All those had a great influence. You absorb everything in your life. If you're an artist, part of your life is synthesizing these elements. But you don't want to know too much about your own past. Subconsciously it's stronger; if you're consciously trying to relive your life, it looks too programmed."[19]

Clarissa Sligh (1961–), Book Artist. "I would say to a student who is thinking about being an artist, 'your life is important; you have something to say and it's important that you say it. Some of the things it takes to be an artist are: 1) support, 2) focus, 3) commitment, 4) willingness to trust yourself, and 5) positive feedback.'"[20]

Faith Ringgold (1930–), Painter, Quilt Maker. "I wanted to do a series of women and bridges. Now a bridge, we all know, looms over the city and commands attention. I wanted to create an image of women as powerful and creative and able to stand up to a bridge. I also associated the design of the bridge, its structure, the ways in which it is interlaced, its triangles and squares and gridwork, with the same kind of design that is often seen in quilts."[21]

"My advice to students is the following: real hard work. See everything. Go to every museum. Look at everything. Look at all the art and then look around you at everything, because what you want to do is art from life, not from other people's art. But you must know about all the other art, so you can look at all the ways that artists have made art from life. Look at everything everybody has done and don't let them tell you that only white men make art. It is not true. Art is made by people all over the world. Important art has been made by all peoples for all time, and all of it is worth looking at and knowing about and thinking about. Then you can go ahead and do yours, because you have all of theirs in your head. Actually the whole world of art belongs to all of us in our hands and in our heads. It's okay to use it. As we make our art from life we can be inspired by everything else."[22]

Thomas Nozkowski (1944–), Painter. "If there is one essential survival skill that you must learn, it is how to sustain yourself and your work over the years. There is really only one way to do this, and that is by loving what you do, being fascinated by your work, and by being obsessed with making art. You will get in trouble if you need the approval of others to keep your work moving forward. After all these years, the one essential element in my practice, the one thing I am sure of is that I need to be interested in and happy about what I am doing in the studio."[23]

John Baldessari (1931–), Conceptual Artist. "My advice? Don't go into art for fame or fortune. Do it because you cannot *not* do it. Being an artist is a combination of talent and obsession. . . . Live in New York, LA, Cologne, or London. As for money: If you're talented and obsessed, you'll find a solution."[24]

Artists' Practices of Making Art

The following quotations from artists and designers are provided as motivation for your continuing process as an artist. They offer ways of getting started, keeping motivated, knowing when a work is finished, and many other things that will confront you as an artist. The ideas that the artists express reinforce what we have discussed so far.

Chris Powell (1957–), Sculptor. "Working in my sketchbooks (**12.2**) is the single most important activity I do. For me the sketchbook is a record of ideas and a lab for experimentation. As a sculptor, my sketchbooks free me from gravity and other physical constraints."[25]

Maria and Charlie Girsch, Toy Designers. "Key qualities of creative people: Willing to generate lots of ideas, curious, aware and observant, improvisers and risk takers, able to see the 'old' in new ways, dreamers, fun-loving, able to live with ambiguity."[26]

"Seven practices of inventivity: dream dreams, be open and prepared, try new and different things, make mistakes, share the dream, let go and trust, find quiet time."[27]

frog design, Design Team. "For many of us, cooking is something we love, but not something we have time for. . . . The home cook and the professional chef were our inspiration and our ideal customers, and we sought ways to bridge the gap between the two in terms of kitchen technology. We spent valuable time with them in their kitchens, cooking meals and getting to know their needs and wants. We listened carefully to their personal values and their life's priorities. They shared with us their fondest memories from the kitchen, their functional needs, and their emotional desires. Listening, understanding, observing, and later analyzing these consumers was vital to our design process. Our team focused heavily on harmonizing the form, function, and

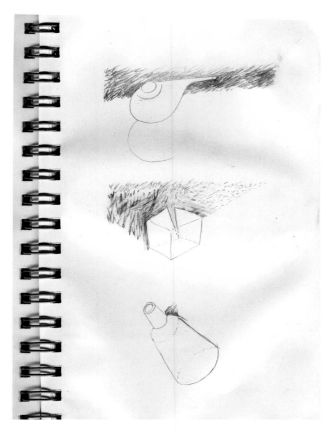

12.2   CHRIS POWELL   Page from sketchbook, 2002.
5½ × 8½ in.

overall experience of the oven, fading technology into the background to bring back memories of cooking in a simpler time. Our design responded to this desire for simplicity, for speed, for a humanized kitchen."[28]

Renzo Piano (1937–), Architect. "Architecture is a complex matter, but one continuously present dimension is the craftsmanship and the way you do things and in some way, if you go around the building you can feel it. Everything is well crafted. Every piece is crafted. The building is actually made piece by piece. Everything is designed, tested, made, and re-made. I think this is one of the most essential and inevitable things in architecture."[29]

Fast Company on Masters of Design. The magazine and website, www.fastcompany.com, want to "empower innovators to challenge convention and create the future of business":

1. Design is the Differentiator: Ford design chief J. Mays believes that only a distinctive look and feel will give customers a compelling reason to buy what is essentially a commodity.
2. Those Who Write the Rules, Rule: All-star architect William McDonough dared to break with the past and create a new road map for manufacturing environmentally sustainable products. In doing so, he's getting the likes of Herman Miller and Berkshire Hathaway's Shaw Industries to play by his rules.
3. Confront the Unfamiliar: BMW Group asks car designers to work on products (from Nokia cell phones to John Deere tractors) and product designers to contribute to cars (BMWs, to be precise). The constant round of fresh, unfamiliar challenges inspires maximum creativity from everyone.
4. Make It Real: Target had the foresight to bring high-concept design to the masses. But it was up to the company's former trend-spotter, Robyn Waters, to help translate Target's inspiration into real products that relate to its customers.
5. Get Emotional: Truly innovative products speak to their users' emotions, counsels Yves Behar, who designs for Nike and Toshiba, among many others. "When you make an emotional connection with your customers, you win their loyalty."

Shigeru Miyamoto, Game Designer. "The most important thing is to create—when I was young, I made comics and puppets. Then take those creations and show them to people so you get feedback. Whether it is positive feedback or even if they make fun of it, repeating that process is a good thing for being prepared to make games."[30]

Philippe Starck (1949–), Product Designer. "The first thing for us to remember is that creativity has a duty of political action and now we have forgotten that, and young designers just think about being a star and making money. They forget their duty to society. Everything you do must be in relation to your civilization, your society, yourself, your life: without that the objects you make are just objects. That's why I try to wake people up a little and say everything you do is a political vote."[31]

Adrian Piper, (1948–), Conceptual Artist. "A lot of the stuff I learned about art and being an artist did not come from visual artists; it came from writers like Keats (in his letters) and composers like Ned Rorem (in his diaries) and outdoorsmen like Ray Bergman (who wrote about fly fishing for trout). So read as much as you can and get into the thick of life whenever you can—learn a foreign language, learn things about other people, go places and do things that have nothing to do with art because it's the stuff that has nothing to do with art that has everything to do with art."[32]

Yoko Ono, (1933–), Artist, Musician. "You, as an artist, will unfold the infinite mystery of life and share it with the world. It may just be two people your work will communicate to. Don't be upset. Be upset if you are not happy with your work. Never be upset about how many people have seen it, or how many reviews it has received. Your work will exist and keep influencing the world. Moreover, your work will keep changing the very configuration of our world no matter what kind of attention it gets or doesn't get. So even when you are an unknown artist, be caring of what you make and what you give out. Your work, no matter what, affects the world, and in return, it brings back 10 times what you've given out. If you give out junk, you get back junk. If you give out confusion, you will give yourself confusion. If you give out something beautiful, you will get back 10 times more beauty in your life. That's how it works.

"If you don't practice, you viscerally feel the gradual process of shutting down, becoming numb, mechanical, unreflective, insensitive, sad; of atrophying that part of yourself that gives you reason to live. Once you stop feeling that process, you're lost, and that part of yourself will sink out of reach. So when you fail to practice, thirst for it, grieve its loss, resolve yet again to give it pride of place in your schedule. It doesn't matter whether you always succeed in this resolve. What's important is making that resolve, each day, with the same determination. The more often you make it, the easier it will get—eventually—to act on it, and the more opportunities to practice you will find."[33]

Squeak Carnwath, (1947–), Painter. A Simple List about Painting:

1. It's simple really! To paint is to trust. To believe in our instincts; to become.

2. Painting is an investigation of being.

3. It is not the job of art to mirror. Images reflected in a mirror appear to us in reverse. An artist's responsibility is to reveal consciousness; to produce a human document.

4. Painting is an act of devotion. A practiced witnessing of the human spirit.

5. Paintings are about: paint, observation & thought.

6. Art is not about facts but about what is; the am-ness of things.

7. All paintings share a connection with all other paintings.

8. Art is evidence. Evidence of breathing in and breathing out; proof of human majesty.

9. Painting places us. Painting puts us in real time. The time in which we inhabit our bodies.

10. Light is the true home of painting.

11. The visible is how we orient ourselves. It remains our principal source of information about the world. Painting reminds us of what is absent. What we don't see anymore.

12. Painting is not only a mnemonic device employed to remember events in our lifetime. Paintings address a greater memory. A memory less topical, one less provincial than the geography of our currently occupied body. Painting reminds us of what we don't know but what we recognize as familiar.

13. Painting, like water, takes any form. Paint is a film of pigment on a plane. It is not real in the way that gravity-bound sculpture is real. It is, however, real. Painting comes to reality through illusion. An illusion that allows us to make a leap of faith; to believe. To believe in a blue that can be the wing of a bug or a thought. It makes our invisible visible.[34]

Jane Hammond (1950–), Painter. Hammond collaborated with John Ashbery, a poet, by asking him to compose a list of titles for her to paint. This is the list he gave her:[35]

Keeping the Orphan

Long Black German Heels and Back Areas

Contra-Zed

Kibosh

Sore Models

A Parliament of Refrigerator Magnets

Midwife to Gargoyles

Bread and Butter

Machine

The Friendly Sea

Tom Tiddler's Ground

A Scratched Itch

Surrounded by Buddies

RSVP

Love You in the Morning

Lobby Card

Irregular Plural

The Peace Plan

The Human Condition Revisited

Long-Haired Avatar

The Stocking Market

Mad Elge

Prevents Furring

Confessions of a Fop

The Wonderfulness of Downtown

The Hagiography of This Moment

Wonderful You

No One Can Win at the Hurricane Bar

Night Stick

Heavenly Days

Pumpkin Soup

Hand Held

Good Night Nurse

Part Time in the Library

The Mush Stage

Forests of Fire

The Soapstone Factory

Do Husbands Matter?

Dumb Show

In Noir et Blanc

The National Cigar Factory

You Saw It First Here

Freezer Burn

Man Overboard

Sea of Troubles

Richard Serra (1939–), Sculptor (see 5.6). Serra wrote the following "Verb List" of more than one hundred processes that could be done to or with a material, in this case, molten lead:[36]

TO ROLL	TO DIFFER	TO SUPPORT
TO CREASE	TO DISARRANGE	TO HOOK
TO FOLD	TO OPEN	TO SUSPEND
TO STORE	TO MIX	TO SPREAD
TO BEND	TO SPLASH	TO HANG
TO SHORTEN	TO KNOT	TO COLLECT
TO TWIST	TO SPILL	OF TENSION
TO DAPPLE	TO DROOP	OF GRAVITY
TO CRUMPLE	TO FLOW	OF ENTROPY
TO SHAVE	TO CURVE	OF NATURE
TO TEAR	TO LIFT	OF GROUPING
TO CHIP	TO INLAY	OF LAYERING
TO SPLIT	TO IMPRESS	OF FELTING
TO CUT	TO FIRE	TO GRASP
TO SEVER	TO FLOOD	TO TIGHTEN
TO DROP	TO SMEAR	TO BUNDLE
TO REMOVE	TO ROTATE	TO HEAP
TO SCATTER	TO JOIN	OF TIDES
TO ARRANGE	TO MATCH	OF REFLECTION
TO REPAIR	TO LAMINATE	OF EQUILIBRIUM
TO DISCARD	TO BOND	OF SYMMETRY
TO PAIR	TO HINGE	OF FRICTION
TO DISTRIBUTE	TO MARK	TO STRETCH
TO SURFEIT	TO EXPAND	TO BOUNCE
TO COMPLEMENT	TO DILUTE	TO ERASE
TO ENCLOSE	TO LIGHT	TO SPRAY
TO SURROUND	TO MODULATE	TO SYSTEMATIZE
TO ENCIRCLE	TO DISTILL	TO REFER
TO HIDE	OF WAVES	TO FORCE
TO COVER	OF ELECTROMAGNETIC	OF MAPPING
TO WRAP	OF INERTIA	OF LOCATION
TO DIG	OF IONIZATION	OF CONTEXT
TO TIE	OF POLARIZATION	OF TIME
TO BIND	OF REFRACTION	OF CARBONIZATION
TO WEAVE	OF SIMULTANEITY	TO CONTINUE

Roy Lichtenstein (1923–1997), Painter. "You put something down, react to it, put something else down, and the painting itself becomes a symbol of this."[37]

Elizabeth Murray (1940–2007), Painter (see 6.18). "I never start a painting from a clear, rational plan or from a complete drawing. I work more impulsively. Often, though, the motivation comes from the desire to make a shape or to get a certain color. The idea is to enact what happens."[38]

"Art making requires a kinetic, coming through the body, revealing other dimensions, making imprints of all that is known but difficult to speak of."[39]

Jasper Johns (1930–), Painter. "Take an object. Do something to it. Do something else to it."[40]

Jenny Saville (1970–), Painter (see 3.32). "I tend to think about each section of the painting in terms of musical passages. I work on areas like one meter by one meter, so I'll think, I've got to get across the nose or the stomach or whatever; how am I going to play it? So I mix up all the colors and think of them as if they were tones. And then I think, How am I going to play that brush mark? Am I going to play it hard, next to some fiddly brush marks? I think of it like that."[41]

Willem de Kooning (1904–1997), Painter. "If you write down a sentence and you don't like it, but that's what you wanted to say, you say it again in another way. Once you start doing it and you find how difficult it is, you get interested. You have it, then you lose it again, and then you get it again. You have to change to stay the same."[42]

Brice Marden (1938–), Painter. "The painting talks to you, you talk to the painting, and it emerges."[43]

Do-Ho Suh (1962–), Sculptor (see 11.34). "Making art is a residue of my life. I'm just slow. My work always comes late, from the first experience. I have to digest. Process-wise, I eliminate many things. I reduce things. Sometimes it takes six months and I just sit, just doing nothing, just think, and try to get to the essential idea. I don't want to add anything unnecessary. And that's how it works."[44]

Robert Rauschenberg (1925–2008), Painter, Print-maker (see 11.17). "I begin by just having an idea and if that idea isn't enough, have another idea and then a third and a fourth; composition could be described as an attempt to mass all these things in such a way that they don't interfere with each other. I never set up cause and effect sequences or action contrasts that are extreme: Calmly or less calmly, episodes just happen to exist at the same time. One of my main problems is how to get a piece started and how to get it stopped without breaking into the sense of the continuation of the whole unit. I work very much the same way—composing in non-sequential relationships—that I do in painting. . . .

"Yet I am not so facile that I can accomplish what I want to explore in one or two paintings. Sometimes a period, such as the all-red paintings or the ones I call 'pedestrian colors', encompassed about fifteen paintings or it may go up to thirty. When I reach a stage where working in a certain way is more apt to be successful than unsuccessful—and it's not just a lucky streak—when I definitely see that this is the case, I start something else. Usually while I'm working one way there's another attitude that's growing up, a reaction to what I'm doing that almost may be the reverse of it."[45]

Frank Stella (1936–), Painter, Printmaker (see 1.17, 10.16). "At this time [1960] I was talking to Darby Bannard down in Princeton—he was working at the Little Gallery—and showed him the drawings, and I just said, 'You know, this seems pretty good. I mean, I really like this, but this part bothers me,' and I showed him some corners, some little squares where the pattern ended in a small block. And I said, 'I really don't like that. I don't like the way that anchors the corner in. It doesn't seem in the right kind of scale relationship. It just doesn't seem right.'

"He said, 'Well, if you don't like it, why don't you take it away? Get rid of it?'

"It was a kind of simpleminded thing, and I said, 'You know, that's a good idea. I'll just take it out.'

"In the drawing it was very easy: I just erased a block in the corner, and I had this kind of slightly shaped or notched format. The more I looked at it, the more I liked it, and that's the way I built the stretchers and painted the series.

"That was the beginning, at least for me, of shaping the outside edge. Once I started on that, once I started thinking about it, then it just sort of ran away with itself for a while. It led through the copper paintings. I guess maybe in some ways I turned back after the copper paintings."[46]

Tom Friedman (1965–), Sculptor. "I really wanted the logic to kind of circle around itself in a way, always come back to itself, and be about itself. I thought more about this circular logic, and this led me to the next piece (*Untitled*, 1990). I made a pendulum out of a string and funnel. I filled it with laundry detergent and then swung the pendulum into a circular path. The funnel sprinkled the detergent on the floor in a spiral pattern. After it made the spiral, I removed the pendulum. So there was the laundry detergent in relation to its form, like a spin cycle of a washing machine, and gravity in relation to a galaxy. One thing that was interesting about using the detergent was the idea of cleansing. I started to look for other materials that had to do with cleaning, or personal hygiene. Because I was thinking about ritual and process, I liked the connection these materials made between daily mundane rituals for spiritual purification."[47]

David Hammons (1943–), Sculptor. "We talked all day about symbols, Egypt and stuff. How a symbol, a shape, has meaning. After that, I started using the symbol of the spade . . . I was trying to figure out why black people were called spades, as opposed to clubs. Because I remember being called a spade once, and I didn't know what it meant; nigger I knew but spade I still don't. So I just took the shape, and started painting it. I started dealing with the spade the way Jim Dine was using the heart. I sold some of them. Stevie Wonder bought one in fact. Then I started getting shovels (spades); I got all these shovels and made masks out of them. It was just like a chain reaction. A lot of magical things happen in art. Outrageously magical things happen when you mess around with a symbol. I was running my car over these spades and then photographing them. I was hanging them from trees. Some were made out of leather (they were skins). I would take that symbol and just do dumb stuff with it, tons of dumb, ignorant, corny things. But you do them, and after you do all the corny things, and all the ignorant things, then a little bit of brilliance starts happening. There's a process to get to brilliancy: You do all the corny things, and you might have to go through five hundred ideas. Any corny thought that comes into your head, do a sketch of it. You're constantly emptying the brain of the ignorant and the dumb and the silly things and there's nothing left but the brilliant ideas. The brilliant ideas are hatched through this process. Pretty soon you get ideas that no one else could have thought of because you didn't think of them, you went through this process to get them. These thoughts are the ones that are used, the last of the hundred or five hundred, however many it takes. Those last thoughts are the ones that are used to make the image, and the rest of them are thrown away. Hopefully you ride on that last good thought and you start thinking like that and you don't have to go through all these silly things."[48]

Eric Fischl (1948–), Painter, Printmaker, Sculptor (see 2.10, 2.17). A painting is "done when I become the audience, when I'm looking at something and don't have a need to fix it. I'm not there saying, 'I can make this arm better' or 'that guy really isn't working so I'll get rid of him.' It's finished when I'm looking and asking, 'what the hell's going on here?' and want to try to figure it out from the audience's point of view."[49]

Lawrence Weiner (1942–), Conceptual Artist. "I practice every day. . . . One thing seems to lead to another."[50]

Maurice Sendak (1928–), Illustrator. "I have been doodling with ink and watercolor on paper all my life. It's my way of stirring up my imagination to see what I find hidden in my head. I call the results dream pictures, fantasy sketches, and even brain-sharpening exercises. They are the only homework I've ever energetically applied myself to, the only school that ever taught me anything. . . . Spontaneous sketching gives me great pleasure. I recommend doodling as an excellent exercise for stirring up the unconscious, just as you would stir up some mysterious soup all the while hoping it tastes good."[51]

Howardena Pindel, (1943–), Painter. "We all isolate ourselves. Try to get together with people you trust. Also keep your mind fresh. I try to read every day from about 11:00 P.M. until 1:00 or 2:00 A.M., or I try to read first thing in the morning. The hard part is finding enough work (a job) to pay the bills—and pay off student loans—so that you can afford to make art. I worked for a museum for twelve years (five days a week or more) before I could find a teaching job. Some artists work in construction, some work on Wall Street, some wait tables or work for other artists. Some teach and some are librarians. Whatever works for you. Try not to get overly discouraged. Isolation can also cause this. One thing that helps is reading about the lives of other artists."[52]

Helen Frankenthaler (1928–), Painter, Printmaker. At age 74, Frankenthaler said, "One is safe if one is still able to risk. I hope I can still do that."[53]

Conclusion: Keep Yourself Motivated

It should be obvious that there are many motivations and processes that artists and designers use to make their works. It should also be clear that professionally mature artists suffer challenges, doubts, and feelings of satisfaction that you may also be experiencing in your efforts.

13 Studio Critiques

13.1   YUKI WAKAMIYA   *Untitled,* 2003. Undergraduate artist, The Ohio State University. Blown glass, fabric, wire, resin, plasticine.

Critiques are an integral part of studio art courses, from undergraduate through graduate level. In a general sense, a studio critique is a discussion of a work of art by art students and an instructor. Critiques can occur while works are in progress or when they are complete. They can be one on one or in a group setting. This chapter defines critiques, offers both students' and instructors' views on what makes a helpful critique, and illustrates different kinds of critiques.

Critiques Defined

There is no single view of the purpose of a studio critique or of a method for conducting one. You will likely find different attitudes and approaches in your courses. Here is a sample of art instructors' definitions of the studio critique:[1]

- An examination of a work of art to determine how successful it is in achieving certain goals or following guidelines previously established.

- An on-site, at-the-moment, in-person evaluation of students' artworks.

- A conversation about why and how a work of art was conceived and created.

- An occasion for students to develop a critical awareness of their own work—or the ability to step outside their own subjectivity regarding the work—and to develop some idea of how the work relates to contemporary art.

- An event during which an artist finds out viewers' responses so that he or she can evaluate how the image is interpreted and judged by others.

- An opportunity for students to get guidance and support from faculty and peers to gain greater consciousness of the hows and whys of their works.

- A means for a group to get at big issues and to form a bond of purpose for a class.

- A public discussion of an individual's aesthetic ideas and tangible results with commentary by both the maker and the viewer.

- Usually a collective group exchange between students and professors about technique, form, concepts, production, theory, and iconography.

Notice the differences in these spontaneous definitions. Some stress that critiques are opportunities for student artists to learn how to improve their art making; others stress the conversational aspects of critiques, in which artists and viewers discuss ideas about a work of art or about issues it raises. The definitions also have commonalities. Critiques are occasions for learning,

Studio Critiques Key Terms

STUDIO CRITIQUES Reflective discussions about works of art, in process or finished, for deeper understanding and appreciation.

GROUP CRITIQUES Discussions of works of art by groups of people, usually but not necessarily including the artist whose work is being considered.

INDIVIDUAL CRITIQUES One-on-one discussions of works of art between the artist who made the work and an instructor, a fellow artist, or other viewer.

DESCRIPTIVE CRITIQUES Discussions of works of art that focus on all that can be observed in a work of art.

INTENTIONALIST CRITIQUES Discussions of works of art that are based on what the artist says a work of art is meant to express; also, discussions of the basis of the instructor's educational purpose in posing a studio project.

INTERPRETIVE CRITIQUES Discussions of works of art that focus on the implied meanings of what is observable in or known about a work of art.

JUDGMENTAL CRITIQUES Discussions of works of art that focus on successful and less than successful aspects of works of art.

ARTISTIC PREFERENCES Personal, psychological reports of likes and dislikes concerning works of art; preference statements reveal more about the speaker than about the work of art.

ARTISTIC JUDGMENTS Statements of value based on explicit reasons and criteria for judging the merit of a work of art.

THEORETICAL CRITIQUES Discussions of works of art that focus on implications for concepts of art evoked by the work being considered.

opportunities for gaining insights, and means of measuring success. For the purpose of this chapter, we will define **studio critiques** as reflective discussions about works of art, in process or finished, for deeper understanding and appreciation. **Group critiques** are discussions of works of art by groups of people, usually but not necessarily including the artist whose work is being considered. **Individual critiques** are one-on-one discussions of works of art between the artist who made the work and an instructor, a fellow artist, or other viewer.

Recommended Attitudes toward Critiques

Critiques, or "crits," as they are colloquially known, are not just school exercises; professional artists also seek responses to their works from fellow artists. Tucson-based artist Alfred J. Quiroz continues to seek out critiques of his work, especially when he has turned to a new direction in his art making: "I want to know if the concept is sound. Did I make my point? Is the work qualitative regarding craftsmanship, composition, and humor? It is very important to me that humor eases the viewer into understanding that there is a very serious side to my work."[2]

Because critiques are often judgmental, and sometimes negatively so, artists are apprehensive about them. Pop Art painter Larry Rivers told of his anxiety when thinking about critiques: "I have a recurring nightmare. I'm working at an easel and a critic walks in, looks at what I'm doing, and says, 'I get it! Forget it!'"[3]

Art instructors hope that students have positive attitudes about critiques. They are aware that critiques can be stressful but want students to be open to receiving feedback. Here is what some instructors said they want students to know about critiques:

- A critique is for learning how to see.
- A critique is an opportunity to see what others are doing, to satisfy your curiosity, and to get new ideas and perspectives.
- We as artists can learn a lot *after* the making of a thing by looking at that thing.
- A critique can only help you think about your work. Crits help you get a distance between yourself and the work. Crits can bring new light to the work.
- Be open to new ideas.
- Try to disregard what you already think you know about your work.
- You can gain insights into your own and others' work. It is not a time to be defensive. You can take or leave what people say.
- You are not your work—a criticism of it is not a criticism of you.
- You learn how to maximize the benefits of the criticism given and, more importantly, decide what is useful and not useful in any feedback you get.
- You can learn how to think and talk about work— others' works—not just your own. Art class is not just about creating a piece. It is about how the piece functions after you have presented it.
- Don't be afraid to talk. What you have to say is important and is never unintelligent.

- Look before you speak. Speak first about what is there, rather than about what is not there. Be honest. Realize that you know more than you think you know.
- Talk about what we are *looking at;* tell us what the object is; go beyond "I like it" or "I don't like it."
- Be aware of your cultural biases.
- Talk of the work itself rather than about the person or the person's ability.

One theme that emerges from these instructors' comments is that you are not your work—it is your work rather than you that is being discussed and sometimes judged.

In your critiques, be honest yet always respectful of your fellow artists. Part of art learning is learning to see and not just make; an aspect of this is to see and understand what you have made once it is finished and displayed. Critiques can provide you with valuable insights. This will happen only if you are not defensive but, rather, open to hearing what is said about your work.

You gain the benefit of many insights only if many students talk: not to talk during a critique is to withhold valuable responses from one another. Instructors want you to trust that you have something important to say, even if you fear that what you have to say is not valuable. When students do not respond to an instructor's questions, critiques become spontaneous monologues by the instructor rather than interactive discussions among the whole group.

What Students Want and Do Not Want from a Critique

When critiquing other students' work, it helps to know what type of feedback they are looking for and what you might be looking for. Here are some requests made by undergraduate and graduate students who have participated in many critiques:

- I want to know if my photographs work visually and what effect they have emotionally and intellectually.
- I want help in considering some of the big questions, for example, what is art, what is good art, how does art affect culture and vice versa?
- I want to feel confident and motivated to continue making art.
- I want to know if I met the criteria of the assignment. I also want to know how people related to or interpreted my work. A critique should be a supportive, positive experience.

- I want to learn what works and what doesn't and why. If something really *shines,* I'd also like to know how and why.

- I want the work to be viewed with respect.

- Tell me what you get from my work and what thoughts it arouses within your mind. Then let me decide whether your feedback is valid to me.

- I want to see things from different points of view and to hear different interpretations.

- I like to hear what people are seeing when they look at one of my pieces. It helps me figure out what I need to do to make it a stronger piece.

- Sometimes I get too close to the work and I need new insights into the work from others.

- I want harsh truth. My work will never progress to its potential unless I am told what appear to be my strengths and weaknesses, what I'm doing both well and not so well.

- I want probing questions that help me expand my thinking, clarifying questions that require factual responses.

- I'd like to hear links between my work and that of other contemporary artists who may have done work similar to mine.

- I want the viewer's first emotional and spontaneous impression.

- I want a thorough interpretation of my artwork.

- I don't want to feel uncomfortable or embarrassed. I do not want to defend my artwork in front of a group of my peers.

- I don't want someone to say, "Oh, I like it," just to be nice and then move on.

- I do not want silence.

- Most of the time my work gets misinterpreted solely on the fact that I have skin color. If I were to submit the work anonymously to an exhibition, color wouldn't be an issue purely because I am a minority. It's extremely frustrating when all people see of my work is a color and nothing else for no other reason than my skin tone. It's like a different version of racism where your work is scaled down and denied its true meaning and labeled a color.

- I don't like to hear what I could have done or should have done if it totally changes my piece.

- I do not want the person critiquing my work to try and change it to look like theirs.

- I love it when I leave the critique with a burst of energy and ideas! I go straight to the studio and get busy.

Kinds of Critiques

You will experience several different kinds of critiques, depending on their purposes. For example, an instructor may want to use a critique to assess what you and your fellow students have learned through the completion of an assignment. Such critiques take the general form of "This is what was assigned; let's see how you did."

Critiques need not be tied to an assignment. Sometimes the art generated from an assignment can be seen and critiqued simply as art, purposely ignoring that it was a response to an assignment in an art class.

Critiques can be conducted in the middle of a project, when the primary purpose is to evaluate different solutions to problems and different directions for work. A discussion of alternative solutions is appropriate. Other critiques discuss work already completed and celebrate the work by talking about it without negatively judging it. This is not the occasion to make suggestions for improvements.

One decision that should be made before a critique begins is whether the work is going to be discussed (1) *as it is* or (2) *as it should be.* Some critiques are set up to accept the work just as it is and to discuss it without making suggestions for changes. In this case, the artist can decide later if he or she wishes to change the work based on what was said. Other critiques are conducted expressly to help the artist improve specific works, and thus comments about how it might be or should be changed are appropriate. Agreeing beforehand on a basic ground rule will greatly facilitate smoother and clearer discussions: (1) "We are accepting the work as it is and are not suggesting changes" or (2) "We are open to suggestions for improvements."

DESCRIPTIVE CRITIQUES

Many instructors believe that a primary purpose of critiques is to increase participants' abilities *to see.* You can learn to see by describing what you are looking at, by observing and choosing words to name what you see, and by hearing what others see and the words they use. Critiques that focus on all that can be observed in a work of art are **descriptive critiques.**

By hearing others talk about a work of art, you can see it through their eyes and hear it in words different from your own. Such an experience can greatly expand your awareness of what is being described. Niketas, a fictional character in one of Italian writer Umberto Eco's novels, reinforces this point: "Niketas was curious by nature. He loved to listen to the stories of others, and not only concerning things unknown to him. Even things he had seen with his own eyes, when someone recounted them to him, seemed to unfold from another point of view."[4]

Students sometimes have difficulty describing what is in front of them. Many students wrongly assume that what they see is what everyone sees, and that to tell what they see is to say what is too obvious. This is not the case, however: we all notice different things because of personal and cultural differences; we use different words to express what we see; and our word choice colors the meanings of our descriptions. For an artist to hear what others do and do not notice about a work can be revealing and helpful in future developments.

Description is not a prelude to criticism. In itself, description is criticism. Sandy Skoglund, a photographer and installation artist, frequently begins the critiques she engages in with the phrase, "I see . . ."[5] Description can be a valuable means to survey what is being critically considered. In this sense, description is a data-gathering process. When in doubt about what to say about a piece, begin by describing what you see: its medium, how it was made, its subject matter if it has subject matter, its form, what it reveals about process, and in what context it is presented.

INTENTIONALIST CRITIQUES

Many critiques assume that the analysis will be based on the stated or implied intent of the artist who made the work. These are implicitly **intentionalist critiques.** Thus many critiques begin with the artist whose work is to be critiqued making a statement about what she or he meant the piece to do. Then the critique proceeds to determine if and how well the artist met the stated intent for the work.

The statement of intent might also include what the artist wished she or he would have done, or an admission of what she or he should have done, could have done if more time had been given, and so forth. Many instructors will want the work to be discussed on the basis of what is actually there rather than imagined.

Sometimes when critiques are based on the intent of the artist, the group must discover the intent. Then the artist does not speak about the intent of the work. Other times the critique is based on what the instructor intended for the assignment. In all cases, it will help if everyone knows that the work is being critiqued in part or in whole on artistic intent.

Intentionalist critiques can take interpretive directions (What does the work express?) or evaluative directions (Is it a good work?). For example, an interpretive intentionalist critique would involve a discussion of whether and how the artist met the intent of the work. The discussion is about what and how the work means. The work might also be judged according to whether it has successfully met the artist's or the instructor's intent for the piece. For example, it is a successful work of art because it accomplished what the artist or instructor wanted it to accomplish; or, conversely, the work fails because it does not adequately provide a visual match between intent and final work. Regarding intentionalist critiques, be aware that the work might adequately meet the maker's intent, but the intent itself might not be a very good idea. Thus the work is probably not a good work.

Intentionalist methods of critiquing work have advantages and disadvantages. If the critique is run to help artists be more articulate about their own work, then examining the stated intent of the work in relationship to the work would seem a sound educational strategy. If, however, the critique aims to have the audience become more insightful critics, it might be better if the artist kept silent and let the viewers decipher the artwork. Relying on stated intents can lead to passive interpreters and overreliance on what the artist says in words rather than what the artwork itself expresses in visual media.

INTERPRETIVE CRITIQUES

Too often, student critics rush to judgment (Is it a good work of art?) much more quickly than professional critics who, when writing about art, spend considerable column space describing and interpreting what they see before (and if) they offer a judgment.

Critiques can be ordered around these three questions, which will pace the discussion and preclude rushing to judgment:

- What do I see?
- What is it about?
- How do I know?

These questions seek interpretations of meaning, not judgments of value. **Interpretive critiques** are discussions of works of art that focus on the implied meanings of what is observable in or known about a work of art. Aesthetician and critic Arthur Danto insists that all art is about something: that art has *aboutness,* which distinguishes an art object from an ordinary, non-art object.[6] The question "How do I know?" asks for evidence and reasons for interpretive claims. A work of art is not about anything we wish it to be about. The meanings of a work are constrained by medium, form, subject matter, process, the time and place in which it was made, and its creator(s). Reexamine Chapter 2 for elaborations on meanings and interpretations.

When American conceptual sculptor Tom Friedman faces a work new to him, he asks these three questions:[7]

- What is it?
- How is it made?
- Why is it like this?

The first question—What is it?—addresses subject matter, medium, form, and contextual presentation. The second question—How is it made?—assumes that the process of forming the work and the way the artist used the medium affect the work's meaning. Friedman's third question—Why is it like this?—directly addresses the artwork just the way it is, accepting it on its own grounds. Later, perhaps, Friedman may make decisions about whether he thinks it should be like it is, but first he gives the artwork the respect of accepting it *as it is.*

Museum educators devised four questions to accompany visitors to an exhibition by Fred Wilson. Wilson is known for rearranging objects in museum collections, giving them new contexts and forcing new associations and interpretations. These questions can also be asked of student work during a critique:[8]

- For whom was it created?
- For whom does it exist?
- Whom does it represent?
- Who is doing the telling? The hearing?

The following list of questions can be used to encourage interpretive thought. A critique could be built around any one of them or a few combined:[9]

- What do you think the artwork is for or against?
- What political, religious, or racial views does the artwork seem to uphold?
- What would the artwork have you believe about the world?
- Does the artwork represent a gendered point of view?
- What does the artwork assume about the viewer?
- Is the artwork directed at a certain age group, a certain class of people?
- Who might most appreciate the artwork?
- Might some be offended by the work?

JUDGMENTAL CRITIQUES

Many people assume that all critiques are judgmental, and worse, that they are *negatively* judgmental, forgetting that judgments can be positive or negative. Critiques can be descriptive and interpretive without entering into explicit judgments such as "It's a good work of art" or "It's not a good work of art."

Judgmental critiques are discussions of works of art that focus on successful and less than successful aspects of works of art. If a work is carefully described and reasonable interpretations of it are offered, judgments usually are implied: "This work has many aspects to it; it generates meaning and offers insight into experience and the world, and by implication, it is therefore a good work of art." Conversely, if we carefully describe and interpret a work and there is not much substance to be found in the work, implicitly it is likely to be judged an unsuccessful work.

Responsible judgments of value contain three aspects:

1. an appraisal of merit
2. reasons for the appraisal
3. criteria on which the reasons are based

These aspects translate into a judgment such as the following:

1. "This is a good work of art"
2. "because it expresses feelings"
3. "and expression of feelings in art is good for humanity"[10]

An appraisal ought to be clear. If you are the appraiser, the artist and audience ought to know what you mean and how you value the work you are judging. To say that a work of art is "cool" may be an appraisal, but not a very clear one. Further, the speaker still needs to explain how and why it is "cool." In addition, reasons for an appraisal ought to be clear. They should also clearly apply to the work being judged.

Criteria for judging art are diverse but generally fall into three major categories: realism, expressionism, and formalism. Realism generally holds that a work of art ought to be true to nature and look like what it represents. Expressionism generally holds that works of art ought to communicate ideas and reveal feelings. Formalism holds that a work need only be compositionally elegant or "right." How well a work is crafted is usually subservient to the major criterion one is using to judge a work. The work's social value to the world is also tied to the three larger criteria.[11]

You can let the work decide by which criterion it shall be judged: if it's a realistic portrayal, you can judge it on realistic grounds. However, you might also ask what is expressed by the use of realism. All works have form: are you going to look only at the form of a work, or are you going to address its social implications? If you personally hold expressionist criteria for art, will you impose these values on all works you see, or will you let the artwork determine how it should be critiqued? Some socially minded critics insist that all works of art be considered for their social impact and not merely their aesthetic value.

Preferences are not judgments. **Artistic preferences** are mere psychological reports on what an individual likes or dislikes. Whether one likes or dislikes a work of art is critically irrelevant in art discourse. We all get to like what we like. When we make **artistic judgments,** however, we are making statements about the work, and not ourselves, and our judgments ought to be backed by reasons that other people can understand. The judgmental question in criticism is not whether one *likes* a work but whether one thinks the work is *good* or not and *for what reasons.* During your next critique, try to ban the word "like" from your vocabulary for the whole critique—you may find this to be a surprisingly difficult limitation, but the exercise can further your critical prowess and intellectual development.

Judgments can be, but need not be, comparative; for example, José uses a high degree of unity in his work, whereas Li-Yan relies on a high degree of variety. To compare and contrast works of art is a standard and effective procedure of analysis used in art history, but the artists who made those works are not present. In a studio critique, one could rephrase the thought and simply say, "This work of art uses unity as an organizing principle very effectively," and then go on to explain how it does that.

Some instructors may state the criterion for success in the assignment. They may then ask that the works be judged by that criterion. In such cases, it would seem fairest to follow that criterion when judging the work. If you are not clear about the instructor's criterion for success, you can ask for clarification.

When the instructor does not set a criterion, then choices emerge. Should the work be judged by any one of many criteria: realism, expressionism, formalism, social value, craftsmanship, originality? Should the work be judged by the critic's criterion? Should the artist (or the artwork) establish the criterion by which it should be judged? To take an obvious example, many viewers think art ought to be representational, realistic, and conventionally beautiful. When such viewers judge an Edward Weston photograph of a nautilus, they will likely conclude that it is a good work of art because it is realistic and of a conventionally beautiful body; and when those same viewers face a Jenny Saville painted nude (see 3.32), they might judge it negatively because it is less than realistic and does not represent conventional beauty of the body. Viewers who are only able to appreciate conventionally beautiful works unfortunately have a very limited repertoire of artworks that they can appreciate. A more generous approach would be to allow the work to determine by what criterion it will be judged. Determining that a nonrepresentational work of art is unsuccessful because it does not realistically represent reality is unreasonable.

Remember that judgmental critiques need not be negative. A critique could be solely judgmental and only positive: "This is a good work of art because . . ."; "The strengths of this piece are . . ."; "An effective aspect of this work is . . . because . . ." Nor do judgmental critiques need to take the form of giving advice to the artist, such as "You should have done this," or "It would be a better piece if . . ." Asking questions such as the following will let the artist decide how to improve the work if he or she thinks that it needs to be improved:

- What is good about this work of art?
- What are the most successful aspects of this work?

- Which (professional) artists might be drawn to this work and why?

THEORETICAL CRITIQUES

Critiques are occasionally designed to engage in theoretical thinking about art. **Theoretical critiques** entertain big questions about art in general that arise from looking at the specific works being examined in the critique. Here are some questions that could be explored:

- Does this work challenge conventional notions of what art is?
- What does this work demand of the viewer if it is to be considered a work of art?
- What prior knowledge does a viewer need to accept this as a good work of art?
- What elements in the culture and times most influence this work?

Samples of Critiques

The following critiques were facilitated by the author with groups of students in art classes at The Ohio State University, tape-recorded, and transcribed. Some of the critiques asked students to respond to other students' work in writing, and these have been quoted.

EXCERPTS FROM AN INTERPRETIVE CRITIQUE

Samantha Hookway's *Self-Conscious Artist* (**13.2**), made of blown glass and mirroring material, was discussed during a critique at the end of a course. It was displayed along with many glass objects made by others during the course. Students participating in the group critique ranged from beginning to advanced glass artists. This particular critique was set up to be interpretive ("What does this work express?") rather than evaluative ("How good is the work?"). The instructor asked Hookway not to speak about her work or to comment on what people said about it but instead to relax and absorb all that she could from the discussion. The instructor directed the group not to ask the artist questions and to address their comments to everyone, not just to Hookway. The group did not have access to Hookway's intentions for the piece or why it looks the way it does. Nor did the group consider any class assignments that may have influenced Hookway's work. This was her second course in glass.

The instructor used the formula given in Chapter 2 to guide the discussion:

Subject Matter + Medium + Form + Process + Contexts = Meanings

To begin, the instructor asked the group to consider the work's medium, including what the work is made of and how the work was made and crafted, so that eventually they could think of medium in relation to what the work might be expressing. Because the student group was a mix of beginning and advanced glassmakers, those who knew most about processes of glass provided technical explanations, and thus beginning glass workers learned about technique while those giving explanations practiced being articulate.

One student noted that Hookway's piece did not have subject matter. The instructor agreed but then asked if it had "associations with subject matter, if it referenced things in the real world." The students then turned the discussion to the mirrored *medium* of the work and said that it did reflect reality and talked about "raindrops," "mercury," "mirrors on a wall," and "Christmas ornaments." They noted that the work was lit and its shadows were also part of its meaning, and especially that it reflected the room and them viewing it. They noticed that the mirrored surfaces were crackled and suggested that the crackles functioned to show "the fragility of the piece and the images it reflected." Someone said that the larger pieces showed larger cracks in the surface and drew the implication that "images of people larger than life are more susceptible to breaking." A student brought up the notion of egos, large and small, transparent and opaque. Someone else shifted the conversation from images of people to thoughts about the fragility of the environment because he saw the three glass balls as planets that were stretching and cracking. Others added to this new interpretive theme. The instructor complimented the students on being able to draw implications about meaning from how the work was crafted.

During the same critique, students discussed Yuki Wakamiya's pedestal of blown-glass objects (see 13.1). Wakamiya was an advanced undergraduate glass major. The first respondent to Wakamiya's piece suggested that the work's subject matter was its form. The instructor then made the distinction between *subject matter* and how the subject matter is treated by the artist. That is, subject matter is the people or things represented in a work of art, but the work is an expression about the subject matter. Further, a piece may not have actual subject matter such as pears, sailboats, and nudes, but a piece may *refer* to subject matter, even though it does not attempt to look like it. The first respondent then rephrased his thought and suggested that the meaning of Wakamiya's piece might be contained in how it is formed. Another student agreed and suggested that the piece was also about "transformation of objects and relationships among the objects." She saw "interconnectedness" among the objects and energy among them. Someone else saw a "young" to "old" relationship.

There was discussion about how many pieces we were discussing, namely, the context in which the parts

13.2 **SAMANTHA HOOKWAY** *Self-Conscious Artist,* 2003. Undergraduate artist, The Ohio State University. Blown glass and mirroring solution, spheres about 8, 7, and 6 in. diameters.

were shown. Some saw five pieces, while others saw four. Those who saw four counted the vertical blue and the horizontal green object as one piece because they were connected by wires. Someone else suggested that we were looking at one piece, that all the individual parts composed a single work of art. Yet another student proposed that she was seeing three pieces plus two pieces. When she attempted to point out which were the three and which were the two, the instructor interrupted her and asked her to "point with her words" rather than her fingers, encouraging her to develop her descriptive vocabulary. She responded by discussing how she saw the two small blue pieces as observers of the three larger and more interconnected pieces. Another person suggested a different idea, namely, that the parts were "individual and disparate, although they shared the same energy field."

This topic of how many works we were looking at was not trivial: the piece does seem to be centrally about how the objects on the table interact. Had the artist been allowed to speak, she probably would have offered an answer, maybe a convincing answer, but that would have likely ended the discussion. Instead, the

13.3 ANONYMOUS *Untitled,* 2002. Undergraduate artist, The Ohio State University. Ceramic sculpture, 7 × 12 in.

discussion continued and deepened when the instructor asked for more summary interpretive comments. Someone suggested that the artwork was "a metaphor for a life cycle and regeneration." Another student added to this idea by saying that she saw "a progress of forms and energy," that the two parts connected by the wires represented "maturity," and the other parts she thought were in "a state of growth."

The instructor asked for comments on the medium in relation to meanings of the work. The students observed that the artist used various media such as blown glass, cut glass, wire, fabric, and small plasticine balls. Someone posited that the parts were united by the artist's use of "candy-coated, saturated hues."

The instructor wanted to bring the discussion to a close before moving on to another piece, and asked a final question about the artwork to elicit personal meaning from the students: "Is there anything in your life like this?" Responses included students' personal experiences such as "floating in water," "being at a carnival," "walking through a magical forest full of spores," and "being at a catered, festive and fancy, but nontraditional wedding reception."

The discussions of both works of art did not conclude with any definitive interpretations of what the works meant, nor were they supposed to, but many students spoke about the works, and each time they did, new interpretive thoughts would emerge from other students. The students did most of the talking; the instructor summarized points, encouraged different students to speak, and generally kept his comments to a minimum. The artists were beneficiaries of the interpretive thoughts about their works, but so, too, were all who spoke, listened, and saw in the works what others said about them.

A WRITTEN CRITIQUE

Following are some comments written by students while examining an untitled ceramic sculpture (**13.3**) by an anonymous student in an entry-level ceramics course. The instructor gave each participant in the critique (about twenty-five students) a blank index card and asked the critics to write in response to this prompt: "When I see this piece I think or feel . . ." After collecting the written cards, the instructor read them aloud and then gave them to the artist for reflection. The writing took about ten minutes of class time. This critique method was designed to give critics practice in articulating their thoughts and to provide the artist with many thoughtful responses to the sculpture.

• "I see movement, inside and outside, shiny glaze, red versus flesh tones, organic form—vaginal or ear canal. It looks fluid, or like it has moved and settled. Intimate space within—some places protecting others exposed. It feels frozen."

• "When I look at this, I think that it is not a functional piece of work. I have to bend down to look at it, or get close up. I am interested in how it looks from far away and how it looks close up. It seems like a lump of clay from far away, but as I approach I can see different areas that are modeled and controlled to some degree. Both far and close up I want to walk around it and look at it from different angles. There is a built-in narrative by the way it changes as I look."

• "When I look at this piece I think of plants and body cavities, of wounds whose edges are not torn and crevices whose boundaries are ribbed and softened. The "blood" has been washed and is neither thick nor dry. The cavity in the center, into which something has dripped, moves toward a sphere, a space set apart."

• "When I look at this artwork I feel like touching it, wearing it on my head or around my foot. It tricks me. Is it soft? Is it hard? It's sexy, like you want to slip your hand into the gaping openings."

This critique was set up to be interpretive rather than evaluative. It is clear in reading, however, that many viewers found the piece to be meaningful and moving and, by implication, successful. It is also clear that even a work in a beginning ceramics class is expressive and

13.4   KRISTEN DESIDERIO   Installation view, 2003. Student artist, The Ohio State University.

can be interpreted, without the benefit, or distraction, of hearing the artist's intent in making the piece.

Assessing Your Own Art

Ultimately, it is your responsibility as an artist to determine the success of your own work. Learning to self-assess is one goal of critiques. An example of a student assessing her own work follows.

For her BFA exhibition, Kristen Desiderio, a sculpture major, built many individual pieces of sculpture, crafting them out of welded steel, wood, plastic, and other materials. She exhibited the pieces not as individual sculptures but as an installation (**13.4**) in a large, empty warehouse space. Individual pieces within the installation featured plastic assault rifles that were stacked on a rack, but they were melted and ineffectual. Desiderio describes her ambitious piece, *War Machine,* which was inspired by live coverage of the bombing of Iraq that she watched on the Cable News Network:

> *War Machine* is a rectangular steel box that measures 5 feet by 2 feet by 1.5 feet high. It is constructed out of angle iron and ⅛-inch sheet steel. It has a lid but the interior of the box can be accessed through peepholes. The box is welded to a steel table 4 feet high with four legs and two steel casters for mobility. It is constructed from angle iron (legs) and square

tubing (cross bracing). In the lower left-hand corner on one end of the box there is an illuminated push-button. On both ends are holes for viewers to look through, but only one end allows the viewers to start the war because only one end has the push-button. Once the viewer looks into *War Machine,* his or her gaze is filtered by night-vision green glass that is present behind the steel. When the button is pushed it starts up a stationary right angle grinder located inside the box. A piece of steel on a hinge rests on the face of a grinding stone, and once started is ground away. The steel applies constant pressure due to its weight on the stone, hence causing sparks to fly around in the box. The grinding process creates a lot of noise as well as the smell of grinding metal that filters out of the two 1.5-inch holes drilled into the lid of the box. When the button is pushed again, the grinder stops and silence resumes, until the next person starts "the war." The *War Machine* is offered up as a parody device to simulate war for soldiers and for those who are watching television trying to grasp a sense of what it is like to experience war in person.[12]

A few weeks after the exhibition was disassembled, Desiderio reflected critically on her work in an instructor-student, one-to-one, discussion:

Instructor: Do you think your installation is good? Why?

Desiderio: I think my installation is good. There is a definite body of work there. There is coherence among the pieces—they play off each other, and more associations and interpretations can be drawn by having a whole group of work as opposed to having pieces standing alone.

I also think that the warehouse space was the perfect setting for the show. I imagined that the pieces were made in some factory (my own factory, I guess) and on display within the factory.

I sought out a space for my senior show, set a date for an opening reception, made flyers, advertised the show using the flyers, considered the space and how my work would look inside the space. Since it was a warehouse, I wanted to block off with curtains stuff that was being stored there. Also lighting was a major deal. I turned off the existing warehouse lights and used spotlights to create a dramatic feel.

Instructor: What was your intent in making the piece? How did you want viewers to receive it?

Desiderio: My intentions were to create a body of work that spoke of the historical moment, things that are occurring now [the American invasion of Afghanistan and Iraq in response to the terrorist attacks of September 11, 2001]. The language of my artwork is fundamentally rooted in an interest in the military and war.

My interests in the military range from the basic objectives of the military, the design and engineering of weapons and equipment, the recruitment of citizens, and the training of soldiers.

I can talk specifically about each piece, but generally I made art that comments, suggests, and pokes fun at the ironies that exist within the realm of defense systems. I make art that sets out to control the viewer's path of response into a certain tributary of thoughts and ideas. My art stages a drama or scenario that evokes a sense of seriousness while at the same time it is comic, much like the inherent paradoxes I find in the defense system.

I want my viewers to be thought-provoked and talk about the work, and to draw associations from the pieces and apply them to life. Viewers told me that my sculptures were thought provoking, coherent, and well made. People came up and told me what they thought a piece

was about, or asked me questions about what some pieces might have been about.

Instructor: Is there anything you would now change, now that it is up and has been seen?

Desiderio: I would make more work.

What is especially inspirational about Desiderio's responses to showing her work and hearing responses to it is that what she saw and heard encouraged her to make more work. This is a desirable goal of any critique.

Conclusion: The Benefits of Critiques

Studio critiques are occasions for art students and instructors to talk about student artworks. Critiques can be held while a work is in process or after it is completed. They can be one on one, between instructor and student, or student to student. They can also be held in small groups or with the whole class.

Critiques are valuable to both those whose works are being critiqued and those critiquing the works. Artists learn how their art is being understood, received, and valued by others. All students learn, through critiques, how to be more articulate about works of art, both when speaking and writing about them.

It is a privilege to have a group of people carefully look at, examine, and talk about your work. Many professional artists have said that they miss such occasions in their professional practice and wish they had the advantage that critiques can bring.

Instructors and students want critiques to be positive learning experiences, even when negative things are said about works of art. Remember that critiques can be positively judgmental and need not be negatively judgmental at all. They can be descriptive, intentionalist, or interpretive, or they can be theoretical and deal with larger issues about art and its role in society. No matter what form a critique takes, or where, when, and how it takes place, a critique should be an occasion for thoughtful feedback.

Notes

CHAPTER 1

1   Susan Dominus, "A Girly-Girl Joins the 'Sesame' Boys," *New York Times Arts & Leisure,* August 6, 2005, 1, 25.

2   Hillary Chute, "Stand Up Comics: Talking with Joe Sacco," *Village Voice,* July 19, 2005.

3   Dave Gilson, "The Art of War," an interview with Joe Sacco, *Mother Jones,* July/August 2005, www .motherjones.com/arts/qa/2005/07/joe _sacco.html.

4   Ibid.

5   Desiree Cooper and Angela Kim, "Joe Sacco's 'Palestine'," Weekend America, December 15, 2007, http://weekendamerica.publicradio .org/display/web/2007/12/12/sacco/.

6   Janet Koplos, "Echoes and Shadows," in *Betty Woodman,* ed. Janet Koplos, Arthur Danto, and Barry Schwabsky (New York: Monacelli Press, 2006), 23.

7   ArtScene, http://artscenecal.com/ ArtistIndex/ArtistsS.html.

8   Dave Hickey, "The Kids Are All Right: *After the Prom,"* in *Norman Rockwell: Pictures for the American People,* ed. Maureen Hennessey and Anne Knutson (New York: Abrams, 1991), 123–125.

9   Ibid., 120.

10   Victoria Combalia, "Sean Scully: Against Formalism," in *Sean Scully: Twenty Years, 1976–1995,* ed. Ned Rifkin (London: Thames and Hudson, 1995), 36.

11   Frederick Hartt, *Art: A History of Painting, Sculpture, Architecture,* 3rd ed. (New York: Abrams, 1989), 592–594.

12   Richard Tansey and Fred Kleiner, *Gardner's Art Through the Ages,* 10th ed. (New York: Harcourt Brace, 1996), 668–669.

13   "Picasso in Conversation," www.bcn.cat/museupicasso/en/picasso/ conversation.html.

14   Ansel Adams and Robert Baker, *The New Ansel Adams Photography Series* (Boston: New York Graphic Society, 1980–1983).

15   Sarah Hood, Jewelry Artist, www .sarahhoodjewelry.com/.

16   Hickey, "The Kids Are All Right," 72.

17   P'kolino, About Us, www.pkolino .com.

18   CI:99/00 (Carnegie International 1999/2000), www.cmoa.org/ international/html/art/sze.htm.

19   *Vanity Fair*, November 2006, 32.

CHAPTER 2

1   Galinsky, "Contemporary Arts Center," www.galinsky.com/buildings/ cac-cincinnati/index.htm.

2   Chandler Burr, "Style: Smoke and Mirrors," *New York Times Magazine,* August 7, 2005, 55–57.

3   Columbus Society of Communicating Arts, *Creative Best,* Columbus, Ohio, 1997.

4   Tom Friedman quoted in "Interview with Dennis Cooper," in *Tom Friedman,* by Bruce Hainley (New York: Phaidon, 2001), 18.

5   Ibid. 19–20.

6   Peter Tauber, "Monument Maker," *New York Times,* February 24, 1991.

7   Louis Menand, "The Reluctant Memorialist," *New Yorker,* July 8, 2002, 62–63.

8   Tauber, "Monument Maker."

9   Carrie Mae Weems in *Artists, Critics, Context: Readings in and Around American Art Since 1945,* ed. Paul F. Fabozzi (Upper Saddle River, NJ: Prentice Hall, 2002), 426.

10   Eric Fischl, *Eric Fischl, 1970– 2000* (New York: Monacelli Press, 2000), 33.

11   Jackson Pollock in *Artists, Critics, Context,* ed. Fabozzi, 3.

12   Miriam Schapiro in *M/E/A/N/I/N/G: An Anthology of Artists' Writings, Theory, and Criticism,* ed. Susan Bee and Mira Schor (Durham, NC: Duke University Press, 2000), 247.

13   Lauren Greenfield, *Girl Culture* (San Francisco: Chronicle Books, 2002), 150.

14   Facts about *Ladder for Booker T. Washington* are provided in a catalog essay, "Martin Puryear," by Margo Crutchfield (Richmond: Virginia Museum of Arts, 2001), 34.

15   Amelia Jones, "Intra-Venus and Hannah Wilke's Feminist Narcissism," in *"Intra Venus,"* by Hannah Wilke, exhibition catalog (New York: Ronald Feldman Fine Arts, 1995).

16   David Revere McFadden and Ellen Napiura Taubman, eds., *Changing Hands: Art Without Reservation, 1* (London: Merrell, 2002), 95.

17   Scott Wittenburg, Mindy Rhoades, Dori Appel, class assignments for Terry Barrett, The Ohio State University, Columbus, summer quarter, 2006.

18   W. K. Wimsatt and Monroe Beardsley, "The Intentional Fallacy," in *The Verbal Icon: Studies in the Meaning of Poetry,* by W. K. Wimsatt (Lexington: University of Kentucky Press, 1954).

19   David Ebony, "9/11 Bronze Brouhaha," *Art in America,* November 22,
2002, http://findarticles.com/p/articles/
mi_m1248/is_11_90/ai_94079478.

20   Jonathan Fisher, personal correspondence, 2002.

21   Carrie Mae Weems in *Artists, Critics, Context*, ed. Fabozzi, 430.

22   Personal correspondence with the
author from students, George Mason
University, Art and Visual Technology
Department, September 19, 2006.

24   *New Yorker,* August 4, 2002, 12.

25   For a fuller and different treatment
of these principles of interpretation, see
Terry Barrett, *Interpreting Art: Reflecting, Wondering, and Responding* (New
York: McGraw-Hill, 2003), 197–228.

CHAPTER 3
1   Personal correspondence with the
artist, April 28, 2009.

2   Richard Marshall and Robert Mapplethorpe, *50 New York Artists* (San
Francisco: Chronicle Books, 1986), 91.

3   Charlotte and Peter Fiell, eds.,
Designing the 21st Century (Cologne,
Germany: Taschen, 2001), 432.

4   Michael Kimmelman, "Art Review:
Jazz Geometry, Cool Quilters," *New
York Times,* November 29, 2002. See
also "The Quilts of Gee's Bend,"
www.quiltsofgeesbend.com/history.

5   Nathan Begaye, *Changing Hands:
Art Without Reservation, 1: Contem-
porary Native American Art from the
Southwest* (London: Merrell, 2002), 33.

6   Robert Taplin, "Hague's Tree-Trunk
Anatomies," *Art in America,* November
2000, 156.

7   Gemma De Cruz, *Art Noises at
the Saatchi Gallery,* exhibition catalog
(London: Saatchi Gallery, 2000), 2.

8   Wassily Kandinsky in *The Grove
Book of Art Writing,* ed. Martin Gay-
ford and Karen Wright (New York:
Grove Press, 1998), 349–350. © 2010
Artists Rights Society (ARS), New
York/ADAGP, Paris.

9   Lorraine Shemesh, "The Artist's
Voice," *National Academy Museum and
School of Fine Art Bulletin* 26, no. 1
(Spring 2008).

CHAPTER 4
1   Julian Schnabel in *Artists, Critics,
Context*, ed. Fabozzi, 389.

2   Jean-Dominique Bauby, *The Diving Bell and the Butterfly* (New York:
Knopf, 1997).

3   The Dan Flavin Art Institute, www
.diacenter.org/ltproj/flavbrid/.

4   Annegret Hoberg, ed., *Wassily Kan-
dinsky & Gabriele Munter: Letters and
Reminiscences, 1902–1914* (Munich:
Prestel-Verlag, 1994).

5   Ralph Mayer, *Dictionary of Art
Terms & Techniques* (New York: Collins, 1981).

6   Johannes Itten, *The Art of Color:
The Subjective Experience and Objec-
tive Rationale of Color* (New York: Van
Nostrand Reinhold, 1978).

7   Mark Rothko in *Conversations with
Artists,* by Selden Rodman (New York:
Devin-Adair, 1957), 93–94.

8   Color, Vision, and Art, "Simultaneous Contrast," www.webexhibits
.org/colorart/contrast.html.

9   Josef Albers in *Color: A Workshop
Approach,* by David Hornung (New
York: McGraw-Hill, 2005), 62.

10   Henry Sayre, *A World of Art*
(Upper Saddle River, NJ: Prentice Hall,
2000), 129.

11   Joel Meyerowitz, *Cape Light:
Color Photographs* (Boston: Museum
of Fine Arts, 1978).

12   Brassaï in *The Grove Book of Art
Writing,* ed. Gayford and Wright, 5.

13   Sayre, *A World of Art,* 119.

14   Victoria Finlay, *A National History of the Palette* (New York: Random
House, 2002), 97, 142, 203.

15   Ibid.

16   Ibid., 287–293.

17   Ibid., 22–23.

18   Nicholas Mirzoeff, *An Introduction to Visual Culture* (London: Routledge, 1999), 55.

19   Josef Albers, *Interaction of Color*
(New Haven, CT: Yale University
Press, 1975), 5.

CHAPTER 5
1   Frank Gehry in *The Annotated
Arch,* by Carol Strickland (Kansas City,
MO: Andrews McMeel Publishing,
2001), 159.

2   Michael Kimmelman, "Abstract
Art's New World, Forged for All," *New
York Times,* June 7, 2005, B1.

3   Valerie Fletcher in *Hirshhorn
Museum and Sculpture Garden* (Washington, DC: Hirshhorn Museum and
Sculpture Garden, Smithsonian Institution, 1996), 163.

4   Fiell, *Designing the 21st Century,*
318.

5   Nancy Princenthal, "Dia: Beacon—
The Imperturbables," *Art in America,*
July 2003, 67.

6   "Art:21, James Turrell," www.pbs
.org/art21/artists/turrell/.

7   Massumeh Farhad in *Rings: Five
Passions of the World,* by J. Carter
Brown (Atlanta, GA: High Museum of
Art, 1996), 86.

8   Cary Welch in *Rings,* by Brown, 58.

9   Metropolitan Museum of Art,
"Works of Art," www.metmuseum.org/
works_of_art/collection_database.

10   *New York Times Magazine,* "The
Sixth Annual Year in Ideas," December
12, 2006.

11   Hartt, *Art,* 3rd ed., 901.

12   Sheldon Museum of Art, "Al
Held," www.sheldonartgallery.org/
collection/index.html?topic=
artistdetail&clct_artist_full_name=
Al+Held&clct_id=3760.

CHAPTER 6
1   Chris Burden in *Artists, Critics,
Context*, ed. Fabozzi, 335.

2   See especially the writings
of French cultural theorist Jean
Baudrillard.

3   Quotes Museum, "Henri Cartier-
Bresson," www.quotes-museum.com/
quote/14211.

4   "The Decisive Moment: Henri
Cartier-Bresson," in *Images of Man*
(New York: Scholastic Magazines,
1975).

5   Campbell Robertson, "She's Got a Date and Only 72 Hours to Prepare," *New York Times,* July 9, 2007, B1.

6   Robert Bersson, *Responding to Art* (New York: McGraw-Hill, 2003), 467.

7   Kenneth Rinaldo, personal correspondence with the author, February 13, 2002.

8   Louise Bourgeois, *Louise Bourgeois* (New York: Phaidon, 2003), 23.

9   Daniel Bergner, "The Other Army," *New York Times Magazine,* August 14, 2005, 50.

10   Elizabeth Thomas in *An International Legacy: Selections from the Carnegie Museum of Art,* by Sheryl Conkelton (New York: American Federation of Arts, 2003), 98.

CHAPTER 7
1   Siggraph, "2000 Art Gallery—Text Rain," www.siggraph.org/artdesign/gallery/S00/interactive/thumbnail21.html.

2   Tansey and Kleiner, *Gardner's Art Through the Ages,* 10th ed., 340.

3   Ann Hamilton, personal correspondence, September 13, 2005.

4   Charles Solomon, "Television," *New York Times,* July 9, 2006, 22.

5   Atom Egoyan, "Janet Cardiff," *Bomb Magazine,* www.bombmagazine.com/articles/search?search=janet+cardiff.

6   Jean Tinguely in *Jean Tinguely: Life and Work,* by Heidi Violand-Hobi (New York: Prestel-Verlag, 1995), 9.

7   Smithsonian American Art Museum, http://americanart.si.edu/collections/search/artwork/?id=36484.

8   Apinan Poshyananda, *Montien Boonma, Temple of the Mind* (New York: The Asia Society, 2003), 94.

CHAPTER 8
1   Arthur Wesley Dow, *Composition: A Series of Exercises in Art Structure for the Use of Students and Teachers* (1899; repr. Berkeley: University of California Press, 1998).

2   Eric Fischl in *Artists, Critics, Context,* ed. Fabozzi, 384.

3   Roy Lichtenstein in *Artists, Critics, Context,* ed. Fabozzi, 104.

4   The Art Institute of Chicago, "Art Access," www.artic.edu/artaccess/AA_Modern/pages/MOD_5.shtml.

5   Suzanne Valenstein, "Figure of Budai Heshang," in *Rings: Five Passions in World Art,* by J. Carter Brown (New York: Abrams, 1996), 250.

6   Roy Sieber in *Rings,* Brown, 184.

7   Philip Pearlstein in *50 New York Artists,* Marshall and Mapplethorpe, 88–89.

8   ARTINFO: LACMA Unveils Plans for Giant Koons Train, www.artinfo.com/news/story/24715/lacma=unveils=plans=for=giant=koons=train/.

9   Richard Misrach, "At Sea," *New York Times Magazine,* July 17, 2005, 24.

10   Minneapolis Sculpture Garden, Claes Oldenburg & Coosje van Bruggen, http://garden.walkerart.org/commissions.wac#head.

11   Jill Britton, "Golden Section in Art and Architecture," http://britton.disted.camosun.bc.ca/goldslide/jbgoldslide.htm.

CHAPTER 9
1   Andy Goldsworthy, *Passage* (New York: Abrams, 2004), 7–8.

2   Anish Kapoor, www.anishkapoor.com/works/index.htm.

3   Kara Walker in *Oprah Magazine,* April 2001, 149.

CHAPTER 10
1   Donald Judd in *Minimalism: Themes and Movements,* ed. James Meyer (London: Phaidon, 2000), 13.

2   Sebastiao Salgado, *Workers: Archaeology of the Industrial Age* (New York: Aperture, 1993).

3   Kiki Smith in *The Portraits Speak: Chuck Close in Conversation with 27 of His Subjects,* by Chuck Close (New York: A.R.T. Press, 1997), 596.

4   Miriam Schapiro in *M/E/A/N/I/N/G,* ed. Bee and Schor, 247.

5   El Anatsui, www.octobergallery.co.uk/microsites/anatsui/.

6   Roy Lichtenstein in *Artists, Critics, Context,* ed. Fabozzi, 104.

7   Nancy Princenthal, "Shape Shifter," *Art in America,* February 2007, 106–109.

8   Hans Haacke in "An Interview with Jeanne Siegel," *Arts Magazine* 45, no. 7 (May 1971): 18–21.

9   Malmö Konsthall, "Tony Cragg: New Sculptures," www.artmag.com/museums/a_suede/malmo/cragg.html.

10   Guardian.co.uk blog, "A New Window on St. Martin's Past," www.guardian.co.uk/artanddesign/artblog/2008/apr/25/throughaglasslightly.

11   CI:99/00, "Sarah Sze," www.cmoa.org/international/html/art/sze.htm.

12   Atlantic Center for the Arts, www.atlanticcenterforthearts.org/artresprog/resschedule/mar/f_rae.html.

CHAPTER 11
1   Terry Barrett, *Why Is That Art?: Aesthetics and Criticism of Contemporary Art* (New York: Oxford University Press, 2008), 109.

2   Arthur Danto in *Criticizing Art: Understanding the Contemporary,* by Terry Barrett, 2nd ed. (New York: McGraw-Hill, 1990), 35.

3   Arcspace.com, www.arcspace.com/architects/venturi/out_of_the_ordinary/.

4   Chuck Close, *The Portraits Speak,* 591.

5   Ibid., 365.

6   Emma Amos in *M/E/A/N/I/N/G,* ed. Bee and Schor, 204–205.

7   Robert Smithson in *Artists, Critics, Context,* ed. Fabozzi, 248–249.

8   J. R. Stromberg, "Nan Goldin," in *Encyclopedia of Twentieth-Century Photography,* ed. Lynne Warren (New York: Routledge, 2006), 621.

9   Elliot Earls, *Bull and Wounded Horse,* www.theapolloprogram.com/BullHorse2.html.

10   Joyce Kozloff in *Mutiny and the Mainstream: Talk That Changed Art, 1975–1990,* ed. Judy Seigel (New York: Midmarch Arts Press, 1992), 7.

11   The author gratefully acknowledges Olivia Gude and her article "Postmodern Principles: In Search of a 21st Century Art Education," *Art Education,* January 2004, 6–13, in which she explores layering, juxtaposition, recontextualization, reinterpretation, metaphor, low/high blur, space, installation, found objects, authentic located voices, reality and representation, (mixed messages) text/image hybridity, advertising strategies, appropriation, and mixing codes of styles.

12   Holland Cotter, "Great Meaning in Asian Small Works," *New York Times,* December 2, 2005, www.nytimes.com/ 2005/12/02/arts/design/02mini.html.

13   Hal Foster, *Recordings: Art, Spectacle, Cultural Politics* (Seattle: Bay Press, 1985).

14   Paraphrase of Baudrillard, "Simulacra and Simulations," in *Jean Baudrillard: Selected Writings,* ed. Mark Poster (Palo Alto, CA: Stanford University Press, 1988), 170.

15   Kobena Mercer, "What Did Hybridity Do?" *Handwerker Gallery Newsletter* 1, no. 4 (Winter 1999), www.ithaca.edu/hs/handwerker/g/ publications/news/200001/hybridy1 .htm.

16   Susan Cahan and Zoya Kocur, eds., *Contemporary Art and Multicultural Education* (New York: Routledge, 1996), 159.

17   Dana Friis-Hansen in *Finders Keepers,* by Marti Mayo et al. (Houston, TX: Contemporary Arts Museum, 1997), 98.

18   See Roni Feinstein, "A Journey to China," *Art in America,* February 2002, 108–113.

19   Gude, "Postmodern Principles," 7.

20   Cahan and Kocur, *Contemporary Art and Multicultural Education,* 80.

21   John Berger, *Ways of Seeing* (London: Penguin Books, 1972), 51.

22   Personal correspondence with Robert Smit, March 10, 2009.

23   "Gran Fury Talks to Douglas Crimp," *Artforum,* April 2003, www .artforum.com/inprint/id=4466.

24   The Jewish Museum, "*Elijah Chair:* Art, Ritual, and Social Action," www.thejewishmuseum.org/ exhibitions/ElijahChair.

25   Ibid.

26   Guillermo Gómez-Peña in *Contemporary Art and Multicultural Education,* ed. Cahan and Kokur, 133.

27   Robert Atkins, *Artspeak* (New York: Abbeville Press, 1990), 107–108.

28   Personal correspondence with Charlotte Schulz, April 7, 1998.

29   Ibid.

30   Do-Ho Suh in *Art: 21: Art in the Twenty-first Century 2,* by Susan Sollins (New York: Abrams, 2003), 49.

31   James Luna in *Contemporary Art and Multicultural Education,* ed. Cahan and Kokur, 138.

32   James Meyer, Preface, *Minimalism,* ed. James Meyer (London: Phaidon, 2000), 42.

CHAPTER 12
1   Karim Rashid in *Designing the 21st Century,* ed. Fiell, 407–408.

2   Peter Schreyer in *Designing the 21st Century,* 446.

3   Business Week, "Baby Products Meet Smart Design" www .businessweek.com/innovate/ content/jul2006/id20060720_263371 .htm.

4   Erik Adams, *Print,* March/April 2007, 48.

5   Cybu Richli, *Print,* March/April 2007, 76.

6   Anne Fabbri, "Anne Seidman, Schmidt-Dean," *Art in America,* February 2009, 136.

7   Julian Schnabel in the *New Yorker,* May 7, 2007, 28.

8   John McCracken in *Letters to a Young Artist,* by Peter Nesbett, Sarah Andress, and Shelly Bancroft (New York: Darte Publishing, 2006), 70.

9   Mierle Ukeles in *Letters to a Young Artist,* ed. Nesbett, Andress, and Bancroft, 75.

10   Roger Brown in *National Museum of American Art,* Smithsonian Institution (Washington, DC: Author, 1995), 118.

11   Stephen Shore in *Letters to a Young Artist,* by Nesbett, Andress, and Bancroft, 35.

12   Barbara Jo Revelle in *Contemporary Art and Multicultural Education,* ed. Cahan and Kocur, 159.

13   Philip Taaffe in *Abstraction, Gesture, Ecriture: Paintings from the Daros Collection,* ed. Peter Fisher (Zurich: Alesco, 1999), 155.

14   Howard Finster in *National Museum of American Art,* 150.

15   "Mark Ryden," http://artbeatstreet .com/html/markryden.html.

16   Ida Applebroog in *Contemporary Art and Multicultural Education,* ed. Cahan and Kocur, 113.

17   Jimmie Durham in *Contemporary Art and Multicultural Education,* 120.

18   Sean Scully in *Sean Scully: Twenty Years, 1976–1995,* ed. Rifkin, 57.

19   David Levinthal in *National Museum of American Art,* Smithsonian Institution, 247.

20   Clarissa Sligh in *Contemporary Art and Multicultural Education,* ed. Cahan and Kokur, 147.

21   Faith Ringgold in *Contemporary Art and Multicultural Education,* 89.

22   Ibid., 147.

3   Thomas Nozkowski in *Letters to a Young Artist,* ed. Nesbett, Andress, and Bancroft, 48.

24   John Baldessari in *Letters to a Young Artist,* 39.

25   Personal correspondence, July 22, 2009.

26   Maria Girsch and Charlie Girsch, *Fanning the Creative Spirit* (St. Paul, MN: Creativity Central, 2001), section 9.

27   Ibid., section 6.

28   frog design, www.frogdesign .com/?p=81&page=1.

29   Archinect, a "Renzo Piano," interview with Liz Martin, January 16, 2006, http://Archinect.com/features/article.php?id=31565_0_23_0_M.

30   "10 Questions," *Time,* July 30, 2007, 4.

31   Julie Taraska, "Philippe Starck's Politique," *Metropolis Magazine,* July 25, 2005, www.metropolismag.com/cda/print_friendly.php?artid=1525.

32   Adrian Piper in *Letters to a Young Artist,* ed. Nesbett, Andress, and Bancroft, 92.

33   Yoko Ono in *Letters to a Young Artist,* 81.

34   Squeak Carnwath, *Lists, Observations & Counting* (San Francisco: Chronicle Books, 1996), 9.

35   Cleveland Center for Contemporary Art, *Jane Hammond: The John Ashbery Collaboration, 1993–2001* (Cleveland, OH: Author, 2001), 13–16, 83; Amei Wallach, "To a Painter, Words Are Worth a Thousand Pictures," *New York Times,* October 13, 2002, 35.

36   Richard Serra, "Verb List," in *Artists, Critics, Context,* ed. Fabozzi, 234–235.

37   Lichtenstein in *Artists, Critics, Context,* 73–74.

38   Elizabeth Murray in *Artists, Critics, Context,* 381.

39   Jasper Johns, "Sketchbook Notes," in *Art and Literature* 4, Spring 1965, 192.

40   Elizabeth Murray in *M/E/A/N/I/N/G,* ed. Bee and Schor, 197.

41   "Jenny Saville," *Interview,* September 2003, 169–171.

42   Willem de Kooning in *50 New York Artists,* ed. Marshall and Mapplethorpe, 34.

43   Brenda Richardson, "Brice Marden: Lifelines," in *Abstraction, Gesture, Ecriture,* ed. Fischer, 103.

44   Do-Ho Suh in *Art: 21,* Sollins, 49.

45   Robert Rauschenberg in *Artists, Critics, Context,* ed. Fabozzi, 71, 73–74.

46   Frank Stella in *Artists, Critics, Context,* 170–171.

47   Bruce Hainley, *Tom Friedman* (New York: Phaidon, 2001).

48   David Hammons in *Contemporary Art and Multicultural Education,* ed. Cahan and Kocur, 128.

49   Fischl, *Eric Fischl, 1970–2000,* 284.

50   Lawrence Weiner in *M/E/A/N/I/N/G,* ed. Bee and Schor, 250.

51   *Wings of an Artist: Children's Book Illustrators Talk about Their Art* (New York: Abrams, 1999), 26.

52   Howardena Pindel in *Letters to a Young Artist,* ed. Nesbett, Andress, and Bancroft.

53   Helen Frankenthaler in "Helen Frankenthaler, Back to the Future," by Ted Loose, *New York Times,* April 27, 2003, 33.

CHAPTER 13

1   The author obtained questionnaires about critiques from art instructors (professors and graduate teaching associates) at many schools, including the American Photography Institute, Austin Peay State University, Ball State University, Boise State University, Colorado State University, George Mason University, James Madison University, Moore College of Art & Design, Mount Mary College, Northern Illinois University, Nova Scotia School of Art and Design, The Ohio State University, Old Dominion University, Portland Community College, Pratt School of Art & Design, Rhode Island School of Art & Design, Redeemer University College (Waterloo, Canada), Southern Connecticut State University, Southern Illinois University at Carbondale, Texas Christian University, The University of Arizona, The University of Central Arkansas, University of Florida, University of Memphis, University of Michigan, The University of New South Wales, The University of Northern Iowa, University of Toledo, and Webster University.

2   Personal correspondence with Alfred Quiroz, 2000.

3   Larry Rivers quoted by Barbara Goldsmith, "When Park Ave. Met Pop Art," *Vanity Fair,* January 2003, 126.

4   Umberto Eco, *Baudolino* (New York: Harcourt, 2000).

5   Based on observed critiques run by Sandy Skoglund at The Ohio State University, 2000.

6   Arthur Danto, *The Transfiguration of the Commonplace: A Philosophy of Art* (Cambridge, MA: Harvard University Press, 1981).

7   Tom Friedman interviewed by Robert Storr in *Tom Friedman,* 123.

8   Terry Barrett, *Criticizing Art: Understanding the Contemporary* (New York: McGraw-Hill, 2000), 55.

9   Terry Barrett, *Talking about Student Art* (Worcester, MA: Davis, 1997), 56.

10   For more on judgment in art criticism, see Barrett, *Criticizing Art.*

11   For more on criteria for judging art, see Barrett, *Why Is That Art?*

12   Kristen Desiderio, "A Portrait of an Artist as a Young Woman," class paper, Art 595, The Ohio State University, 2003.

Glossary

A

THE ABJECT   What is considered base about being human; things a culture thinks of as shameful and wishes to hide.

ACHROMATIC VALUE   Value without color, ranging from white to black, with variations of gray in between.

ACTUAL BALANCE   An arrangement of weight and force that allows a three-dimensional object to stand on its own.

ACTUAL LINE   A series of points made by a tool moving across a surface.

ACTUAL SPACE   An expanse having depth, height, and width that surrounds an object or that an object occupies.

ACTUAL TEXTURE   The tactile quality of the material used to make an artifact.

ACTUAL TIME   The duration of a real-time event as measured by a clock.

ACTUAL WEIGHT   A term measure of the heaviness of an object.

ADDITIVE COLOR PROCESS   The mixing of colored lights so that when some colored lights shine on a surface, they combine (add) to make other colors.

AESTHETIC EXPERIENCE   A unique reaction to an artifact or event that is disengaged, disinterested, and removed from practical concerns.

AFTERIMAGE   An image that appears after looking away from a strong stimulus, such as seeing a halo after looking at a bright light.

AMORPHOUS SHAPE   A shape that lacks clear edges and is ambiguous and indistinct.

AMPLIFIED PERSPECTIVE   A dramatic illusionist effect that occurs when an object is angled toward the viewer.

ANALOGOUS COLOR SCHEME   Variations in color based on colors adjacent to one another on the color wheel.

APPROPRIATION   Possessing, borrowing, copying, quoting, or excerpting images that already exist, are made by other artists, or are available in the public domain.

APPROXIMATE SYMMETRICAL BALANCE   Equilibrium that is almost but not exactly symmetrical.

ARBITRARY COLOR   A color chosen for expressive qualities rather than representational qualities that correspond to the world.

ART HISTORICAL CONTEXT   The artifact in relation to all other artifacts past and present.

ART WORLD   The people and institutions that circulate art and discourse about it.

ARTFORM   A kind of artifact, such as a painting, drawing, sculpture, textile, photograph, product, or graphic design.

ARTISTIC JUDGMENTS   Statements of value based on explicit reasons and criteria for judging the merit of a work of art.

ARTISTIC PREFERENCES   Personal, psychological reports of likes and dislikes concerning works of art; preference statements reveal more about the speaker than about the work of art.

ARTIST'S CONTEXT   The life history, experiences, and time influencing an artist's work.

ARTIST'S STATEMENT   A written commentary by artists about their own work to help them clarify their own *intent* and give viewers an entry point to understanding their artifacts.

ASYMMETRICAL BALANCE   Visual or actual equilibrium of a composition not dependent on one side mirroring the other.

ATMOSPHERIC PERSPECTIVE, AERIAL PERSPECTIVE   The technique of representing dimensional space by making objects close to the viewer appear crisp and vibrant and making them fuzzy and less intense in color and tone as they recede.

B

BACKGROUND   On a two-dimensional surface, what appears farthest from the viewer in a three-dimensional representation.

BALANCE   An equilibrium of weight and force; distribution of weight enabling someone or something to remain upright and steady.

BIRD'S-EYE VIEW   A point of view from a very high level looking down at a space or object.

C

CALLIGRAPHY   The art of fine handwriting.

CHROMATIC GRAY   A neutral gray produced by mixing complementary colors in order to change intensity and value.

CHRONOLOGY   The order of events as they unfold in time.

CIRCULAR FORCE   An arrangement of elements along a circular path or radiating from a central point, often expressing fullness, harmony, joy, and inner stability.

COHERENCE   The criterion that interpretations ought to make sense as thoughts in themselves independent of the artifact.

COLLABORATION   Working as part of a team rather than as a sole creator.

COLOR   The effect on our eyes of different wavelengths or frequencies of an electromagnetic spectrum that is infinite and continuous. Color consists of hue, intensity, and value.

COLOR SPECTRUM   The portion of the electromagnetic spectrum that is visible to the human eye.

COLOR WHEEL   A circular arrangement of the colors of the visible spectrum.

COMPLEMENTARY COLOR SCHEME   Variations in color based on colors opposite each other on the color wheel.

COMPLETENESS   The criterion that interpretations ought to account for all that is in an artifact.

CONCEPTUAL CONTRAST   An implied opposition of ideas to emphasize unexpected differences.

CONE OF VISION   In linear perspectival rendering, a 45- to 60-degree angle that includes the artist's vision from the artist's point of view when depicting an illusion of a three-dimensional object or scene.

CONNOTATIONS   What an image implies or suggests beyond what it shows.

CONTOUR   An actual or implied outline bounding a shape.

CONTOUR LINE   An actual line or implied line that defines the outer limits of a three-dimensional object or two-dimensional shape; sometimes synonymously used with "outline."

CONTRAST   1. The degree of value difference in an image; high contrast is a wide separation between dark and light; low contrast is a narrow range of values in an image. 2. The use of opposing aspects of the elements of art to produce an intensified effect.

COPY   See *text* (2.).

CORRESPONDENCE   The criterion that interpretations ought to match what we see in and know about an artifact.

CRAFTSMANSHIP   The skill with which an artifact is made.

CROSS-HATCHING   Crisscrossing straight lines, one atop the other.

CUT   In film or video, the immediate change from one shot to another; as a verb, to stop the camera from recording.

D

DENOTATIONS   What an image actually shows; its surface meanings.

DESCRIPTIVE CRITIQUES   Discussions of works of art that focus on all that can be observed in a work of art.

DESIGN ELEMENTS   Visual components of artifacts, including point, line, texture, shape, mass, volume, space, color, value, time, motion, words, and sound.

DESIGN PRINCIPLES   Compositional means by which artists arrange design elements of artifacts for effective visual expression.

DIAGONAL FORCE   An arrangement of elements along a diagonal axis, often expressing dynamism, agitation, and vigor.

DIRECTIONAL FORCE   Arrangements of elements that can move the viewer's eyes in, around, or through a work of art.

DIRECTIONAL LINES   Visible or implied lines that move the viewer's attention to an artifact's focal point.

DISSONANCE   Lack of harmony or agreement between elements in a work.

DURATION   How long an actual or recorded event lasts, or seems to last.

DYE   An intensely colored compound that dissolves in a medium (usually water) and is absorbed by the material it touches.

E

EDIT (IN FILM OR VIDEO)   To arrange a series of shots to convey and put in order a cohesive sequence or to convey a narrative.

EMPHASIS   Arrangement of elements of art to make some areas the primary focus of a viewer's attention.

EYE LEVEL   The position from which an artist shows a scene.

F

FIGURE   A shape on a background.

FOCAL POINT   An area of an artifact that grasps and holds a viewer's attention.

FOREGROUND   On a two-dimensional surface, what appears closest to the viewer in a three-dimensional representation.

FORESHORTENING   In linear perspective, making things close to the viewer appear disproportionately large for expressive purposes.

FORM   How an artwork is composed structurally according to its intended functional and expressive purposes, which affect its meanings and uses.

FUNCTION   How an artifact is meant to be used.

G

THE GAZE   Positioning the maker and the viewer of an image as the active subject, and what is represented as the passive object.

GEOMETRIC SHAPE   A regular or standard shape such as a rectangle, triangle, circle, polygon, often human made.

GESTALT PSYCHOLOGY   An aspect of cognitive psychology developed in the early twentieth century by German psychologists and philosophers investigating how the mind seeks unity and closure. The gestalt of an artifact is the general feeling it evokes in viewers—their response to the whole object.

GESTURAL LINE   Line that conveys the energy of the artist's hand as it moves across the drawing surface.

GOLDEN RECTANGLE, ROOT 5 RECTANGLE   A rectangle derived by the ancient Greeks from the Golden Section; its length is the square root of 5.

GOLDEN SECTION, GOLDEN MEAN   A line sectioned so the ratio of the shorter section is to the larger section as the larger section is to the whole; the so-called perfect ratio in ancient Greek art and architecture.

GRID   A mathematically designed series of horizontal and vertical lines in which to organize elements.

GROUND   A background on which marks, shapes, or figures are placed.

GROUP CRITIQUES   Discussions of works of art by groups of people, usually but not necessarily including the artist whose work is being considered.

H

HATCHING   A series of thin parallel lines.

HEXAD   Six colors obtained by choosing every other color on the color wheel.

HIGH AND LOW ART   A contested distinction between "fine art" and artifacts made for and used in daily living. Postmodernists collapse the distinction between "high" and "low."

HIGHLIGHT   The area of an image that appears lightest to the viewer.

HORIZON LINE   Where the sky meets the ground in the world or in a perspectival representation of it.

HORIZONTAL FORCE   An arrangement of elements along a horizontal axis, often expressing peace, restfulness, and stability.

HUE   A name of a color family or an area on the color spectrum.

HYBRIDIZATION   Mixing diverse cultural influences in an artwork to make a new, distinct statement.

I

IDENTITY POLITICS   Political action through artifacts to advance members of groups who are underrepresented, misrepresented, or oppressed because of race, religion, gender, and other social conditions.

ILLUSIONAL SPACE   The appearance of depth, height, and width on a two-dimensional surface.

IMPLIED LINE   A series of points that the eye recognizes as a line; a perceived line where areas of contrasting color or texture meet.

IMPLIED MOTION   The illusion of movement and the passage of time or distance.

IMPLIED SOUND   A depiction that suggests sound but is actually silent.

IMPLIED TEXTURE   The tactile quality of elements in an artifact rendered in a way that gives the impression of texture.

IMPLIED TIME   The illusion of time and its passing.

IN RELIEF   Meant to be seen from the front and sides, not in the round. Relief building or sculpting entails carving away or building up a flat surface.

IN THE ROUND, FREESTANDING   Made to be seen from 360 degrees.

INDIVIDUAL CRITIQUES   One-on-one discussions of works of art between the artist who made the work and an instructor, a fellow artist, or other viewer.

INTENSITY, SATURATION, CHROMA   The strength or weakness of a color.

INTENTIONAL FALLACY   The false belief that an artifact means only what its maker meant it to mean.

INTENTIONALIST CRITIQUES   Discussions of works of art that are based on what the artist says a work of art is meant to express; also, discussions of the basis of the instructor's educational purpose in posing a studio project.

INTERNAL CONTEXT   The juxtaposition of parts within a whole artifact and the meanings they evoke through proximity to one another.

INTERPRETATION   A process and result of deciphering what an artifact is about, means, or expresses.

INTERPRETIVE CRITIQUES   Discussions of works of art that focus on the implied meanings of what is observable in or known about a work of art.

INTERTEXTUALITY   The shaping of one sign's meaning by other signs in a single work of art.

INVENTED TEXTURE   The illusion of tactility through the arrangement of lines, colors, and other design elements.

IRONY   The use of words and images to convey the opposite of what they say and show.

IRREGULAR RHYTHM   A rhythm that omits expected stresses or adds unexpected stresses.

ISOMETRIC PERSPECTIVE   A means of rendering three-dimensional objects without reliance on vanishing points or converging lines; scale of objects remains the same regardless of the distance from the foreground and background.

J

JOUISSANCE   A French term adopted by postmodernists to express the joy of losing oneself in an artwork; a term used in contrast to "aesthetic experience."

JUDGMENTAL CRITIQUES   Discussions of works of art that focus on successful and less than successful aspects of works of art.

K

KEY   In a scale of values, high-key colors are lighter than colors in the middle of the scale; low-key colors are darker than colors in the middle of the scale; used synonymously with "value".

KINETIC ART   Artifacts that are designed to move.

L

LAYERING   Placing images on top of images in artworks to make new associations and meanings.

LINE   A series of connected points. Lines can be actual or implied.

LINEAR PERSPECTIVE   A system of rendering the appearance of three dimensions on a two-dimensional plane by making objects appear smaller as they recede and by making parallel lines converge in the distance at a vanishing point on a horizon line.

LOCAL COLOR   The color that an object reflects in the real world.

M

MASS   Actual or illusionary three-dimensional bulk.

MEANINGS   Expressive content of an artifact and the artifact's inferred implications.

MEDIUM, MEDIA   The material of which an artifact is made; also, an artform, such as painting, sculpture, or product design.

METAPHOR   A direct comparison between two or more seemingly unrelated subjects; showing something with the attributes of another thing.

MIDDLE GROUND   On a two-dimensional surface, the area of a representation between foreground and background in a three-dimensional representation.

MIXED CODES   Different conventional means of communication used in a single work of art, such as a combination of words and images.

MIXED MEDIA   Different media used in a single work of art.

MONOCHROMATIC COLOR SCHEME   Variations in color based on one color.

MOTION   The actual or implied changing of position.

MULTIPLE PERSPECTIVE   More than one view of the subject simultaneously in the same picture.

N

NARRATIVE   A representation of an event or story.

NEGATIVE SHAPE   A shape "left over" from or around a dominant shape.

NEGATIVE SPACE   An empty area surrounded and shaped so that it acquires form or volume.

NEUTRALS   Blacks, whites, and grays made from mixing black and white. In some media, earth tones are also considered to be neutrals.

NONREPRESENTATIONAL ART, NONOBJECTIVE ART   Artifacts that use colors, textures, shapes, and brushstrokes, for example, to express thoughts and feelings in themselves rather than to make representational artifacts.

O

ONE-POINT PERSPECTIVE   The use of only one vanishing point on the horizon line of a representational picture made in linear perspective.

OPAQUE   Impenetrable to light; preventing underlying images and colors from showing through, or the illusion of this phenomenon.

OPTICAL COLOR MIXING   Placement of different colors in such a way that the human eye mixes them to form new colors.

ORGANIC SHAPE, BIOMORPHIC SHAPE   A shape that resembles irregular shapes often found in nature.

ORTHOGONAL LINES   Lines or edges in a picture that lead the viewer's eyes to the vanishing points in an illusional three-dimensional space.

P

PARODY   A mockery of an artifact, an event, or type of representation.

PATTERN   A systematic repetition of an element in a work.

PERSPECTIVE   The illusion of space on planar surfaces, created by techniques to represent three dimensions on a two-dimensional surface.

PICTURE PLANE   The actual flat surface on which the artist makes marks or representations of three dimensions.

PIGMENT   Ground-up color material, such as powdered minerals, that is suspended in a medium such as oil or acrylic to make paint.

PLANE   A form that has height and width but very little depth; also a flat or level surface.

POINT   A dot or small, circular shape.

POLYCHROMATIC   Many different colors in one composition.

POSITIVE SHAPE   A dominant shape on a ground.

POSITIVE SPACE   An area filled with elements of design.

PRIMARY COLORS   In a color system, the basic colors that cannot be broken down into other colors and that can be combined to create other colors.

PROCESS   The series of activities and decisions that lead to a finished artifact.

PROPORTION   The relationship of the sizes of parts to one another and to the whole artifact.

PROXIMITY   The relative distance between elements in an artifact.

PURPOSE, FUNCTION   How an artifact is meant to be used.

R

RADIAL BALANCE   Equilibrium achieved by elements emanating from a point, usually the center, in a composition.

RECONTEXTUALIZATION   Placing what is usually seen in one venue into a different venue to create new associations and meanings.

RECORDED MOTION   The capture of movement with lens-based media.

RECORDED SOUND   Sound that is saved to be replayed as part of an artifact.

RECORDED TIME   Duration, tempo, scope, and sequence captured and preserved in media such as film, video, and computer-based technologies and in paint or ink.

REPETITION   Use of any element or object more than once in an artifact in order to structure a viewer's experience of that work.

REPRESENTATIONAL ART   Artifacts that render figures, objects, or scenes as they appear in the real or visible world and as they might appear in the imagined world, with varying degrees of accuracy, distortion, and stylization.

RHYTHM   The movement, fluctuation, or variation marked by a regular recurrence of related elements.

RUNNING TIME   The *duration* of an event recorded on sequential media such as video or film; the duration of a performance.

S

SCALE   The comparative size of an element of art or object in relation to other elements or objects and expectations about what is normal.

SCOPE   A range of events shown or implied in a temporal artifact.

SECONDARY COLORS   The colors created from mixing two primary colors.

SEMIOTICS   An area of study concerned with how a sign means.

SEQUENCE   The order of a series of events or images.

SHADE   A color that has black added to it.

SHADOW   The darker value in an image in relation to the highlight of the image.

SHAPE   A two-dimensional area with defined or implied boundaries that can be measured by height and width.

SHOT   In film or video, a continuous series of images of one action from one camera position.

SIGN   An entity that signifies another entity.

SIMULACRUM, SIMULACRA   Representations of things that no longer have an original or never had one; insubstantial semblances of real things or events.

SIMULATION   Imitating, copying, or reproducing an experience of the real.

SIMULTANEOUS CONTRAST   An effect achieved by placing highly contrasting colors, values, and intensities next to one another; the contrast between colors increases when they are placed next to one another.

SIZE   The physical dimensions of an object or element of art.

SOCIAL CONTEXT   The time and place in which an artifact is made.

SOUND   A vibratory disturbance capable of being detected by the ear.

SPACE   An expanse of three-dimensionality in which objects and events occur.

SPECTRAL COLOR   Color that becomes visible when white light passes through a prism: red, orange, yellow, green, blue, indigo, and violet.

STORYBOARD   A sequence of images representing the shots for a scene in a film or television show; a plan for a sequence of artifacts.

STUDIO CRITIQUES   Reflective discussions about works of art, in process or finished, for deeper understanding and appreciation.

SUBJECT MATTER   The representation of people, animals, plants, places, and things depicted in representational art; the shapes, colors, brushstrokes, and other elements in nonrepresentational art.

SUBORDINATION   Arrangement of elements of art to support a larger visual theme, idea, or motif.

SUBTRACTIVE COLOR PROCESS   The mixing of pigments and dyes so that all colors of light except the desired color are absorbed (subtracted).

SYMBOLIC COLOR   Color that invokes cultural meanings, which can vary with time and place.

SYMMETRICAL BALANCE   Visual or actual equilibrium of two halves of a composition mirroring each other in size, shape, and placement of elements of art.

SYMMETRY   Mirroring of elements on both sides of a horizontal, vertical, or diagonal dividing line.

T

TEMPO   The speed at which an activity takes place, or seems to take place.

TERTIARY COLORS, INTERMEDIATES   The products of mixing a primary and a secondary color.

TETRAD   Four colors that are equidistant from one another (form a square or rectangle) on the color wheel.

TEXT   1. A conception of artifacts as webs of references to other artifacts; postmodernists prefer it to "work of art" because the latter implies singular artifacts independent of other artifacts and ideas. 2. In graphic design, a body of words, as distinguished from images, in a graphic artifact such as a book or poster; also called *copy*.

TEXTURE   The actual or implied tactile quality of a surface.

THEORETICAL CRITIQUES   Discussions of works of art that focus on implications for concepts of art evoked by the work being considered.

THREE DIMENSIONAL   Having height, width, and depth.

THREE-POINT PERSPECTIVE   The use of three vanishing points on, above, or below the horizon line of a picture made in linear perspective.

TIME   The continuum of experience in which events actually or apparently take place. It is used to specify events.

TINT   A color that has white added to it.

TONE   A color that has gray added to it.

TRANSLUCENT   Penetrable by light but diffusing it so that underlying images are blurry, or the illusion of this phenomenon.

TRANSPARENT   Able to transmit light and underlying colors and images, or the illusion of this phenomenon.

TRIAD   Three colors that are equidistant from one another (form an equilateral triangle) on the color wheel.

TRIANGULAR FORCE   An arrangement of elements relying on a triangular structure that provides actual or illusional stability.

TWO-DIMENSIONAL SPACE   A planar surface area bound by height and width.

TWO-POINT PERSPECTIVE   The use of two vanishing points on the horizon line of a picture made in linear perspective.

TYPEFACE   A particular style of letters used in typography or text.

TYPOGRAPHY   The art of making and using movable type.

U

UNITY   The feeling that a composition holds together well visually and is designed to be experienced as a whole.

V

VALUE   The relative degree of light or dark; the degree of lightness or darkness in a color.

VALUE SCALE   A series of progressively changing values from light to dark or dark to light.

VANISHING POINT   Where converging lines drawn in linear perspective seem to disappear into a distant dot on the horizon line of a three-dimensional scene on a two-dimensional surface.

VARIETY   Visual diversity to avoid an unintended monotonous composition and to hold the viewer's interest.

VERTICAL FORCE   An arrangement of elements along a vertical axis, often expressing height, power, and grandeur.

VIEWING CONTEXT   Where and how an artifact is placed for viewing.

VIRTUAL SPACE   Artificial, computer-based, three-dimensional environments and objects allowing viewer experiences that seem real.

VISUAL BALANCE   The appearance of equilibrium in a work of art.

VISUAL CONTRAST   Degree of visual difference among elements of art in a composition as a means of visual emphasis.

VISUAL HIERARCHY   Arrangement of design elements in terms of their importance to the expressive purpose of the work.

VISUAL RHYTHM   The ordered repetition of design elements within an artifact to move a viewer's attention.

VISUAL WEIGHT   The appearance of heaviness of elements in a work of art.

VOLUME   The measurable area that an object occupies—its height, width, and depth.

W

WORD   A sound or combination of sounds, or its representation in writing or printing, that communicates a meaning.

WORK OF ART   A modernist term that implies a notion of an artifact as singular and unique and the product of isolated genius.

WORM'S-EYE VIEW   A point of view from a very low level looking up at a space or object.

Bibliography

Albers, Josef. *Interaction of Color.* New Haven, CT: Yale University Press, 1975.

Archinect. "Renzo Piano." Interview with Liz Martin, January 16, 2006. http://archinect.com/features/article .php?id=31565_0_23_0_M.

Arcspace.com. "Out of the Ordinary: The Architecture and Design of Robert Venturi, Denise Scott Brown and Associates." www.arcspace.com/architects/venturi/ out_of_the_ordinary/.

Art Beat Street. "Mark Ryden." http:// artbeatstreet.com/html/markryden.html.

The Art Institute of Chicago. "Art Access." www.artic.edu/artaccess/AA_Modern/pages/ MOD_5.shtml.

Atkins, Robert. *Artspeak.* New York: Abbeville Press, 1990.

Atlantic Center for the Arts. www .atlanticcenterforthearts.org/artresprog/ resschedule/mar/f_rae.html.

Barrett, Terry. *Why Is That Art?: Aesthetics and Criticism of Contemporary Art.* New York: Oxford University Press, 2008.

————. *Interpreting Art: Reflecting, Wondering, and Responding.* 2nd ed. New York: McGraw-Hill, 2003.

————. *Criticizing Art: Understanding the Contemporary.* New York: McGraw-Hill, 2000.

————. *Talking about Student Art.* Worcester, MA: Davis, 1997.

————. *Lessons for Teaching Art Criticism.* Bloomington: ERIC, Social Studies Development Center, Indiana University, 1995.

Bauby, Jean-Dominique. *The Diving Bell and the Butterfly.* New York: Knopf, 1997.

Bee, Susan, and Mira Schor, eds. *M/E/A/N/I/N/G: An Anthology of Artists' Writings, Theory, and Criticism.* Durham, NC: Duke University Press, 2000.

Begaye, Nathan. *Changing Hands: Art Without Reservation, 1: Contemporary Native American Art from the Southwest.* London: Merrell, 2002.

Berger, John. *Ways of Seeing.* London: Penguin Books, 1972.

Bergner, Daniel. "The Other Army." *New York Times Magazine,* August 14, 2005.

Bourgeois, Louise. *Louise Bourgeois.* New York: Phaidon, 2003.

Britton, Jill. "Golden Section in Art and Architecture." http://britton.disted.camosun .bc.ca/goldslide/jbgoldslide.htm.

Brown, J. Carter. *Rings: Five Passions of the World.* Atlanta, GA: High Museum of Art, 1996.

Burr, Chandler. "Style: Smoke and Mirrors." *New York Times Magazine,* August 7, 2005.

Cahan, Susan, and Zoya Kocur, eds. *Contemporary Art and Multicultural Education.* New York: Routledge, 1996.

Cameron, Dan. "Paul McCarthy." New Museum, 2001. www.newmuseum.org/more _exh_p_mccarthy.php.

Carnwath, Squeak. *Lists, Observations & Counting.* San Francisco: Chronicle Books, 1996.

Chute, Hillary. "Stand Up Comics." *Village Voice,* July 19, 2005.

Cleveland Center for Contemporary Art. *Jane Hammond: The John Ashbery Collaboration, 1993–2001.* Cleveland, OH: Author, 2001.

Close, Chuck. *The Portraits Speak: Chuck Close in Conversation with 27 of His Subjects.* New York: A.R.T. Press, 1997.

Color, Vision, and Art. "Simultaneous Contrast." www.webexhibits.org/colorart/ contrast.html.

Columbus Society of Communicating Arts. *Creative Best.* Columbus, OH: Author, 1997.

Conkelton, Sheryl. *An International Legacy: Selections from Carnegie Museum of Art.* New York: American Federation of Arts, 2003.

Cooper, Desiree, and Angela Kim. "Joe Sacco's 'Palestine'." Weekend America, December 15, 2007. http://weekendamerica .publicradio.org/display/web/2007/12/12/ sacco/.

Cotter, Holland. "Great Meaning in Asian Small Works." *New York Times,* December 2, 2005.

Crutchfield, Margo. "Martin Puryear." Richmond: Virginia Museum of Arts, 2001.

Danto, Arthur. *The Transfiguration of the Commonplace: A Philosophy of Art.* Cambridge, MA: Harvard University Press, 1981.

De Cruz, Gemma. *Art Noises at the Saatchi Gallery.* London: Saatchi Gallery, 2000.

Desiderio, Kristen. "A Portrait of an Artist as a Young Woman." BFA thesis paper, Department of Art, The Ohio State University, 2003.

Dia Art Foundation. "The Dan Flavin Art Institute." www.diacenter.org/ltproj/flavbrid/.

Dominus, Susan. "A Girly-Girl Joins the 'Sesame' Boys." *New York Times Arts & Leisure,* August 6, 2005.

Dow, Arthur Wesley. *Composition: A Series of Exercises in Art Structure for the Use of Students and Teachers.* 1899. Berkeley: University of California Press, 1998.

Ebony, David. "0/11 Bronze Brouhaha." *Art in America,* November 22, 2002. http:// findarticles.com/p/articles/mi_m1248/is _11_90/ai_94079478.

Eco, Umberto. *Baudolino.* New York: Harcourt, 2000.

Egoyan, Atom. "Janet Cardiff." *Bomb Magazine.* www.bombmagazine.com/articles/ search?search=janet+cardiff.

El Anatsui. www.octobergallery.co.uk/ microsites/anatsui/.

Fabbri, Anne. "Anne Seidman, Schmidt-Dean." *Art in America,* February 2009.

Fabozzi, Paul F., ed. *Artists, Critics, Context: Readings in and Around American Art Since 1945.* Upper Saddle River, NJ: Prentice Hall, 2002.

Feinstein, Roni. "A Journey to China." *Art in America,* February 2002.

Fiell, Charlotte, and Peter Fiell, eds. *Designing the 21st Century.* Cologne, Germany: Taschen, 2001.

Fischl, Eric. *Eric Fischl, 1970–2000.* New York: Monacelli Press, 2000.

Fisher, Peter, ed. *Abstraction, Gesture, Ecriture: Paintings from the Daros Collection.* Zurich: Alesco, 1999.

Foster, Hal. *Recordings: Art, Spectacle, Cultural Politics.* Seattle: Bay Press, 1985.

Friedman, Tom. *Tom Friedman.* New York: Phaidon, 2001.

frog design. www.frogdesign.com/?p=81&page=1.

Galinsky. "Contemporary Arts Center." www.galinsky.com/buildings/cac-cincinnati/index.htm.

Gavin, Francesca. "Boxes, Boxes Everywhere." *Collective.* www.bbc.co.uk/dna/collective/A6112289.

Gayford, Martin, and Karen Wright, eds. *The Grove Book of Art Writing.* New York: Grove Press, 1998.

Gilson, Dave. "The Art of War." *Mother Jones,* July/August 2005. www.motherjones.com/arts/qa/2005/07/joe_sacco.html.

Girsch, Maria, and Charlie Girsch. *Fanning the Creative Spirit.* St. Paul, MN: Creativity Central, 2001.

Goldsmith, Barbara. "When Park Ave. Met Pop Art." *Vanity Fair,* January 2003.

Goldsworthy, Andy. *Passage.* New York: Abrams, 2004.

"Gran Fury Talks to Douglas Crimp." *Artforum,* April 2003. www.artforum.com/inprint/id=4466.

Greenfield, Lauren. *Girl Culture.* San Francisco: Chronicle Books, 2002.

Guardian.co.uk blog. "A New Window on St. Martin's Past." www.guardian.co.uk/artanddesign/artblog/2008/apr/25/throughaglasslightly.

Gude, Olivia. "Postmodern Principles: In Search of a 21st Century Art Education." *Art Education,* January 2004.

Hartt, Frederick. *Art: A History of Painting, Sculpture, and Architecture.* 3rd ed. New York: Abrams, 1989.

Hickey, Dave. "The Kids Are All Right: After the Prom." In *Norman Rockwell: Pictures for the American People,* ed. Maureen Hennessey and Anne Knutson. New York: Abrams, 1991.

Hirshhorn Museum and Sculpture Garden. Washington, DC: Hirshhorn Museum and Sculpture Garden, Smithsonian Institution, 1996.

Hoberg, Annegret, ed. *Wassily Kandinsky & Gabriele Munter: Letters and Reminiscences, 1902–1914.* Munich: Prestel-Verlag, 1994.

Hood, Sarah. www.sarahhoodjewelry.com/.

Hornung, David. *Color: A Workshop Approach.* New York: McGraw-Hill, 2005.

Hunter Museum of American Art, Chattanooga, Tennessee. www.huntermuseum.org.

"An Interview with Jeanne Siegel." *Arts Magazine* 45, no. 7 (May 1971): 18–21.

Itten, Johannes. *The Art of Color: The Subjective Experience and Objective Rationale of Color.* New York: Van Nostrand Reinhold, 1978.

"Jenny Saville." *Interview,* September 2003, 169–171.

Kapoor, Anish. www.anishkapoor.com/works/index.htm.

"Kara Walker." *Oprah Magazine,* April 2001, 149.

Kimmelman, Michael. "Abstract Art's New World, Forged for All." *New York Times,* June 7, 2005.

Konsthall, Malmö. "Tony Cragg: New Sculptures." www.artmag.com/museums/a_suede/malmo/cragg.html.

Loose, Ted. "Helen Frankenthaler, Back to the Future." *New York Times,* April 27, 2003.

Marshall, Richard, and Robert Mapplethorpe. *50 New York Artists.* San Francisco: Chronicle Books, 1986.

Mayer, Ralph. *Dictionary of Art Terms & Techniques.* New York: Collins, 1981.

Mayo, Marti, et al. *Finders Keepers.* Houston, TX: Contemporary Arts Museum, 1997.

McFadden, David Revere, and Ellen Napiura Taubman, eds. *Changing Hands: Art Without Reservation, 1.* London: Merrell, 2002.

Menand, Louis. "The Reluctant Memorialist." *New Yorker,* July 8, 2002.

Mercer, Kobena. "What Did Hybridity Do?" *Handwerker Gallery Newsletter* 1, no. 4 (Winter 1999). www.ithaca.edu/hs/handwerker/g/publications/news/200001/hybridy1.htm.

Merkel, Jayne. "The Restoration Era." The Architects Newspaper, February 15, 2006. www.archpaper.com/feature_articles/03_06_rera.html.

Metropolitan Museum of Art. "Works of Art." www.metmuseum.org/works_of_art/collection_database/photographs/the_road_west/objectView.aspx?&OID=190017984&collID=19&vw=0.

Meyer, James, ed. *Minimalism: Themes and Movements.* London: Phaidon, 2000.

Mirzoeff, Nicholas. *An Introduction to Visual Culture.* London: Routledge, 1999.

Nesbett, Peter, Sarah Andress, and Shelly Bancroft. *Letters to a Young Artist.* New York: Darte Publishing, 2006.

Pattin, Thomas, and Jennifer McLerran. *Artwords: A Glossary of Contemporary Art Theory.* Westport, CT: Greenwood Press, 1997.

Pogrebin, Robin. "Extreme Makeover: Museum Edition." *New York Times,* September 18, 2005.

Poshyananda, Apinan. *Montien Boonma, Temple of the Mind.* New York: The Asia Society, 2003.

Poster, Mark, ed. *Jean Baudrillard: Selected Writings.* Palo Alto, CA: Stanford University Press, 1988.

Princenthal, Nancy. "Shape Shifter." *Art in America,* February 2007.

———. "Dia: Beacon—The Imperturbables." *Art in America,* July 2003.

The Quilts of Gee's Bend. "Quilters Collective History." www.quiltsofgeesbend.com/history/.

Rifkin, Ned, ed. *Sean Scully: Twenty Years, 1976–1995.* London: Thames & Hudson, 1995.

Robertson, Campbell. "She's Got a Date and Only 72 Hours to Prepare." *New York Times,* July 9, 2007.

Rodman, Selden. *Conversations with Artists.* New York: Devin-Adair, 1957.

Rosenthal, Mark, ed. *The Robert and Jane Meyerhoff Collection 1945 to 1995.* Washington, DC: National Gallery of Art, 1996.

Salgado, Sebastiao. *Workers: Archaeology of the Industrial Age.* New York: Aperture, 1993.

Sayre, Henry. *A World of Art.* Upper Saddle River, NJ: Prentice Hall, 2000.

Seabrook, John. "Master's Voice." *New Yorker,* May 7, 2007, 28.

Seigel, Judy, ed. *Mutiny and the Mainstream: Talk That Changed Art, 1975–1990.* New York: Midmarch Arts Press, 1992.

Sheldon Museum of Art. "Al Held." www.sheldonartgallery.org/collection/index.html?topic=artistdetail&clct_artist_full_name=Al+Held&clct_id=3760.

Shemesh, Lorraine. "The Artist's Voice." *National Academy Museum and School of Fine Art Bulletin* 26, no. 1 (Spring 2008).

Siggraph. "2000 Art Gallery—Text Rain." www.siggraph.org/artdesign/gallery/S00/interactive/thumbnail21.html.

"The Sixth Annual Year in Ideas." *New York Times Magazine,* December 12, 2006.

Smithsonian Institution. *National Museum of American Art.* Washington, DC: Author, 1995.

Sollins, Susan. *Art: 21: Art in the Twenty-first Century 2.* New York: Abrams, 2003.

Solomon, Charles. "Television." *New York Times,* July 9, 2006, 22.

Strickland, Carol. *The Annotated Arch.* Kansas City, MO: Andrews McMeel Publishing, 2001.

Stromberg, J. R. "Nan Goldin." In *Encyclopedia of Twentieth-Century Photography,* ed. Lynne Warren. New York: Routledge, 2006.

Tansey, Richard, and Fred Kleiner. *Gardner's Art through the Ages.* 10th ed. New York: Harcourt Brace, 1996.

Taplin, Robert. "Hague's Tree-Trunk Anatomies." *Art in America,* November 2000.

Taraska, Julie. "Philippe Starck's Politique." *Metropolis Magazine,* July 25, 2005. www.metropolismag.com/cda/print_friendly.php?artid=1525.

Tauber, Peter. "Monument Maker." *New York Times,* February 24, 1991.

"10 Questions." *Time,* July 30, 2007, 4.

Violand-Hobi, Heidi. *Jean Tinguely: Life and Work.* New York: Prestel-Verlag, 1995.

Wallach, Amei. "To a Painter, Words Are Worth a Thousand Pictures. *New York Times,* October 13, 2002, 35.

Wilke, Hannah. "Intra Venus." New York: Ronald Feldman Fine Arts, 1995.

Wimsatt, W. K., and Monroe Beardsley. "The Intentional Fallacy." In *The Verbal Icon: Studies in the Meaning of Poetry.* Lexington: University of Kentucky Press, 1954.

Wings of an Artist: Children's Book Illustrators Talk about Their Art. New York: Abrams, 1999.

Woodman, Betty. *Betty Woodman.* New York: Monacelli Press, 2006.

Credits

CHAPTER 1

1.1 Courtesy of John Cederquist, Photo: Mike Sasso; **1.2** Sesame Workshop ® Sesame Street ® and associated characters, trademarks, and design elements are owned and licensed by Sesame Workshop. © 2010 Sesame Workshop. All Rights Reserved; **1.3** © Joe Sacco, courtesy of Fantagraphics Books; **1.4** Betty Woodman, Winged Figure Obi. Ceramic. Courtesy of the artist & Max Protech Gallery, NY; **1.5** © Horacio Salinas; **1.6** Courtesy of Christopher Wool and Luhring Augustine, New York; **1.7** Collection of Bill and Marie Prater. Courtesy of Richard Shaw and the Frank Lloyd Gallery; **1.8** Printed by permission of the Norman Rockwell Family Agency. © 1957 Norma Rockwell Family Entities. Image courtesy of Norman Rockwell Museum; **1.9** Alberto Giacometti, Three Men Walking (II), 1949. Bronze, $30^{1}/_{8}$ × 13 × $12^{3}/_{4}$ in. (76.5 × 33 × 32.4 cm). Jacques and Natasha Gelman Collection, 1998 (1999.363.22). The Metropolitan Museum of Art, New York, NY, U.S.A. Photo: Malcolm Varon. Art Resource, NY. © 2010 Artists Rights Society (ARS), New York/ADAGP/FAAG, Paris; **1.10** © Sean Scully. Public Collection: Von der Heydt-Museum, Wuppertal, Germany; **1.11** Courtesy of Jessica Stockholder and 1301PE. Photo: Fredrik Nilsen; **1.12** XM Satellite Radio Inc; **1.13** Laurie Simmons, Black Bathroom (April 16, 1997), 1997. Cibachrome; edition of 5 with 2 APs, 28 × 40 inches (71.1 × 101.6 cm). Courtesy of Sperone Westwater, New York; **1.14** Erich Lessing/Art Resource, NY. Museo del Prado, Madrid Spain; **1.15** Ansel Adams, Aspens, Northern New Mexico, 1958. © Ansel Adams Publishing Rights Trust/Corbis; **1.16** Private Collection, Courtesy of Cheim & Read, New York. Photo: Frédéric Delpech. Art © Louise Bourgeois/Licensed by VAGA, New York, NY; **1.17** Frank Stella, La vecchia dell'orto (The Witch in the Garden), 2000. Columbus Museum of Art, Ohio © 2010 Frank Stella/Artists Rights Society (ARS), New York; **1.18** Courtesy of Kettering Skate Plaza; **1.19** Courtesy of Mike and Doug Starn; **1.20** Courtesy of Sarah Hood, photo by Doug Yaple; **1.21** ENV Bike by Intelligent Energy, Great Britain, 2006. © Intelligent Energy; **1.22** Courtesy P'kolino, LLC; **1.23** Galerie für Zeitgenossische Kunst, Leipzig, August 23–October 3, 1999. © Sarah Sze and Frank Oudeman; **1.24** Courtesy of Wangechi Mutu; **1.25** Art © Estate of Leon Golub/Licensed by VAGA, New York, NY; **1.26** Robert Colescott, George Washington Carver Crossing the Delaware: Page From an American History Textbook, 1975. Courtesy of Phyllis Kind Gallery; **1.27** Emanuel Gottlieb Leutze. Washington Crossing the Delaware, 1851. Oil on canvas, 149 × 255 in. (378.5 × 647.7 cm). Gift of John Stewart Kennedy, 1897 (97.34). The Metropolitan Museum of Art, New York, NY, U.S.A. Image copyright © The Metropolitan Museum of Art / Art Resource, NY; **1.28** Frida Kahlo, What the Water Has Given Me (Lo que el agua me dio), 1939. Oil on canvas, 69 × 88 cm. Private Collection. Photo: Schalkwijk/Art Resource, NY. © 2010 Banco de México Diego Rivera Frida Kahlo Museums Trust, Mexico, D.F./Artists Rights Society (ARS).

CHAPTER 2

2.1 Martin Puryear, Ladder for Booker T. Washington, 1996. Wood (ash and maple), 432 × $22^{3}/_{4}$ (narrowing to $1^{1}/_{4}$ at top) × 3 inches. Gift of Ruth Carter Stevenson, by Exchange. Collection of the Modern Art Museum of Fort Worth; **2.2–2.3** Photos: Roland Halbe; **2.4** © Mitchell Feinberg; **2.5** Viktor & Rolf Flower Bomb, 2005. Photo: Frederick Leiberath. Design: Fabien Baron; **2.6** Courtesy of Peter Kwok Chan, chan.179@osu.edu and Riley Hawk Galleries, Columbus, Ohio; **2.7** © Tom Friedman, courtesy of Gagosian Gallery, New York; **2.8** Photodisc/Getty Images; **2.9** Courtesy of Kerry James Marshall and Jack Shainman Gallery; **2.10** Courtesy of Eric Fischl and Mary Boone Gallery; **2.11** © Lauren Greenfield/VII/AP Images; **2.12** Courtesy of Nicole Brugnoli; **2.13** Hannah Wilke, Intra-Venus Series No. 4, February 19, 1992. Courtesy of Donald and Helen Goddard and Ronald Feldman Fine Arts, New York; **2.14** © Jacquie Stevens; **2.15** Courtesy of the Anne Seidman and Marc and Susan Howard, Philadelphia; **2.17** Courtesy of Eric Fischl and Mary Boone Gallery; **2.18** Courtesy of Jonathan Fisher; **2.19** The Whitney Museum of American Art, New York. July 3–October 9, 2003. © Sarah Sze and Frank Oudeman.

CHAPTER 3

3.1 © Douglas Kirkland/Corbis; **3.2** © WMATA; **3.3** Courtesy of Hannah Whitaker; **3.4** © Chuck Close, courtesy of PaceWildenstein, New York; **3.5** © Loretta Lux, courtesy of Yossi Milo Gallery, New York and Torch Gallery, Amsterdam. © 2010 Artists Rights Society (ARS), New York/VG Bild-Kunst, Bonn; **3.6** © George Steinmetz/Corbis. Art © Estate of Robert Smithson/VAGA, New York; **3.7** Cy Twombly, Untitled, 1970. Oil-based house paint and crayon on canvas, 13 ft. $3^{3}/_{8}$ in. × 21 ft. $^{1}/_{8}$ in. Acquired through the Lillie P. Bliss Bequest and the Sidney and Harriet Janis Collection (both by exchange). (614.1994). The Museum of Modern Art, New York, NY, U.S.A. Digital Image © The Museum of Modern Art/Licensed by SCALA / Art Resource, NY. © Cy Twombly; **3.8** Bryan Bedder/Getty Images; **3.9** Victoria and Albert Museum, London/Art Resource, NY. © 2010 Artists Rights Society (ARS), New York/ ADAGP, Paris; **3.10** Sol LeWitt, Wall Drawing #260 On Black Walls, All Two-Part Combinations of White Arcs from Corners and Sides, and White Straight, Not-Straight, and Broken Lines, 1975. Crayon on painted wall. Dimensions variable. Gift of an anonymous donor. (517.1978) (IN2060.07) The Museum of Modern Art, New York, NY, U.S.A. Digital Image Photo: The Museum of Modern Art/Licensed by SCALA / Art Resource, NY. © 2010 The LeWitt Estate/Artists Rights Society (ARS), New York; **3.11** Michelangelo Buonarroti, The Holy Family with the Infant Saint John the Baptist, c. 1530. Black and red chalk with pen and brown ink over stylus, 27.9 × 39.4 cm (11 × $15^{1}/_{2}$ in.) The J. Paul Getty Museum, Los Angeles; **3.12** Vincent van Gogh, Portrait of Joseph Roulin, 1888. Reed and quill pens and brown ink and black chalk, 32.1 × 24.4 cm ($12^{5}/_{8}$ × $9^{5}/_{8}$ in.) The J. Paul Getty Museum, Los Angeles; **3.14** Saul Steinberg, The New Yorker Magazine, Cover, November 23, 1968. © Drawing by Saul Steinberg, © Condé Nast Publications. © 2010 The Saul Steinberg Foundation / Artists Rights Society (ARS), New York; **3.15** Courtesy of Premier Rides Inc; **3.16** Art © Deborah Butterfield/Licensed by VAGA, New York, NY; **3.17** Art © Judy Pfaff/Licensed by VAGA, New York, NY; **3.18** Peter Dazeley/Stone/Getty Images; **3.19** Marta Sansoni, Alessi S.p.a, Crusinallo, Italy; **3.20** Henri Matisse, Blue Nude II, 1952. © Succession H. Matisse, Paris / ARS, NY. Musée National d'Art Moderne, Centre Georges Pompidou, Paris, France. CNAC/MNAM/Dist. Réunion des Musées Nationaux/Art Resource, NY. © 2009 Succession H. Matisse/Artists Rights Society (ARS), New York; **3.21** Courtesy of Mary Ann Pettway; **3.22** Ellsworth Kelly, Red White, 1961. Oil on canvas, $62^{1}/_{2}$ × 85 inches. Hirshhorn Museum & Sculpture Garden, Washington DC. © Ellsworth Kelly; **3.23** Courtesy of CBS; **3.24** René Magritte, The False Mirror, 1928. Oil on canvas, $21^{1}/_{4}$ × $31^{7}/_{8}$ in. Purchase. (133.1936). The Museum of Modern Art, New York, NY, U.S.A. Photo: Digital Image © The Museum of Modern Art/Licensed by SCALA / Art Resource, NY. © 2010 Herscovici, London/Artists Rights Society (ARS), New York; **3.25** Courtesy of Brad Norr Design; **3.26** © Cecily Brown. Courtesy of Gagosian Gallery, New York; **3.27** © Philip Taaffe, courtesy of Gagosian Gallery, New York; **3.28** Nathan Begaye, Reconstructed Vessel, 1998. From "Changing Hands: Art Without Reservation". Museum of Arts and Design, New York; **3.29** Adobe product box shot reprinted with permission from Adobe Systems Incorporated; **3.30** Designed by Ted Warren; Courtesy of Warren Light Craft, Salem, MA; **3.31** Art © Raoul Hague Foundation/Licensed by VAGA, New York, NY **3.32** © Jenny Saville, courtesy of Gagosian Gallery, New York; **3.33** Sandy Skoglund, The Cocktail Party, 1992. Installation and photograph, cheese snack food embedded in epoxy resin, furniture, sculpted figures from mannequins, live models; **3.34** Getty Images; **3.35** Auguste Rodin, Danaid, 1889. Photo: Bulloz. Musee Rodin, Paris, France. Réunion des Musées Nationaux/Art Resource, NY; **3.36** Meret Oppenheim, Object (Le Dejeuner en fourrure), 1936. Fur-covered cup, saucer and spoon. Cup, $4^{3}/_{8}$ in. diameter; saucer, $9^{3}/_{8}$ in. diameter; spoon, 8 in. long; overall height $2^{7}/_{8}$ in.. (130.1946a–c). The Museum of Modern Art, New York, NY, U.S.A. Photo: Digital Image © The Museum of Modern Art/Licensed by SCALA/Art Resource, NY. © 2010 Artists Rights Society (ARS), New York/ProLitteris, Zürich; **3.37** Photo: Elke Estel/Hans-Peter Klut. Gemaeldegalerie, Staatliche Kunstsammlungen, Dresden, Germany. Bildarchiv Preussischer Kulturbesitz/Art Resource, NY; **3.38** Courtesy of Tom Lang; **3.40** Ansel Adams, Moonrise, Hernandez, New Mexico, 1941. © Ansel Adams Publishing Rights Trust/Corbis; **3.41** Kathe Kollwitz, Arbeiterfrau (Working woman), 1906. Facsimile of a charcoal drawing on laid paper. Impression from the 1921 Richter portfolio. Sheet size: $22^{3}/_{4}$ in. × $17^{1}/_{4}$ in.. Catalogue reference: Nagel 406, Inventory# 5176. Pasquale Iannetti Art Galleries, Inc. Dealers since 1969 in original prints, paintings & other works of art from the 15th century to the present. © 2010 Artists Rights Society (ARS), New York/VG Bild-Kunst, Bonn; **3.42** Sid Chafetz, Freud, 1962. Woodcut. Columbus Museum of Art, Ohio: Gift of the Artist, 2001.034.423; **3.43** Wassily Kandinsky, Yellow-Red-Blue, 1925. Oil on canvas, 128 × 201.5 cm. Inv. AM1976-856. Photo: Adam Rzepka. Musee National d'Art Moderne, Centre Georges Pompidou, Paris, France. Photo: CNAC/MNAM/Dist. Réunion des Musées Nationaux/Art Resource, NY. © 2010 Artists Rights Society (ARS), New York/ ADAGP, Paris; **3.44** Lorraine Shemesh, LINK, 1999. 67 × $66^{3}/_{4}$ inches, Private Collection, courtesy of Allan Stone Gallery, New York.

CHAPTER 4

4.1 Pathe/The Kobal Collection; **4.2** Dan Flavin, Untitled (in honor of Harold Joachim) 3, 1977. Kirsty Wigglesworth/AP Images; **4.3** Apple iPod nanos, 2008. Courtesy of Apple Computer, Inc.; **4.5** Thinkstock/Index Stock Imagery; **4.9** Courtesy of Kara Walker and Sikkema Jenkins & Co.; **4.10** Courtesy of e-cloud9, Barcelona, Spain; **4.13** Courtesy of NE14 Design; **4.15** Otto Maier Verlag; **4.16** Courtesy of the Munsell Store; **4.17** Ellsworth Kelly, Blue Green Yellow Orange Red, 1966, and Orange Red Relief, 1959. Collection The Solomon R Guggenheim Museum, New York. Installation view from Singular Forms (Sometimes Repeated): Art from 1951 to the Present, Solomon R. Guggenheim Museum, New York, March 5–May 19, 2004. Photo: David Heald © The Solomon R. Guggenheim Foundation, New York; **4.19** Philip Gatward/Dorling Kindersley/Getty Images; **4.21** Courtesy of Behr.com; **4.22** The Textile Museum, Washington, D.C., 2001.5.1. Ruth Lincoln Fisher Memorial Fund; **4.23** PLEATS PLEASE ISSEY MIYAKE, Spring Summer 2001, Photo: Francis Giacobetti; **4.24** © Marvin Lipofsky. Photo: b.v. Koninklijke Nederlandsche Glasfabriek Leerdam (Royal Leerdam); **4.25** Art © Janet Fish/Licensed by VAGA, New York, NY; **4.30** Collection of Michael and Ninah Lynne, New York. Courtesy of Mary Boone Gallery, New York; **4.32** Mark Rothko, Orange and Yellow, 1956. Oil on canvas, framed: $93^{1}/_{2}$ × $73^{1}/_{2}$ × $2^{3}/_{4}$ in. (237.5 × 186.7 cm.); support: 91 × 71 in. (321.12 × 180.34 cm.) Gift of Seymour H. Knox, Jr. 1956. Albright-Knox Gallery, Buffalo, New York. © 1998 Kate Rothko Prizel & Christopher Rothko / Artists Rights Society (ARS), New York; **4.34** National Archives; **4.37** Frederic S. Remington, His First Lesson, 1903. Oil on canvas, $27^{1}/_{4}$ × 40 inches. Amon Carter Museum, Fort Worth, Texas, 1961.231; **4.38** Frederic S. Remington, The Fall of the Cowboy, 1895. Oil on canvas, 25 × $35^{1}/_{8}$ inches. Amon Carter Museum, Fort Worth, Texas, 1961.230; **4.41** Richard Misrach, Dead Animals #1, 1987. © Richard Misrach, courtesy of Fraenkel Gallery, San Francisco, Marc Selwyn Fine Art, Los Angeles, and Pace/MacGill Gallery, New York; **4.42** Courtesy of Adidas; **4.43** © Trenton Doyle Hancock, courtesy of James Cohan Gallery, New York; **4.44.** Installation view of Sol LeWitt: New Wall Drawings. PaceWildenstein, 32 East 57th Street, New York. September 3–October 12, 2002. Photo: Ellen Page Wilson, courtesy of PaceWildenstein, New York. © 2010 The LeWitt Estate/Artists Rights Society (ARS), New York; **4.45** Courtesy of the University Art Gallery / Art Resource, NY; **4.49** Art © Larry Poons/Licensed by VAGA, New York, NY; **4.50** © Chuck Close, courtesy of PaceWildenstein, New York; **4.51** © Estate of Duane Hanson, courtesy of Van de Weghe Fine Art, New York. Licensed by VAGA, New York, NY; **4.52** © Joel Meyerowitz, courtesy of Edwynn Houk Gallery, NY; **4.53** Pierre Bonnard, Nude in Bathtub, c.1941–1946. Oil on canvas, 48 × $59^{1}/_{2}$ inches. Carnegie Museum of Art, Pittsburgh; Acquired through the generosity of Sarah Mellon Scaife Family. Photo: Richard Stoner. Photograph © 2009 Carnegie Museum of Art, Pittsburgh. © 2010 Artists Rights Society (ARS), New York/ ADAGP, Paris; **4.54** © Glenn Ligon, courtesy of Regen Projects, Los Angeles; **4.55** © Lynn Goldsmith/Corbis; **4.56** Courtesy of Seymour Chwast and Pushpin Group; **4.57** Poster for traveling exhibition, "Coexistence". Museum on the Seam, artist: José Rementeria; **4.58** The Nativity, c.1475, from the church of Saint Nicholas, Gostinople. Banca Intesa Collection of Russian Icons. NOVGOROD School. The Art Archive/Palazzo Leoni-Montanari Vicenza/Gianni Dagli Orti; **4.59** Michelangelo Buonarroti, The Entombment, about 1500–1. Oil on wood, 161.7 × 149.9 cm. Bought 1868, (NG790). National Gallery, London, Great Britain. © National Gallery, London/Art Resource, NY; **4.60** Luis Vaquero, Vaquero. Modeled 1980, cast 1990. Acrylic urethane, fiberglass, steel armature, 199 × 114 × 67 in. (505.5 × 289.6 × 170.2 cm.). Gift of Judith and Wilbur L. Ross, Jr., Anne and Ronald Abramson, Thelma and Melvin Lenkin. Smithsonian American Art Museum, Washington, DC/Art Resource, NY. © 2010 Estate of Luis A. Jimenez, Jr./Artists Rights Society (ARS), New York; **4.61** Courtesy of Kerry James Marshall and Jack Shainman Gallery.

CHAPTER 5

5.1 © Tim Hawkinson, courtesy of Pace/Wildenstein, New York. Photo: Philipp Scholz Rittermann. Stuart Collection, University of California, San Diego; **5.2** Hemis /Alamy Images; **5.3** Vito Palmisano/Photographer's Choice/Getty Images; **5.4** Courtesy of Red Feather Development Group; **5.5** Donald Nausbaum/Photographer's Choice/Getty Images; **5.6** RAFA RIVAS/AFP/Getty Images/Gagosian Gallery; **5.7** Roxy Paine, Conjoined, 2007. Stainless steel and concrete, 46 × 42 × 28 feet. Originally commissioned by the Madison Square Park Conservancy. Modern Art Museum of Fort Worth, Texas, museum purchase. © Roxy Paine, courtesy of James Cohan Gallery, New York. Photo: Modern Art Museum of Fort Worth, Texas/David Wharton; **5.8** Photo: Anthony Cunha. Courtesy of the Ralph Bacerra Estate and the Frank Lloyd Gallery; **5.9** Mireille Vautier/Alamy Images; **5.10** Louise Nevelson, Installation view of Dawn's Wedding Feast (1959) in The Jewish Museum, New York exhibition The Sculpture of Louise Nevelson: Constructing a Legend (May 5–September 16, 2007). Photo by David Heald. The Jewish Museum, New York, NY/Art Resource, NY. © 2010 Estate of Louise Nevelson/Artists Rights Society (ARS), New York; **5.11** Nice children's furniture, designed by Michael Marriott; **5.12** Courtesy of Rachel Whiteread and Luhring Augustine, New York; **5.13** Michael Heizer, North, East, South, West, 1967/2002 (Detail: North). Installation view at Dia: Beacon, Beacon, NY. Photo: Tom Vinetz. Collection Dia Art Foundation; **5.14** James Turrell, Afrum I (White), 1967. Projected light, dimensions variable. Solomon R. Guggenheim Museum, New York. Panza Collection, Gift, 1992. 92.4175. Photo: David Heald © The Solomon R. Guggenheim Foundation, New York; **5.15–5.16** Courtesy of EA SPORTS; **5.17** Renaissance Revival Parlor, Meriden, Connecticut, American, 1870. Architect: Augustus Truesdell. The Metropolitan Museum of Art, Gift of Josephine M. Fiala, 1968 (68.133.7). Photo: Richard Cheek. Image © The Metropolitan Museum of Art; **5.17** Room from the Hart House, Ipswich, Massachusetts, American, before 1674. The Metropolitan Museum of Art, Munsey Fund, 1938 (36.127) Image © The Metropolitan Museum of Art; **5.18** General Egyptian Book Organization, Cairo; **5.19** Radha and Krishna in a Bower, c. 1780. Opaque watercolor and gold on paper; 17.5 × 27.2 cm ($6^{7}/_{8}$ × $10^{11}/_{16}$ in.) Harvard Art Museum, Arthur M. Sackler Museum, Private Collection, TL32253.2. Photo: Imaging Department © President and Fellows of Harvard College; **5.20** Kunsthistorisches Museum, Vienna, Austria. Erich Lessing/Art Resource, NY; **5.21** SPIDER-MAN: TM & © 2010 Marvel Characters, Inc. Used with permission; **5.22** George Seurat, Trees (study for La Grande Jatte), 1884. Black Conté crayon, on white laid paper, laid down on cream board, 620 × 475 mm. Helen Regenstein Collection, 1966.184 Reproduction © The Art Institute of Chicago; **5.23** Robert Motherwell, Elegy to the Spanish Republic No. 34, 1953–1954. Oil on canvas, support: 80 × 100 in. (203.2 × 254 cm.) Albright-Knox Gallery, Buffalo, New York, Gift of Seymour H. Knox, Jr. 1957. Art © Dedalus Foundation, Inc./Licensed by VAGA, New York, NY; **5.24** From Dinh Q. Le's exhibition "A Quagmire This Time", September 6–October 11, 2008 at the Shoshana Wayne Gallery, Santa Monica, CA. Photo: Gene Ogami; **5.25** Georgia O'Keeffe, Petunia No. 2, 1924. Oil on canvas, 36 × 30 in.. 1996.03.02. Gift of The Burnett Foundation and Gerald and Kathleen Peters. Photo: Malcolm Varon, 2001. © 2009 Georgia O'Keeffe Museum/Art Resource, NY/ Artists Rights Society (ARS), New York; **5.27** © Annie Leibovitz/Contact Press Images; **5.28** The Library of Congress; **5.31** Scala/Art Resource, NY; **5.33** Cover of Amazing Spider-Man #512. Characters: Spider-Man, the Stacy Twins. Artist: Mike

Deodato Jr. SPIDER-MAN: TM & © 2010 Marvel Characters, Inc. Used with permission; **5.36** Ed Ruscha, Standard Station, 1966. Screen-print, printed in color, composition: $19\frac{1}{2} \times 36\frac{15}{16}$ in. John B. Turner Fund. (1386.1968). The Museum of Modern Art, New York, NY, U.S.A. Photo: Digital Image © The Museum of Modern Art/Licensed by SCALA / Art Resource, NY; **5.38** M.C. Escher, Ascending and Descending. © 2009 The M.C. Escher Company-Holland. All rights reserved. www.mcescher.com <http://www.mcescher.com>; **5.39** Cover of Captain Marvel #3. Penciler: Ed Mcguiness, Inker: Dexter Viens, Colorist: Jason Keith. TM & © 2010 Marvel Characters, Inc. Used with permission; **5.40** SPIDER-MAN: TM & © 2010 Marvel Characters, Inc. Used with permission; **5.41** Courtesy of Tony's Pizza; **5.44** Courtesy of Chester Jenkins; **5.45** Pablo Picasso, Guernica, 1937. Museo Nacional Centro de Arte Reina Sofia, Madrid, Spain. Art Resource, NY. © 2010 Estate of Pablo Picasso/Artists Rights Society (ARS), New York; **5.46** Al Held, Phoenicia VI, 1969, Acrylic on canvas, 114 × 114 inches, AHE.704. Art © Al Held Foundation/Licensed by VAGA, New York, NY; **5.47** Jackson Pollock, Blue Poles, 1953, also known as Number 11, 1952. Oil, enamel, aluminium paint, glass on canvas. 212.1 × 488.9 cm. National of Australia, Canberra. Purchased 1973. © 2010 Pollock-Krasner Foundation. Licensed by Artists Rights Society (ARS), New York & VISCOPY, Australia; **5.48** Helen Frankenthaler, The Bay, 1963. The Detroit Institute of Arts, USA/ Founders Society Purchase, Dr & Mrs Hilbert H. DeLawter Fund/The Bridgeman Art Library.

CHAPTER 6

6.1 Star Wars: Episode VI - Return of the Jedi (TM) & © 1983 and 1997 Lucasfilm Ltd. All rights reserved. Used under authorization. Unauthorized duplication is a violation of applicable law. Courtesy of Lucasfilm Ltd.; **6.2** Robert Irwin, detail of the Getty Garden, 1997–present. © Robert Landau/Corbis; **6.3** © Andy Goldsworthy/© Julian Calder/Corbis; **6.4** "BUNNY" © 1998 Twentieth Century Fox. All Rights Reserved; **6.5** Photofest; **6.6** Courtesy of Pepsico; **6.7** © Duane Michals, courtesy of Pace/MacGill Gallery, New York; **6.8** Courtesy of Gregory Crewdson and Luhring Augustine, New York; **6.9** Sally Mann, Immediate Family, 1993. Courtesy of Aperture; **6.10** Henri Cartier-Bresson, Greece, Cyclades, Islands of Siphnos, 1961. Magnum Photos; **6.11** © 2010 William Wegman / Artists Rights Society (ARS), New York; **6.12** © Bill Viola. Photo: Kira Perov; **6.13** Lián Amaris Sifuentes, Fashionably Late for the Relationship, 2007. Photo: Casey Kelbaugh. New York Times, July 9, 2007; **6.14** Louvre, Paris, France. Erich Lessing/Art Resource, NY; **6.15** Alexander Calder, Tower with Pinwheel, 1951. Painted steel wire, painted wood, painted sheet metal and string, 1.016 × .914 × .864 cm (40 × 36 × 26 in). Gift of Mr. and Mrs. Klaus G. Perls. Image © 2009 Board of Trustees, National Gallery of Art, Washington, 1951. © 2010 Calder Foundation/New York/ Artists Rights Society (ARS), New York; **6.16** Kiasma Museum, Helsinki, Finland. Courtesy of Ken Rinaldo; **6.17** Alexander Calder, Vertical Constellation with Bomb, 1943. Painted steel wire, painted wood, and wood, .775 × .756 × .610 cm. $30\frac{1}{2} \times 29\frac{3}{4} \times 24$ in. Gift of Mr. and Mrs. Klaus G. Perls. © 2009 Board of Trustees, National Gallery of Art, Washington, 1943. © 2010 Calder Foundation/New York/ Artists Rights Society (ARS), New York; **6.18** © Estate of Elizabeth Murray, courtesy of PaceWildenstein, New York; Photo: Ellen Page Wilson; **6.19** © Bridget Riley. All rights reserved. Courtesy of Karsten Schubert London; **6.20** Courtesy Cheim & Read, Galerie Karsten Greve, and Hauser & Wirth. Photo: Allan Finkelman. Art © Louise Bourgeois/Licensed by VAGA, New York, NY; **6.21** Courtesy of Kehinde Wiley; **6.22** Marcel Duchamp, Nude Descending a Staircase (No. 2), 1912. Oil on canvas, $57\frac{7}{8} \times 35\frac{1}{8}$ inches (147 × 89.2cm). The Louise and Walter Arensberg Collection, 1950. Philadelphia Museum of Art, Philadelphia, Pennsylvania, U.S.A. Photo: The Philadelphia Museum of Art / Art Resource, NY. © 2010 Artists Rights Society (ARS), New York/ ADAGP, Paris/Succession Marcel Duchamp; **6.23** Marjane Satrapi, Persepolis: The Story of A Childhood, Pantheon: New York, 2003, p. 104. Used by permission of Pantheon Books, a division of Random House, Inc; **6.24** Robert Capa, Omaha Beach, Normandy Coast, France, 1944. Magnum Pictures; **6.25** Courtesy of Nathan Fox; **6.26** The Library of Congress; **6.27** © Harold & Esther Edgerton Foundation, 2009, courtesy of Palm Press, Inc.; **6.28** Courtesy of T & C Edition AG; **6.29** © Chen Kai/Xinhua Press/Corbis.

CHAPTER 7

7.1 Seduction: Form, Sensation, and the Production of Architectural Desire symposium poster designed for the Yale School of Architecture, 2007. Designed by Michael Bierut/Pentagram and Marian Bantjes; **7.2** Xu Bing, Book from the Sky, 1987–1991. Hand printed books, ceiling and wall scrolls printed from wood letterpress type using false Chinese characters, dimensions variable. Installation view at Three Installations by Xu Bing, Elvehjem Museum of Art, University of Wisconsin-Madison, Madison, WI; **7.3** René Magritte, La Trahison des images (Ceci n'est pas une pipe), 1929. Oil on canvas, 60 × 81 cm. Los Angeles County Museum of Art, Los Angeles, CA, U.S.A. Photo: Banque d'Images, ADAGP / Art Resource, NY. © 2010 Herscovici, London/ Artists Rights Society (ARS), New York; **7.4** Jenny Holzer, Truisms (detail), 1977–1979 © 2010 Jenny Holzer, member Artists Rights Society (ARS), New York; **7.5** Courtesy of the Camille Utterback and Romy Achituv; **7.6** Bruce Nauman, One Hundred Live and Die, 1984. Neon tubing mounted on four metal monoliths. 118 × 132 × 21 inches. Collection Benesse Corporation, Naoshima Contemporary Art Museum, Kagawa, Japan. © 2010 Bruce Nauman/Artists Rights Society (ARS), New York; **7.7** Glenn Ligon, Warm Broad Glow, 2005. © Glenn Ligon, courtesy of Regen Projects, Los Angeles; **7.8** Calligraphy, Iranian or Turkish, Islamic, Ottoman period (ca. 1280–1924), 16th century. Page of Poetry from an Anthology of Poetry, author: Amir Shahi of Sabzavar, d. 1453; artist: Maulana Nur al-Din 'Abd al-Rahman Jami, 1414–92; author: Nasir Khusrau, 1003–ca 1066. The Metropolitan Museum of Art, Gift of Mrs. Lucy W. Drexel 1889 (89.2.2152) Image © The Metropolitan Museum of Art; **7.9** Courtesy of Seymour Chwast and Pushpin Group; **7.10** Ann Hamilton and Ann Chamberlain, (detail) San Francisco Public Library Public Art Project, 1996. Annotated paper library index cards, size variable. Courtesy of the artists; **7.11** Courtesy of Malcolm Cochran; **7.12** © Lalla Essaydi, courtesy of Edwynn Houk Gallery, New York; **7.13** From MAUS I: A SURVIVOR'S TALE/MY FATHER BLEEDS HISTORY by Art Spiegelman. © 1973, 1980, 1981, 1982, 1984, 1985, 1986 by Art Spiegelman. Used by permission of Pantheon Books, a division of Random House, Inc; **7.14** Vicki Daiello, Silences between words and world: Deconstruction and the evolution of an inquiry, 2007. Courtesy of the author; **7.15** Courtesy of Lorna Simpson and Salon 94; **7.16** Barbara Kruger, Untitled (Thinking of you), 1999–2000. Photographic screenprint on vinyl, Overall: 123 × 101in. (312.4 × 256.5cm). Photo: Sheldan C. Collin. Purchase with funds from the Katherine Schmidt Shubert Purchase Fund 2000.217. Whitney Museum of American Art, New York. © Barbara Kruger: Courtesy Mary Boone Gallery, New York; **7.17** © José Luis Giménez del Pueblo, courtesy of the artist; **7.18** Steve & Ghy Sampson/Digital Vision/Getty Images; **7.19** Courtesy of Janet Cardiff and George Bures Miller and Luhring Augustine, New York; **7.20** Courtesy of Nick Cave and Jack Shainman Gallery; **7.21** Photo: Felicitas Timpe. Division of Images and Maps. Bayerische Staatsbibliothek, Munich, Germany. Bildarchiv Preussischer Kulturbesitz / Art Resource, NY; **7.22** Smithsonian American Art Museum, Washington, DC / Art Resource, NY; **7.23** Edvard Munch, The Scream, 1893. Tempera and pastels on cardboard, 91 × 73.5 cm. Erich Lessing/Art Resource, NY. © 2010 The Munch Museum/The Munch-Ellingsen Group/Artists Rights Society (ARS), New York; **7.24** Montien Boonma, Lotus Sound, 1992. Reproduced by permission, from the Collection of the Queensland Art Gallery, Brisbane.

CHAPTER 8

8.1 © Richard Misrach, courtesy of Fraenkel Gallery, San Francisco, Marc Selwyn Fine Art, Los Angeles, and Pace/MacGill Gallery, New York; **8.2** Grant Wood, American Gothic, 1930. Oil on beaver board, $30\frac{11}{16} \times 25\frac{11}{16}$ in. (78 × 65.3 cm) unframed. Friends of American Art Collection, 1930.934. Photo: Bob Hashimoto. Reproduction © The Art Institute of Chicago; **8.3** The Library of Congress; **8.4** Alison Saar, Nocturne Navigator, 1998. Copper, wood, and neon. Columbus Museum of Art, Ohio: Museum Purchase with partial funds donated by the Columbus Chapter of Links, Inc. 1998.005; **8.5** Courtesy of Thomas Muir; **8.6** Grant Wood, Spring Turning, 1936. Oil on masonite panel, $18\frac{1}{4} \times 40\frac{1}{4}$ in.. 1991.2.2. Reynolda House Museum of American Art, Winston-Salem, North Carolina. Gift of Barbara B. Millhouse. Art © Estate of Grant Wood/Licensed by VAGA, New York, NY; **8.7** Eva Hesse, Right After, 1969. Fiberglass, approximately 5 × 18 × 4 feet. Photo: Larry Sanders. Gift of Friends of Art, M1970.27, Milwaukee Art Museum; **8.8** Courtesy of Charles Csuri; **8.9** Cai Guo-Qiang, Installation view of Inopportune: Stage One, 2004. Nine cars and sequenced multi-channel light tubes, dimensions variable. Seattle Art Museum, Gift of Robert M. Arnold, in honor of the 75th Anniversary of the Seattle Art Museum, 2006. Exhibition copy installed at The Solomon R. Guggenheim Museum, New York, 2008 for the exhibition Cai Guo Qiang: I Want To Believe, February 22–May 28, 2008. Photo: David Heald © The Solomon R. Guggenheim Foundation, New York; **8.10** Conan ® and © 2009 Conan Properties International LLC; **8.11** Figure of Budai Heshang, China, early Qing dynasty (1644–1911). The Metropolitan Museum of Art, The Michael Friedsam Collection, Bequest of Michael Friedsam, 1931 (32.100.422). Image © The Metropolitan Museum of Art; **8.12** Judy Chicago, Emily Dickinson Place Setting, The Dinner Party, 1974–1979. © 2010 Judy Chicago/Artists Rights Society (ARS), New York. © 2010 Photo: Donald Woodman/Artists Rights Society (ARS), New York; **8.13** Judy Chicago, The Dinner Party, 1974–1979. © 2010 Judy Chicago/Artists Rights Society (ARS), New York. © 2010 Photo: Donald Woodman/Artists Rights Society (ARS), New York; **8.14** Courtesy of Tribal Arts, Brussels, Belgium; **8.15** © Philip Pearlstein, courtesy of Betty Cuningham Gallery, New York; **8.16** © Joan Snyder, courtesy of Betty Cuningham Gallery, New York. Collection of The Francis Young Tang Teaching Museum and Art Gallery at Skidmore College, Saratoga Springs, NY (2001.23). Photo: Steven Sloman; **8.17** Courtesy of Gretchen Cochran; **8.18** © Jeff Koons; **8.19** Collection Walker Art Center, Minneapolis. Gift of Frederick R. Weisman in honor of his parents, William and Mary Weisman, 1988. © Claes Oldenburg and Coosje van Bruggen; **8.20** © Duane Michals, courtesy of Pace/MacGill Gallery, New York; **8.21** Jacob Lawrence, Typists, 1966. Tempera and gouache on paper, 22 × $29\frac{1}{4}$ in.. Cornell University, Ithaca, NY. Photo: The Jacob and Gwendolyn Lawrence Foundation / Art Resource, NY. © 2010 The Jacob and Gwendolyn Lawrence Foundation, Seattle/Artists Rights Society (ARS), New York; **8.25** Salvador Dali, The Sacrament of the Last Supper, 1955. Oil on canvas, 1.667 × 2.670 ($65\frac{5}{8} \times 105\frac{1}{8}$ in.); framed: 2.026 × 3.020 ($79\frac{3}{4} \times 118\frac{7}{8}$). Chester Dale Collection, Image courtesy of the Board of Trustees, National Gallery of Art, Washington, 1955. 1963.10.115.(1779)/PA. © 2010 Salvador Dali, Gala-Salvador Dali Foundation/Artists Rights Society (ARS), New York; **8.27** Brand × Pictures/Punchstock; **8.28** Thomas J. Abercrombie/ National Geographic/Getty Images.

CHAPTER 9

9.1 © Philip Taaffe, courtesy of Gagosian Gallery, New York; **9.2** Graphic courtesy of South Florida SunSentinel; **9.3** © Chris Hellier/ Corbis; **9.4** Courtesy of Rossi di Albizzate; **9.5** © The Keith Haring Foundation. Used by permission; **9.6** From Sparkle and Spin ©1957 by Ann Rand Ozbekhan and Paul Rand. Used with permission of Chronicle Books LLC, San Francisco. Visit ChronicleBooks.com; **9.7** Eugene Richards, Mariella, East New York, 1992. From Cocaine True, Cocaine Blue (Aperture, 1994); **9.9** Hulton Archive/Getty Images; **9.10** Rubin Museum of Art, New York, NY. © Rubin Museum of Art / Art Resource, NY; **9.12** © Nivia González; **9.13** © 1995 www.gerlovin.com <http://www.gerlovin.com>; **9.14** Photograph courtesy of Pace-Wildenstein, New York. © Joel Shapiro/Artists Rights Society (ARS), New York; **9.15** Courtesy of Sam Gilliam and Marsha Mateyka and Essie Green Galleries; **9.16** Damien Hirst, The Most Beautiful Thing in the World, 2003 © 2010 Damien Hirst, courtesy of Gagosian Gallery. All Rights Reserved/Artists Rights Society, New York/DACS, London; **9.17** Courtesy of Twin Rocks Trading Post; **9.19** Courtesy of Susie Rosmarin and Danese, New York; **9.20** Courtesy of Julian Stanczak and Danese, New York; **9.21** Art © The Estate of Ronald Bladen, LLC/Licensed by VAGA, New York, NY; **9.22** © 2009 Sally Michel / Artists Rights Society (ARS), New York; **9.23** Courtesy of April Gornik and Danese, New York; **9.24** Courtesy of Kay WalkingStick; **9.25** F.C. Ware, from Jimmy Corrigan, The Smartest Kid on Earth, 2000. Used by permission of Pantheon Books, a division of Random House, Inc; **9.26** Robert Irwin, Untitled, 1968. Synthetic polymer paint on aluminum and light, disc: $60\frac{3}{8}$ in. in diameter. Mrs. Sam A. Lewison Fund. (235.1969) Digital Image © The Museum of Modern Art/Licensed by SCALA/Art Resource, NY. © 2009 Robert Irwin/Artists Rights Society (ARS), New York; **9.27** Ellsworth Kelly, Installation, 52nd Venice Biennale, 2007. Photo © Jack Shear. Artwork © Ellsworth Kelly; **9.28** © Anish Kapoor. Photo: Dave Morgan. Courtesy of the Lisson Gallery; **9.29** © John Tremblay. Photo: Adam Reich. Courtesy of the Paula Cooper Gallery, New York; **9.30** Courtesy of Thames & Hudson Ltd.; **9.31** © Meg Webster. Photo: Seth Erickson. Courtesy of the Paula Cooper Gallery, New York; **9.32** Courtesy of Kara Walker and Sikkema Jenkins & Co; 9.33 Courtesy of OOOMS, www.oooms.nl <http://www.oooms.nl> .

CHAPTER 10

10.1 Miriam Schapiro, Untitled, ca.1975. Oil on canvas. 40 × 40 in. Courtesy of the Pennsylvania Academy of the Fine Arts, Philadelphia and Gertrude Stein Gallery; **10.2** Russian State Museum, St. Petersburg, Russia. Scala/Art Resource, NY; **10.3** Courtesy of Seymour Chwast and Pushpin Group; **10.4** © Emmet and Edith Gowin, courtesy of Pace/MacGill Gallery, New York; **10.5** © Sebastiao Salgado/Contact Press Images; **10.6** © Kiki Smith. Photo: Ellen Page Wilson. Courtesy of PaceWildenstein, New York; **10.7** Courtesy of Carrie Ruby; **10.8** Courtesy of Marimekko Corporation; **10.9** © British Museum/Art Resource, NY; **10.10** Richard Freeda/Aurora/Getty Images; **10.11** Courtesy of Lorna Simpson and Salon 94; **10.12** Amos Ferguson, Beaded Hair, 1984. Plio-lux enamel on cardboard, $35\frac{3}{4} \times 29\frac{3}{4}$ inches. The Ella Gallup Sumner and Mary Catlin Sumner Collection Fund. 1984.8. Wadsworth Atheheum Museum of Art, Hartford, CT; **10.13** El Anatsui, Fading Cloth, 2005. Aluminium and copper wire, 320 × 650 cm. Collection St. Louis Art Museum. Photo: October Gallery, London; **10.14** © Trenton Doyle Hancock, courtesy of James Cohan Gallery, New York; **10.15** Allan McCollum, The SHAPES Project, 2005–2006. 7,056 SHAPES Monoprints, each unique. Framed digital prints, 4.25 × 5.5 inches each, on acid-free bond. Each print signed and numbered. Installation: Friedrich Petzel Gallery, New York, 2006; **10.16** Frank Stella, Flin-Flon IV, 1970. Acrylic on canvas. 274.5 × 274.5 cm. AM1974-DEP7. Photo: Christian Bahier/Philippe Migeat. Musée National d'Art Moderne, Centre Georges Pompidou, Paris, France. CNAC/MNAM/Dist. Réunion des Musées Nationaux/Art Resource, NY. © 2010 Frank Stella/Artists Rights Society (ARS), New York; **10.17** © Todd Roeth: www.toddroeth.com <http://www.toddroeth.com>; **10.18** Hans Haacke,Wide White Flow, 1967–2008. Electric fans, white silk fabric, dimensions variable to space. Edition 1 of 3. © Hans Haacke. Photo: Ellen Wilson. Courtesy of the Paula Cooper Gallery, New York. © 2009 Artists Rights Society (ARS), New York / VG Bild-Kunst, Bonn; **10.19** Courtesy of Tony Cragg; **10.20** Courtesy of Steven Finke; **10.21** Courtesy of Wooden Radio GbR; **10.22** Courtesy of Sitepoint, Victoria, Australia; **10.23** Agnes Martin, Untitled, 1998. Portfolio of 4 offset lithographs on GilClear paper. 12 × 12 in.. Edition of 75. Detail 1. Photo: Kerry Ryan McFate, courtesy of PaceWildenstein, New York. © 2009 Agnes Martin / Artists Rights Society (ARS), New York; **10.24** © James Siena, courtesy of PaceWildenstein, New York. Photo: Aram Jibilian; **10.25** Courtesy of Shirazeh Houshiary and Pip Horne and Lisson Gallery; **10.26** "Sarah Sze: Tilting Planet," Malmö Konsthall, Malmö, Sweden, December 1, 2006–February 18, 2007.© Sarah Sze and Helen Toresdotter; **10.27** © Fiona Rae, courtesy of PaceWildenstein, New York. Photo: Aram Jibilian; **10.28** © Fred Prouser/Reuters/Corbis; **10.29** Courtesy of Angela De La Cruz and Lisson Gallery; **10.30** © Mary Heilmann. Courtesy of the artist; **10.31** Courtesy of Georg Heimdal; **10.32** Courtesy of Ken Price; **10.33** © Bill Viola. Photo: Kira Perov; **10.34** Courtesy of Spencer Finch and Lisson Gallery; **10.35** F.C. Ware, from Jimmy Corrigan, The Smartest Kid on Earth, 2000. Used by permission of Pantheon Books, a division of Random House, Inc.

CHAPTER 11

11.1 Barbara Kruger, Untitled (Are we having fun yet?), 1987. Photographic silkscreen/vinyl, 147 in. by 103 in. Courtesy of Mary Boone Gallery, New York; **11.2** Courtesy of Venturi, Scott Brown & Associates, Inc; **11.3** © Guerilla Girls; **11.4** © Chip East/Reuters/Corbis; **11.5** © Jeff Koons; **11.6** Frank Franklin II/AP Images; **11.7** Elliott Earls Design, and Photography, Abraham and Isaac, 2002. Dye sublimation print, 80 in. × 42 in. © 2002, all rights reserved; **11.8** © Nan Goldin. courtesy of Matthew Marks Gallery, New York; **11.9** Courtesy of Mona Hatoum and Alexander and Bonin Gallery; **11.10** Alamy Images; **11.11** Image courtesy of the artists and Green Cardamom; **11.12** Marcel Duchamp, Fountain, 1950 (replica of 1917 original). Porcelain urinal, 12 × 15 × 18 inches (30.5 × 38.1 × 45.7 cm). Gift (by exchange) of Mrs. Herbert Cameron Morris, 1998. Philadelphia Museum of Art, Philadelphia, Pennsylvania, U.S.A. Photo: The Philadelphia Museum of Art / Art Resource, NY. © 2010 Artists Rights Society (ARS), New York/ ADAGP, Paris/Succession Marcel Duchamp; **11.13** © Richard Prince; **11.14** Betty Boop-Fleisher Studios. King Features Syndicate; **11.15** Courtesy of Gregory Crewdson and Luhring Augustine, New York; **11.16** Sangeeta Sandrasegar, Details: Untitled (no. 22) from the series, Goddess of Flowers, 2003–04. Paper, glitter, sequins. Courtesy of Johnston Gallery; **11.17** Masami Teraoka, AIDS Series / Vaccine Day Celebration, 1990. Courtesy of Catharine Clark Gallery; **11.18** Robert Rauschenberg, First Landing Jump, 1961. Combine painting: cloth, metal, leather, electric fixture, cable and oil paint on composition board; overall, including automobile tire and wooden plank on floor, 7 ft. $5\frac{1}{8}$ in. × 6 ft. $8\frac{7}{8}$ in.. Gift of Philip Johnson. (434.1972). The Museum of Modern Art, New York, NY, U.S.A. Photo: Digital Image © The Museum of Modern Art/Licensed by SCALA/Art Resource, NY. Art © Estate of Robert Rauschenberg/Licensed by VAGA, New York, NY; **11.19** Courtesy of Rachel Hecker; **11.20** Collection and courtesy of the artist, Ah Xian; **11.21** © Michael Ray Charles; **11.22** © Fred Willson, courtesy of PaceWildenstein, New York; **11.23** © Yolanda M. Lopez; **11.24** Courtesy of Fitzgerald & Co. Advertising, Atlanta. Art Director: Fernando Lecca; Copy writer: Jerry Williams; Photographer: Arian Camilleri; **11.25** Musée des Beaux-Arts, Strasbourg, France. Giraudon/Art Resource, NY; **11.26** Courtesy of Cindy Sherman and Metro Pictures; **11.27** Tracey Emin, Everyone I Have Ever Slept With 1963–1995. Appliquéd tent, mattress and light. 48 × $96\frac{1}{2} \times 84\frac{1}{2}$ in. (122 × 245 × 215 cm.) Photo: Stephen White. Courtesy of White Cube. © 2009 Tracey Emin. All rights reserved, DACS, London/Artists Rights Society (ARS), New York; **11.28** Courtesy of Cecilia Cortes-Earle; **11.29** Courtesy of Robert Smit; **11.30** Dirck Halstead//Time Life Pictures/Getty Images; **11.31** Courtesy of Melissa Shiff; **11.32** Guillermo Gómez-Peña, from a performance, Binational Boxer. Courtesy of La Pocha Nostra; **11.33** Courtesy of Charlotte Schulz; **11.34** Courtesy of Altoids and Wrigleys Company; **11.35** Courtesy of Do Ho Suh and Lehmann Maupin Gallery, New York; **11.36** © Stephen Althouse; **11.37** Courtesy of Janine Antoni and Luhring Augustine, New York.

CHAPTER 12

12.1 Courtesy of Adidas; **12.2** Courtesy of Chris Powell.

CHAPTER 13

13.1 Courtesy of Yuki Wakamiya; **13.2** Courtesy of Samantha Hookway; **13.3** Courtesy of the author; **13.4** Courtesy of Kristin Desiderio.

Index